Intellectual Property, Finance and Corporate Governance

AF695689

IP law has evolved from being a little pool to a big ocean. Corporate governance needs to respond to society's rising expectations of directors and boards as the impact of the global intellectual property ecosystem is felt. How can a responsible corporate culture of IP transparency be stimulated to create a rosy future to connect corporate communication with the desires of shareholders, investors and other stakeholders? The astonishing lack of material quantitative and qualitative information that companies report about their IP assets makes it difficult for shareholders and other stakeholders to assess directors' stewardship of those assets – a pressing corporate governance issue in the 21st century. This book advances IP reporting in alignment with the key corporate governance principles of transparency and disclosure. It analyses the juncture between the IP ecosystem; corporate finance and accounting for intangibles; and corporate governance. Patents, mini-case studies and an original business triage style model for assessing IP disclosures are used to illustrate the gaps corporate governance theory needs to address. Focussing on the common law tradition of corporate governance in England and Wales, intangibles and IP reporting developments in other jurisdictions are also explored.

Janice Denoncourt is a senior lecturer in intellectual property law and company law at Nottingham Law School, Nottingham Trent University in the United Kingdom.

Routledge Research in Intellectual Property

Titles in this series include:

Copyright Industries and the Impact of Creative Destruction
Copyright Expansion and the Publishing Industry
Jiabo Liu

Health Technologies and International Intellectual Property
A Precautionary Principle
Phoebe Li

Intellectual Property, Traditional Knowledge and Cultural Property Protection
Cultural Signifiers in the Caribbean and the Americas
Sharon Le Gall

Intellectual Property and Traditional Knowledge in the Global Economy
Translating Geographical Indications for Development
Teshager W. Dagne

The Object of Copyright
A Conceptual History of Originals and Copies in Literature, Art and Design
Stina Teilmann-Lock

Well-Known Trade Marks
A Comparative Study of Japan and the EU
Hiroko Onishi

Contemporary Issues in Pharmaceutical Patent Law
Setting the Framework and Exploring Policy Options
Bryan Mercurio and Daria Kim

Intellectual Property, Finance and Corporate Governance
Janice Denoncourt

Intellectual Property, Finance and Corporate Governance

Janice Denoncourt

Routledge
Taylor & Francis Group
LONDON AND NEW YORK

First published 2018 by Routledge

2 Park Square, Milton Park, Abingdon, Oxfordshire OX14 4RN
52 Vanderbilt Avenue, New York, NY 10017

Routledge is an imprint of the Taylor & Francis Group, an informa business

First issued in paperback 2020

British Library Cataloguing in Publication Data
A catalogue record for this book is available from the British Library

Library of Congress Cataloging in Publication Data
Names: Denoncourt, Janice, author.
Title: Intellectual property, finance and corporate governance / Janice Denoncourt.
Description: New York : Routledge, 2018. |
Series: Routledge research in intellectual property | Includes bibliographical references and index.
Identifiers: LCCN 2017050794 | ISBN 9781138186255 (hbk)
Subjects: LCSH: Intellectual property—Great Britain. | Corporate governance—Law and legislation—Great Britain.
Classification: LCC KD1269. D465 2018 | DDC 346.4104/8—dc23
LC record available at https://lccn.loc.gov/2017050794

ISBN: 978-1-138-18625-5 (hbk)
ISBN: 978-0-367-59141-0 (pbk)

Typeset in Galliard
by Keystroke, Neville Lodge, Tettenhall, Wolverhampton

Contents

Foreword

To many observers of companies, such as financial analysts, investors and auditors, corporate IP assets remain complex. This is true despite the fact that IP rights are mentioned in any management or finance report as the main asset of a company. IP is the driver of the future company incomes and the tracker of its innovation capacity. This is the paradox: IP is the main asset but IP is left out of the corporate governance and corporate financial analyses.

The first explanation for this paradox rests on the fact that IP is left off the balance sheet. From an accounting point of view, IP assets created internally by the company should not be included in the balance sheet (also true for IP licences). Without direct information on IP assets in the financial documents, they are not taken into consideration in the financial analysis. There is a lack of normative culture on the IP value and approaches to IP valuation. The financial analyst is focused on operational expenditure (Opex) and is not able to see the shadow of IP.

The second explanation is based on the lack of IP culture in many companies and lack of awareness by managers. IP is seen narrowly as patents, trade mark, copyrights only, and considered as a bundle of rights. It is perceived as a cost more than as an asset. The overall quality of an IP portfolio is rarely considered. Few companies have an IP office and an IP global transversal strategy drawn up by the top management. From a corporate analysis perspective, the annual report could be the best place to propose a clear presentation of the corporate IP assets, on one hand; and of the portfolio coherence, on the other. It could be a solution for the management to show the quality of their actions to create shareholder value. If a company is listed, the market tries to integrate this IP quality in the share price. But for all the other companies, there is no tool to show the quality and value of the corporate IP portfolio and its contribution to the company's development.

One of the consequences of this situation – echoed around the world – is that the ignorance by the company itself and of its stakeholders as to the quality and the value of the corporate IP assets has become a limitation especially when financing the company's development. The company loses the leverage offered by the IP assets, which may even be its main competitive advantage. A key goal of corporate governance in the new economic era is to have a real global management of corporate IP assets and to include them in the financial quantitative reports and narrative communication as a criterion of the quality of the management and as a basis for corporate finance. IP assets are certainly the best way to ascertain a mid-to-long term analysis of any company when the Opex and earnings before interest, taxes, depreciation and amortization (Ebitda) approaches provide short term information.

In this context, the work of Janice Denoncourt, through this research publication, is a major contribution to the analysis of the current situation. This publication is a strong tool, demonstrating the barriers and providing new perspectives for the articulation between Intellectual Property, Finance and Corporate Governance.

Professor Nicolas Binctin,
Université de Poitiers, Paris
4 September 2017

Preface

In the late 1990s, as in-house legal counsel for a publicly listed West Australian mining technology company, I became interested in the clash between three cultures: intellectual property (IP) law, finance and corporate governance. We had acquired a patent portfolio of certain non-explosive rock breaking technology inventions based on NASA rocket technology at a bargain price from an American firm in Chapter 11 insolvency proceedings. Although it owned a substantial patent portfolio, the American firm was in financial dire straits and had exhausted its ability to finance its operations and was wound up. On insolvency, the patent portfolio was still valuable technologically and financially. It was perplexing why the firm was unable to borrow, stabilise its cash flow to continue trading. At that time, the factors inhibiting access to finance were unclear. Indeed, it is still the case that most lenders are reluctant to accept patent assets as security (loan collateral), and this remains a barrier to business growth and survival. While modern capitalism is propelled forward by innovation, financing innovation is seen as high-risk speculation with lenders are more likely to ration credit – undermining innovation, rather than supporting it.

At the same time, in my in-house role I drafted announcements for the Australian Stock Exchange and company annual reports containing statements to the public about the company's growing IP portfolio and how it contributed to business performance. This information was increasingly of interest to shareholders and others. Making appropriate material corporate IP asset and strategy disclosures was challenging as there were few examples of good practice, even by long-established publicly listed companies. Little was known about the intersection between IP law, finance and corporate governance, despite its increasing relevance to the modern business environment. Fortunately, the level of corporate IP awareness has increased since then, but there is still much to learn. Depending on their business model and corporate objectives, companies add value via their corporate IP assets in different ways to achieve their business goals. This reflects growing corporate complexity in a world where intangible IP assets can be used strategically. However, the astonishing lack of quantitative and qualitative public information about the growing magnitude of corporate IP assets makes it difficult to assess strategic value ("the IP value story") and directors' stewardship of those assets – a pressing corporate governance issue in the 21st century. A failure to identify, assess, protect, manage and enforce IP rights can expose a company to risk and threaten business continuity. Corporate IP information (mostly known to internal management) is needed to triangulate intangibles financial data contained in the traditional accounts through cross verification with corporate narrative disclosure. Effective corporate governance is generally seen as crucial for the creation of a proficient global financial architecture. Narrative reporting of IP information and strategy is a new frontier in corporate governance – thinking and practice in this field will continue to evolve, as will the drive toward global standards. Similarly, our assumptions about the importance of IP rights have changed since the 1980s and 1990s. IP law is developing, but there are still large gaps in our understanding of the impact of IP rights on other disciplines and vice versa. This is where the problems arise – we lack some understanding of the consequences of the rise of IP rights, especially when they are owned by companies. In essence, this book analyses how corporate disclosure principles fit with the dynamic world of intangible IP rights. If law is to be fit for the purpose of managing dynamic IP ecosystems, the approach to corporate reporting of IP assets and strategy may have to change. The question then is: how should it change? The multidisciplinary insights in this book aim to provide a deeper level of legal analysis concerning the intersection between: (1) the IP ecosystem; (2) accounting for intangibles; and finally, (3) corporate governance and reporting requirements. Although there are many types of IP rights, this book focuses mainly on patents to illustrate corporate governance theory. It includes an original business triage-style *Essential, Desirable & Optional* narrative corporate material patent disclosure evaluation model to assist companies make advances in how they communicate the role and value of their IP portfolios in alignment with the key governance principles of transparency and disclosure.

This book will be useful to a wide range of professionals: company directors, IP and R&D managers, managers working with boards and other governing bodies, corporate and banking regulators, company secretaries, auditors, accountants, lawyers, corporate governance consultants, business advisors, bankers and financiers, IP professionals (patent and trade mark attorneys, licensing professionals), inventors and creators, shareholders, business journalists, market analysts and of course, academics.

The subject of corporate governance is continually changing and expanding, particularly society and shareholders' rising expectations of directors and boards as the impact of the IP ecosystem on business is felt. Consequently, readers are encouraged to explore developments through the references to many relevant sources and websites. The book is partly based on material that I developed in my PhD thesis entitled, "Patent-backed Debt Finance: Should Company Law Take the Lead to Provide a True and Fair View of SME's Patent Assets?" awarded by the University of Nottingham in 2015 and my other related research. Although the focus is on the common law tradition of corporate governance in England and Wales, the corporate disclosure of IP assets in other jurisdictions is explored by way of comparison.

Abbreviations

ABS	Alternative Business Structure
ACCA	Association of Chartered Certified Accountants
AIM	Alternative Investment Market
Basel II & III	The second and third of the Basel Accords issued by the Basel Committee on Banking Supervision
BBA	British Banking Association
BEIS	Department for Business, Energy and Industrial Strategy
CA 2006	Companies Act 2006
CDB	China Development Bank
CIPA	Chartered Institute of Patent Attorneys
CIPO	Chief Intellectual Property Officer
CJEU	Court of Justice of the EU
Companies House	An executive agency of DTI which registers and provides information on all UK companies under the Companies Acts
CPC	Community Patent Convention
CTO	Chief Technology Officer
DATI	Danish Agency for Trade and Industry
DMSTI	Danish Ministry of Science, Technology and Innovation
DTI	Department of Trade and Industry (United Kingdom)
EPC	European Patent Convention
EPO	European Patent Office
ESV	Enlightened shareholder value
EU	European Union
EUIPO	European Union Intellectual Property Office
EUR	Euro
FASB	Financial Accounting Standards Board
FRC	Financial Reporting Council
GAAP	Generally Accepted Accounting Principles
GBP	Great Britain Pound
GIPID	Guidelines for IP Information Disclosure (Japan)
HMRC	Her Majesty's Revenue & Customs
IAS	International Accounting Standard

IASB	International Accounting Standards Board
IASC	International Accounting Standards Committee
IN	Intellectual Capital
ICS	Intellectual Capital Statement
IFRS	International Financial Reporting Standards
ILF	Institute of Law and Finance (Germany)
INTIPSA	International IP Strategists' Association
IPEC	Intellectual Property Enterprise Court
IPFI	Intellectual Property Finance Institute
IPR	Intellectual Property Rights
KPI	Key Performance Indicator
LGST	Legislative Guide on Secured Transactions
LLP	Limited Liability Partnership
LSE	London Stock Exchange
NESTA	National Endowment for Science, Technology and the Arts
NHS	National Health Service
NPE	Non-practising entity(ies)
OFT	Office of Fair Trading
PA 1997	Patents Act 1977
PCC	Patents County Court
PLC	Publicly listed company
PRC	People's Republic of China
PTC	Patent Co-operation Treaty
R&D	Research and Development
RM	Malaysian Ringgit is the official currency of Malaysia
RMB	The renminbi is the official currency of PRC
SIPO	State Intellectual Property Office of the PRC
SME	Small and Medium-Sized Enterprise
TRIPS	Agreement on Trade Related Aspects of Intellectual Property Rights
UKHL	House of Lords (United Kingdom)
UKIPO	United Kingdom Intellectual Property Office
UKSC	United Kingdom Supreme Court
UPC	Unified Patent Court
UN	United Nations
UNCITRAL	United Nations Commission on International Trade Law
US	United States
USD	United States Dollar
WIPO	World Intellectual Property Organization
WTO	World Trade Organization

List of figures

Table of legislation

Bubble Act (UK) 1720
Civil Procedure (Amendment No 7) Rules 2013 (SI 2013/1974)
  CPR 63.1 A
Companies Act 2006
  Sections 92, 171–177, 172, ss 232–235, 382, 386, 389, 393, 394, 396, 397, 414A–D, 414C(14), 415, 417, 444(1), 444(a), 463 (2), 447(1), 494, 495, *853A (1),* 854, 859A–Q, 859D(e)(ii), 859A(7), 859H
Companies Act 2006 (Strategic Report and Directors' Report) Regulations 2013 No. 197
Copyright Designs and Patents Act 1988
County Courts Act 1984
Disclosure Transparency Rules
Enterprise Act 2002
European Patent Convention
Finance Act 2004
  Section 50
Financial Services and Markets Act 2000
G20/OECD Principles of Corporate Governance 2015
Insolvency Act 1986
Intellectual Property Act 2014
Patents Act 1977
  Sections 1(2)(c), 2(2), 5(1), 14, 25(1), 30(1), 32(2), 33, 33(3), 60, 68, 121
Patents Act 2004
Patent Amendment Act 1952
Patent Rules 2007 SI 2007/3291
  Rules 39, 44(6), 77
Personal Property Securities Act 2009
Senior Courts Act by the Constitutional Reform Act 2005
Small Business, Enterprise and Entities Act 2015
Small Companies and Groups (Account and Directors' Report) Regulations 2008
Small Companies (Micro Entities' Accounts) Regulations 2013

International

Agreement on Trade Related Aspects of Intellectual Property Rights (TRIPS) (1994)
  Article 41
Agreement on the UPC (2013)
Austria University Act 2002
Company Law Directives (EU)
  Article 2 (3) of the 4th Company Law Directive
  Article 16 (3) of the 7th Company Law Directive
Danish Act No 448 of 7 June 2001
Danish Financial Statements Act (2001)
  Chapter 11, s 99(2)
Directive 2007/47/EC of the European Parliament of the Council, OJ L 247/21
Directive 2012/6/EU of the European Parliament and of the Council of 14 March 2012 amending Council Directive 78/660/EEC on the annual accounts of certain types of companies as regards micro-entities
European Communities Act 1972
European Patent Convention
German Commercial Code as translated by A.F. Schuster, Barrister of the Inner Temple at www.archive.org/stream/germancommercial00germuoft/germancommercial00germuoft_djvu.txt
  § 342
Patent Co-operation Treaty
Sarbanes-Oxley Act (SOX 2002) (US)
  Sections 302, 401, 401(c), 404
  Regulation S-K 101(c)(1)(iv)
Treaty on the European Union
  Article 50
Unified Patent Court Agreement (2013)
Unified Patent Court Rules of Procedure (2015)

Accounting standards

Generally Accepted Accounting Practice (GAAP) UK
Generally Accepted Accounting Practice (GAAP) US
Financial Reporting Standards (FRS)
International Accounting Standard (IAS) 38 Intangibles
International Accounting Standard Regulation 1606/2002
  Article 3(2)
UK Financial Reporting Standard (FRS) 102

Table of cases

ALK Abello v Meridian [2010] EWPCC 014
258/03 *HITACHI/Auction method* [2004] EPOR 548
Balloon Promotions Limited v Wilson (Inspector of Taxes) 3 March 2006 SPC00524
Carlen v Drury (1812) 1 Ves & B 149
Electric & Musical Industries Ltd v Lissen Ltd (1939) 56 RPC 23
Gallagher v Jones (Inspector of Taxes) [1994] Ch 107
HMRC v William Grant & Sons Distillers Limited [2007] UKHL 15
Hospital Products Ltd v US Surgical Corporation (1984) 156 CLR 41, 68
Hutton v West Cork Railway (1883) 23 Ch D 654
Kelly & Chiu v GE Healthcare Ltd [2009] EWHC 191 (Pat)
McDonald v Graham [1994] RPC 407
Minsterstone Ltd v Be Modern Ltd [2002] FSR 53
National Guild of Removers & Storers Ltd v Christopher Silveria [2010] EWPCC 015
Odeon Associated Theatres v Jones (Inspector of Taxes) [1971] 1 WLR 442
Packer v Packer [1953] 2 All ER 127
Percival v Wright [1902] 2 Ch 421
Re Aro Company Ltd [1980] Ch 1986
Re Brightlife Ltd [1987] Ch 200
Re David Lloyd & Company (1977) 6 Ch D 339
SmithKline Beecham Plc's (Paroxetine Methanesulfonate) Patent [2006] RPC 10
Suh v Ryu [2012] EWPCC 20
T 931/95 *PBS Partnership/Controlling Pension Benefits System* [2002] EPOR 522
York Building Co v MacKenzie (1795) 3 Pat 378
Your Response Limited v Datateam Business Media Limited [2014] EWCA 281

International

Basic Inc. et al v Levinson et al 485 U.S. 224 (1988) at 234 (US)
Marksman Partners L.P. v. Chantal Pharm., 927 F. Supp. 1297, 1305–06 (US)
Santa Fe Industries, Inc. v. Green, 430 U.S. 462, 477-478 (1977) (US)
SEC v. Capital Gains Research Bureau, Inc., 375 U.S. 180, 186 (1963) (US)
Werner v. Werner, 267 F.3d 288, 297 (3d Cir. 2001) (US)

Part I

The corporate IP landscape

1 Corporate governance and IP assets

Corporate governance is concerned with holding the balance between economic and social goals and between individual and communal goals. The governance framework is there to encourage the efficient use of resources and equally to require accountability for the stewardship of those resources. The aim is to align as nearly as possible the interests of individuals, corporations and society.

Sir Adrian Cadbury, UK Commission Report: Corporate Governance 1992

An enterprise's assets may be broadly divided into two categories: physical assets and intangible assets. Intangible assets range from human capital and know-how to inventions, brands, designs and other intangible fruits of a company's creative and innovative capacity. Some intangible assets may be legally protected as forms of intellectual property (IP), as legally constructed monopoly rights, some of which must be formally registered to exist. Our assumptions about the importance of key IP rights such as patents, trade marks and copyright have changed since the 1980s and 1990s. IP law continues to develop, but there are still large gaps in our understanding of the impact of IP rights on other disciplines and vice versa. IP is hardly a liquid asset; it is gained through a long, methodical process that eventually creates value for the company. This is the space in which less obvious problems arise. We lack some understanding of the consequences of the rise of IP rights: how accountants value IP assets and record that value in traditional financial accounts; how, when, where and how much companies should report about their IP assets and their strategies to optimise those assets in the best interests of the company; and finally, how the disclosure of IP asset information should be regulated to protect the interests of shareholders and other stakeholders. This is the great challenge facing corporate governance. For centuries, people have struggled to predict, control, manage and understand the future. IP rights, as a form of intangible property, create multiple possibilities for creating future corporate value during their periods of existence and company directors do not have a crystal ball. Evaluating and reporting timely, reliable and accurate corporate IP asset information is undoubtedly complex. However, some people have much greater power and influence than others to access the company's internal IP information. Shareholders and other stakeholders seek more relevant, accurate and timely information about corporate IP assets – the type of information often only known to internal management. At the same time, public disclosure of IP asset information and strategy invites both accountability and competitive exposure. Corporate disclosure of IP information and strategy is not as straightforward as reporting traditional financial information. Accounting dominates IP valuation. Accounting standards affect valuation and recording and unintentionally result in a lack of information about corporate IP assets (the IP information gap). Nevertheless, company directors have a legal obligation to provide "true and fair" information about corporate assets they manage on behalf of shareholders in the mandatory corporate reports. Consequently, even contemplating making dynamic corporate IP information more transparent causes company directors to bury their heads in their hands. Existing corporate governance principles aimed at increasing shareholder value demand greater transparency and better public disclosure. Transparency, disclosure and accountability are core corporate governance issues and over the centuries, a body of law has evolved to control and shape the conduct of responsible corporations. Directors have access to and are a primary source of internal corporate IP asset and strategy information. Accordingly, they need to distinguish between the available financial data which may present incomplete snapshots of events and the reality behind the facts. A "true and fair" view of corporate performance requires accountants, auditors and company directors to be in a position to triangulate traditional financial performance reports with narrative legal and strategic IP asset information. Triangulation is a powerful technique that facilitates validation of data through cross verification from two more sources.[1]

How do corporate disclosure principles fit the dynamic world of intangible IP rights? The author has heard anecdotal accounts of large corporate patent portfolios where each patent was valued at £1as those involved found patents too complex to value. Even now, corporate disclosure principles for this class of asset are embryonic. By analogy, disclosures related to corporate IP assets and strategy are akin to an early incomplete map of the world. For example, the discipline of cartography builds on the premise that reality can be modelled in ways that communicate spatial information effectively. In comparison to spatial information, the communication of the integral role of abstract legally constructed IP rights in corporate value creation is possibly even more difficult. Imagine that the map also needs to predict the weather. Weather forecasting involves using reoccurring astronomical and meteorological events and personal observation to help monitor changes in the weather. By integrating IP reports into the existing system of corporate reporting, shareholders and other stakeholders will be able to monitor the impact of corporate investment in IP rights. However, those involved in corporate

1 Triangulation has its origins in geometry and is a method developed over centuries for navigation and surveying. It provides a basis for modern satellite navigation. Triangulation establishes a position by taking bearings on three or more known landmarks. The same method is used in politics research to obtain an efficient corroboration of any crucial account. Triangulation involves seeking accounts from three or more perspectives.

narrative reporting and disclosure of IP strategy and material assets face several fundamental problems. First, the material corporate IP assets required to be publicly disclosed to comply with corporate regulations must be selected. This is the concern of editing. Second, irrelevant information must be eliminated. Third, the complexity of the IP assets to be reported must be reduced. This is the concern of generalisation. Finally, the elements of the corporate disclosure that best convey the company's message to its audience need to be orchestrated while complying with the body of corporate regulatory law. Continuing with the analogy, the corporate IP asset and strategy disclosure map is beginning to emerge. Certain countries such as Denmark, Germany, the United States (US) and Japan have a more advanced approach and have introduced specific laws requiring companies to disclose certain corporate IP asset information, while the majority of others do not. That is the starting point. New three-dimensional and four-dimensional maps now exist in other fields that improve users' ability to understand complex information by dynamically displaying changing data, over time. While that type of corporate disclosure model is blue-sky thinking[2] for now, what is needed is a more holistic approach to inform shareholders involved in governance of companies.[3] In expounding on the way in which the system of corporate governance works in the context of IP assets, it is possible to gain a better understanding of the difficulties faced by IP rights owners and the company directors responsible for managing these corporate assets on behalf of their shareholders. It is clear that although some legal structures and norms exist, there are significant holes in the corporate governance system, a system which does not, at least in the United Kingdom (UK), contemplate or expressly address intangibles and corporate IP assets directly. Denmark, the US and Japan have implanted different approaches to regulate how to fill the gap in corporate IP asset and strategy information, to better meet the needs of shareholders and other stakeholders. Even so, these approaches leave much to interpretation and may be considered "vague". While no best practice in corporate IP asset disclosure has yet emerged, the form of disclosure is less important than the content. More corporate IP asset and strategy information is needed. Moreover, there will not be a one-size-fits-all corporate narrative reporting solution, as IP rights are used differently in diverse business sectors depending on their role in the business model as a tool for value creation. Nevertheless, corporate disclosure and transparency norms will help to promote more widespread trust in the potential value of IP rights and how they can be deployed to support commercial objectives, create high quality employment and better pay.

The research presented is multidisciplinary, drawing on academic fields such as law, economics, accounting and finance. The traditional approach to valuation

2 The phrase "blue-sky thinking" refers to original or creative thinking, unfettered by convention and not grounded in reality.

3 Shareholders usually have the same basic rights regardless of whether the company is private or public. The rights of shareholders depend on the rights attaching to their shares under the company's articles of association. In particular, shareholders have the important power of appointing and removing directors under Companies Act 2006 (CA 2006).

and corporate accountability for IP assets will be contrasted with the more holistic, ecosystem approach. In doing so, the author explores the gaps and problems that remain and the ability of corporate law to govern naturally dynamic IP rights that are of increasing economic importance. The aim of this book is to support a framework for better corporate narrative reporting of IP asset and strategy information. This type of narrative will complement the traditional quantitative information contained in company accounts with a view to enhancing the level of truth and fairness of corporate IP asset valuations. This chapter provides a synthesised understanding of IP rights, IP finance and corporate governance principles to inform the direction of future corporate IP asset reporting and the need for systemic change in the post-recession economy.

Let's step back in time for a moment – intangible IP assets have existed for centuries and have been used by companies to raise finance to commercialise innovation since the late 19th century. An early IP-backed finance corporate success story involves a high value patent-backed loan made to American small business owner Lewis Waterman[4], who invented a superior fountain pen that made inkwells and dip pens obsolete. Waterman, an insurance agent, is said to have vowed to invent a better writing instrument when an inferior pen leaked on an important insurance contract, causing a delay which led to him losing the client.[5] In 1884, he borrowed the significant sum of $5,000 US backed by his fountain pen patent[6] to start the Ideal Pen Company in New York. This is the first known reported example of corporate IP debt finance. Five years later he opened a factory north of the border in Montreal, Canada. When he died in 1901, his nephew Frank D Waterman took over the company, renamed it the L E Waterman Company and proceeded to increase sales to 350,000 pens per annum. The fountain pens were widely used until the Great Depression made them a luxury item.[7] Now, more than 130 years later, the Waterman Paris[8] company continues to design and sell luxury writing instruments, inks and refills and the Waterman brand is globally renowned for its luxury products. The point of this century old example is to illustrate the crucial role corporate IP assets play in creating value for a business, and how they can be used to access finance and sustain long term growth. Nevertheless, it is well-known that many early stage innovation firms fail due to under-capitalisation. Imperfect access to funding and investment is an important barrier to commercialising innovation. Corporate governance principles may be able to improve this situation by creating greater transparency as to the

4 Lewis Edson Waterman (18 November 1837–1 May 1901) was the inventor of the capillary feed fountain pen and founder of the famous Waterman Pen Company. He was inducted into the US National Inventors Hall of Fame in 2006.

5 US Inventors Hall of Fame Biography of Lewis Edison Waterman, at www.invent.org/Hall_Of_Fame/308.html.

6 US Patent 293,545 Fountain Pen, 12 February 1884.

7 After World War II the invention of the disposable ballpoint pen dominated.

8 Since 2000 Waterman Paris has been a wholly owned subsidiary of the American group Newell Rubbermaid.

role of corporate IP assets in value creation. Analysis of corporate finance, which takes into account the value of the company's IP portfolio, provides the scaffolding to support the corporate governance discussion that ensues in later chapters. Core company law focuses on equity financing: the relationship between the company and its shareholders. Equity financing occurs where a company issues shares to one or more investors who become members of the company, or "shareholders". The other main form of corporate finance is debt finance, which occurs when a company enters into a contract to borrow money from another person, typically a bank, which lends money to the company. In this book we consider IP-backed finance, using IP assets as security (or collateral) for lending. For the sake of simplicity, we narrow the spotlight and focus on patents as corporate IP assets, as patents protect innovation. Both equity and debt finance require the company's IP assets to be valued by applying relevant accounting standards. This application of International Accounting Standard (IAS) 38 Intangibles will be critically discussed in Chapter 4.

As corporate investment in acquiring and exploiting IP rights continues to increase, across the world the mainstream financial press is now more aware of the value of IP assets as a core component of business strategy. High profile IP corporate finance stories with global impact have been widely reported in recent years. These involve multinational companies operating in a variety of industrial sectors, including Apple, Disney, Facebook, GSK, Lucasfilm, IBM, Microsoft, Samsung, Sony, Toshiba, Panasonic and Pfizer, to name a few. According to research commissioned by the UK Intellectual Property Office (UKIPO) published in autumn 2016, investment in UK intangibles such as inventions, brands, content, code, data, know-how and confidential information reached an incredible £133 billion. This is 9% higher than traditional "tangible" investment such as such as real estate, machinery and information technology (IT) hardware. The research confirmed that 53% of intangible investments are protected by IP rights, the most economically important of which are patents, followed by copyright and trade marks, highlighting their increasingly critical role in the UK and global "knowledge economy".[9] The central corporate governance questions are: who is empowered to make decisions about the company's affairs, and how are those decisions taken and communicated to shareholders, stakeholders and the public? The key organs of governance of a company are the board of directors and the shareholders. Shareholders are sometimes referred to as "residual controllers" of the company when they act collectively as a part of the decision-making governance body of the company (as opposed to acting in an individual capacity to enforce their personal rights). Directors have many duties with respect to the company for which they have been appointed to act. In the UK, directors have

9 Goodridge, P., Haskell, J. and Wallis, G. *UK Intangible Investment and Growth: New Measures of UK Investment in Knowledge Assets and Intellectual Property Rights* (September 2016) Independent Report commissioned by the UK Intellectual Property Office ISBN: 978-1-910790-25-0.

statutory duties as set out in the Companies Act 2006 (CA 2006) to keep accounting records to record the value of company assets and transactions, prepare the accounts, circulate corporate reports and accounts, prepare the Directors'Report, promote the success of the company and exercise reasonable care, skill and diligence with regard to the company's affairs whilst acting within their powers, among other things. In other words, they are accountable to the company for managing its portfolio of IP assets to preserve and maximise its value. Protecting rights, particularly property rights such as intangible IP rights, and establishing standards for human conscience when individuals in the company are entrusted to protect the rights of third parties (e.g. stakeholders with an interest in the company, such as shareholders, creditors, employees, customers, suppliers and the community at large) are legal matters dealt with by corporate governance principles. The aim of good corporate governance under the CA 2006 is to align what is good for the company with what is good for society at large. The concept of "enlightened shareholder value" is enshrined in the section 172 duty that requires directors to "have regard to" the interests of the plurality of stakeholders and "the likely consequences of any decisions in the long term" (section 172(1)(a)). This introduction squarely sets the scene for the discussion as to good corporate governance and the nature and form of corporate IP information and strategy disclosure to shareholders and stakeholders.

1.1 IP rights and corporate governance

The fundamental value of IP arises from its exclusivity. The law confers a monopoly right – ability of the IP owner to exclude others – assuring its uniqueness. This gives the owner the time to monetise the innovations by the route that creates greatest corporate value without undue concern that third parties will copy them without permission. IP rights also confer pricing power. The value of an IP right (or portfolio of IP rights) is basically the value of supra-normal profits earned from exploiting the innovation or creation, compared with what might be earned without the IP right. The commercialisation of innovations and creations and the IP rights that protect them are therefore two different issues. For example, if a patent is granted, the IP owner may get to market quicker than its competitors thus earning revenue (through sales) from the invention. Conversely, if the owner fails to develop the invention, a revenue stream can still be earned from the patent by licensing out to others the right of its use.[10] In theory, young IP-rich small to medium size enterprises (SMEs) are less likely to suffer margin erosion, and this should be an important factor in an holistic financial valuation of the IP rights as corporate assets.

Turning to the UK, more than 99% of its companies are SMEs and do not issue publicly tradable securities, making them reliant on credit from banks to grow their businesses. Traditionally, the nature of assets used as security in loan

10 Walmsley, J. *Patenting Finance: Financing Patents* (2001) International Securities Market Association, Zurich.

transactions mainly included land, plant, stock, inventories and receivables. Gold, jewelry and other tangible assets including antiques and works of art are also used as security. Whilst in quoted (publicly listed on a stock exchange offering shares to the public) and large private companies, the value of intangible patent assets is recognised in their market value, for unquoted SMEs there is no comparable mechanism for them to measure and demonstrate the value of the patent assets inherent in their business to use as security or collateral[11] for bank loans.[12]

Fortunately, important and meaningful recent developments in IP-backed finance in the UK and Europe have recently provided impetus to consolidate knowledge with respect to corporate governance and IP assets. In the UK, research focusing specifically on IP-backed debt finance has been published in the independent *Banking on IP?* Report (2013).[13] The EU's *Final Report from the Expert Group on IP Valuation* (2014) relates to future actions on IP policy, especially with respect to the European Commission's review of Europe 2020.[14] These publications indicate that both the UK and the EU seek to achieve a better understanding of the interplay between IP and finance, increasing confidence in IP valuation with the goal of facilitating financing to innovating SMEs. Accordingly, there is now momentum in the region to learn more about how corporate governance principles can support corporate IP information and strategy disclosure. The UKIPO stated:

> In 2014/15 the UKIPO will therefore focus attention on improving the ability of IP-rich businesses to secure access to growth finance – by building understanding of IP in the business and the financial services communities, by enabling a more productive dialogue between businesses and lenders, and by building greater confidence in the value of IP assets as collateral.[15]

Similarly, this book focuses on a practical commercial problem within a legal context, namely to support a framework for better corporate narrative reporting of IP asset information and stewardship of company assets to complement the traditional quantitative information in company accounts, leading to true and fair corporate IP asset valuations.

One problem that has not been studied sufficiently is the ***unintended effect*** of the "small companies' regime"[16] aimed at reducing administrative regulatory burdens by exempting directors of SMEs from providing a narrative corporate

11 Collateral is the US term for security.

12 Garrett, J. F. *Banks and Their Customers* (1995) Oceana Publications, Dobbs Ferry NY p 99.

13 Brassell, M. and King, K. *Banking on IP? The role of Intellectual Property and Intangible Assets in Facilitating Business Finance Final Report* (6 November 2013) Independent report commissioned by the UKIPO.

14 *Final Report from the Expert Group on Intellectual Property Valuation* (2014).

15 *Banking on IP: An Active Response* (31 March 2014) UKIPO p 20.

16 Small Companies and Groups (Accounts and Directors' Report) Regulations 2008 as amended by the Small Companies (Micro Entities' Accounts) Regulations 2013. This means that SMEs can take advantage of some exemptions to disclose less information.

report concerning their stewardship of company assets. The combined effect of traditional accounting principles (with respect to intangibles) and corporate disclosure laws has created a void of publicly available corporate IP and especially patent information. This is particularly problematic for stakeholders such as lenders who receive very little corporate IP asset and strategy information from a company applying for a loan, information that would assist them in assessing the corporate assets available as potential security. This book adopts a multidisciplinary approach, in particular, by adding a company law and corporate disclosure layer into the analysis. It investigates the deficiencies in traditional accounting for intangibles which can, it is argued, be potentially solved by increased corporate narrative disclosure concerning those IP assets. Enhanced narrative IP information and strategy disclosure could help to reduce the information gap, making corporate IP assets more visible to shareholders and other stakeholders such as financiers and investors. Another alternative that will be considered is a test case to judicially consider whether International Accounting Standard (IAS) 38 provides a "true and fair" view with respect to the financial value of internally generated IP assets. This could result in legal authority to depart from the IAS 38 standard. Thus, it is argued, company law should take the lead to provide a true and fair view of SMEs' IP and patent assets.

1.2 The corporate IP owners' perspective

From a corporate perspective, the advantage in applying for and being granted a patent, for example, is that in addition to creating a new asset which can be used as a source of security for loans, patents have the potential to create a royalty revenue stream, bolster financial statements and provide a shield against aggressive competitors. However, applying for a patent requires a largely upfront financial investment by the owner. This has a comparatively greater negative impact on SMEs at the beginning of the business life cycle because of their limited access to finance compared to larger firms who have more finance options. Further, for firms to benefit from their valuable IP rights they have to cultivate a greater awareness and understanding of them and this begins by embedding them into business decisions. Timely, accurate and reliable IP information is crucial to good corporate management as it will help firms determine what IP already exists, avoid infringement and duplication, keep track of competitors, identify potential partners and collaborators and spot market trends. Business decision making that systemically embeds corporate IP knowledge will drive the corporate "IP value" story that may need to be voluntarily or statutorily reported to shareholders and the public.

1.3 Users of IP asset information: the financiers' perspective

This book also investigates how certain risks inherent in intangible patent assets can be managed by producing better corporate IP information to assist in reducing the level of uncertainty perceived by lenders. The following statement by Scott Bell, Head of UK Investment Banking at DeutscheBank, clarifies the lenders' perspective about the lack of corporate IP asset information and the impact on lending decisions:

> Without data about value and risk, ownership, strategy and information allowing us to make market comparisons, it is hard to see how a functional and active market can be developed; and while data is not the only ingredient, transparency, visibility and understanding of the patent world has to be the starting point.[17]

Jiang Lurong, the general manager of the Shandong branch of Bank of Communications in the People's Republic of China (part of the consortium that syndicated a large patent-backed loan in that country), publicly stated:

> IP seems intangible, but it reflects the ability of value creation and sustainable operation of enterprises. Banking risk is not increased, but may be able to get a hold of high-quality customers early and improve the structure/makeup of the client base.[18]

In this book, we will investigate the level of transparency, visibility and understanding of potentially valuable corporate IP rights as commercial assets managed by company directors. This would assist companies to better forecast the growth potential and future cash flow of their business with greater precision and accuracy and put a probability on the forecast. As noted by Phillips:

> There [is a] paucity of information on which banks can assess the nature of the risk they take in lending on intangible securities.[19]

Another barrier to corporate reporting of IP assets and strategy is the uncertainty inherent in the boundaries and enforceability of legally constructed IP rights. Analysing the underlying value of corporate IP assets and associated risks is still difficult. IP monopoly rights are constructed by legal rules and the rules that define patent monopolies, for example, are the subject of constant change via case law and the doctrine of judicial precedent, which in the short term reduces certainty although in the long term the *stare decisis*[20] legal method increases

17 Phillips, J. (Ed.) *The Trillion Dollar Tipping Point AISTEMOS Report* (September 2014) AISTEMOS, London, p 8.

18 'Chinese company's $1.3 billion patent and trade mark loan enters the IP deal Pantheon' (4 April 2014) *Intellectual Asset Magazine* blog at www.iam-media.com/blog/Detail.aspx?g=481b76b6-637f-427f-b8d6-78d06cece504.

19 Supra n [17].

20 The phrase "stare decisis" is an abbreviation of the Latin phrase *stare decisis et non quieta movere* which translates as "to stand by decisions and not to disturb settled matters". The doctrine provides that the decision of a higher court acts as binding authority on a lower court within that same jurisdiction.

certainty. The more complex the uncertainties, the higher the risks for shareholders, investors, creditors and other stakeholders. This and other factors make it difficult, but not impossible, to give a true and fair value to IP rights (if the valuer has adequate and sufficient information). In order to estimate present and ***potential*** value of the IP assets, an analysis of non-financial qualitative indicators is beginning to develop in the UK but there is as yet no conceptual standard. This lack of transparency can be addressed by corporate governance theory and principles.

1.4 The corporate regulators' perspective

According to the Organization for Economic Cooperation and Development (OECD): Good corporate governance is not an end in itself. It is a means to support economic efficiency, sustainable growth and financial stability. It facilitates companies' access to capital for long-term investment and helps ensure that shareholders and other stakeholders who contribute to the success of the corporation are treated fairly.[21]

First issued in 1999, updated in 2004 and revised in 2015, the *G20/OECD Principles of Corporate Governance* have become the international benchmark in corporate governance. These principles have been adopted as one of the Financial Stability Board's Key Standards for Sound Financial Systems, are endorsed by the G20[22] and have been used by the World Bank Group in more than 60 country reviews worldwide. The principles also form the basis for the corporate governance of banks issued by the Basel Committee on Banking Supervision. The six key G20/OECD corporate governance principles are as follows:

I. Ensuring the basis for an effective corporate governance framework;
II. The rights and equitable treatment of shareholders and key ownership functions;
III. Institutional investors, stock markets, and other intermediaries;
IV. The role of stakeholders in corporate governance;
V. Disclosure and transparency; and
VI. The responsibilities of the board.

All companies must balance conformance with law and commercial performance to ensure the long-term success of the company. Corporate governance is about the relationship between a company's management, its board of directors, its

21 *G20/OECD Principles of Corporate Governance* (30 November 2015) ISBN: 9789264236882. See http://dx.doi.org/10.1787/9789264236882-en.

22 The G20 is the central forum for international cooperation on financial and economic questions. The "Group of Twenty" is made up of 19 countries and the European Union. The countries are: Argentina, Australia, Brazil, Canada, China, France, Germany, India, Indonesia, Italy, Japan, Mexico, Russia, Saudi Arabia, South Africa, South Korea, Turkey, the United Kingdom and the USA.

auditors (and their influence on traditional financial statements), its shareholders, its creditors and other stakeholders. The historic need for corporate governance arises out of the disconnect in corporations between the rights of shareholders and other suppliers of capital on the one hand and the operational control, which is in the hands of professional managers, on the other.[23] The corporate governance conundrum is whether the professional managers will or should run the corporation exclusively for the long-term benefit of the shareholders. For example, shareholders seek to ensure that the company is run to maximise long-term shareholder wealth and that directors put shareholders, rather than their own, interests first. Auditors need protection from the undue influence of management in their role as guardians of the accuracy of financial statements in order to give shareholders and other stakeholders a true and fair view of the financial performance of the company. Corporate governance is therefore a legal framework designed to monitor performance against the strategic corporate objectives set, and ensure that risks are managed appropriately and the company's resources are used responsibly. [24] The six key G20/OECD principles of corporate governance exist to ensure this ethical conduct. In this book we focus squarely on the fifth principle, that of disclosure and transparency.[25]

Corporate governance principles have developed to provide a legal framework for managing companies that embodies best practice, rather than relying on the integrity of individual company directors. For example, in the UK the annual financial reports ordinarily contain a corporate governance statement. This statement is vital for interpreting financial statements – a company with a fragile corporate governance system will provide opportunities for the manipulation of financial statements, resulting in undesirable consequences for users.

As IP rights no longer play solely the role of legal instrument, but also form potentially valuable commercial property, there is a pressing need to ensure good corporate governance. The increase in the number of patents filed worldwide over the last two decades and the growth of the markets for these assets has convincingly confirmed this trend.[26] While there are volumes of material concerning IP law, patent law, patent litigation, patents and economics (Italy and Germany); non-practising entities (NPEs) and the patent transactions market, there remains a significant deficit in the current research and literature related to best practice in transparency and disclosure of reliable and accurate information about the value of corporate IP assets and strategy. This is largely due to the fact that in material

23 *Influences on Corporate Governance B853-2 Issues in International Financial Reporting* (1 March 2016) The Open University, Amazon Media EU S.à r.l., section 1.1.

24 International Federation of Accountants (2004).

25 The 'Corporate governance, value creation and growth' initiative was launched in 2013 by the OECD Corporate Governance Committee to address how better corporate governance policies can support corporate access to capital, value creation and economic growth.

26 Munari, F. and Oriani, R. (Eds) *The Economic Valuation of Patents: Methods and Applications* (2011) Edward Elgar Publications Ltd p *xi*.

and voluntary corporate IP disclosure neither common principles nor best practice have emerged. How these limiting factors should be addressed to develop standards for corporate reporting of IP information and strategy will be discussed in more detail in the chapters that follow.

1.5 The need for a multidisciplinary approach to corporate IP

Recent global attention on IP rights as commercial tools has led to a greater focus on the need for research that addresses complex questions that cannot be answered within a single discipline. As such, law and finance is emerging as a new discipline. The issues arising extend to corporate governance of the IP assets owned by companies and require detailed research and efforts by policymakers, and those in the accounting, legal and patent attorney professions in order to overcome the corporate IP information gap. This reflects the weak corporate governance in terms of the lack of transparency of corporate IP assets. This book integrates the insights of the traditional disciplines of law, finance and accounting to create new knowledge with respect to enhancing corporate governance theory and principles as applied to IP rights as corporate assets.

The legal profession has always learned about business and finance as a function of legal practice, and finance professionals learn about business law as a requirement of their professional accreditation. Indeed corporate lawyers and financiers are professional cousins who interact closely over the course of their careers. It is not surprising that important research into IP finance (specifically IP-backed finance) and corporate governance transcends the scope of the single discipline. Research integrating information, perspectives and concepts derived from bodies of specialised knowledge is required in order to advance fundamental understanding and solve problems that are beyond the scope of the single discipline.[27] In this research, multidisciplinarity brings patent law, accounting and corporate law to the same table and has the goal of connecting the disciplines in pursuit of an increased understanding of the barriers to IP-backed debt finance and how shareholders can better identify and evaluate emergent corporate IP assets value to make better business decisions. Published research on the subject of law and finance is beginning to emerge, mainly in the field of financial regulation (law) and economics.[28]

27 Adapted from the definition created by the Committee on Facilitating Interdisciplinary Research, Committee on Science, Engineering and Public Policy (2004). *Facilitating interdisciplinary research*. National Academies. Washington: National Academy Press, p 2.

28 See UK law journals such as the *Law and Financial Markets Review* (Hart Publishing) and *Butterworths Journal of International Banking and Financial Law*.

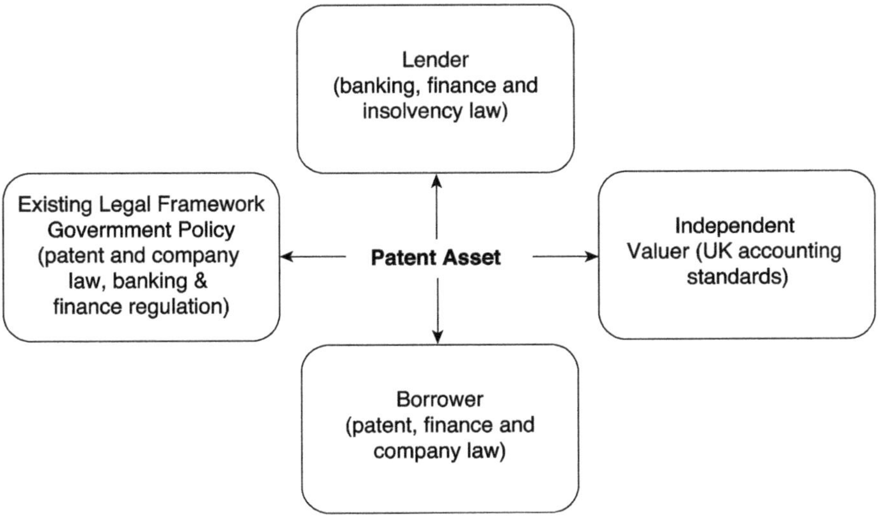

Figure 1.1 The IP asset as a tool to secure finance and the interplay of the academic disciplines

1.6 Corporate IP assets in the business environment

There is little academic literature concerning corporate narrative reporting of IP per se. However, in the US several professional publications became bestsellers in the American business community and captured worldwide attention. These included Rivette and Kline's *Rembrandts in the Attic: Unlocking the Hidden Value of Patents (2000)*[29] which addressed the corporate challenge of how to strategically use patents as business assets. In 2001 Baruch Lev's *Intangibles Management, Measurement, and Reporting*[30] was followed by another bestseller, *Einstein in the Boardroom: Moving beyond Intellectual Capital to I-stuff*.[31] The former advances the literature in three dimensions relevant to this book: the economics of intangibles (an accounting term that encompasses IP rights); the empirical record of intangibles; and the harms arising from the lack of information regarding intangibles. In 2017 an important work that increased knowledge in the field of IP finance was published by Canadian lawyer and academic, Kiriakoula Hatzikiriakos, *Secured Lending in Intellectual Property*, a comprehensive best practice guide for commercial transactions involving IP rights in Canada and the

29 Rivette, K., G., and Kline, D. (2000).
30 Lev, B. (2001).
31 Harrison, S. Sullivan, P.H. (2006).

United States.[32] Turning to the scant interdisciplinary literature on the subject of IP and accounting, legal scholar and economist, Dr Roya Ghafele[33] studied how the highly formalised language of accounting deals with the concept of intangibles. In 'Accounting for IP?'[34] she notes that accounting processes and terminology document past performance rather than expectations of the future, resulting in accounting statements that inadequately reflect how IP rights relate to business performance. Dr Ghafele's work was a springboard for the development of the thinking in this research, which argues that law, rather than accounting, should take the lead to ensure a "true and fair" view of patent assets and to overcome the invisibility of those assets in the traditional financial accounting statements. Dr Ghafele participated in the Panel of Experts that produced the 2014 "IP Valuation" report.[35] For the most part, until 2014, the literature did not obviously address or assume a multidisciplinary approach from either a financiers' or corporate regulators' perspective. Recent exceptions to this are the *Banking on IP?*[36] and "IP Valuation" reports. While both of these reports adopt a multidisciplinary approach, only the latter directly addresses corporate narrative reporting, but not corporate governance or regulatory issues.

Professor Toshiyuki Kono's edited collection *Security Interests in Intellectual Property: Perspectives in Law, Business and Innovation* offers a comprehensive analysis of IP and debt financing from Asian, European and American, points of view. The use of IP as collateral in practice, through a survey conducted in Japan on IP and debt financing, is also analysed. It identifies various obstacles in the proper use of IP and debt financing and some projects to facilitate its use are illustrated.[37] Most recently, the 2017 *Hidden Value: A Study of the UK IP Valuation Market*[38] report commissioned by the UKIPO confirms the demand for increased and better disclosure of corporate IP information.

This book further develops the author's doctoral thesis research,[39] published in 2015, which suggested that as a matter of modern corporate governance, it is

32 Second edition (2017) LexisNexis, Canada.

33 Fellow at the Said Business School, Oxford University

34 Ghafele, R. 'Accounting for Intangibles' (2010) 5(7) *Journal of Intellectual Property Law & Practice* 521–530.

35 *Final Report from the Expert Group on Intellectual Property Valuation* (2014).

36 Brassell, M. and King, K. *Banking on IP? The role of Intellectual Property and Intangible Assets in Facilitating Business Finance Final Report.*

37 Kono, T. (Ed.) *Security Interests in Intellectual Property: Perspectives in Law, Business and Innovation* (2017) Springer Verlag Singapore. See also Denoncourt, J. 'IP Debt Finance and SMEs: Revealing the Evolving Conceptual Framework Drawing on Initiatives from Around the World' in Kono, T. (Ed.) *Security Interests in Intellectual Property: Perspectives in Law, Business and Innovation* (2017).

38 Brassell, M. and Maguire, J. *Hidden Value: A Study of the UK IP Valuation Market* (August 2017) Independent Report Commissioned by the UK Intellectual Property Office Chapter 5.

39 Denoncourt, Janice A. *Patent-backed Debt Finance: Should Company Law Take the Lead to Provide a "true and fair" View of SME Patent Assets?* (2015) PhD thesis, University of Nottingham.

timely to introduce company law and corporate law regulators into the debate, examining company directors' stewardship and existing legal obligations to deal with intangible IP assets in their corporate reporting and recommending that voluntary statements in the Strategic Report section of the Directors' Report could be beneficial to highlight to stakeholders the existence and value of intangibles in the company.

1.7 Communicating how IP creates value

The rest of this book aims to guide companies as to how to communicate their IP value story to their shareholders, the public (if legally required to do so) and other stakeholders. It attempts to answer the following questions:

- How should additional narrative corporate disclosure of IP information and strategies be presented in order to give a "true and fair" view of the future value creating potential of the patent assets?
- What is the role of company law and corporate governance in this respect?
- How does a global company with access to the best advice present its IP and patent information and strategy in its company annual return?
- Is the Intellectual Capital Statement (ICS), mandated in Denmark, an appropriate form of disclosure? Or, should disclosure be by way of a management report, a growth report or integrated with the existing Strategic Report?
- Should the disclosure be voluntary or mandatory under the CA 2006 with respect to innovating SMEs?
- What international developments are taking place that may inform UK policy?

Part I: The corporate IP landscape, provides a political, economic, social, technological and legal (PESTL[40]) analysis and critically analyses the IP and patent ecosystem in which businesses must operate to create value. Part II: The IP finance dimension: corporate governance and transparency, demonstrates the role of corporate governance to support access to innovation finance (using corporate IP assets for debt and equity finance). Part III: Accounting for IP: corporate IP assets and transparency, illuminates the historic reasons for the corporate IP assets information gap and invisibility on the accounting balance sheet. The intersection between accounting practice and the corporate governance transparency principle, in other words, the reasons why "true and fair" IP information is a corporate governance issue is clarified. The impact of international corporate accounting rules, UK corporate legislation and case law is evaluated. Part IV: The corporate governance dimension: developing a normative practice in IP reporting, sets out corporate reporting obligations in the UK under the Companies Act 2006 and the concept of a material IP disclosure illustrated by two mini-case studies. It

40 Aguilar, F. *Scanning the Business Environment* (1967) Macmillan, USA.

explores the importance of non-financial narrative corporate IP information and benefits that accrue to companies that make public disclosures.

Chapter 2 introduces the political, economic, social, technological and legal environment in which IP monopolies operate in the UK. This will provide an IP ecosystem context and a foundation for the corporate finance and corporate governance issues arising. In Chapter 3 we analyse why reliance on debt finance (borrowing), as compared with other types of funding (selling shares), is critically important for innovation firms at the early stage of the business life cycle. We also explore the need for financial institutions to have a better IP awareness and develop more institutional trust in corporate IP assets, analysed from a behavioural finance perspective. In Chapters 4–6 a comparative functional analysis of narrative corporate IP asset disclosure using the US, Canada, Japan, Denmark and Germany as comparators is carried out, evaluating key principles with a view to establishing the boundaries of a conceptual framework for solving the intangibles reporting problem. In Chapter 7, the substance and form of corporate narrative IP asset disclosures is analysed. Using another mini-case study, we consider corporate narrative patent disclosure in practice, to investigate one company's approach to reporting its IP value story and business strategy in a real-life context.[41] Actual corporate IP and patent information narrative disclosures are hermeneutically interpreted and evaluated. The analysis begins to develop a normative practice, adopting the principles espoused in the UK Financial Reporting Council's guidance on the Strategic Report within the Directors' Report. In Chapter 8, criticisms of narrative IP disclosures are evaluated and a new business triage-style "materiality evaluation model" for IP and patent disclosures is presented. Chapter 9 offers final reflections on the new unofficial class of company, the IP-rich company, whether small or large, public or private and the role of corporate governance in shaping corporate behaviour.

41 Robson, C. *Real World Research* (1993) Blackwell, Oxford p 53

2 Corporate governance

The IP and patent ecosystem

The patent system introduces some of the greatest complexities in the capitalist ules of the game and leads to many anomalies.

J. Robinson, *The Accumulation of Capital*, 1956

The corporate IP assets of innovation firms are part of the IP ecosystem, whether they are large or small. Governments provide the legal framework by enacting legislation that facilitates, regulates and constrains the activities of IP owners. The IP ecosystem is the subject of this chapter and a broad overview of the environment in which innovation firms operate is presented. This serves as a theoretical framework, adopting a multidisciplinary approach, to examine specific factors that affect the evolving scope of corporate governance and the range of stakeholders involved. Stakeholders may include shareholders, the board of directors, the management, external auditors, investors, financiers and creditors. For public companies, institutional investors may include a range of financial institutions such as pension funds, investment funds, life assurance funds, unit trusts, hedge funds and other investment houses. There may be many intermediary institutions between the company and the ultimate investor in its shares. Investment bankers may act as underwriters in launching shares in an initial public offering (IPO) of shares. Brokers, merchant bankers and other institutions can hold shares in innovation firms on behalf of others. Sometimes financial institutions that hold shares in innovation firms lend them as security for other transactions. In contrast, in the smallest innovation companies, one person may be the director, shareholder and employee of the IP-rich company.

As patents are widely regarded as the most important type of IP right in economic terms, this chapter focuses on the patent ecosystem and the need to access capital to acquire and exploit patents as corporate assets. An effective patent granting and enforcement system is vital for companies that own or license the use of patents. The UK patent ecosystem is well developed to support companies, their directors and management to maximise corporate patent assets. However, many issues could be improved to support IP-rich companies to thrive. Section 2.1 explores the strategic commercial reasons for patenting inventions. Section 2.2 introduces the Political, Economic, Social, Technological and Legal (PESTL) analysis[1] to give an overview of the external macro-environment factors that collectively impact companies. Section 2.3 evaluates the political factors affecting UK patent policy. Section 2.4 studies economic factors that affect access to debt finance, especially for early stage innovating SMEs. Section 2.5 adopts a behavioural finance[2] approach to critically analyse the social factors influencing access to finance. Section 2.6 considers emerging technologies, patent backlogs, Horizon 2020: The EU International Strategy for Research and Innovation and finally, Technology Readiness Levels (TRLs) as a tool for corporate reporting.

2.1 Why firms invest in IP and patents

Although corporate agreement principles apply to all corporate IP assets, this book uses patent rights to illustrate the finance and corporate governance issues. In essence, patent rights protect new, industrially applicable inventions and give the inventor or proprietor ("the patentee") a legally recognised monopoly to work the invention for a period of up to 20 years.[3] A UK patent is governed by national laws, and also by international treaties, when those treaties have been given effect in UK domestic law, providing exclusive rights only in the UK and not in any other country. Patents are legal instruments intended to encourage innovation by providing a limited monopoly to the inventor (or their assignee) in return for the disclosure of the invention. Publication of the invention is mandatory in order to be awarded a patent.[4] The patent law system recognises that innovation and technological developments, both crucial tools for a country's financial and social wealth, cannot be motivated solely by market competition. IP rights and patents in particular, are increasingly reshaping the landscape of modern business. A key commercial advantage of a patent monopoly is that it can prevent unauthorised third parties from using the invention for a limited period. While under monopoly protection, the Patent Act 1977 (PA 1977) provides that only the patentee is lawfully allowed to commercially exploit the invention.[5] The scope of that right in any particular case is determined by the claims in the patent specification.[6] Further, there is strong evidence pointing to a positive association between patenting and measures of firm performance,[7] as indicated, for example,

1 Professor Francis Aguilar of Harvard University is credited with being the creator of PEST Analysis. He included a scanning tool called ETPS in his book, *Scanning the Business Environment* (1967) Macmillan. The name was later updated to include legal factors in the current acronym.

2 Baltussen, G. 'Behavioural Finance: An Introduction' (13 Jan 2009) Available at SSRN: http://ssrn.com/abstract=1488110.

3 Section 25(1) PA 1977.

4 Phillips, J. 'The English Patent as a Reward for Invention: The Importance of an Idea' (1982) 3 *Journal of Legal History* 71.

5 Section 60 PA 1977.

6 Section 14 PA 1977.

7 Hall, B., Helmers, C., Rogers, M. and Vania, S. 'The Importance (or not) of Patents to UK Firms' p1 at: *http://niesr.ac.uk/sites/default/files/publications/dp410.pdf.*

by a firm's sales of innovative products and growth in employment.[8] Firms with innovations that are *new* to the market are considerably more likely to patent.[9] Further, firms usually prefer patents over the cost and inconvenience of keeping their inventions secret (although unpatentable "know-how" may need to be kept confidential). Typically, firms that apply for patents have undertaken a commercial analysis of the pros and cons of patenting and arrived at a considered conclusion that the benefits of obtaining a monopoly over their invention exceed the costs and that patent rights will provide stronger protection than keeping the invention confidential[10] or defensive publication.[11] Strong patents (certain validity) are preferred over weak patents (at risk of being invalidated). However, even weak patents can be used anti-competitively and have their strategic uses which should be borne in mind. In addition, firms patent their inventions because they wish to: (1) prevent others from copying or free-riding; (2) block other firms from competing; (3) use them in cross-licensing negotiations and raise licensing revenue; and (4) enhance their business reputation.[12] These IP management strategies are important information from a corporate governance standpoint to assist to assess the directors' strategic direction of the company and policy making; supervision of executive management; stewardship of corporate patent (and other IP) assets; assessment of risk; and accountability to shareholders and other stakeholders.[13]

2.2 The Political, Economic, Social, Technological and Legal (PESTL) model

It is a legal requirement for most company financial accounts to be audited. Inevitably, questions arise during an audit such as the valuation of patent and other corporate IP assets; whether certain expenditures should be on or off-balance sheet, capitalised or written off to the profit and loss account; or concerns about the financial control systems.[14] Every company director should be aware of significant matters that have been raised during the audit by the independent,

8 Ibid p 4.
9 Supra n [7] at p 10.
10 The key disadvantage of a trade secret is its vulnerability to reverse engineering.
11 The act of publishing a detailed description of a new invention (without patenting it) to disclose prior art and public identification as the originator (or it can be done anonymously). A defensive publication prevents others from later being able to patent the invention.
12 Corporate Patent Strategy, WIPO p 33; Pletscher, T. 'Corporate Strategies for Managing, Exploiting and Enforcing IP Rights' (December 1988) WIPO pp 1–6.
13 Academics, economists, STEM (science, technology, engineering and mathematics) professionals and policymakers have conflicting views on patents and there is contentious debate in the field. These critical debates form part of an extensive discourse on IP protection beyond the scope of this thesis.
14 See Brassell. M. and Maguire, J., *Hidden Value: A Study of the UK IP Valuation Market* (August 2017) report for more detailed information on IP valuation methodology.

external auditor with respect to the company's financial statements (interim and annual) prior to publication. This includes but is not limited to accounting policies; material issues arising in or from the financial statements; compliance with accounting standards, company law, stock exchange reporting requirements (if applicable); ensuring the integrity of judgments made in the accounts; and ensuring the Directors' Report and Operating Statement is consistent with the audited financial statements. The UK Smith Report (2002), reflected in the UK Combined Corporate Governance Code (2010) suggests that management has the responsibility for "the identification, assessment, management and monitoring of risk, for developing, operating and monitoring the system of internal control and for providing assurance to the board that it has done so".[15] This general statement is broad and there is no reason why it would not extend to corporate IP assets. However, a company, on its own, cannot improve the IP ecosystem in order to reduce corporate risk or make IP-backed finance more accessible, many factors will play a part. By scanning the environment, we will have a better understanding of the positive and negative influences that impact on the IP ecosystem in which companies with patent portfolios operate. The PESTL framework is commonly used in a business context and represents one of the vertebrae of the backbone of strategic analysis, providing a broad overview of the factors that are beyond the control of innovation companies and financiers (an external perspective), yet which play an important role in value creation potential of patents in the UK.

2.3 Political factors that impact on UK IP and patent policy

Over the past two decades, the patent system has experienced significant changes worldwide. Consequently, the UK's patenting behaviour and legislation are prominent public policy themes. Analysis of the political environment will focus on patent law regime policy as it relates to innovating companies. The UKIPO[16], an Executive Agency of the Department for Business, Energy and Industrial Strategy (BEIS) is responsible for IP rights granting, formulating and delivering policy on patent law topics.[17] It has direct administrative responsibility for examining, issuing or rejecting patents, and maintaining the UK patent register. Several reports are published annually, including a Patent Office Annual Report

15 The UK Corporate Governance Code (from here on referred to as "the Code") is a part of UK company law with a set of principles of good corporate governance aimed at companies listed on the London Stock Exchange. It is overseen by the Financial Reporting Council and its importance derives from the Financial Conduct Authority's Listing Rules. The first version was published in 1992 by the Cadbury Committee and it has been updated in 1995, 1998, 1999, 2003, 2005, 2006, 2008, 2010, 2012, 2014 and 2016. See www.frc.org.uk/directors/corporate-governance-and-stewardship/uk-corporate-governance-code/history-of-the-uk-corporate-governance-code

16 www.ipo.gov.uk.

17 The Patents Law Amendment Act 1852 established the first patent office in the UK on 1 October 1852.

and Accounts[18], a Corporate Plan and a Facts and Figures report. The latter provides statistical data on annual trends for patents. The UKIPO actively engages with BEIS, supporting the wider BEIS agenda. It has been a key delivery partner in the BEIS Knowledge and Innovation Group, and contributed directly to the Government's Growth Agenda by improving the accessibility of the IP system to UK businesses at home and abroad.

In June 2007, the position of Minister of IP was created making the UK the only country in Europe to have a dedicated Minister with an IP portfolio, though it is a junior ministerial role, showing the UK is a leading nation within the global patent ecosystem. For all practical purposes however, the impact of the Minister of IP has not been very visible to date. This is likely because since 2007 there have been eight ministers and little continuity in policy implementation.[19] There is a need for the IP Minister to play a more active role in coordinating policies relating to innovation finance, regulation of corporate IP assets and raising awareness of IP. In 2008 the UKIPO appointed its first IP economist (the European Patent Office (EPO) appointed its first Chief Economist in 2004) and in 2009 developed a complementary work programme to build economic evidence for the development of IP policy. This unit is important for quantifying and analysing IP-related data.[20] Key issues in the government's policy agenda, currently being dealt with by the UKIPO include:

(1) substantive patent law harmonisation;
(2) patent backlogs;
(3) the proposed EU (Community) Patent;
(4) the reform of the Patent Convention Treaty (PCT) system;
(5) computer-implemented inventions i.e. software patents;
(6) collaboration with the EU to create a European Patent Court (EPC); and
(7) the impact on the IP ecosystem of the UK's exit from the European Union (BREXIT).

Political factors play a key role in shaping the UKIPO's activities and priorities in the public interest and key appointments have a direct influence on the government's national and international objectives and priorities. The need to educate businesses, company directors, business managers and finance professionals to increase awareness of the value of IP assets and support a constructive dialogue is ongoing, yet lacks visibility in terms of policy. In conclusion, the government needs to demonstrate more effectively that its structures and appointees are coordinating policies in relation to innovating firms, especially start-ups and

18 The Annual Report is presented to Parliament pursuant to section 121 of the PA 1977.

19 The current Director of Innovation and Chief Economist at the UKIPO is Pippa Hall appointed in April 2015.

20 Phillips, J. 'Katenomics 4: Where to look for an IP-oriented economist' (28 November 2008) *The IPKat* blog at http://ipkitten.blogspot.co.uk/2011_11_01_archive.html.

SMEs, IP, finance and in particular corporate regulation (to be discussed in the following chapters). Next, as part of our review of the IP ecosystem, we consider patent monopoly rights from an economic perspective.

2.4 Economic factors that impact IP as a driver for innovation

Everyone in the UK has an important stake in the modern market economy as it has the potential to continue to create prosperity and maintain a high standard of living. From a 21st century economic point of view, an IP right is an instrument of competition[21] that has grown in value in an increasingly knowledge-based economy. For example, a patent offers individuals the short-term right to exclude others from practising an invention and so provides them with the opportunity to earn royalties or supra-normal profits, i.e. higher than they would earn if there were immediate free entry into imitation of their invention.[22] This is why the patent system is widely believed to stimulate inventive and economic activity. However, there are weaknesses in the market system. Both economic theory and practical experience have established many examples of where markets, free and unfettered, bring inefficiency.[23] Where the distant future is concerned, or where rational decision making involves making a careful assessment of risk, or where shareholders and other stakeholders such as lenders have asymmetric information (an imbalance in the quality and quantity of information) about the future potential economic value of patents, the transactions between them are distorted and lending transaction costs increase.[24] Many market-oriented patent owners suffer frustrations as they attempt to educate their shareholders, government, the judiciary and financiers as to the role their innovations should play in supporting the regional, national and global economy. Companies need sufficient funds to develop their innovations. Corporate finance relates to the sources of funding, the capital structure of companies and the action that directors and managers take to increase the value of the firm to the shareholders. The primary goal of corporate finance is to increase shareholder value. The two main types of corporate finance are equity finance and debt finance. Investors provide funds to the company in return for equity (shares) which they hope will provide a return on investment (dividend and/or capital growth). Debt is the main alternative to equity within the wider context of corporate finance and can be used for both short and long terms purposes. Debt usually involves the payment of interest and may or may not be secured. Defects in information regarding IP rights as business assets are

21 WIPO Competition and Patents: Introduction, Studies and Articles.

22 McEachern, W.A *Economics: A Contemporary Introduction* (2012) Tenth edition, Cengage Learning Chapters 9 and 10.

23 Fulcher, J. *Capitalism: A Very Short Introduction* (2004) Oxford University Press, Oxford p 41.

24 Barkley Rosser, J. 'A Nobel Prize for Asymmetric Information: The Economic Contributions of George Akerlof, Michael Spence, and Joseph Stiglitz' (2003) 15(1) *Review of Political Economy*.

potentially serious considerations for shareholders and financiers, but they are also fairly tractable as shall be argued in the chapters that follow. The way most banks and lenders have dealt with corporate IP assets as potential security has been to restrict access to borrowing, as IP value is perceived as too uncertain to be covered by a reasonable risk premium, or charge higher interest rates. However, if the information asymmetry problem could be improved, in terms of economic theory,[25] this should have a positive impact on lenders' aversion to IP-backed lending as illustrated in the *Banking on IP?* report (2013), which concluded:

> The main obstacle is that IP is generally regarded as being too complex an asset class to finance within the constraints of normal lending margins, mainly due to the difficulties in understanding what it is, how it relates to cash, and were its value can be realised independently of a business. However, this is a perception that is open to challenge, not least because these are the primary assets modern businesses own and use.[26]

In this book, we adopt the view that in most Western democracies such as the UK, the market system has been most successful when supported by government regulation, including corporate regulation.[27] However, within the financial market system lenders are prone to "herd behaviour".[28] Currently, the "lender herd" continues to ration lending against patents and other IP assets because they are not comfortable with those assets as security. The "herd mentality" concept was first introduced by German philosopher Friedrich Nietzsche and suggests that (some) people tend to follow what others do without giving it much thought of their own, just like a herd of cows would follow one cow that starts to walk in a certain direction. Herd mentality is much more common and prevalent in society than might appear and plays an important role in business and human interaction. Groupthink[29] is a natural consequence of human social nature because we cannot predict the future. However, predicting the future is of overwhelming importance to present decision making, so people cling to what has worked in the past when attempting to forecast the future. Lenders have developed a strategy for dealing

25 Ibid.

26 Brassell, M. and King, K. *Banking on IP? The role of Intellectual Property and Intangible Assets in Facilitating Business Finance Final Report* (6 November 2013) Independent report commissioned by the UK Intellectual Property Office, p 210.

27 Stilwell, F. *Political Economy: The Contest of Economic Ideas* (2002) First Edition. Oxford University Press, Melbourne, Australia.

28 Shiller, R.J. 'Human Behaviour and the Efficiency of the Financial System' in Taylor, J.B. and Uhlig, H. (Eds) *Handbook of Macroecomics* (2016) Vol. 1, Elsevier; Bannerjee, A. V. 'A Simple Model of Herd Behaviour' (1992) 107 *Quarterly Journal of Economics* 797–817.

29 Allison, S.T and Messick, D.M. 'The Group Attribution Error' (1985) 39(4) *Journal of Experimental Social Psychology* pp 578–589. The biased belief that the characteristics of an individual group member are reflective of the group as a whole, even when information is available that clearly suggests otherwise.

with uncertainty by adopting the *conventional* view that patents as an asset class are not suitable as security for loans. It is critically important to shift this type of thinking by lenders for two reasons. First, because of the increasing amount of IP asset value that resides in firms. Second, because access to finance enables inventors and innovating firms with ideas, inventions, technical ability and opportunity – but no cash – to invest profitably, using the money of others who do not have the ideas, inventions or technical abilities. This mechanism ultimately leads to economic growth and better standards of living. Consequently, it is vital to realign business lending (a key type of corporate finance) from the industrial age to the modern age of the innovation economy. Funding is an essential building block of economic development, yet innovation companies, especially SMEs, find it challenging to secure loans from the retail banks using corporate IP assets such as patents. UK lenders should consider expanding their lending portfolios to include IP assets enabling them to diversify risk by spreading and minimising it. This will help to safeguard their position by lowering lending risks in the long term as some portion of their lending portfolio will perform favourably during economic cycles.[30] Fortunately, lenders such as the Clydesdale Bank, Santander and the Silicon Valley Bank UK branch are not following the herd[31] and are actively taking steps as early entrants in the intangibles lending market. The talent of these lenders is to see what others do not, or to see it earlier. They regard IP assets as an alternative asset category, affording the opportunity for greater diversification. To do this successfully requires skill, which is honed by becoming aware of valuable IP assets, learning about them and practising the skill in taking security over IP assets to develop expertise in the field.[32]

Turning to the borrower, the first management decision it makes is whether to invest in patenting its invention at all. This is an economic decision that depends on the impact investing resources in the patent will potentially have on profits. Further, according to the CA 2006, the board of directors now also has a statutory obligation to have regard to promoting the success of the company, which includes the likely consequences of any decision in the long term (CA 2006 section 172). According to ministerial statements,

> The words "have regard to" mean "think about"; they are absolutely not about just ticking boxes. If "thinking about" leads to the conclusion, as we believe it will in many cases, that the proper course is to act positively to

30 Tier, M. *The Winning Investment Habits of Warren Buffett & George Soros* (2005) St. Martin's Press, NY pp 296–298.

31 The Silicon Valley Bank opened its first UK branch, offering a full range of services in June 2013.

32 Maubussin, Michael J. *The Success Equation: Untangling Skill and Luck in Business, Sports, and Investing* (2012) Harvard Business Review Press. For further information on Clydesdales Growth Fund see *Banking on IP?* Report (2013) pp 135–136; *Final Report from the Expert Group on Intellectual Property Valuation* (2014). p 29.

> achieve the objectives in the clause, that will be what the director's duty is. In other words "have regard to" means "give proper consideration to".[33]

For example, the revenue generated by the invention should cover the costs of making a patent application as well as the renewal costs of maintaining any patent subsequently granted, so there is a net profit. This will depend on the success and value of the invention. At this point, the innovating firm has already made a preliminary assessment of the economic value of the patent to the business. Yet, while the IP ecosystem is effective in terms of encouraging innovation, it stalls at the decision-making level by external financiers. This is problematic when the UK is a key patent-intensive region in the EU with more than 2,000 UK patents a year being granted in the region during the period 2010–2013.[34] Indeed, there is patent activity across virtually every sector of the UK economy as patentees seek to gain proprietary market advantages. The top ten companies with the most patents granted by the UKIPO in 2013 are unsurprisingly all large companies.[35] However, the more patents issued, the greater both the public's awareness of them and the pressure on innovating SMEs to apply for them. Companies increasingly realise that neglecting to patent an invention may result in losing it to someone more proactive, who would demand a royalty for its continued use or production. Investment by UK business in intangible assets (including patents) totalling £137 billion has outstripped investment in tangible assets of £104 billion (approximately 25%).[36] This investment in intangibles led the *UK IP Ministerial Forum on the Economic Value of IP* held in 2009 to further understand the impact of intangibles on the economy. Due to the level of patenting activity, there is a scramble for both public and private funds in a harsh economic climate.[37] IP-intensive industries report that little money is available to support innovation, and it comes with onerous conditions.[38]

Turning our economic analysis to corporate debt finance and innovation, the National Endowment for Science, Technology and the Arts (NESTA) studied innovating firms' ease of access to loans in the UK, confirming that firms found it difficult to obtain a bank loan with only a good business plan and no tangible

33 Horrigan, B. *Corporate Social Responsibility in the 21st Century: Debates, Models and Practices Across Government, Law and Business* (2010) Edward Elgar Publishing p 245.

34 UKIPO Facts and Figures 2010 and 2011 Calendar Years, p1; UKIPO Facts and Figures 2012 and 2013 Calendar Years p 4.

35 IBM Corporation, Broadcom Corporation, Baker Hughes Incorporated, Dyson Technology Ltd., Schlumberger Holdings Ltd., GM Global Technology Operations, Inc., Hewlett-Packard Development Company, L.P., General Electric Company, Canon and Rolls-Royce. Source: Facts and figures for 2012–2013 Calendar Years (2014) UKIPO p 9.

36 Goodridge, P. et al *UK Investment in Intangible Assets: Report for NESTA* (2011) NESTA Working Paper No. 14/02, p 15.

37 Sunjata, D. 'Protecting ideas is crucial for eco-technology to succeed' (4 June 2010) *The Environment and Intellectual Property Financial Times Special Report* p 2.

38 Harvey, F. 'Scramble for funds in a harsh climate' (4 June 2010) *The Financial Times* p 1.

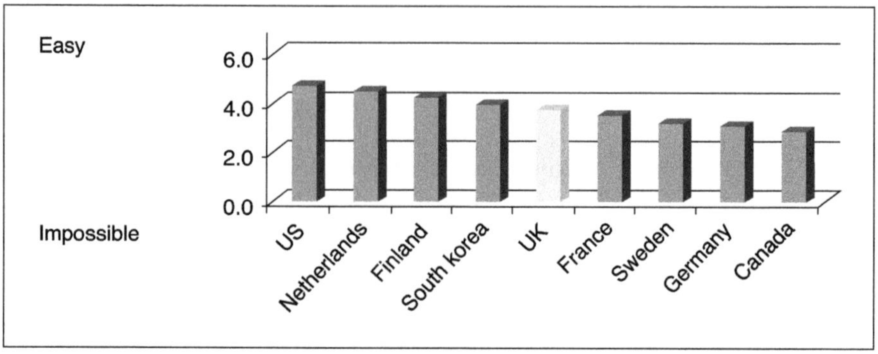

Figure 2.1 Access to loans

This chart shows the results of a business survey measure of respondents' views on how easy it is in different countries to obtain a bank loan with only a good business plan and no security (1 = impossible, 7 = easy).

Source: The Innovation Index NESTA (2009) p 23

security. The UK has declined in terms of access to loans and the current economic environment with tightening credit conditions adversely impacts new businesses as set out in Figure 2.1.

From the standpoint of innovating firms as borrowers, access to corporate debt finance is the most significant barrier to economic growth, as shown in Figure 2.2.

In its innovation report, NESTA concluded that:

> The UK is a relatively good place to innovate, but has some important shortcomings. On the basis of available internationally comparable data . . . the UK performed less well on three important indicators: access to finance, demand for innovation (in particular, the use of government procurement to encourage innovation), and skills for innovation.[39]

While the UK has a highly sophisticated corporate finance sector, research confirms that access to credit is a pressing concern. SMEs were particularly vulnerable as their size prevented them from accessing alternative sources of corporate finance.[40] BEIS has strategically prioritised and committed to improving the interface between innovation SMEs and lenders to assist them to commercialise their inventions.[41] It reported that over half of SMEs used finance in the last three

39 *The Innovation Index: Measuring the UK's Investment in Innovation and the Effects* (2009) p 7.

40 Pierrakis, Y. and Collins, L. *Banking on Each Other: Peer-to-Peer Lending to Business: Evidence from the Funding Circle* (April 2013) NESTA pp 3–7.

41 Ibid p 21.

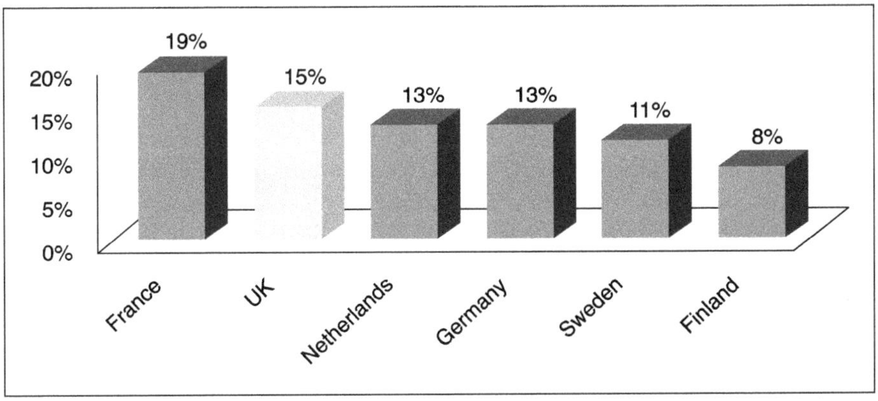

Figure 2.2 Companies identifying access to finance as the most pressing problem they face

This chart shows that 15% of UK firms (Eurobarometer survey) report access to loan finance as their most pressing business development problem.

Source: The Innovation Index NESTA (2009) p 23

years. Bank overdrafts, credit cards and a loan from an individual were the most common forms of debt finance used, followed by a bank loan or commercial mortgage or leasing/hire purchase.[42] SMEs that sought finance did so to obtain working capital or for cash flow.[43] The preferred source of corporate finance overall, regardless of reason, was a bank loan or commercial mortgage followed by a bank overdraft and loan/equity from friends and family.[44] Strategic realignment to evaluate the effects of alternative patent policies on the relationship between IP and economic development and IP debt finance would be beneficial.

2.5 Social impact: a behavioural economics approach and barriers to innovation

Behavioural economic research is regularly featured in top academic journals in economics and science. It studies the effects of psychological, social, cognitive and emotional factors on economic decisions.[45] Behavioural economics extends economic principles by demonstrating that economic decisions are affected by social and psychological influences, as well as a rational calculation of the benefits

42 *Small and Medium-Sized Enterprise (SME) Journey Towards Raising External Finance* (October 2013) A Report by BMG Research for BIS, Chapter 3.

43 Ibid Chapter 4.

44 Supra n [41] Chapter 7.

45 Lin, Tom W. C. 'A Behavioral Framework for Securities Risk' (2012) 34 *Seattle Law Review* 325

and costs. It provides a more intuitive and less mathematical account of decision making.[46] Although psychology has been used to support economic analysis since the early 20th century, it was in the 1960s that cognitive psychology shone a light on how the brain processes information. Psychologists such as Amos Tversky and Daniel Kahneman began to compare their cognitive models of decision-making under risk and uncertainty to economic models of rational behaviour.[47] Social factors and norms in the finance industry contribute to the barriers faced by innovation companies who seek access to debt finance. This section explores the interface between innovating companies (especially SMEs and their inventors) and access to corporate debt finance. We consider the lender mindset to cogitate their underlying social and cultural values at the point at which an innovating firm applies for debt finance. With regard to the social motivation of professional lenders, they typically take pride in carrying out their professional duties and want to provide a good service to their customers, while acting in a prudent way to balance making money from their lending activities and protecting the bank's position. Lenders' attitudes and behaviour are enshrined in professional codes of conduct and via laws regulating banking and finance and they risk loss of reputation and fines if they fall short of their professional standards. Lenders do not see themselves in an adversarial relationship with their customers until the customer defaults on its loan. What needs to be fostered as between innovating corporate borrowers and lenders who can distribute capital is a "team spirit" so that they worked cooperatively rather than in a dysfunctional manner. As for banks, they are part of the institutional structure of society[48] and are social constructs.[49] How lenders think about the IP ecosystem and how they behave are social phenomena.[50] The corporate finance environment is part of the financial system and is inherently fragile because it depends on trust. Trust is important because it is based on the ability to predict the future. In the paragraphs that follow, a short introduction to the research on human decision-making relevant to lending is presented. Before they will lend, lenders need to trust the IP-rich firm and have confidence that the loan will be repaid.[51] IP-rich firms also need to acknowledge that gaining a lender's trust is the key to an affirmative lending decision in their favour. Trust is an elusive element in many business dealings and is a critical aspect of a lending decision, because trust is a feeling. Trust is crucial in building long term success with a lender and vice versa (mutual functional trust). The trust the

46 Baddeley, M. *Behavioural Economics: A Very Short Introduction* (2017) Oxford University Press p 1.

47 Kahnemann, D. Slovic, P. and Tversky, A. *Judgment under Uncertainty: Heuristics and Biases* (1982) Cambridge University Press, Cambridge, MA.

48 Stein, H. *Beyond the World Bank Agenda: An Institutional Approach to Development* (2008) University of Chicago Press p 125.

49 Burr, V. *An introduction to Social Constructionism* (1995) Routledge, London, UK.

50 Social phenomena include all behaviour influences.

51 Tronnberg, C., Hemlin, S. 'Bankers' Lending Decision Making: A Psychological Approach' (2012) 38(11) *Managerial Finance* 1032–1047.

lender needs to feel lies not only with the borrower, but also in the patent asset and the patent system, which currently are not appreciated in mainstream UK corporate finance.[52] The author submits that lenders suffer from a cognitive bias in relation to patents as a form of intangible personal property capable of securing a loan as explained by an interviewee in the *Banking on IP?* Report:

> Our credit team was inclined to turn down anything they didn't understand and which didn't have the sort of assets that were familiar. However, we did manage to turn round a lot of decisions that were initially declined.[53]

Generally speaking, they do not see IP rights and patents as a functioning asset class. This cognitive bias includes being risk averse with respect to corporate IP assets.[54] Trust is a form of faith in that the lender also has to believe in what the IP-rich firm is doing and their plans for the future. Lenders need relevant, useful and reliable qualitative information about the firm's IP strategy for generating future value from those assets. For example, lenders may trust the firm as a business, but not have faith in the value or quality of the patent(s) as a business asset. Alternatively, the lender may believe in the value and quality of the patent asset, but not trust the borrower (based on past lending experience or credit history).

A common misconception is the view that numeric (quantitative) accounting information is more trustworthy than qualitative formats[55] because it is less vulnerable to "spin". It will be argued in the chapters to follow that improving the communication of the "patent value story" to lenders supported by corporate narrative IP information and strategy disclosure within the company's annual Strategic Report filed with Companies House is needed to garner lenders' trust. Corporate annual and quarterly narrative reports are the most credible and compelling medium for telling a company's "IP value story". They are also corporate reporting documents with which lenders and other stakeholders in the commercial environment are familiar. Further, disclosure made within the company law framework substantially increases the legitimacy and authority of the information disclosed, which comforts lenders and other stakeholders, e.g. shareholders and corporate regulators.

In essence, lenders need to have a high level of trust in borrowers because they are contemplating lending money and want to know it is safe and will be repaid. Trusting a borrower is a risk. The lender will typically examine the possibility of the company defaulting on the loan within a one to two year time frame, taking into consideration current information about the borrower.[56] Defaulting on a loan

52 Supra n [25] at p 13.

53 Supra n [25] at p 67.

54 Supra n [46].

55 McLeod, S. A. 'Qualitative Quantitative' (2008). Qualitative research gathers information that is not in numerical form and may require a degree of expert knowledge to interpret.

56 Tronnberg, C. and Hemlin, S. 'Bankers' Lending Decision Making: A Psychological Approach' (2012) 38(11) *Managerial Finance* 138.

is trust lost and lenders will be reluctant to trust again for a period of time. If a lender loses faith in a borrower's ability to repay debt, even though it may not be the borrowers fault, the lender's trust evaporates and the lender does not really care what caused the default. When trust is present, banks will lend because lending is a core business. The provision of relevant, useful and reliable information about the borrower's proposed IP and patent assets to secure a loan is economically sound and will increase trust.

In a social context, a lender's trust initially is tentative and must be earned – this is the case for any borrower.[57] Lenders use different methods to assess the risk of default. They use either quantitative methods, such as financial statement lending and credit scoring, or more qualitative methods, such as relationship lending, to assess the borrower and its business strategy.[58] Quantitative credit appraisal methods involving numbers are potentially problematic to the extent that they give the illusion of providing more truth than they actually do (especially in relation to internally generated corporate patent assets, to be discussed in Chapter 4). They favour what is easiest to measure, not necessarily what is the most important.[59] They can easily be used to dress up failure as success.[60] A combination of quantitative and qualitative methods would complement each other and assist to reduce lending risk, assisting experienced loan officers to undertake a more thorough evaluation before making a lending decision.[61] It is fair that lenders are sceptical about intangible corporate IP assets because they generally do not have a great deal of experience with them as an asset class with collateral potential. Both the amount of financial information and the type of information influence lending decisions.[62] In traditional bank lending decision making is guided by the "5Cs of lending" that apply to both transactional and relationship lending. The 5Cs, which should be evaluated equally, are:

(1) character (i.e. evaluation of the prospective borrower's personal characteristics, in other words those of its company directors and managers);
(2) capital (i.e. the borrower's net worth);

57 Deszo, L. and Loewenstein, G. 'Lenders' Blind Trust and Borrowers' Blind Spots: A Descriptive Investigation of Personal Loans' (2012) 33(5) *Journal of Economic Psychology* 996–1011.

58 Berger, A.N. and Udell, G.F. 'A More Conceptual Framework for SME Finance' (2006) 30(11) *Journal of Banking & Finance* 2945–2966.

59 Bornstein, D. *How to Change the World: Social Entrepreneurs and the Power of New Ideas* (20 Sept 2007) Second edition, Oxford University Press, USA..

60 Ruddick, G. 'Suspended Tesco executive to return as Dave Lewis overhauls team' (1 December 2014) *The Telegraph*. The well-known UK supermarket Tesco plc financial statement scandal uncovered a profit black hole amounting to £263 million which is presently being investigated by the Serious Fraud Office.

61 Supra n [55] at p 1040.

62 Biggs, S.F., Bedard, J.C., Gaber, B.G. and Linsmeier, T.J. 'The Effects of Task Size and Similarity on the Decision Behaviour of Bank Loan Officers' (1985) 31(8) *Management Science* 970–986.

(3) collateral (i.e. the borrower's pledge of property to secure the debt);
(4) capacity (i.e. the borrower's ability to service the debt out of current income); and
(5) conditions (i.e. present market conditions for both the borrower and the general economy).[63]

However, according to Hedelin and Sjo'berg it appears that the borrower's personal characteristics are overemphasised in lending-decision making.[64] The author considers that conversely, it is likely that the borrower's collateral is underemphasised if it comprises IP rights with which lending officers have little expertise. It may be they neglect to take into account important IP information as it does not usually form part of any common corporate information or other documentation used to approve loans. This is detrimental to corporate finance in general.

Financial herding has arguably disrupted innovation firm access to corporate debt finance with a consequent impact on the ability to develop and commercialise innovation, a public good. Lending money involves assessing risk. However, it may be that when contemplating making a decision to lend to an innovation company, lenders inflate the impact of losses relative to gains. Reducing herding and groupthink depends on decision makers having all the information (timely, accurate and relevant) they need to arrive at a sound decision. Currently, lenders and other stakeholders are not receiving sufficient information about the financial value of the innovation firm's corporate IP assets and their role in value creation. Disclosure and transparency of the value of corporate assets is a matter for corporate governance. Analysing how to improve the quality and amount of corporate IP asset information that companies disclose is the subject of later chapters.

Humans dislike change and this dislike goes further than fear of material loss. A practical solution for corporate finance and IP-backed lending is for the innovating firm to seek relatively small loans initially. Lenders learn from experience and may draw conclusions from earlier situations and can match these with present situations.[65] As the lender becomes more comfortable it will consider increasing the amount of funds advanced, as with credit card limits which are only increased once the borrower has shown discipline by meeting the monthly repayments and developing a positive credit history. Lenders test borrowers this way because they want to feel safe, breeding confidence in future favourable lending decisions.

Another solution is for innovating firms to approach smaller banks that form closer relationships with their client-borrowers and taker greater risks, relying more heavily on traditional relationship lending and qualitative lending risk

63 Thomas, L.C. 'A Survey of Credit and Behavioural Scoring: Forecasting Financial Risk of Lending to Consumers' (2000) 16(2) *International Journal of Forecasting* 149–172.

64 Hedelin, E. and Sjo'berg, L. *Risk Assessments – Loan Officers' Assessment of New Entrepreneurs' Personal Characteristics)* (1993) NUTEK, Stockholm.

65 Supra n [55] at p 1039.

assessment.[66] In *How to Change the World,* concerning social entrepreneurs and the Ashoka Foundation, Bornstein states:

> funders should remain cautious when embracing numerical assessments. The quest for quantifiable social returns or outcomes has become an obsession in a sector that envies the efficiency of business capital markets. Given this obsession, it is important to remember that a number has an unfortunate tendency to supersede other kinds of knowing. The human mind is a miracle of subtlety: It can assimilate thousands of pieces of information – impressions, experiences, intuition – and produce wonderfully nuanced decisions.[67]

The positive benefits of relationship lending were experienced by Sir James Dyson, inventor, billionaire, engineer, industrial designer, founder of the Dyson company and knight of the realm, who experienced cash flow pressures with his fledgling innovation business:

> Dyson vacuum cleaners would not exist were it not for Mike Page, my bank manager, who personally lobbied an initially reluctant Lloyds Bank to loan me the £600,000 I needed for tooling – the only way to start out on my own.[68]

Mr Page possibly used an intuitive approach[69] and rated Dyson's managerial and business experience as an important factor in the credit assessment.[70] Nevertheless, the status quo is that lenders are averse to IP finance and patent-backed lending and this is a barrier to overcome. Lenders currently trust in tangible assets, intangible equity assets (shares) and all kinds of other tricky, risky and complex financial products (derivatives and hedge funds etc.). Nobel prize-winning Grameen Bank has even pioneered and popularised a methodology for extending small collateral-free loans for self-employment to some of the world's poorest people which has had an enormous impact.[71] Microfinance is an example of systemic change in the field of finance to solve a problem. Academic Muhammed Yunus challenged banking theory showing how to systematically extend security-free loans on a cost-effective basis to poor villagers on a large scale. The Grameen Bank has 7.1 million borrowers in 77,000 villages in India. Microfinance is now a global movement and has been taken up by banking giants like Citigroup. If it

66 Supra n [57].

67 Bornstein, D. *How to Change the World: Social Entrepreneurs and the Power of New Ideas* (20 Sept 2007) Second edition, Oxford University Press, USA.

68 Dyson, J. *Ingenious Britain Making the UK the Leading High Tech Exporter in Europe: A Report by James Dyson* (March 2010) Commissioned by the UK Conservative Party p 42.

69 Khatri, N. and Ng, H.A. 'The role of intuition in strategic decision making' (2000) 53(57) *Human Relations* 57–86.

70 Supra n [55]at p 1040.

71 See www.grameen.com.

is possible to make cost-efficient loans to borrowers with no security at all, surely it should be feasible to make loans to innovating firms against patents to create time-limited monopolies that have an existing and potential future value?

In 2010 the UK's Conservative Party invited James Dyson to help them reawaken Britain's innate inventiveness and creativity to generate and export more technology. This resulted in Dyson's *Ingenious Britain: Making the UK the Leading High Tech Exporter in Europe* report[72] which recommended the UK government tackle the issue of "[f]inancing high tech start-ups".[73] Dyson's report identifies that as the vast majority of high tech innovating SMEs rely on debt financing for growth it is vital to examine better routes to access such financing as it will have a high impact on the domestic economy.[74] The report recommends the government address the apparent unwillingness of banks to lend to small businesses:

> Clearing banks[75] have a unique understanding of small businesses and have the infrastructure to monitor small debt financing. The process of obtaining a clearing bank loan is simpler and more easily understood by fledgling start-ups. A loan guarantee scheme similar to the National Loan Guarantee Scheme to stimulate small business lending, especially to those exploring new technology, should also be explored.[76]

Dyson's report reiterates the need to improve access to debt finance to assist the UK maintain and improve its status as a nation at the forefront of technologies of the future. Unfortunately, what lenders and banking regulators are really saying to corporate IP rights owners is "we trust borrowers who own other classes of asset more". But is this trust in other assets classes misplaced and are patent assets really riskier? Banks perceive less risk in lending against land, shares and other financial products and even to the poor, but the global financial crisis 2007–2012[77] tells a different story. Traditional forms of security are riskier than commercial lenders originally perceived. In time, lenders' trust in corporate patent assets will develop and the patent asset class will mature and foster a solid reputation (a past credit history). The corporate governance theories of transparency and disclosure directly support the goal of earning trust.

72 Supra n [67] foreword.

73 Ibid.

74 Supra n [67] at pp 46–47.

75 In the UK the five largest clearing banks (institutions which clear bankers' cheques) in England and Wales were Barclays, HSBC, Lloyds Banking Group and Natwest.

76 Supra n [67] at p 42.

77 *The Run on the Rock Fifth Report of Session 2007–2008 House of Commons Treasury Committee* (2008) Vol. 1, House of Commons, The Stationer Office Ltd, London pp 4–20. Also known as a credit crunch, it is a decline in the general availability of loans (or credit) coupled with a tightening of the conditions required to obtain bank loans. A credit crunch is accompanied by a "flight to quality" by lenders, as they search for less risky investments, often at the expense of SMEs.

Gaining the lenders' trust does not mean innovating firms will always successfully commercialise innovations, however it does provide the funding to move forward at a significantly increased rate than would otherwise be the case. A favourable lending decision means that over the term of the loan, the innovating firm will deliver more detailed information about its business strategy, positively impacting on the lender/borrower relationship. This takes place through the bank's loan risk monitoring procedures under the loan documentation applicable to all loans. A dynamic risk monitoring system provides an intelligence framework for collecting real-time information by scanning for events relevant to loan quality, as opposed to a creditor scoring system which relies on historical data about the borrower to predict loan quality. [78] Loan monitoring systems directly benefit the bank's shareholders by enhancing the value of the bank's loan portfolio.[79] More importantly for the development of corporate finance and IP-backed lending, banks have increased incentives to hold "risky" loans when they can monitor such "riskier" loans in real time.[80] This is where the "missing" narrative corporate disclosure regarding IP, patent information and strategy will be felt in the long term, by improving the business relationship. The challenge for the innovating firm, as a trusted borrower, is to provide real-time information that is accurate, visible and has value to the lender, making the value of their IP assets more transparent, thus breeding confidence.

Trust is the highest level of human and social interaction and it is also the most complex.[81] The simplicity of trust is that if lenders do not have trust in corporate IP assets, it is because that trust has yet to be earned. Lenders must be confident that the innovating firm trusted to repay the loan will do what is expected. It is important to analyse the IP ecosystem to understand why lenders do not generally trust in IP assets and then to work to lower the barriers to gain that trust.[82] In economic terms, trust is viewed as an economic lubricant, reducing the cost of transactions between parties, enabling new forms of cooperation and generally furthering business activities and prosperity.[83] Without trust in corporate IP rights as an asset class, lenders are paralysed. The *Banking on IP?*[84] report confirmed that

78 Instefjord, N. and Nakata, H. 'Loan Monitoring and Bank Risk' (17 April 2014) First Draft, p 2.

79 Ibid p 4.

80 Ibid pp 6–7.

81 Mayer, R.C., Davis J.H., Schoorman, F.D. An Integrative Model of Organizational Trust (1995) 20(3) *Academy of Management Review* 709–734. Definitions of trust typically refer to a situation whereby one party (trustor) is willing to rely on the actions of another party (trustee) and the situation is directed to the future.

82 Kosfeld, M., Heinrichs M., Zak, P. J., Fischbacher, U. and Fehr, E. 'Oxytocin Increases Trust in Humans' (2005) 435 *Nature* 673–676. It can be demonstrated that humans have a natural disposition to trust and to judge trustworthiness that can be traced to the neurobiological structure and activity of a human brain.

83 Morgan, R. and Hunt, S. 'The Commitment-Trust Theory of Relationship Marketing' (July 1994) 58(3) *The Journal of Marketing* 20–38.

84 Supra Brassell and King n [13].

the role of IP in facilitating corporate finance was not appreciated in mainstream UK lending and that IP was therefore a missed opportunity.

A problem facing lenders is that borrowers can be dishonest and provide less than accurate information. Fraud is a risk with respect to intangibles, as with any asset. There is risk with regard to genuine uncertainty as to the future. Dishonest or misleading IP valuations may involve collusion with accountants, solicitors, patent attorneys and other professional intermediaries who inflate the value of the asset. This is why making IP information disclosure in the Strategic Report of a company's annual return, a tool to ensure good corporate governance, is critically important. It is argued that if lenders and other company stakeholders are in a position to triangulate[85] quantitative, qualitative and strategic IP information, this promotes validity, reliability and accuracy – increasing predictability and decreasing the volatility of quantitative IP asset values. This should enhance lenders' trust in IP rights as an asset class for use as security. The information must meet the "true and fair" standard set by corporate disclosure regulations. Having reliable information will facilitate lenders' due diligence. Further, having both types of information will also assist the lender to dynamically monitor the loan by triangulating the information with the borrower's current account activity. Thus, to enhance corporate governance and innovation finance, it would be beneficial for lenders to introduce effective dynamic monitoring systems to align the banks' and banking regulator's interests.[86]

Finally, another way for innovating firms to gain a lender's trust is to demonstrate competency, superior skills and passion. As a legal construct, patents for example, demonstrate a degree of novelty and inventive step over the state of the art, in other words, over the competition. Innovating firms need to show lenders and other stakeholders their value by showing the problem the invention solves, not just how the patented invention works – this is part of the "Patent Value Story". Patents granted in countries with a thorough system of examination carried out by highly qualified patent examiners, demonstrate a high degree of validity. Winning prizes or professional accolades, writing publications, being invited by peers to speak at conferences and being perceived as an authority on the issue to which the patent relates also demonstrates superior skills and builds a valuable corporate reputation (non-financial indicators of value). Thus, IP and patent-backed debt finance can be thought of as a mixture of applied economics and human nature. Lenders cannot trust in what they do not understand, therefore the UKIPO agenda to raise awareness and understanding of IP and IP-backed corporate finance methods is the right approach. Measures to enhance the interface between corporate IP owners and equity and debt financiers will be addressed throughout this book from a corporate governance perspective. If we do nothing, innovation firms will continue to struggle to thrive and grow without access to

85 Triangulation is a powerful technique that facilitates validation of data through cross verification from three or more sources applying several methodologies to the same phenomenon.

86 Supra Instefjord and Nakata n [77] at p 6.

debt finance. Financial lending institutions should re-think the way they evaluate corporate IP assets and their economic value for security (collateral) purposes.

2.6 Technology issues that affect the patent ecosystem

Emerging technologies underpin the creation of a sustainable and resilient future for the UK and are at the heart of the inventive patentable subject matter of the future. This section considers the external technology issues that affect the patent ecosystem in which innovation firms operate.

2.6.1 Emerging technologies

The *Summit on the Global Agenda* is organised annually by the World Economic Forum's (WEF) Global Agenda Council on Emerging Technologies.[87] It is the world's largest global brainstorming event, assembling thought leaders comprising eight expert groups from business, academia, government and civil society to advance knowledge and jointly explore critical issues shaping the world. Technology has a critical role to play in the global economy, yet it also poses significant risks of which companies need to remain cognizant.

In 2016, the Summit determined that the following five technology trends would make the greatest impact on the world in the near future:

- Nanosensors and the Internet of nanothings;
- Next generation batteries (advances in energy storage);
- The Blockchain (distributed electronic ledger behind the online currency Bitcoin);
- Two-dimensional materials (such as graphene);
- Autonomous vehicles.[88]

However, without appropriate systems and capabilities to develop and commercialise inventions, their safe and successful development is not guaranteed. The UKIPO will need to ensure its human resources plan enables it to recruit suitable and sufficient patent examiners, who have expertise in the emerging technology fields identified above to support innovation companies.

2.6.2 Patent application examination backlogs and corporate asset value

Technological pressures are also at work in the patent system due to the high level of patent applications. The World Intellectual Property Organization (WIPO)

87 See www.weforum.org/events/summit-global-agenda-2015.

88 Global Agenda on Emerging Technologies blog at www.weforum.org/agenda/2016/06/top-10-emerging-technologies-2016/.

reported that in 2011 global patent applications reached the two million mark evidencing almost constant growth spanning more than two decades.[89] In the UK and other patent-rich jurisdictions, this is leading to problems of patent office backlogs and the emergence of so called "patent thickets", which obstruct entry to some markets and so impede innovation. A "patent thicket" is a strategy whereby a patent owner develops a dense collection of overlapping patent rights which means that innovators need to license multiple patents to use the technology. From a strategic point of view, patent thickets are also used to defend against competition from third parties who might otherwise design around a single patent.[90] This is normal according to Sir Robin Jacob:[91]

> every patentee of a major invention is likely to come up with improvements and alleged improvements to his invention . . . it is in the nature of the patent system itself that [patent thickets] should happen and has always happened.[92]

The *Hargreaves Review*[93] took the view that patent thickets could reduce technological development and innovation. It is important the UK continues to engage in international cooperation to address the backlogs and thickets. The UKIPO published *Patent Thickets – An Overview*[94] and *A Study of Patent Thickets*[95] to gain a better understanding of:

(1) whether thickets deter new competitors, especially innovating SMES, from entering a field of technology; and
(2) the effect pending patents have as a barrier to entery to a technology area and their relationship with patent thickets.

The latter concluded that the growth of patent thickets in the European patent system negatively impacts on entry into certain fields of technology, coupled with

89 'To hack or not to hack? A new report on patent thickets' (22 August 2013) UKIPO *Facto blog* at www.ipo.gov.uk/blogs/ipofacto/2013/08/22/to-hack-or-not-to-hack-a-new-report-on-patent-thickets/.
90 Rubinfeld, D. and Maness, R. 'The Strategic Use of Patents: Implication for Antitrust' in Leveque, F. Shelanski, H. *Antitrust, Patents and Copyright: EU and US Perspectives* (2005) Edward Elgar, Northampton pp 85–102.
91 Formerly Lord Justice Jacob of the Court of Appeal, admitted to the IP Hall of Fame in 2006.
92 Jacob, R. '*Patents and Pharmaceuticals*' (29 November 2008) Paper given at the Presentation of the Directorate-General of Competition's *Preliminary Report of the Pharma-sector Inquiry*.
93 Hargreaves, I. *Digital Opportunity: A Review of IP and Growth* (May 2011) Independent report commissioned by the UK Prime Minister.
94 *Patent Thickets – An Overview* (25 November 2011) UKIPO Informatics Team.
95 Hall, B., Helmers, C., Rogers, M. and Vania, S. 'The importance (or not) of patents to UK firms' p 1 at:http://faculty.haas.berkeley.edu/neil_thompson/Innovation_Seminar/Papers/HHRS12_UK_patenting.

a "lack of resources and misaligned incentives in patent offices faced with a flood of patent applications".[96] How to reduce patent pendency and uncertainty in the patent ecosystem is an administrative issue of key concern to innovation companies and other stakeholders. Over the past two decades, the number of UK patent applications filed annually has mostly grown in an upward trajectory. However, the volume of patent applications outpaces the UKIPO's capacity to examine them. As a result, a substantial backlog of unprocessed patent applications has accumulated resulting in longer periods of patent pendency. This problem is affecting patent offices worldwide.

In terms of corporate asset value, patent applications are less valuable than granted patents. Backlogs in processing and examining patent applications cause delays in patents being granted, together with the rights afforded by granted patents (which in turn increase their economic value). Delays in processing patent applications also impede new products and processes from being commercialised, as the incentive to create and innovate is reduced.

Investors and are reluctant to invest, and lenders reluctant to lend against new technologies that are not protected by a granted patent. Further, corporate patent owners cannot take legal action for patent infringement until their patent is granted. The expressions "patent pending" or "patent applied for" are notices that companies are entitled to use indicting that they have filed a patent application, but the application has not yet been officially granted. This puts potential infringers on notice that they may be liable for damages (including damages back-dated to the priority date of the patent) as well as other remedies available under the Patent A Act 1977. Lengthy periods of patent pendency also lead to greater uncertainty about the potential validity of the inventions and whether they will in fact ever be patent-protected which in turn impacts on corporate asset value.

One legal issue arising is that the claims which define the patent monopoly are not available to the public, nor can they be searched until published. This is the period from the priority date until publication date of the patent, part of the period of "pendency". The content of the patent claims therefore remains confidential as between the patent applicant and the UKIPO and is not able to be searched, creating a "black box" of claims. Thus, later patent applicants may not be aware of the earlier confidential claims and their own patent application may fail for lack of novelty or worse, they risk infringing the pending patents. The greater the patent backlog, the greater the risk for patent applicants and companies who invest in filing patents to protect their innovations. This creates uncertainty regarding the patent asset, lowering its value. Simply put, longer pendency periods reduce the value of the patent. Although pending patents cannot be enforced, they still have value, although not as much as either a granted patent or a granted patent that has been successfully challenged and held to be valid. Voluntary narrative corporate disclosure confirming the existence of patents applied for and

96 Ibid p 3.

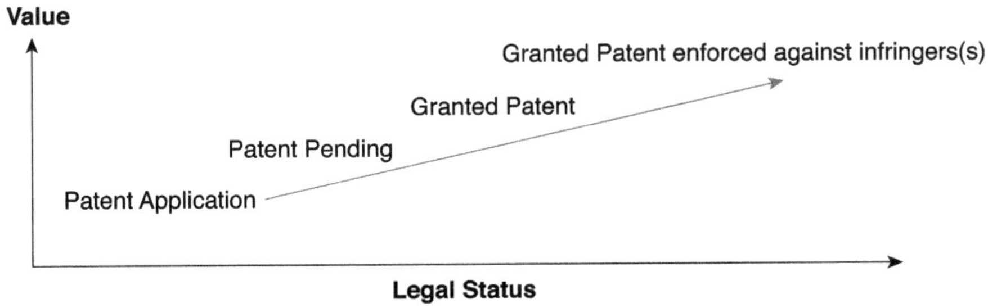

Figure 2.3 The patent value continuum

undergoing examination can provide a basic level of factual information for investors, lenders and other stakeholders. Figure 2.3 depicts the patent value continuum.

The increasing complexity of technology and volume of prior art that needs to be examined is making the role of patent examiners more difficult. However, if the average period of patent pendency remains constant, the UKIPO backlog will continue to grow as patent applications grow and the system becomes even more backlogged. The EPO estimates that it will take *over four years to clear its patent backlog*. A recent economic study entitled, *Patent Backlogs and a System of Mutual Recognition*[97] made two important conclusions. First, backlogs reduce the effectiveness of the patent system by creating costs for the applicant. Costs arise because any uncertainty about validity complicates planning and formulating business strategy, investment decisions and access to funding. Second, backlogs impact on patent quality. Uncertainty over the scope of patent quality deters shareholders from investing and lenders from granting loans as a pending patent has less value than a granted patent. If the backlog stretches the UKIPO's resources and patent quality decreases, more applicants are encouraged to "try their luck" by making low quality patent applications. This predictably means patent litigation will increase.[98]

The UKIPO recognises this operational challenge stating that "it is playing an active role in encouraging international cooperation between IP offices through work-sharing to reduce backlogs".[99] This is sensible as it is estimated that approximately one third of patent applications worldwide are duplicate applications. A mutual recognition system will allow the UKIPO to reduce the time it spends examining duplicate applications also being reviewed by foreign patent examiners,

97 *Patent Backlogs and a System of Mutual Recognition* (2010) Prepared by London Economics for the UK Intellectual Property Office.

98 *Patent Backlogs and a System of Mutual Recognition* (2010) Prepared by London Economics for the UK Intellectual Property Office, p 14.

99 Ibid p 14.

with a knock-on effect on the backlog. However, even with work-sharing programmes, without sufficient resources and suitably qualified and experienced patent examiners, this will remain a challenge for the foreseeable future.

For the reasons set out above, it is important to ensure that the UKIPO is adequately funded to train and employ patent examiners to overcome the UK's patent backlog and reduce pendency times in the interest of further developing innovation firms' access to corporate debt finance and patent-backed lending.

2.6.3 Corporate finance and Horizon 2020: the EU's international strategy for research and innovation

The latest financial development to impact on the patent landscape is *Horizon 2020*, the *EU Framework Programme for Research and Innovation.*[100] *Horizon 2020* is the public funding financial instrument that implements the "Innovation Union", an initiative aimed at positioning Europe as a top global competitor in terms of research and innovation as well as creating new economic growth and jobs within the EU. The *Horizon 2020* programme will proceed from 2014 to 2020 with a massive €80 billion budget. The major advantage for innovating firms is that *Horizon 2020* simplifies the availability of public funding through the use of a single set of rules. It is envisaged that a significant percentage of the budget will be allocating to SMEs. *Horizon 2020* will be complemented through additional measures to advance the European Research Area by breaking down barriers to develop a unified EU market for knowledge, research and innovation. In terms of corporate finance, this market-driven strategic approach provided the UK with a tremendous opportunity to access funds to support innovation. The *Horizon2020 SME Instrument* is an entirely new line of EU funding to support innovating SMEs with high potential and high risk research and development (R&D) projects by providing direct financial support and indirect support to increase their innovation capacity. However, all projects must be at Technology Readiness Level 6 (TRL 6) or more.[101] TRL 6 requires a system/subsystem model or prototype demonstration in a relevant environment.

2.6.4 The Technology Readiness Level (TRL) system

Methods for valuing corporate IP need to advance and draw on other disciplines to supplement traditional accounting theory and practice. The TRL system is a well-established method of estimating the maturity of critical technology elements on a scale of one to nine with nine being the most mature technology. It was originally developed by the US National Aeronautics and Space Agency (NASA) in the 1980s to assist allocation of public funding. See figure 2.4.

100 http://ec.europa.eu/research/horizon2020/index_en.cfm.

101 'UK SMEs Earmarked for EU Grants to Help Them Innovate' (27 July 2014) EC press release.

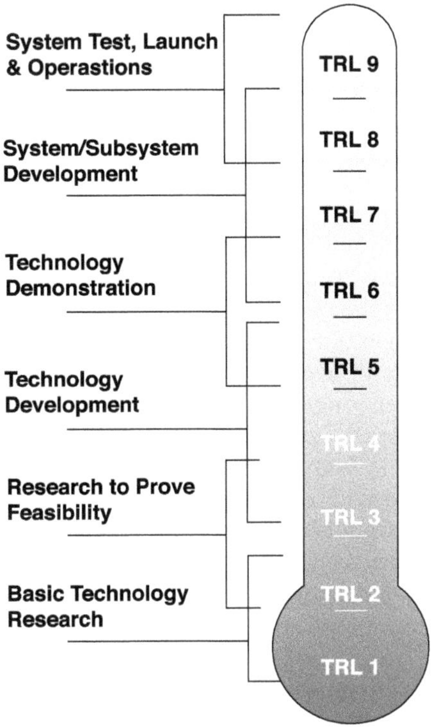

Figure 2.4 NASA's Technology Readiness Levels

Source: Adapted from NASA public domain

The use of TRLs enables consistent uniform discussions of technical maturity across different types of technology. Although common in the R&D and public finance field, it is less well known in corporate finance and banking. It is also used in the European Commission, the European Space Agency (ESA), NASA and the Canadian Innovation and Commercialization Program. The latter provides financial assistance by awarding contracts to entrepreneurs with pre-commercial innovations, provided the innovation is between TRL 7 and 9. The TRL system already facilitates cross-sector communication regarding technology and could help to improve communication in the IP ecosystem. It could be used by innovating firms (see the model in Chapter 8) to communicate with their shareholders, investors, financiers and other stakeholders in order to promote transparency of corporate IP assets.

In summary, changes in the technological environment have a direct impact on innovating firms and the UK's IP and patent ecosystems. There is also the opportunity for innovating firms to communicate with stakeholders using the well-established TRL system, a tool to support the assessment of investment and funding risks.

2.7 The legal factor: enforcing IP and patent rights

It is commonly said that IP rights are only as valuable as the ability to enforce them. However, IP infringements are often difficult for companies to identify, involve considerable expense to gather evidence of infringement, and arduous to litigate. IP and, in particular, expensive high tech patent disputes present an enormous business risk for innovating firms, licensees and lenders with IP assets as security for loans. At stake is the ability to sell products, gain or maintain market share for products, receive possible licensing royalties, the validity and thus the commercial value of the IP or patent itself, and potential liability for damages and costs as the result of unsuccessful litigation. Prudent management of corporate IP assets is essential for the sustainability of the innovating firm, but knowing how to proactively enforce IP rights is far from intuitive. The ability to enforce IP rights is a key legal factor that impacts on the development of corporate innovation finance and IP-backed lending to support companies.

Patents, regarded as the most valuable IP rights, are governed by the Patents Act 1977 (as amended), the Patents Act 2004, the Patent Rules 2007 and the Intellectual Property Act 2014, the modern UK national legislation that creates the patent law framework. These derive from a hybrid of national, European and international agreements.[102] As a minimum, the UK is required to ensure its patent rights enforcement system complies with the Agreement on Trade Related Aspects of IP (TRIPS)[103] which provides:

> Article 41
> Members shall ensure that enforcement procedures as specified in this Part 1 are available under their law so as to permit effective action against any act of infringement of IP rights covered by this Agreement, including expeditious remedies to prevent infringements and remedies which constitute a deterrent to further infringements. These procedures shall be applied in such a manner as to avoid the creation of barriers to legitimate trade and to provide for safeguards against their abuse.
>
> Procedures concerning the enforcement of IP rights shall be fair and equitable. They shall not be unnecessarily complicated or costly, or entail unreasonable time-limits or unwarranted delays.

Enforcing patent rights is a major concern for innovating firms. In 2000, the EU study entitled, *Enforcing Small Firms Patent Rights*[104] found that every single valuable EU invention that an innovating SME held had been copied at least once

102 Such as the 1994 TRIPS Agreement, part of the World Trade Organization (WTO) founding treaty.

103 An international agreement administered by the WTO that sets down minimum standards for many forms of IP regulation as applied to nationals of other WTO Members.

104 Kingston, W. *Enforcing Samll Firms Patent Rights* (2000) Publications Office of the Commission of the European Communities, Luxembourg.

(in every case at least once) yet not one EU innovating SME had been able to successfully enforce their patent. This is a depressing statistic for innovation firms. Fortunately, recent legal reforms level the playing field for innovating SMEs who wish to take enforcement action in the specialist IP Enterprise Court (IPEC), the High Court and the new Unified Patent Court (UPC).

2.7.1 The UK IP Enterprise Court (IPEC) and the High Court, Chancery Division

As of 1 October 2013, the Patents County Court (PCC) was reformulated as a specialist list of the High Court as the IP Enterprise Court (IPEC).[105] Thus, currently in the legal system of the Courts of England and Wales, IPEC (previously the Patents County Court) in London is an alternative venue to the High Court for bringing legal actions involving IP matters including patent rights.[106] The IPEC provides access to justice for litigants who are unable to afford the costs of litigation in the High Court.

Revitalised rules of procedure require more detailed particulars of claim,[107] no disclosure (discovery), no examination-in-chief of expert witnesses and tight control by the Judge of the issues that go to trial. Financial ceilings were introduced to both the recoverable damages (at £500,000) and the legal costs (at £50,000, with an additional cap per stage). Trials should last no more than two days. IPEC judges have specialist IP and patent knowledge and can order the full range of IP remedies including financial compensation/damages, an account of profits, final injunction to prevent future infringements, search and seizure and freezing of assets. Although the IPEC is now part of the High Court, patent and trade mark attorneys retain their rights of audience and to conduct litigation.[108]

Within IPEC there are two systems: the multi-track described above and the small claims track for claims of less than £10,000 with restrictions on costs orders. However, the latter is not appropriate for patent claims.

The creation of IPEC, a junior IP court, in 2010 is a positive development supporting innovating SME access justice in respect of their IP rights as a low cost forum for IP litigation. IPEC deals with smaller, less complex, lower value actions with procedures specifically designed for these types of cases, aimed at ensuring IP owners are not deterred from enforcing their patents due to potential litigation costs. Longer, more complex, higher value actions, as is often the case with patent litigation, are heard in the High Court. IPEC aims to strike a balance between swift, low cost, streamlined litigation and ensuring a proper investigation of the

105 Civil Procedure (Amendment No 7) Rules 2013 (SI 2013/1974).

106 Civil Procedure Rules 63.1 A The CPR are designed to improve access to justice by making legal proceedings cheaper, quicker, and easier to understand for non-lawyers.

107 The document that sets out the claimant's case.

108 *Rights to Conduct Litigation and Rights of Audience and Other Reserved Legal Activities Certification Rules 2012*, IP Regulation Board (IPReg).

claim in an informal courtroom environment. In 2017, it was reported that cases brought by SMEs to IPEC were up by 68%.[109]

Corporate IP asset owners should take comfort in the high quality of the specialist IP courts and judges available in the UK to enforce IP rights and resolve disputes.

2.7.2 The impact of Brexit[110] on the UK's IP legal framework

To date, the UK's EU membership has had a huge impact, in particular the PA 1977 which harmonised UK patent law with the European Patent Convention (EPC).[111] The EPC is not a piece of EU legislation and will be unaffected when the UK leaves the EU, as will representation rights of UK-based European Patent Attorneys, who will still be able to represent clients in all work before the EPO, and European patent holders whose rights will remain unaffected. Consequently, the fusion of UK and European patent law and practice remains and to date has been largely positive in practical terms, resulting in a solid degree of legal certainty in the patent legal framework. However, the impact of Brexit on other aspects of the UK's IP and patent legal frameworks are far from settled. After Brexit, EU Regulations will cease to be applicable in the UK as they only have effect throughout the EU of which the UK will no longer be a member. Directives that have already been implemented into UK law by primary legislation are likely to remain in effect unless the UK Parliament decides to repeal or amend the national laws that transposed them. The position of Directives that have been implemented by secondary legislation is unclear. Some commentators consider that these will survive, while others consider that they will fall when the empowering legislation, namely the European Communities Act 1972, is repealed.

The Court of Justice of the European Union (CJEU) will cease to have jurisdiction over UK matters and to be binding authority. In practice however, their decisions may still indirectly influence the UK courts. For example, the Boards of Appeal (BoA) of the EPO will continue to follow the CJEU rulings on the Biotech Directive and the UK Courts may continue to pay attention to the BoA decisions.[112]

109 White, C. 'SME cases up by 68%' (24 May 2017) *Intellectual Property Magazine*, available at www.intellectualpropertymagazine.com/patent/sme-cases-up-by-68-at-ipec-124252.htm accessed on 30 May 2017.

110 The British Exit from the European Union (Brexit). In a referendum on 23 June 2016, 51.9% of the participating UK electorate voted to leave the EU. On 29 March 2017, the British government invoked Article 50 of the Treaty on the European Union and the UK is now on course to leave the EU on Friday, 29 March 2019.

111 The EPC came into force in 1974.

112 'The Impact of Brexit on Intellectual Property' (23 February 2017) Chartered Institute of Patent Attorneys (CIPA) at www.cipa.org.uk/policy-and-news/briefing-papers/the-impact-of-brexit-on-intellectual-property/.

Patent Co-operation Treaty (PCT) applications will remain unchanged as the PCT is not an EU treaty. There will also be no effect on UK patents granted by the UK Intellectual Property Office (UKIPO).

2.7.3 The UK and the European Unified Patent Court (UPC)

Although the EPO provides single patent grant procedures, the ability to enforce European patents is in the process of change with the advent of the UPC. Consequently, the UK's Intellectual Property Act 2014 streamlined parts of existing laws, including improvements to the patent law regime. The Act provided the foundation for the UK to sign the UPC Agreement and lays out the groundwork for introducing the UPC.

"Patent prosecution" refers to the interaction between patent applicants, their representatives and the relevant patent granting office and is divided into: (1) pre-grant prosecution which involves negotiating with the patent office for the patent to be granted; and (2) post-grant prosecution which relates to post-grant amendments to the patent or responding to opposition to the patent by third parties. This is distinct from "patent litigation" which is legal action taken to enforce the patent monopoly against an infringing third party.

The *Agreement on the UPC* signed by 24 EU Member States on 19 February 2013 creates a specialised patent court with exclusive jurisdiction for litigation relating to European patents and European patents with unitary effect. According to the EPO, the UPC was needed to address the problem of the high legal costs that ensue when patent litigation has to be undertaken in two or more national courts, with the risk of diverging decisions and lack of legal certainty. Forum shopping also occurred as the parties sought to take advantage of differences between national courts' interpretation of harmonised European patent law and procedure.[113] The new court system paves the way for the implementation of a unitary patent system in Europe. EPO President Benoît Batistelli stated:

> The signing of the UPC agreement is a decisive step towards the long-awaited introduction of a truly supranational patent system in Europe. Following the endorsement of the unitary patent package by the European Parliament and Council in December 2012, the creation of a European court specialised in patent matters will be a tremendous boost for the completion of the European patent system.[114]

This was the most dramatic change in the patent landscape across most of Europe in the last 30 years. A unified patent system should reduce the cost of acquiring patents in Europe. It will be similar to the existing system in that one can apply

113 www.epo.org/law-practice/unitary/patent-court.html.

114 'EPO Welcomes Historic Signing of the Unified Patent Court Agreement' (2013) EPO press release.

centrally to the EPO in Munich, but rather than choosing to acquire a bundle of single national patent monopolies, the applicant will acquire a single monopoly covering the relevant EU member states. Existing UK national patent rights will not change.

For the patent owner, the unitary patent system meant that in the near future, when filing a UK patent application, the applicant would obtain a single European patent that would stand or fall across the whole of Europe. There would be a transition period for the first seven years during which the applicant could choose to opt-in its existing portfolio, or not opt-in for strategic reasons e.g. uncertainty as to implementation of the new system with the patent owner preferring to remain in the existing, more predictable, national-based UK system.

The UPC will be one court but will sit in a number of different locations and will hear disputes pertaining to the unitary patent. It will be composed of a central division with its main seat in Paris, with further seats in London and Germany. The London court is to hear patent disputes relating to chemistry and pharmaceutical patents, with the German court hearing mechanical engineering cases. The UPC system aims to reduce complexity and increase legal certainty for patent owner, however, this remains to be seen as it has yet to be fully implemented. The Preparatory Committee has however published the UPC's 18th draft of the Rules of Procedure in March 2017 (which have yet to be agreed).[115] Judges may only be formally appointed once the UPC is established.[116] For innovating firms who choose to file a unitary patent, it appears they will obtain an advantage through simpler administration processes for patent prosecution.

Since the EU patent system was formulated in the 1970s, there has been a desire to have a single EU patent and single European court for resolving disputes. It has taken four decades to create such a system, largely due to the key stumbling block, language. Overall, the development is a positive step for the EU in the long term, although there will be a period of uncertainty for business (and other stakeholders) in the short term. A key decision to be made by innovating firms in the short term will be whether to opt-in or opt-out. At the moment it is still not possible to apply for a unitary patent. After the UPC Agreement comes into force, there will be a transitional period of seven years that may be extended to 14 years.[117]

The impact of Brexit on the UPC Agreement is not settled.[118] The UPC, as explained above, is a pan-European project and the UK Government has

115 See www.unified-patent-court.org/news/draft-rules-procedure-updated-march-2017.

116 'Progress on implementing the UPC and the Unitary Patent' (23 September 2014) *Allen & Overy*.

117 The UK must pass secondary legislation to ratify the UPC Agreement and deposit the instrument of ratification in Brussels.

118 Arnold, R., Bently, LA.F., Derclaye, E. and Dinwoodie, G.B. 'The Legal Consequences of Brexit Through the Lens of IP Law' (15 February 2017) 101(2) *Judicature*; Oxford Legal Studies Research Paper No. 15/2017; University of Cambridge Faculty of Law Research Paper No. 21/2017 available at SSRN: https://ssrn.com/abstract=2917219.

confirmed its intention to continue its preparations to ratify the UPC Agreement such that the UK will be a member of the UPC when it comes into operation. The conferral of legal capacity and immunities and privileges is necessary to enable the UPC to function as an international organisation in the UK and this involves Parliamentary approval of the Protocol on Privileges and Immunities and the UPC Agreement. The UK House of Commons Sixth Delegated Legislation Committee will consider the UPC legislation on 29 November 2017.[119] The UPC Agreement will finally come into force when the Protocol comes into force. This will be 30 days after the last of France, Germany, Luxembourg and the United Kingdom has deposited its instrument of ratification. According to CIPA, for the UK to continue participating after Brexit, a new international agreement with the participating EU Member States and the UK will be needed to provide compatibility with EU law. This will be a political challenge for the UK. However, if the UK does not remain a member of the UPC, transitional provisions will need to be agreed and drafted to protect rights acquired or cases in progress at the time the UK leaves the EU. CIPA has a strong preference for the UK to continue to participate in the unitary patent and the UPC system, "if a solid legal basis for this can be agreed."[120]

In terms of best practice in corporate governance of IP assets, on balance, a pan-European approach should create greater certainty (single system, single patent, single court, single renewal fee) and thus value in the medium to long term. This should be viewed as a positive development by innovation firms and their stakeholders. However, a unitary patent will be vulnerable across Europe to a single unfavourable UPC decision which is a new risk that both innovating firms and stakeholders will need to take into account.

Finally, the Taylor Wessing Global IP Index 2016 (GIPI16) provides a comprehensive assessment of how important international IP regimes compare. The fifth edition assessed the regimes of 43 jurisdictions, using more than 8,500 individual assessments from senior industry figures, balanced with 61 objective factors. Each jurisdiction is rated in relation to obtaining, enforcing and exploiting five key IP rights: patents, trade marks, copyright, design and data protection. The UK IP regime ranks first for its patent regime. The Netherlands is top overall, closely followed by former winners Germany (GIPI3) and the UK (GIPI1, GIPI2 and GIPI4).[121] This is a strong endorsement of the overall quality of the UK's IP legal regime. The impact of BREXIT and ensuing uncertainty in relation to the IP legal framework will likely reduce the UK's ranking next year.

119 See https://calendar.parliament.uk/calendar/Commons/All/2017/11/29/Daily.

120 'The Impact of Brexit on Intellectual Property' (23 February 2017) Chartered Institute of Patent Attorneys at www.cipa.org.uk/policy-and-news/briefing-papers/the-impact-of-brexit-on-intellectual-property/.

121 *Taylor Wessing Global IP Index 2016* at https://united-kingdom.taylorwessing.com/en/taylor-wessing-launches-fifth-gipi-report.

2.8 Corporate governance and IP: concluding remarks

All corporate entities, including profit-oriented companies, both public and private, such as joint ventures, cooperatives, and partnerships, and not-for-profit organisations such as voluntary and community organisations, charities and academic institutions, as well as government corporate entities have to be governed by a governing body. Corporate governance is different to management. Executive management is responsible for running the enterprise, but the governing body ensures that it is running in the right direction and being well run and adheres to the norms of good corporate governance. Modern growth industries are intrinsically linked to those that are IP-rich and IP-intensive. As commercial success is increasingly dependent on effective protection, management and strategic application of corporate IP assets, corporate governance needs to respond. Many believe that IP and patent ecosystems are too complex and have too many variables to take into consideration. The PESTL analysis is a widely-used tool that provides a fuller picture of the political, economic, socio-cultural, technological and legal environment facing corporate entities. It sets out the "state" of the ecosystem. It identifies areas of concern and weakness to assist with corporate governance and support other stakeholders to deal with forecasted changes and design policy for the future of the IP ecosystem. Minimizing the weaknesses and limitations will increase certainty in IP rights as an asset class. In theory, this should improve access to innovation finance and IP-backed debt finance as the UK's IP ecosystem is comparatively well developed. At a political level, the UK government needs to demonstrate more effectively that its structures and ministerial appointees are coordinating policies in relation to innovating firms, IP, finance and corporate regulation and that UKIPO, BEIS and Companies House efforts are synergised. Companies House and corporate regulators do not appear to feature in the IP finance discussions. From the economic standpoint, the government should ensure that public funding remains available until corporate IP -backed debt finance is more accessible. In terms of the impact of social factors, investors and financiers need a higher level of trust in IP rights as an asset class. It was argued that triangulating quantitative, qualitative and strategic IP information should improve validity, reliability and accuracy (thus increasing predictability and decreasing volatility) of quantitative corporate IP and patent asset values. Addressing the increasingly complex high-tech nature of patent applications and reducing patent backlogs are important aspects of improving legal certainty with respect to granted patents (which are more valuable than patent applications). Cross-pollinating the TRL system to estimate the maturity of critical technology elements may assist investors, shareholders, financiers and other stakeholders with technology risk assessment and valuation.

The evolving pan-European patent law framework should create greater legal certainty (single system, single patent, single court, single renewal fee) and thus "value" in the medium to long term and should be viewed as a positive development. Introducing behavioural finance analysis to IP-backed debt finance transactions is a new way of thinking that could improve access to corporate innovation finance in the future. Where an IP portfolio contains international rights, a PESTL analysis could be performed on a country-by-country basis.

In conclusion, the idea of corporate governance is ancient. Shakespeare (1564–1616) understood its vital importance. In his famous play *The Merchant of Venice*, Antonio the merchant agonised as he watched his ships sail out of sight, with his fortune entrusted to others.[122] Adam Smith, in *The Wealth of Nations* published in 1776 stated, "The directors of companies, being the managers of other people's money rather than their own, cannot well be expected to watch over it with the same anxious vigilance with which (they) watch their own."[123] The 19th century concept of the corporation still underpins corporate governance practice today.[124] Corporate governance now has to respond to the new class of corporate IP assets and evolve. The PESTL analysis carried out in this chapter has provided a vital overview of the factors that impact on the ability of IP-rich and intensive innovation firms to thrive in the UK. It has identified many of the hurdles to be addressed by corporate boards and the relevant policy makers to facilitate business models reliant on IP rights. It is understandable that shareholders and other stakeholders are questioning the reliability of traditional financial statements for reporting on the value of corporate IP assets (and in particular patents) and their role in value creation for the business. Historically, the limited liability of companies is a privilege granted by society, not a right. The way in which increasingly IP-rich companies are managed or governed must comply with corporate governance principles and meet society's expectations. Before a satisfactory corporate governance model can be developed to deal with corporate IP assets, a fundamental issue needs to be resolved: what level of IP asset information does society believe companies should publicly disclose? The PESTL context for patent monopolies is certainly vastly different from that of the 19th century when the limited company was first invented. The scale and significance of corporate IP assets to value creation are of a different order. These prized assets do not just happen – they are the result of thoughtful planning and responsible stewardship. How should corporate governance principles respond to the increased need for the disclosure of corporate IP information and strategy to inform stakeholders? How, when and where should companies make that disclosure? In the early 19th century, the need to access capital without exposing external investors to the threat of bankruptcy led to a form of limited liability incorporation that spread across the globe leading to huge industrial growth. The growing separation of power between executive management and shareholders, identified by Berle and Means (1932), and the corporate collapses of the 1980s have reinforced the need for effective corporate governance. The emergence of IP-rich and IP-intensive

122 Tricker, B. 'Re-inventing the Limited Liability Company' (July 2011) 19(4) *International Review*.

123 Smith, A. *The Wealth of Nations*, (1776) revised edition., George J. Steigler (Ed.), University of Chicago Press, Chicago.

124 Supra Tricker n [119].

companies is a new dimension for corporate governance and the core principles of disclosure and transparency. Companies feature prominently in the news. They are the most successful legal invention in history and are the most common form of business organisation. Their activities permeate every aspect of our society. Everything which is done in the name of the company has to be done by humans. However, the ease with which shares in an enterprise can be bought and sold has a major disadvantage. It distracts attention from the important fact that the value of the shares depends on the value of the company itself. As investors, shareholders and stakeholders become more IP aware, so will IP activist shareholders who will want to ensure that the company is getting a good return on corporate IP assets and increasingly, that corporate investment in IP assets can be used as security for debt finance to fund operations. Company directors and auditors will need to carefully consider and address corporate IP asset valuations. However, there has been a mixed response from the global multidisciplinary community on the issue of corporate IP transparency and disclosure, fundamental principles of company law, that underpin IP-rich firms' access to finance and value creation.

Chapter 3 explains why debt finance, given the range of corporate finance options available, remains critical to the commercial success of innovating firms. This will set the scene for the corporate governance issues that arise in relation to company reports, traditional financial reporting and valuation of intangibles and IP assets which shareholder and other stakeholders use to determine whether to engage with the innovation firm.

Part II

The IP finance dimension: corporate governance and transparency

3 Bridging the gap between corporate finance and corporate governance

"The difficulty lies not so much in developing new ideas as in escaping from old ones."

John Maynard Keynes (1883–1946)
(Influential economist of the 20th century)

Introduction

All corporate entities need capital to finance their operations. Corporate governance has a role to play in regulating the conduct of directors who act as stewards of corporate assets. Most company law and corporate governance codes encourage transparency in reporting specific corporate and financial information including the business model and overall financial strategy. This chapter uses the difficulties faced by innovating SMEs in accessing debt finance as an example to illustrate the corporate IP asset transparency problem.

Corporate finance refers to the sources of funding and the capital structure of corporate entities, the actions taken by directors and managers to increase the value of the firm to the shareholders. Corporate entities raise capital and deploy it for productive purposes such as to develop and commercialise innovation. A corporate entity has many choices, a key choice is whether to raise equity capital (sell shares) or debt capital (borrow money). Any decision by a corporate entity that involves the use of money is a corporate financial decision that needs to comply with corporate governance principles relating to the nature and extent of accountability to members (shareholders) and creditors, for example. In this chapter, our focus is early in the classic business life cycle, between the initial start-up and the critical early growth stages of the innovating SME. It is at this stage that increased access to debt-finance is needed. This chapter aims to bridge the gap between corporate finance and corporate governance by introducing the modern corporate IP asset dimension.

In terms of debt finance, banks lend funds based mainly on a borrowers' balance sheet, financial history, cash flow and available security. One argument why IP-backed debt finance is rarely used is because the traditional financial statements analysed by lenders to determine a borrowers' creditworthiness – the treasure map – do not map well onto "intangibles" (the accounting term that includes IP).

In simple terms, the way corporate financial statements report IP and other intangibles presents difficulties for users. This is a corporate governance problem.

Although there are many public and private avenues for financing a business, debt finance is the critical method of financing innovating SMEs for four reasons. First, the pool of public finance is limited. Second, the power of debt-funded working capital to generate financial returns is formidable. Third, debt finance is less expensive than equity finance. Fourth, debt finance is a more strategic financing method as it does not involve diluting equity in the business, or selling or losing control of the patents. The UK's "innovation sector" requires a debt finance banking service specific to its needs which are presently unmet.[1] This is thought to be because banks are traditionally conservative and process-driven in terms of risk assessment; they deem IP value to be uncertain, volatile and thus unable to be covered by a reasonable risk premium. This view will be examined in more detail and in doing so we cannot avoid touching on the fallout from the global financial crisis that began in August 2007 which affected access to finance generally.[2] While innovating SMEs may have some working capital, large pools of readily available funds to self-fund a business are rare. As such, the role of credit providers in the early stage of the business life cycle is crucial.

Section 3.1 explains the power of debt finance to generate returns. Section 3.2 analyses the stakeholders involved in the development of IP-backed lending and the innovation business life cycle. Section 3.3 discusses the current funding landscape as well as newer funding options. Section 3.4 analyses data from the WIPO *IP Advantage Database* to provide evidence that IP-backed debt finance is underused. Section 3.5 enlightens our understanding of the negative impact of banking capital adequacy requirements and Basel III on IP-backed debt finance. Section 3.6 examines the lenders' triad of concerns, introduces the issue of legal risk, uncertainty in patent valuation and the process for registering security interests in patents. Section 3.7 considers the issue of transparency in the context of registering security interests in IP and finally, section 3.8 reflects on the role of corporate governance in supporting access to IP finance.

3.1 The power of debt finance to generate returns for innovation firms

Debt finance is critical given the power of debt to generate returns. Compare and contrast a capital investment with a loan. If an innovating firm invests £100 capital in its business and the return is 10%, then the profit is £10 gross. If it invests

1 There is an opportunity for the new UK Government-backed British Business Bank, which supports "challenger" banks and other alternatives to the main UK lenders, to play a role in facilitating patent-backed debt finance in the future.

2 *The run on the Rock Fifth Report of Session 2007–2008 House of Commons Treasury Committee* (2008) Vol.1, House of Commons London: The Stationer Office Ltd pp 4–20.

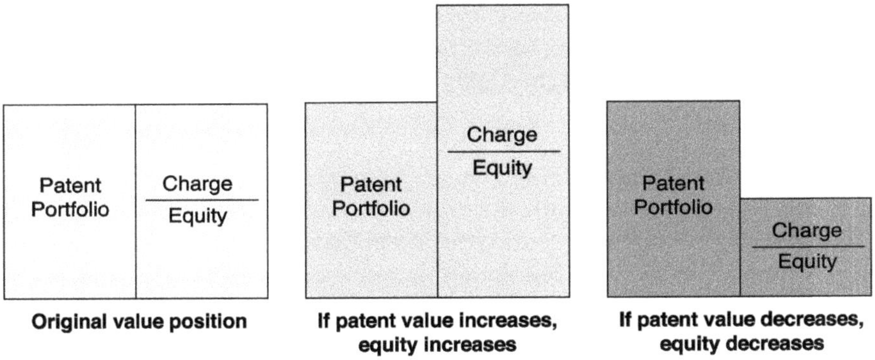

Figure 3.1 Balance sheet diagrams for funding a patent and selling it a year later

£100 but also borrows £900 at 5% per annum interest, then the return will be £55 (calculated as £100 gross (10% of £1,000) minus £45 interest). Leverage transforms a return of 10% into one of 55%. Financial institutions are in the business of lending: receiving deposits and lending the funds, lending much more capital than they are legally required to hold (capital adequacy requirements). Private equity firms act in an analogous way. However, when an asset declines in value, leverage wipes out equity capital at a faster rate than the rate of fall in asset value.[3] This is the dark side of borrowing that an innovating firm faces when seeking to develop and commercialise its corporate IP assets as illustrated in Figure 3.1.

Debt finance is usually the preferred option for innovating SMEs because it costs less and due to the increase in the value/equity upside demonstrated above. Borrowers benefit from the full upside of risks being taken, while the downside is shared by the creditors (both trade and finance) if there is a possibility of default. We also know that it is difficult for innovating SMEs to access debt financing in the current economic climate. Consequently, the upside in equity necessary to fund the growth stage of the business is lacking. Next, we consider the existing innovation finance paradigm.

3.2 Corporate innovation finance and the business life cycle

To commercialise an invention, working capital (money) is typically needed for a variety of business activities including: market research; patent and prior art searches; prototype development; patent filing and legal fees; professional advisers (e.g. patent attorneys, accountants and lawyers); and patent renewal fees. Many of

3 Bootle, R. *The Trouble with Markets: Saving Capitalism from Itself* (2009) Nicholas Brealey Publishing, London, p97.

these costs are unique to innovation. The principles of corporate finance are broadly the same for innovating SMEs as for any larger organisation. Innovating SMEs have a predictable life cycle and we will use the term to mean firms that have a potentially patentable invention. In short, they start with an idea leading to a potentially patentable invention, search for a business model, then build an appropriate infrastructure via the legal forms of business organisation (e.g. partnership or company) and then grow as they commercialise their invention and bring it to market generating profits. Figure 3.2 depicts the classic business life cycle.

The seed or start-up stage is when the invention is simply a thought or an idea which can lead to the very conception of a new business. There is no proven market or customers for the invention, so the start-up will rely on seed capital (cash) usually self-funded by the owner/inventor, friends and family. Debt-finance is not a viable option. Using internal finance to reduce transaction costs is the

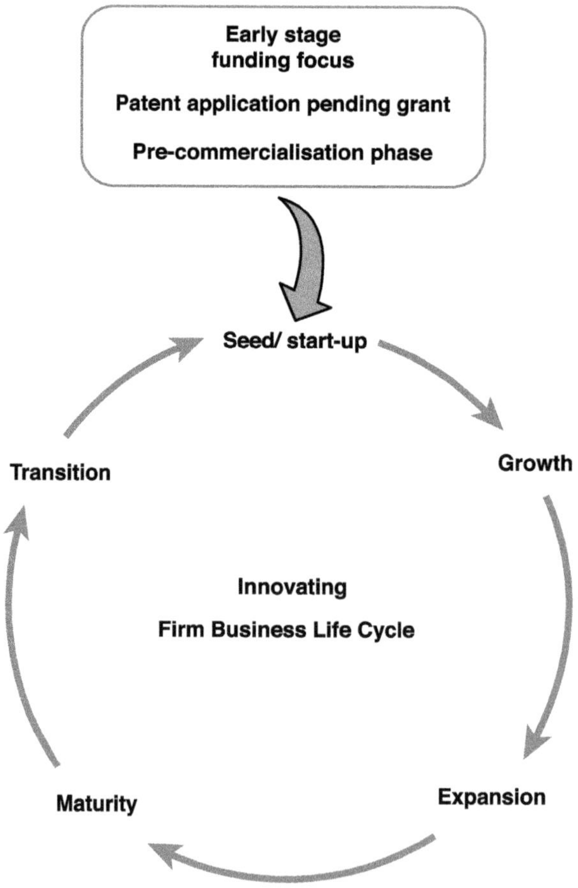

Figure 3.2 The business life cycle: the journey between concept and commercialisation

cheapest option. Famous examples of firms that relied solely on self-funding[4] during the seed stage include Apple, Inc., Google and Starbucks.[5] While inventor entrepreneurs may have some savings, large pools of readily available savings set aside to self-fund a business are rare which is why the role of credit providers and how they enter the business life cycle is critical.

3.3 Financing innovation: the existing paradigm

An innovation business comes into existence when it has a legal structure and a business plan – it is usually small and privately owned. During the first year of existence, R&D and the creation of prototypes for the invention are in progress. Patents applications are also being pursued. At this point the financial burden on innovating SMEs who wish to develop and commercialise an invention is particularly high, given the costs of applying for patents, patent attorney fees and prototype development, all necessary steps before a product can be launched. The startup innovating SME is only just beginning to establish a market presence and develop a customer base. Meanwhile, although the patent applications are valuable business assets, they are invisible on the firm's balance sheet as they are classified as "intangibles" for accounting purposes making successfully applying for a loan and receiving a favourable lending decision difficult. The subject of accounting for intangibles and valuation methodology is explored in more depth in Chapter 4. Inevitably, this means that early growth stage SMEs who internally generate IP have "fragile" balance sheets. During the growth stage, the biggest challenge facing the innovating SME is dealing with the range of issues that demand more money. Growth stage businesses focus on running the business in a more formal manner, improving accounting systems and hiring more staff to deal with the influx of business activities.

3.3.1 Managing accounting for innovation from the date of incorporation

All companies have an incorporation date, the date on which the company's financial year will begin. The directors are responsible for preparing the company's first of set annual accounts, based on the company's accounting records. In managing accounting for innovation, essentially, the corporate accounts must comply with the International Accounting Standard (IAS) 38 for Intangibles. However, the balance sheet is often unable to adequately capture internally-generated

4 'Self-financing' (18 February 2014) *Trizle* at www.trizle.com/tips/20-self-financing.

5 History of Apple: The Story of Steve Jobs and the Company he Founded, available at www.macworld.co.uk/feature/apple/history-of-apple-steve-jobs-mac-3606104/. Apple, Inc. founder Steve Jobs (1955–2011) with minimal personal savings of about $1,300 US resulting in the personal computer that ignited the digital age.

corporate IP assets which are regarded as off-balance sheet and therefore invisible to stakeholders. While, in the author's view, the lack of corporate IP asset transparency across all companies, small and large, is a corporate governance issue, there is also a negative impact on those in the corporate finance ecosystem e.g. lenders and financiers, who rely on accounts and annual reports to evaluate the creditworthiness of company. Without more detailed narrative IP asset disclosure to explain the role of IP assets in future value creation, IP-rich innovation SMEs will be subject to a "rustic" valuation where the focus is primarily on tangible assets and cash flow as there are no or few historic financial transactions. As such, the financial valuation of the innovating SME will be heavily influenced by norms in the relevant business sector e.g. medical, pharmaceutical, aeronautics etc. because the balance sheet is only really useful for companies that have a trading history.

It is therefore *crucial* for innovating SMEs to identify and record IP assets as an additional line item in the accountant's spreadsheet, *even if* they are off-balance sheet items, as they will undoubtedly become more important and valuable to the enterprise as it matures. Moreover, to ensure the integrity of the accounts, the financial value of IP assets should be traced back to the day the company came into existence in the management accounts. Increasing and improving the use of "notes" to the accounts would assist to provide additional relevant IP asset information and their history within the entity. Accordingly, it makes sense that as a matter of good corporate governance, finance directors become better integrated in R&D, IP and business strategy. This finance information will then be available both to internal management who determine strategy, and as the basis for future accurate corporate disclosure to the public, counteracting the negative impact of off-balance sheet IP assets. If corporate IP assets are captured in the accounts from the date of incorporation, this baseline of information will provide the basis for transparency and future corporate disclosures throughout the business life cycle of the company.

In conclusion, traditional financial accounts on their own, in the author's opinion, struggle to provide a true and fair view of an IP-rich enterprise. Indeed, it could be argued in some cases, the accounts may even give third parties a misleading view. In terms of future corporate governance and accounting policy, company directors should consider recording off-balance sheet early stage IP asset financial information from the date of incorporation to ensure traceability and integrity of financial accounting information. These management accounting records support the Directors' Strategic Report which should also contain contextual narrative corporate IP asset and strategy information to provide a true and fair view of the financial position of an enterprise. Corporate disclosure of IP assets and the reason why internally-generated corporate IP assets are regarded as off-balance sheet will be discussed in more detail in later chapters of this book.

3.3.2 Sources of funding for innovation

Additional sources of funding may become available from retained profits, suppliers, customers, government grants and partnerships (public funding e.g. the

Creative England Business Loan Fund, Start Up Loans etc.),[6] banks, private investors, venture capitalists (VCs) and investment funds.[7] However, each type of funding has advantages and disadvantages coupled with availability and accessibility issues. The funding needs of innovating SMEs are typically high, but their ability to raise external debt finance funding is limited because they have insufficient traditional tangible assets to offer as security to lenders. Directors of innovating SMEs who own their homes and have equity by paying off a mortgage may be able to re-finance past mortgages or obtain a home equity line for the business. This is a low cost finance method. However, for those with family obligations using the family home as security is a least favoured innovation finance method. Sir James Dyson[8], the world famous British inventor, had no other option to finance his fledgling business.[9] Dyson is an industrial designer best known as the inventor of the Dual Cyclone bagless vacuum cleaner which works on the principles of cyclonic separation. His current net worth stands at £7.8 billion according to the Sunday Times Rich List 2017.[10] In an article entitled, "Big Achievers Share the Greatest Risks They Ever Took"[11] Kirdahy interviewed Dyson who stated:

> Every year I was getting further and further into debt. In the end, I owed something like $4 million US. I took out two or three mortgages on my house.[12] If I failed, everything I owned would've gone to the bank. Everybody thought I was completely mad. [As it turned out] I repaid the bank loan within about four or five months of selling the product. The bank kept using me in their advertising as an example of how they loan money.

Dyson was only able to obtain the business loan using his home (traditional tangible security) rather his company's burgeoning patent portfolio.

6 Grant funding schemes in the UK have included Catalysts, Collaborative Research & Development, Enterprise Investment Scheme (EIS) Growth Vouchers, IC Tomorrow, Innovation Vouchers, Launchpads, Seed Enterprise Investment Scheme, the Small Business Research Initiative and SMART.

7 *A Guide to Funding Innovation* (2013–2014) Oxford Innovation Ltd.

8 Sir James Dyson OM, CBE, FRS, FREng, born 2 May 1974.

9 Partly supported by his wife's salary as an art teacher, after five years and an incredible 5,127 prototypes, Dyson launched the "G-Force" vacuum cleaner in 1983. However, no manufacturer or distributor would take on the product in the UK, as it was considered "disruptive technology" that would disturb the valuable market for replacement dust bags. This account of Dyson's innovation financing experience is largely constructed from James Dyson's autobiography, Coren, G. *Against the Odds* (1997).

10 Watts, Robert (7 May 2017). 'Brexit brings bonanza for billionaires', *The Sunday Times* pp. 1–2. Sir James Dyson's fortune has increased to £7.8 billion – up from £5 billion last year.

11 Lee, J. 'Big Achievers Share the Greatest Risks They Ever Took' (3 July 2011).

12 To finance the development of the cyclone vacuum invention, Dyson raised £25,000 self-funding, the same amount from a friend, Jeremy Fry and £18,000 raised by selling a small parcel of land (the vegetable garden) as part of this family home.

Some may be tempted to use credit cards (especially those introductory 0% interest free periods), however this is a finance method of last resort as the interest rate ultimately charged typically exceeds 16% and can be as high as 30%. The high monthly interest payments would become a significant drain on cash flow. The obstacles to accessing debt finance regularly cause innovating SMEs to seek alternative funding. At this juncture, they face a funding strategy choice – should they pursue debt, equity or a combination of both?

3.3.3 Debt finance: the simple business loan contract

Debt finance involves a bank advancing money that will be repaid with interest over an agreed term or through a rolling arrangement such as an overdraft. The bank makes a profit on the loan transaction by charging interest. Debt finance can be more complex than a simple loan but for our purposes we will limit our discussion to simple loans. In legal terms, it is a contractual arrangement between a business and the lender whereby the borrower pays a predetermined amount of interest that is not a function of its operating performance, but which is treated in accounting standards as an expense for tax purposes and is therefore tax deductible. The debt has a fixed life and has a priority claim on cash flows in both operating periods and insolvency. This is because interest is paid before the claims of equity holders (e.g. shareholders), and, if the business defaults on interest payments and the loan is secured, the lender will sell the secured asset and the amount owed will be repaid before any payments are made to equity holders (see section 3.7).

Before making the loan, lenders will want to know what the firm will do with the money advanced and how it intends to allocate funds to develop the business. A borrower needs to show: (1) what the money will be used for; (2) how long the money will last; and (3) how much revenue will be generated by the business to cover repayments. In a conventional business loan, lenders perform careful analyses to make sure the borrower can repay the loan based on the business generating a positive cash flow. In most cases, banks want security for the loan which it can take possession of and sell in the event of default in repayment. As we know, this is particularly difficult for an innovating SME whose key assets are intangible inventions with patent protection potential. Further, most lenders do not fund start-ups with seed capital, preferring to see a positive track record of revenue and a solid repayment track record (a credit history). In almost all cases, lenders will require a personal financial guarantee as additional security (e.g. over real property, shares, mutual funds etc.) for the loan. Lenders will routinely require a statement of personal assets and liabilities. Ideally, they prefer to take a fixed charge on personal assets, such as the company director's house.[13] As more people in the UK struggle to become home owners, traditional tangible forms of

13 See section 3.7 for a detailed discussion of the legal characteristics of a fixed charge as a security device.

personal security for business loans will decline. In *Banking on IP?* the authors stated that, "traditional fixed assets simply no longer exist" [14] The author, predicts that the lack of fixed assets will continue as involvement of entrepreneurial millennials in the digital economy continues to grow. Inevitably, this will lead to lenders contemplating lending against modern intangible forms of personal property including IP. The cost of a standard debt finance business loan includes interest, administrative "transaction" costs, legal fees and the impact of the proposed loan on the firm's tax position.

3.3.4 Debt finance: the overdraft facility

Another common type of debt or loan financing is an unsecured overdraft facility attached to the firm's bank account.[15] Some SMEs will switch banks in order to obtain a larger unsecured overdraft facility. It is a "facility" because it is an arrangement available at the borrower's discretion i.e. whether and when to "draw down" on the pre-authorised funds. It is a "revolving facility" because the borrower can repay sums borrowed and draw down further sums at will over the life of the facility. When the company's account becomes overdrawn, the bank becomes a financial creditor of the company and the company becomes a debtor. As a minimum, the terms of the overdraft facility will state the maximum the company may owe the bank at any point in time (the limit), the interest rate payable and the circumstances in which the bank can require the company to repay the sum borrowed/overdrawn.

While lenders provide general business advice, they do not become directly involved in managing the business. As the global financial crisis worsened in 2008–2009, the availability of debt finance fell and the cost of borrowing increased.[16] The situation in 2014 had not improved significantly. Alisdair Steele, Head of the Financial Sector Group, Nabarro LLPO confirms:

> It is widely acknowledged that banks are no longer meeting the funding needs of businesses, particularly of SMEs. The scale of the funding gap is huge, with estimates of £29bn to £59bn cited for SME financing alone. While the debate over exactly why this has happened (and what can be done to reverse it) continues, small businesses need to find the funding that will allow them to deliver growth and jobs.[17]

14 Brassell, M. and King, K. *Banking on IP? The role of Intellectual Property and Intangible Assets in Facilitating Business Finance Final Report* (6 November 2013) Independent report commissioned by the UKIPO p 13.

15 McLaughlin, S. *Unlocking Company Law* (2013) Routledge p141.

16 Eccles, L. 'How bank lending fell by £365 billion in five years' (7 September 2014).

17 Davis, A. 'Seeds of Change: Emerging Sources of Non-bank Funding for Britain's SMEs' (2012) *Centre for the Study of Financial Innovation* p 1.

The next section analyses several types of finance: equity, hybrid, mezzanine, online crowd and pension-led funding, explaining their advantages and disadvantages relative to patent-backed debt finance.

3.3.5 Private equity finance and venture capital

When conventional bank lending is not available for innovation projects that a lender might classify as "speculative", many innovating SMEs seek alternative sources of funding from private equity investors who make their return from the high growth of the business. An innovating SME needs to show they have a viable business plan for an invention with high commercial potential. One method of equity financing involves bringing in shareholders for partial ownership in exchange for money and expertise. Another form involves selling part of the business by issuing shares in the private limited company (possibly a subsidiary Special Purpose Vehicle) in exchange for money. While the investors may receive a dividend on the shareholding, in the early stages of a business most profits are usually retained by the company to grow the business. The important return for equity investors is when the success of the innovating SME allows their shares to be sold at a substantial profit. In return for their cash, private investors will insist on a large equity stake. The cost of capital is typically in the range of 20% to 40%. As with commercial lenders, equity investors are often more interested in larger companies with a business track record than start-up or early growth stage firms. Equity investors often, but not always, add value in addition to the funding they provide by facilitating contacts from their business network; offering the benefit of their commercial experience; or potentially by serving as non-executive directors on the innovating SME's board.

3.3.6 Venture capital

Venture capital (VC), a form of private equity investment, was a critical component of financing innovation in the 1980s. However, the amounts funded and the number of companies supported by such funding continues to decline.[18] Venture capital financing is the exception rather than the norm.[19] In the 1980s, the VC model comprised mostly wealthy individuals investing funds in a business. As such, investors were able to maintain a patient outlook for a significant return on their investment within a timeframe of ten years or more. However, as institutions became more prevalent as VCs, they amassed a greater quantum of money by syndicating. This changed their focus from nurturing growth to increasing fees based on larger investment syndicates. To keep shareholders content, VC funds

18 European venture capital fundraising declined from 2Q 2014 but managed to exceed 3Q 2013 levels. See 'Europe 3Q 2014' (2014) *Dow Jones Venture Source*, p 2.

19 Mulcahy, D. 'Six Myths About Venture Capital Offer Dose of Reality to Start-ups' (16 April 2013).

aim for maximum liquidity, creating early pay-off via premature "exits" rather than long term investment.[20] Further, VCs favour investment in information technology as this type of technology has a lower capital investment requirement. This preference is problematic for the UK, because in contrast to the US, generally only information technology hardware is patentable in the UK. Patents are not granted for business methods,[21] nor computer programs or software unless they provide a technical effect: section1(2)(c) Patents Act 1977. Such technical effect or character lies not in the simple operation of computers but in effects which go further than normal computer operations and involve computer implemented inventions. A consequence of the VC model is that to attract capital, innovating SMEs seek to file patents as early as possible, to accommodate the VC's early exit preference. The UK's laws on patentable subject matter may act as a disadvantage in terms of access to VC investment when compared to the US. It is predicted that in the future, VCs both in the UK and abroad, will continue to play a significant, but smaller, role in channelling capital to start-up firms[22] and new hybrid methods of funding will become more common. The type of funding an innovating SME ultimately pursues largely depends on the answers to the questions set out in Figure 3.3.

3.3.7 Mezzanine finance

Mezzanine finance combines elements of debt financing and equity investment (hybrid finance) and can provide a relatively inexpensive financing alternative for early growth stage SMEs where there is an element of risk.[23] It is not a source of start-up funding and is now available from lenders who acknowledge the "funding gap" and the need to adapt the traditional lending model to the unusual dynamics of innovation. One is Santander plc,[24] a UK bank wholly owned by the Spanish Santander Group. Mezzanine finance providers typically (although not universally) seek to share in the firm's growth by building an element of equity investment as part of the finance transaction. Figure 3.4 illustrates the tiers of finance available at different stages of the business life cycle (the percentage figures indicate the approximate cost of the finance as a percentage of the amount borrowed).

20 Schramm, C. and Bradley, H. 'How Venture Capital Lost Its Way' (2009) *BusinessWeek* at www.kauffmann.org.

21 See T 931/95 *PBS Partnership/Controlling Pension Benefits System* [2002] EPOR 522 and T 258/03 *HITACHI/Auction method* [2004] EPOR 548, decisions of the Board of Appeal of the EPO.

22 Mulcahy, D. 'Six Myths About Venture Capital Offer Dose of Reality to Startups' (16 April 2013).

23 www.santanderbreakthrough.co.uk/advice/finance/funding-options-mezzanine-finance.

24 The bank was established on 11 January 2010 when Abbey National plc, which also by then included the savings business and branches of Bradford & Bingley plc, was renamed Santander UK plc. Alliance & Leicester plc merged into the renamed business in May 2010.

Debt finance	Does the firm have tangible or intangible assets available as security for the business loan? Is the firm in a position to risk losing the secured assets should the business weaken or collapse? Does the firm have the cash flow necessary to meet the required loan repayments and interest obligations? Do the company and its directors (if personal guarantees are required) have a good credit history or personal assets that can be used as security?
Equity finance	How important is unfettered control over company decision making? Is the firm comfortable trading a percentage of the company's shares in return for funding? Is a member, director or employee of the firm skilled in pitching the business model to potential investors? Is the firm willing to disclose critical information to enable investors to decide whether to invest in shares in the firm? What will be the position of the new investor (shareholder) in the firm? NB: There are usually no repayment obligations and no interest payments due to equity investors. If the firm becomes insolvent, the equity investor will make a loss.

Figure 3.3 Sources of finance: selecting debt or equity finance

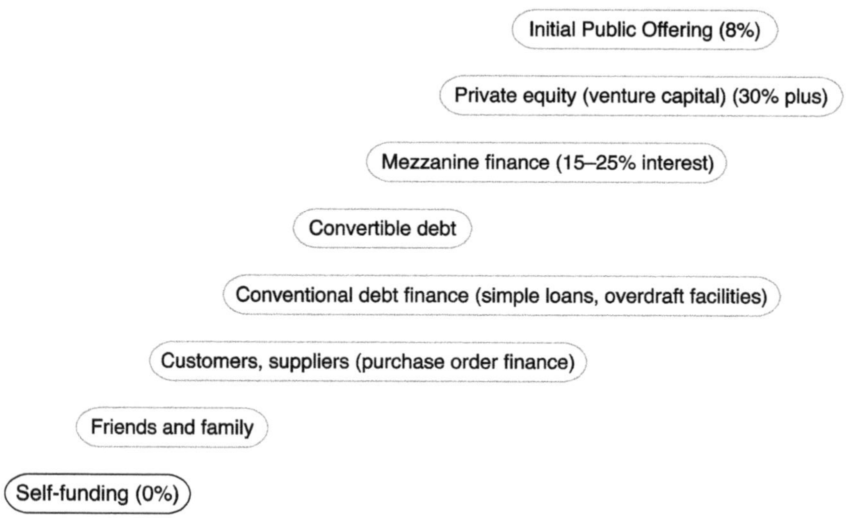

Figure 3.4 Tiers of finance

This equity component means that mezzanine providers are much more comfortable with risk. The cost of equity is lower, in the range of 15%–25%, less than in a conventional VC investment, but higher than a commercial bank loan. Mezzanine finance sits between conventional debt finance and private equity and may be more "cash flow friendly". In contrast with a term loan that requires regular repayments (monthly or quarterly), which reduces cash available to the firm, mezzanine loans are usually repaid at annual intervals. The mezzanine loan is structured so that a high proportion of the money is repayable towards the end of the life of the loan agreement. This funding strategy enables the innovating SME to implement its growth strategy with lower loan repayments and consequently less impact on cash flow at the front end of the term of the loan. However, Santander advises, "this can be a double-edged sword, as a company that fails to deliver on its growth protections will nevertheless be looking at large repayments towards the end of the term".[25] The problem for innovating SMEs is that most mezzanine finance providers operate at the larger end of the market and few offer loans less than £10 million. Accordingly, mezzanine finance, despite its advantages, is currently not a feasible option for the majority of innovating SMEs in the early stage of their business life cycle.

3.3.8 Debt finance by way of a syndicated loan

A sophisticated method of debt finance is the syndicated loan. This method was used by the People's Republic of China's China Development Bank, which led a consortium of lenders to fund Quanlin Paper resulting in the largest ever patent-backed loan made in the world to date. A loan is entered into between a company and more than one lender, who are then known as the "syndicate" of lenders or "bank syndicate". The loan is usually substantial and the contractual arrangements between the various lenders and the borrowing company can be complex and require professional legal advice. There is usually a lead lender or "underwriter" of the loan which is often the bank providing the largest proportion of the funds. The main reason for syndicated loans is to reduce the risk to the lenders by sharing between them the risk of the company not being able to repay the large sum of money borrowed. The loan transaction costs will be higher given the various parties that need to be involved, which makes such loans only viable if a large sum is to be borrowed. London continues to be one of the most active centres for the arrangement of syndicated loans.[26] Such loans would appear to have solid potential for patent-backed lending given the reduced level of risk to each lender, however the transaction costs involved may be high for the innovating SME at the early growth stage.

25 www.santanderbreakthrough.co.uk/advice/finance/funding-options-mezzanine-finance.

26 Rhodes, T. and Campbell, M. *Syndicated Lending: Practice and Documentation* (2009) Fifth edition, Euromoney Institutional Investor, Inc. Foreword by Sir Andrew Large.

3.3.9 Convertible debt

A convertible debt is another form of hybrid finance whereby the loan can convert to equity (shares in the business) instead of being repaid.. A better interest rate is usually available. However, if the loan is not repaid, equity in the business will be lost. American financier Peter Thiel entered into a convertible debt finance arrangement with entrepreneur Mark Zuckerberg at an early stage in Facebook, Inc.'s business life cycle.[27]

3.3.10 Financing options beyond the growth stage

Expanding companies are those that have succeeded in attracting clients and establishing a market presence. They are likely to be financed by private equity and/or VC in addition to owners' equity and bank debt – in other words, a mix of funding sources. *High growth companies* with rapidly growing revenues may seek to publicly trade shares, for example on the London Stock Exchange (LSE) or Alternative Investment Market (AIM). Firms issue equity in the form of shares and other financial instruments, known as an initial public offering (IPO). However, substantial fees and charges are involved in floating a new company as well as additional expenses in connection with a variety of professional advisors. Companies pay an admission fee to join each of the Exchange's markets and an annual fee thereafter. [28] In reality, few SMEs have the opportunity to float via AIM or achieve a full listing on the LSE main market. A public listing is a more realistic funding option for firms in the expansion phases of the business life cycle, whereas in this book we focus on start-up and early stage SMEs. *Mature companies* typically finance their activities by a combination of internal financing, debt and equity.

3.3.11 New financing models: CrowdFunding[29], Peer-to-Peer Lending and pension-led funding

If traditional lenders fail to move with the times, they may find that their out-dated lending model will be swept away by alternatives such as online "CrowdFunding" and "Peer-to-Peer Lending".[30] These are e-platforms via websites whereby IP owners can pitch their ideas, outlining to members of the public exactly how much funding they require to develop and commercialise

27 Kirkpatrick, D. *Facebook Effect: The Real Inside Story of Mark Zuckerberg and the World's Fastest Growing Company* (2012) The Random House Group.

28 See www.londonstockexchange.com/companies-and-advisors/listing/fees/fees.htm.

29 See also CrowdSourcing, CrowdLending, and CrowdInvesting.

30 A form of crowd funding that involves the practice of lending money in the form of an unsecured personal loan to unrelated individuals (without going through a traditional financial intermediary such as a bank), using online credit checking tools.

their inventions, inviting them to lend (debt CrowdFunding) or invest small amounts of money in shares (equity CrowdFunding). The funds raised are then used as seed or start-up capital.

The CrowdFunding model is rapidly evolving now that more online platforms are being formally regulated by the UK's Financial Services Authority (FSA) to protect investors. In July 2011, Abundance Generation was the first debt finance online CrowdLending platform regulated by the FSA. This online private equity platform does not facilitate direct investment in small businesses as such, rather it holds shares in a company as a nominee and manages them on investors' behalf. The public are able to invest small amounts (as little as £10) in unlisted businesses (usually with no upper limit) without the need to use a traditional stock exchange such as the LSE. Such websites create a public market minus some of the traditional market control mechanisms that are required when listing on a stock exchange and are a low cost option for attracting investment. Costs are further reduced as the companies hoping to attract investment do not necessarily even have to sell equity, instead they can give "discounts" and "rewards" in the form of free goods in exchange for funding. According to the FSA, most CrowdFunding platforms require a specified target to be reached during the fundraising period before the money is passed to the business – the "all or nothing" model – with contributions returned to investors if the target is not met.[31] In February 2013, the FSA authorised CrowdCube with more e-platforms to follow. The main advantage is gaining direct access to an enormous pool of investors at a much lower cost than private equity investors or lenders are willing to offer.

3.3.11.1 Crowdfunding and IP issues

While it is positive that the UK financial services industry and the FSA are reacting dynamically to this new funding model,[32] the advantages for patent-rich innovating SMEs are not so clear-cut. This is due to the unique features of the patent law system and the requirement of "absolute novelty" as a criterion for obtaining patent monopoly protection. A basic requirement under section 2 PA 1977 is that the invention be novel (new) and if a patent application does not satisfy this condition, it will not be granted by the UKIPO. This legal requirement cannot be fully understood without first being aware of another fundamental concept in patent law. The priority date of the patent application is the date on which it is tested against the "state of the art",[33] normally the filing date of the application. The "state of the art" comprises all matter made available to the public before the priority date of the invention.[34] This includes all knowledge anywhere in the world

31 www.fsa.gov.uk/consumerinformation/product_news/saving_investments/crowdfunding.

32 Berges, A., Guillen, M.F., Moreno, J.P, Ontiveros, E. *A New Era in Banking: The Landscape After the Battle* (2014) Bibliomotion, Inc.

33 Section 5 (1) PA 1977.

34 Section 2(2) PA 1977.

on the subject matter of the invention. Novelty-destroying prior art could include information that is part of common general knowledge, or information disclosed by an earlier user of the invention, in a single copy of a published document or by oral communication. A business must keep a potentially patentable invention absolutely confidential until a patent application is filed. Only then will they be able to freely disclose the invention to the public, for example via the online funding platform. Therefore, a key challenge is that the patentable details of the invention could be exposed to the public, fall into the public domain, or become part of common general knowledge thereby destroying novelty and the potential to acquire both a patent monopoly and create a valuable business asset. The practical answer to the loss of novelty problem is to file any patent application(s) before accessing a CrowdFunding platform.

A further IP law issue arises if the innovating SMEs (pitch creator) accidentally and/or unknowingly incorporates IP from a third party IP rights holder for which a user licence is needed, giving risk to an infringement claim. The risk of potential IP infringement could result in loss of business, revenue, reputation and competitive advantage. However, if the required licences are obtained, higher funding levels may be achieved.[35] At present, however, many innovating SMEs have a low level of knowledge or understanding of patent law principles and patentability requirements.[36] Those with knowledge of patent law principles will be best positioned to secure funding without compromising their existing or future patent rights. Further, if the funds are actually needed to pay patent application costs and patent attorney fees, innovating SMEs using CrowdFunding platforms may risk being unable to patent their invention if "novelty" is destroyed by disclosing how it works online. Nevertheless, CrowdFunding is a new option with considerable potential. As yet, no data is available in the UK about innovating SMEs financed via regulated platforms. In the US, one success story is that of Dan Provost and his partner Thomas Gerhardt who raised $137,000 US (although they initially only asked for $10,000 US) in 2010 via the Kickstarter[37] platform for their simple yet well designed The GLIF iPhone 4 Tripod Mount and Stand invention. They received financial support to commercialise their prototype from over 5,000 investors who could buy shares and pre-order based on the prototype.[38] No doubt more successful examples of how CrowdFunding has assisted inventors and innovating SMEs will continue to materialise. Supporters of this funding method assert that it enables: (1) ideas, which conventional financiers spurn, an avenue through which to attract funding via the "wisdom of the crowd"; and (2) a receptive market to be identified.[39]

35 *Copyright and the Value of the Public Domain: An Empirical Assessment* (February 2015) Independent Report Commissioned by the UKIPO carried out by CREATe p 5.

36 Pitkethly, R. 'Intellectual Property Awareness and SMEs: UK IP Awareness Survey 2010' (2010) UKIPO, which concluded that UK SMEs are effectively unaware of the IP system.

37 www.kickstarter.com, the world's largest funding platform for creative projects.

38 http://blog.crowdfunder.co.uk/2010/11/08/147/.

39 Surowiecki, J. *The Wisdom of Crowds: Why the Many are Smarter than the Few* (2005) Abacus, New York.

However, innovating SMEs will need patent law advice to protect their position and invention before pitching to raise money on CrowdFunding platforms.

3.3.11.2 Pension-led funding

Many businesses are considering non-bank lending finance options, given the barriers to bank loans. Pension-led funding uses the owner's accrued pension funds to invest in their own innovating SME or larger company. It enables the owner (typically a director/shareholder) with a good size pension pot to obtain funding, essentially a commercial loan from the pension fund, without having to provide a personal guarantee to a lender (e.g. over the home or other personal assets) by using IP assets to secure the loan. Once the value of the patent assets has been established, the pension fund's trustees agree to lend money to the firm secured against the patent assets, or buy some or all of the patents. As the innovating SME generates an income stream from its business activities, it repays the pension scheme. It applies to directors' and/or senior executives' accumulated pensions and does not affect employee pensions. In the event of non-payment, only those pensions are at risk. Thus, pension-led funding shifts business risk to the individual directors/senior executives.

If the innovating SME defaults, the pension scheme is protected from external creditors. However, as a creditor itself to the business, the pension scheme will suffer a loss or be written off entirely. One view is that pension-led funding is less risky for the innovating SME than a traditional bank loan which is only viable as long as the lender is willing to supply funds. With pension-led funding the directors may be appointed as trustees and have more control. In addition, there will be no bank charges although there will be legal costs in drafting the pension loan documentation. If a pension scheme member retires, the value of the IP may be adversely affected depending on his or her role within the business. This type of non-bank lending only has potential for pension-rich innovating SMEs.

3.3.12 Evolving trends in corporate finance for innovation

Financing a business is not static. Rather, the financing models change over time in response to the business life cycle; the relative costs of different types of financing; and their impact on control or ownership of the business. The *amount* of funding depends on business needs, whereas the *type* of financing arrangement used to obtain the required funding will largely by determined by the relative costs of different types of financing. Assuming a key corporate objective is to maximise profits, then a business will prefer the least expensive finance and no loss of control or ownership of the business. At present, debt finance is available for well-run, profitable companies of any size provided they generate regular cash flows with traditional assets to act as security e.g. property, machinery, other capital assets, cash, stock, receivables, etc. The problem for innovating SMEs is when they are only able to provide intangibles as security. Commercialising an invention is a lengthy process and establishing regular cash flows, either via purchasing orders or a licensing revenue streams is challenging. In light of the global financial crisis,[40] lenders are more cautious about the scale of their commercial lending and quality of the assets offered as security.[41] In April 2013 the International Monetary Fund (IMF) pointed out that a continuing problem for UK fiscal policy is that growth in the private sector is still being hampered by a lack of debt finance:

> In the euro area, real GDP is projected to contract by about ¼ percent this year before growing again in 2014. Credit channels are broken: better financial conditions are not yet passing through to companies and households because banks are still hobbled by poor profitability and low capital.[42]

The Big Innovation Centre's Entrepreneurial Finance Hub[43] has developed QuantIPly, an investment and trading finance platform (physical and digital) to finance high-growth firms through critical phases of growth.[44] A group of high profile banks, business incubators, universities, global corporates, alternative finance providers, VCs, business angels and government agencies are participants. The next section investigates the types of funding innovation that firms surveyed by WIPO *actually* used to develop their inventions and get them to market.

3.4 WIPO *IP Advantage* database analysis

In 2010, WIPO launched *IP Advantage*[45] a database of over 100 case studies covering 48 different countries which profiles the experiences of inventors, creators, entrepreneurs and researchers – the only database of its kind that has an innovation finance component, as far as the author is able to ascertain. It provides an intuitive interface that enables one to search according to type of IP and the focus (e.g. R&D, financing). *IP Advantage* is a valuable and unique resource as

40 *The run on the Rock Fifth Report of Session 2007–2008 House of Commons Treasury Committee* (2008) Vol.1, House of Commons London: The Stationer Office Ltd pp 4–20.

41 Fraser, S. *The Impact of the Financial Crisis of Bank Lending to SMEs: Economic Analysis from the EU Survey of SME Finances* (July 2012) University of Warwick, Report prepared for the Breedon Review of Business Finance for the Department of Business Innovation and Skills at pp 4–6.

42 www.imf.org/external/pubs/ft/survey/so/2013/RES041613A.htm.

43 www.biginnovationcentre.com/entrepreneurial-finance-hub.

44 "QuantIPly helps companies whose business models are primarily driven by innovation and technology and which have high growth aspirations. Companies may be looking for their first third party funding round of £250,000, or for a Series B round of £5,000,000. We are sector-agnostic. The QuantIPly process is free to join. Quantiply charges a success fee when funding occurs". See www.biginnovationcentre.com/entrepreneurial-finance-hub.

45 The *IP Advantage* is based on a proposal and funding from the Japanese government and is one of the first concrete deliveries of the WIPO Development Agenda project that was agreed by member states at the end of 2009. French and Spanish versions are under development. See www.wipo.int/pressroom/en/articles/2010/article_0037.html .

the case studies provide a rare opportunity to analyse how innovating SMEs obtain finance to commercialise their inventions. A database search was made selecting "patents" and "financing" as the focus, returning 19 case studies for evaluation, including four from the UK. The dataset captures the financing experience of a collection of innovating SMEs in the recent past. The basic proposition is that patent-backed debt financing will feature rarely, if at all, as a funding method given lenders' apparent aversion to using patents as security. Figure 3.5 contains a table summarising the *IP Advantage* results. The country, company name and industry sector are set out for each entry, followed by the finance method used: self-finance, public, private or debt.

The pilot study provides quantitative data on the type of financing successfully sourced by international innovating SMEs in their home countries which are all WIPO members and adhere to TRIPS.[46] A summary is shown in Figure 3.6.

In 12 out of the 19 case studies (63%) the evidence shows the importance of public funding in the form of grants and financial assistance to support R&D and other business expenditure. This was closely followed by equity finance which featured in nine cases (47%); then to a lesser extent, self-financing in four cases (21%); and lastly, debt finance obtained in only one case (5%). This pattern follows the traditionally held view that early growth stage businesses primarily rely on public funding. Debt finance features rarely (as predicted). However, in most cases the firms accessed a funding mix. Figure 3.7 sets out the statistics depicting the funding mix sourced by the firms.

The data reveals that only two out of the 19 firms even applied for banks loans. Of those two, only one case (6%), the Italian firm GEOX, successfully accessed debt finance. This figure makes the author's argument, that debt finance is underused, powerful and persuasive. Even more importantly, none of the UK cases studied obtained debt finance, although Faveo Ltd documented that it unsuccessfully applied. It is recommended that UKIPO/BEIS collect similar innovating SME case studies to shed more light on the debt-finance situation in the UK. In the author's view, it is likely that the firms participating in WIPO's *IP Advantage* database would have described both negative and positive attempts to obtain bank loans as they were directly asked to report on "their experience in financing their innovations". A further outcome of the dataset analysis demonstrates that debt finance *did not even feature* as part of a funding mix nor was there a single documented instance of patent-backed debt finance. These are the most significant aspects of the *IP Advantage* multi-case study in relation to innovating SMEs and patent-backed debt finance. The results of the *IP Advantage* database analysis are compelling, providing a portrait of the bleak environment facing innovating SMEs. This is preliminary evidence that change is required and that a shift in the innovating SME-lender relationship is desperately needed. Funding is

46 The TRIPS Agreement is Annex 1C of the *Marrakesh Agreement Establishing the WTO*, signed in Marrakesh, Morocco on 15 April 1994 to which the UK is a signatory.

Country	Name/Industry	Financing Type
Argentina	**Descorjet SA** – Durable Household Products	Private funding
Australia	**ITL Limited** – Health Care Equipment and Services	Self-financing Public funding
Brazil	**FK Biotecnologia S.A** – Pharmaceuticals and Biotechnology	Private funding (VC)
Chile/USA	**Florencio Lazo Barra** – Farming, Fishing & Engineering	Public funding
Colombia	**Ecoflora S.A.S Corporation Colombia**	N/A
Denmark	**Borean Pharma A/S** – Pharmaceuticals and Biotechnology	Public funding Private funding (VC syndicate)
India/ USA	**Dr Ashok Gadgil** – Durable Household Products	Public funding
Indonesia	**Indonesian Planters Association for R&D (IPARD), Dept. of Agriculture** – Pharmaceuticals and Biotechnology	Public funding
Italy	**GEOX S.P.A.** – Clothing, Footwear	Debt finance
Japan	**Tefco Aomori Co Ltd** – Chemicals, Clothing and Accessories	Private funding
Japan	**Yamanashi Hitachi Construction Machinery Co. Ltd.**	Private funding
Nigeria	**EAT-SET Industries** – Health Care Equipment and Services	Self-financing Public funding Private funding
Nigeria/ USA	**Bioresources Development and Conservation Programme** – Pharmaceuticals and Biotechnology	Public funding Private funding
Singapore	**iTwin Ptd. Ltd / The Institute for Infocomm Research (I2R)** – Technology Hardware and Equipment	Public funding Private funding (VC)
UK	**Surface Processing Limited** – Chemicals	Public funding
UK	**Faveo Ltd** – Clothing and Accessories	Public funding Debt finance refused.
UK	**Junkk.com Ltd** – Packaging	Public funding
UK	**MakMarine** – Industrial Engineering	Self-financing Public funding
Zimbabwe	**Algorhythm Private Limited** – Industrial Engineering	Self-financing Private funding including (VC)

Figure 3.5 Evaluation of WIPO's *IP Advantage* case studies focussing on patents and financing

Sources: WIPO *IP Advantage* database

Type of finance	Number of firms	Percentage
Public finance	12	71%
Private Finance	9	53%
Self-financing	4	24%
Debt finance	1	6%

Figure 3.6 Statistical analysis of the types of finance used

Mix of funding	Number of firms	Percentage
Self-financing only	Nil	0%
Public funding only	5	29%
Debt finance only	1	6%
Private finance only	4	23%
Self-financing & Public funding	2	12%
Public funding & Private funding	3	18%
Self-financing & Private funding	1	6%
Self-financing, Public funding & Private funding	1	6%

Figure 3.7 Mix of financing types used in the case studies

critical to the survival of innovating SMEs as they face unique overheads that simply do not exist in other creative businesses. Further, innovation usually requires several prototypes to bring the invention to market, a process which can take years. Commercialisation will take even longer if the new technology "disrupts" existing markets. Yet, it is precisely disruptive technology that has the most positive impact on society in the long term and the biggest returns. These overheads are unique to patent innovation and are not required for other types of creative businesses, resulting in a less favourable finance environment for innovating SMEs.

Over the past decade there has been a growing interest in the SME "funding gap" and how to facilitate access to patent-backed debt finance necessary for innovation firms to grow. The evidence from the *IP Advantage* database analysis confirms that for innovation SMEs banks are not important sources of credit. Large financial institutions are costly to run and are geared to serving the needs of customers for whom the volume of activity justifies the costs of acquiring information about the innovating SME's prospects, intangible patent assets and ability to repay. Even if one assumes that the cost of ascertaining creditworthiness was not a decreasing function of the borrower's size and number of years in operation, the cost to the bank per pound (£) loaned is greater for SMEs than for large-scale enterprises. The difficulties are likely to be greater for innovating SMEs outside the main financial centres. The author feels strongly that debt finance holds significant untapped potential for both innovating SMEs and lenders. The pilot study has clear implications for policy makers, lenders and borrowers despite the small sample size. Innovating SMEs require additional public finance support to enable them access private debt finance. Commercial banks do engage in patent-backed lending to larger firms with significant patent portfolios and other assets, but that lending experience needs to flow downstream to innovating SMEs. Other barriers to overcome relate to banking capital adequacy requirements that apply to intangibles and their impact on IP-backed lending.

3.5 Basel III banking capital adequacy requirements: an adverse impact on IP finance

Research has identified that the global financial crisis[47] actually had little to do with traditional banking, commercial lending or, indeed, bankruptcies. In 2008–2009, banks that were vulnerable because they had too much debt simply cut back sharply on their lending. The severe credit crunch was caused by a combination of excessive bank borrowing, thus carrying too much debt, coupled with the rise and fall of "securitised" lending, which enabled banks to originate loans but then repackage and sell them on coupled with a lack of transparency.[48] In response, bank regulators imposed tighter restrictions. Capital regulation requires that a sufficient fraction of a bank's investments or assets be funded with un-borrowed money. This is similar to the requirement that a home buyer make a minimum down payment when buying a house. Having a minimal ratio of un-borrowed funds relative to total assets is a way to limit the share of assets that is funded by borrowing. Because un-borrowed funds are obtained without any promise to make specific payments at particular times, having more equity enhances the banks' ability to absorb losses on its assets.[49]

The Basel III (the Third Basel Accord) mandates the capital adequacy requirements with which banks need to comply when lending against intangible assets. Basel III is the third in a series of comprehensive reform measures developed by 27 member countries of the Basel Committee on Banking Supervision, to strengthen the regulation, supervision and risk management of the global banking sector. It includes a global, *voluntary* regulatory standard on capital adequacy.

47 *The run on the Rock Fifth Report of Session 2007–2008 House of Commons Treasury Committee* (2008) Vol.1, House of Commons London: The Stationer Office Ltd pp 4–20.

48 Final Report of the National Commission on the Causes of the Financial and Economic Crisis of in the United States (January 2011) *The Financial Crisis Inquiry Commission Pursuant to Public Law 111–21* Washington, DC at p *xvii*; Ferguson, N. *The Ascent of Money* (2012); Admati, A. and Hellwig, M. *The Banker's New clothes: What's wrong with Banking and What to Do about It (2013) Princeton University Press p 4.*

49 Admati, A. and Hellwig, M. *The Bankers' New clothes: What's wrong with Banking and What to Do about It* (2013) Princeton University Press pp 5–6.

It originated in response to deficiencies in banking regulation that emerged during the global financial crisis.[50] The aim is to make banks better placed to absorb financial shocks in the long term, by increasing the size of capital reserves a bank must hold against losses.[51] Under the new reforms, banks must progressively reach a minimum solvency ratio of 7% by 2019. The solvency ratio is calculated by dividing Regulatory Capital by Risked Weighted Assets. Before Basel III the solvency ratio was 2%. The new 7% minimum is being phased in and implementation is now extended to 31 March 2018.[52] Under Basel III, intangibles are rated as riskier types of assets and are treated as lower quality security. The definition of capital means that intangibles (e.g. patents) must be deducted from the regulatory capital. As such, intangible assets are not usually counted toward the loan's security because these intangible IP assets are considered too difficult to value.[53] Set out below is the regulatory adjustment to be applied to Common Equity Tier 1 regulatory capital according to the Basel Committee for Banking Supervision:

> Goodwill and other intangibles (except mortgage servicing rights) 67. Goodwill and all other intangibles must be deducted in the calculation of Common Equity Tier 1 capital, including any goodwill included in the valuation of significant investments in the capital of banking, financial and insurance entities that are outside the scope of regulatory consolidation. With the exception of mortgage servicing rights, the full amount is to be deducted net of any associated deferred tax liability which would be extinguished if the intangible assets become impaired or derecognized under the relevant accounting standards.[54]

Basel III includes a voluntary bank loan rating standard which indicates the degree of risk regarding timely payment of the bank facility being rated. The guidelines also require banks to provide capital on the credit exposure as per the credit rating assigned by approved credit assessment institutions. The implications of Basel III for IP-backed debt finance is the higher level of "risk-weighting" that applies to intangible assets in contrast with other forms of assets such as cash or currency that are zero risk. If loans are secured against intangibles such as patents, the bank is legally obliged to make appropriate capital adequacy provision. This is unhelpful with respect to nurturing the development of patent-backed lending. In simple

50 *The run on the Rock Fifth Report of Session 2007–2008 House of Commons Treasury Committee* (2008) Vol.1, House of Commons London: The Stationer Office Ltd pp 4–20.

51 *International Regulatory Framework for Banks (Basel III): Capital* (June 2011) Basel Committee for Banking Supervision, Bank for International Settlements.

52 *Basel III: A Global Regulatory Framework for more Resilient Banks and Banking* Systems (December 2010, Revised June 2011) Basel Committee for Banking Supervision, Bank for International Settlements pp 6–23.

53 'Using Patents as Collateral Can Free Up Funds for Growing Businesses' at www.ipnav.com/blog.

54 *International Regulatory Framework for Banks (Basel III): Capital* (June 2011) Basel Committee for Banking Supervision, Bank for International Settlements p 21–22.

terms, Basel III regards intangibles as "toxic" assets that should be treated carefully.[55]

Basel III capital regulation is perceived by banks to be a major a barrier to the development of innovation finance and IP-backed lending in the UK. Richard McCarthy, UK head of banking at KPMG said, "We have to remember that banking requires risk-taking, yet in the rush to clean up the past, both banks and regulators have lost sight of this."[56] Greater understanding of the implications of capital adequacy requirements, intangible asset risk weightings and improved dialogue between the stakeholders is necessary. The impact of Basel III on intangibles and commercial lending should be addressed by future research carried out by a multidisciplinary panel of experts, beyond the scope of this book.

3.6 The lenders' triad of concerns: uncertainty, risk and liquidity

> The more visible it [IP] becomes in public accounts, the easier its value becomes to realise. This will lead to greater opportunities for lenders – and higher risks of inaction.
>
> Martin Brassell and Kelvin King, *Banking on IP?* (2013)[57]

A lender has a well-established triad of concerns when carrying out a credit appraisal: (1) uncertainty of valuation; (2) legal risks; and (3) liquidity, as illustrated in Figure 3.8.

This book focuses on the initial stage of credit appraisal, when the innovating SME's patent assets are identified and then quantitatively and qualitatively valued, although it is acknowledged that legal risks and liquidity issues form part of a comprehensive credit appraisal. The mechanics of a simple patent-backed debt finance transaction are set out in Figure 3.9.

At the outset of the credit appraisal, a key area of uncertainty from the lender's point of view is that nothing exists to quickly tell the lender how to *value* the patent or small patent portfolio. This is a corporate disclosure and transparency problem resulting in uncertainty and impacting on the level of legal risk assigned to the particular patent asset. A determining factor in the decision to lend is the availability of security, especially in the case of innovating SMEs with no established track record.[58] Further, small firms are most likely to fail and produce the

55 Definition of Basel III, Financial Times Lexicon at http://lexicon.ft.com/term?term=basel-iii.

56 Eccles, L. 'How bank lending fell by £365 Billion in five years' (7 September 2014) *Daily Mail.*

57 Brassell, M. and King, K. *Banking on IP? The role of Intellectual Property and Intangible Assets in Facilitating Business Finance Final Report* (6 November 2013) Independent report commissioned by the UKIPO p 15.

58 *Finance for Small Firms* (1999) Bank of England Sixth Report p 25.

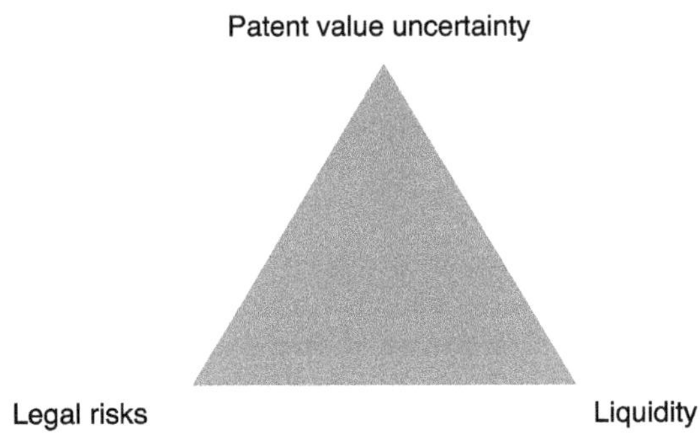

Figure 3.8 Lenders' triad of concerns

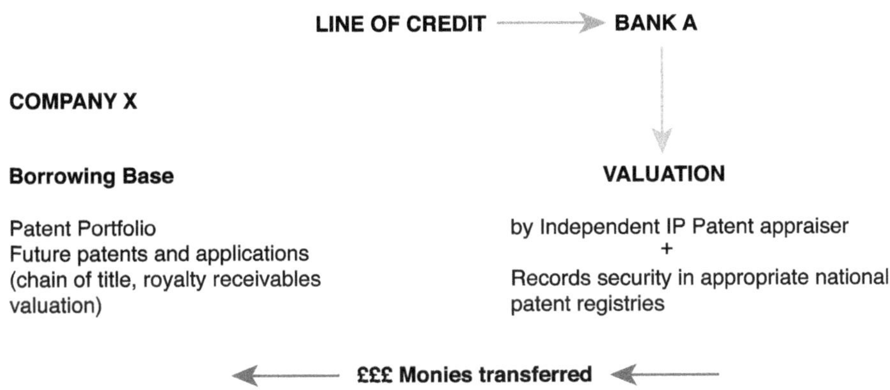

Figure 3.9 Example of a secured transaction involving a patent portfolio

least asset recovery value.[59] This demonstrates the importance of available security. IP rights are a form of property that can be mortgaged and licensed. The lender needs more relevant accurate information about the innovating SME's patent(s) and the potential to generate an income stream to lend prudently and appropriately. If the valuation is favourable and the lender proceeds with the patent-backed loan, then creating an effective security interest in the patent(s) is a primary concern.

3.7 Transparency and registering security interests in patents

In particular, the transparency of security interests in patent assets could be streamlined. This section examines the existing UK legal framework and outlines

59 *Corporate insolvency in the UK: A Decade of Change* (2002) Association of Business Recovery Professionals Tenth Report p 9.

the specific legal issues and risks arising when using patents and/or patent applications as security. The distinction between secured and unsecured lending is important because of the enhanced legal rights afforded the secured creditor relative to an unsecured creditor. The starting point is the PA 1977 which qualifies a patent as personal property,[60] a registrable right that can be used to secure obligations. The PA 1977 and the Patents Rules 2007 (SI2007/3291) also govern the security interest voluntary registration regime for UK patents which are registrable in the specialist UK Register of Patents (the Patents Register). The Patents Register is maintained by the Comptroller-General of Patents, Designs and Trade Marks at the UKIPO.

Banks are unwilling to lend significant sums of money to small companies on an unsecured basis. In general, the key concepts in the field of secured transactions are: (1) creation of the security interest; (2) registration; and (3) priority. "Creation" is the process by which the lender obtains security interests in the debtor's assets via a security agreement documenting the terms and conditions. "Registration" is the process by which the lender ensures that, by giving notice, its security interest will be effective against third parties – especially against the insolvency administrator or other creditors of the debtor. "Priority" means the relative rights of one creditor with a security interest in the debtors' asset vis-à-vis other creditors with claims to the same asset.[61]

3.7.1 Secured versus unsecured transactions

A lender contemplating a loan transaction with the innovating SME will carry out certain actions to protect its position as a creditor. Secured creditors are those who, in addition to having a contractual right to sue the innovating SME for the return of any money owed, have taken a property interest in one or more items of the company's property as security for the credit they have made available to the borrower.[62] The customary security devices include: the possessory lien, pledges, the mortgage and equitable charges.[63] In practice, in relation to Intellectual Property Rights (IPRs) and patents:

> The creation of an equitable charge requires neither transfer of ownership of the [patent(s)] taken as security nor delivery of possession . . . Rather, it is a "shadow" cast over the collateral until the obligation is discharged or the security is realized. This legal device has a linear structure and offers great

60 Section 30(1) PA 1977.

61 Flack, J.H. 'Secured Transactions: Practical Things Every Business Law Should Know About UCC Article 9' (March 2011) *American Bar Association Newsletter*.

62 McLaughlin, S. *Unlocking Company Law* (2015) Third edition, Routledge p 442.

63 *Registration of Security Interests: Company Charges and Property other than Land* (2002) Law Commission Consultation Paper No 164 at paras 2.6–2.19.

> flexibility with regard to the type of property which can be used and the rights and remedies it can offer to the lender. In practice the security agreement creating the may be drafted as a deed, providing the secured lender with both a right of sale and a right to appoint a receiver in the event of default. For these reasons, the charge is compatible with IPRs and appears to be the most efficient security device available in English law.[64]

The creation of an equitable charge is the most efficient security device to protect the lender in a patent-backed secured transaction involving patents and innovating SMEs.[65] The principal reason why the lender should take a security interest in the innovating SMEs asset(s) is so that it will have priority over competing creditors if the innovating SME becomes insolvent. Further, a security interest in the patent(s) may also afford the lender the valuable right to sell or license the patent(s) and apply the proceeds to repay the debt, although this right is likely to be subject to an automatic stay, on the innovating SME's insolvency, from which the lender would be required to seek relief. However, this will depend on the insolvency procedure in question. If liquidation, the secured creditor is entitled to enforce his right over his own property.[66] If administration, the secured creditor cannot take steps to enforce the security unless the administrator consents or the court gives leave.[67] The point is that if the lender has registered a security interest in the innovating SMEs patent asset(s), it will be in a much stronger position to recover monies to repay the loan than it would as an unsecured creditor. However, simply ensuring priority for creditors is not the only important issue at stake:

> The control rights provided by security will be important to a financier and this is especially the case with technologically-driven SMEs as the line between equity and debt finance may become blurred. When [an] SME is in financial difficulty, creditors care about issues of management capability or the threat of the business over-extending itself. A security interest gives creditors a voice in these decisions.[68]

Consequently there are myriad advantages for both the innovating SME in offering its patent assets as security and to the lender in taking security over same.

64 Tosato, A. 'Security Interests over Intellectual Property' (2011) 6(2) *Journal of Intellectual Property Law and Practice* 95.

65 The situation may differ for international patents as the relevant jurisdiction may not permit equitable charges, only mortgages, or may have other security device regimes in place.

66 *Re David Lloyd & Company* (1977) 6 CH D 339; *Re Aro Company Ltd* [1980] CH 1986.

67 Paragraph 43, Schedule B1 Insolvency Act 1986.

68 Davies, I.R. 'Secured Financing of Intellectual Property Assets and the Reform of English Personal Property Security Law' (Autumn 2006) 26(3) *Oxford Journal of Legal Studies* 559–583, 563.

3.7.2 Registering security interests: where patent, company and insolvency law meet

The gist of the problem for IP rights as an asset class (registered IP assets such as patents, trade marks and designs) is how the IP security registers operate. To illustrate, presently there are two security registers for recording property interests in patent assets used as security and this can give rise to "priority dilemmas". First, notice of the security interest should be registered on the Patent Register under section 33 PA 1977. Second, as an innovating SME is a company the security interest should also be registered at Companies House as required by sections 859 A–Q, CA 2006.[69] This is problematic as the specialist Patent Register alone (an external legal factor) cannot be considered a one-stop source of information. This gives rise to a degree of legal uncertainty for the lender when searching the Patent Register for competing interests and registering its own security interests. The general rule of priority is that the first creditor to register obtains priority as to the security (collateral). However in the UK, security interests in respect of patents or patent applications take priority according to the date on which they were registered in the Patents Register, regardless of whether or not the security was also perfected by registration at Companies House.[70] This is important for lenders in the UK to understand – they need to engage with two registration systems, namely, the Patents Register and Companies House. This may not be the case in other jurisdictions. The dual registration system is a weakness of the UK system that may need to be reformed.

3.7.3 When a competing interest exists

For a lender to protect its position, as a matter of due diligence during the credit appraisal process it should verify whether any competing interests encumber the patent assets offered as collateral by the innovating SME. If a search of either register reveals an earlier competing interest, would the lender proceed with the transaction? According to the author's discussions with Dr Sandra Frisby[71] the answer depends on the estimated value of the patent(s) and whether an agreement could be reached between lender one and lender two to subrogate lender one's security to that of lender two. In the right circumstances, if the patents are of sufficient value to cover both lenders' loans and costs, this is a possibility. Nevertheless, the existence of a prior ranking security interest would be problematic for lender two and increase its risk. However, the possibility of

69 A charge is defined in section 859A(7) CA 2006 and registration requires a statement of particulars (section 859D). Registration is voluntary – there are no criminal sanctions for non-registration (c.f. the old regime) – and can be effected by either chargor or chargee, but if it is not effected the charge is void against the administrator, liquidator or creditor of the company.

70 Bezant, M. and Punt, R. 'The Use of Intellectual Property as Security for Debt Finance' (1997) *Intellectual Property Quarterly* 297; Henry, M. 'How Effective is Your Security over Intellectual Property?' (1991) *Journal Business Law* 507.

71 Associate Professor in Corporate and Insolvency Law, The University of Nottingham.

lending against patents on fixed charge security, if lender one has only a floating charge over the patents, should also be considered. In any event, it is crucial for the lender to acquire an indisputable position in terms of priority. The Patent Register plays a decisive role in this regard.[72]

3.7.4 Registering a charge over a patent application or granted patent

A lender is advised to register the charge at the UK Intellectual Property Office *first*. This is because the granting of security over a UK patent or patent application is a registrable "transaction, instrument or event" under section 33 PA 1977. A failure to register the fixed charge at the UKIPO would mean that a subsequent assignee, licensee or chargee of the patent would take free of charge if they were not aware of the fixed charge. A security interest in respect of a patent or an application for a patent is registrable in the Patent Register under sections 32(2) and 33(3) PA 1977 using Form 21. Registration is voluntary and there is no time limit for registration, but as a matter of best practice the security should be registered as soon as possible.[73] The most important outcome of registering a security interest is on priority between competing security interests. Thus, a security interest registered on the Patent Register will bind any party which acquires a security interest in the same patent at a later date. If a security interest is not registered, it will not bind another secured creditor which later acquires a conflicting security interest without knowledge of the existing unregistered security interest.[74] There are also certain practical administrative benefits of registration on the Patent Register that flow to the chargee where it becomes owner of the patent by virtue of the security (e.g. by an assignment by way of security). The chargee will receive patent renewal notices (to ensure that patent does not lapse)[75] and notices of proceedings concerning the patent.[76] Further, the chargee (as registered owner of the patent) will be entitled to be awarded costs in any proceedings.[77] Whereas, if the chargee has not registered its security on the Patent Register, it will only be entitled to be awarded costs in any proceedings for infringement of the patent if:

- it was not practicable to register its security within the six-month period beginning on the date of the security document; or
- if the court or Patent Comptroller is satisfied that it was not practicable to register the security before the end of the 6 month period but the security was registered as soon as practicable thereafter.

72 Tosato, A. 'Security Interests over Intellectual Property' (2011) 6(2) *Journal of Intellectual Property Law and Practice* 97.
73 SI 2007/3291, r ule 44(6) The Patent Rules also provide that notice of any security interest should be entered in the Patent Register as soon as possible after the security interest is granted.
74 Section 33(1) PA 1977.
75 SI 2007/3291 rule 39.
76 SI 2007/3291, rule 77.
77 Section 68 PA 1977.

3.7.5 The Companies Register

The role of Companies House in the UK (England and Wales) is to register company information and make it available to the public. The registration regime for security created by a UK company is governed by CA 2006, Part 25 is optional but the consequences of non-registration are severe on insolvency. The register is maintained by the Registrar of Companies at Companies House.[78] Section 859DE(ii) CA 2006 makes it clear that a charge over any intangible or incorporeal property, such as an IP right, can be registered. This includes any patent or any licence under or in respect of any such right. Where a UK company creates security of a patent right, for example, the security is perfected by registration within 21 days of its creation at Companies House. The registration process simply involves submitting the prescribed form together with a certified copy of the security agreement (charging document) which can be done online through the Companies House portal.[79] Failure to register security over a patent right at Companies House in the correct way and on time will mean that the security is void against a liquidator, an administrator or a creditor of the security provider.[80]

The relationship between the two registers in respect of patent-backed security operates to achieve different aims with respect to each register. Where security over a patent is created, registration on the Patent Register safeguards the *priority* of the security, whereas the security is *perfected* by registration at Companies House. This ensures that the security will be valid in the event of the innovating SME's insolvency and against other creditors of the SME.[81] Failure to register on the Patent Register does not make the security interest void in the event of the innovating SME's insolvency. Rather, it puts the security at a disadvantage to competing security taken by other secured creditors without notice of the existing security.[82] In contrast, failure to register security at Companies House seriously undermines the value of that security for many practical purposes because it will be void against the liquidator, an administrator or a creditor of the innovating SME.[83]

Registering the charge over the patents on both registers is a straightforward exercise in practice. However, potential problems may arise if the lender has to confirm whether competing interests encumber the patents as the Patent Register alone cannot be considered a one-stop source of information and there is a degree

78 As amended by CA 2006 (Amendment of Part 25) Regulations 2013, SI 2013/600.

79 Denoncourt, J. 'Reform to the UK Company Registration of Charges Scheme, CA 2006 (amendment of Part 25) Regulations 2013 (SI 2013/600)' (2013) 22 *Nottingham Law Journal* 138–140.

80 'Perfecting Security over Intellectual Property Rights and Registering Security at an Intellectual Property Register' LexisPSL Banking & Finance; section 859H CA 2006.

81 Graham, P. *'Registration of Company Charges'* [2014] *Journal of Business Law* 175.

82 The priority of perfected security is always determined by the normal rules on priority.

83 Section 859H CA 2006; Supra n [81] at p 361 .

of legal uncertainty.[84] This means that lenders need to carry out preliminary due diligence and subsequently, over the course of the negotiations, monitor both registers. Once the security agreement with the innovating SME has been finalised, the lender must register it on the Patent Register and on the Company Register. The costs associated with carrying out searches of the two registers and registering notice of security quickly mount up. An extra layer of cost applies to patent assets that do not arise in respect of most other assets, especially if the lender needs to deal with numerous UK patents and applications. Further, as the procedures are not routine, the lender may require specialist legal advice. Lenders and their legal advisors are simply not at ease when registering security interests over IP assets. The recent Intellectual Property Act 2014 did not take the opportunity to address the issue of harmonising the specialists IPR security registers[85] or modernising the legal framework governing security interests over IPRs. Presently, no government agency such as the UKIPO, Companies House, BEIS or the British Banking Association (BBA) publish a practical yet comprehensive user guide for registering notice of security interests in patents or other IPR. No doubt stakeholders in the finance community would find such a guide beneficial.

In conclusion, without the ability to offer valuable security the innovating SME will find it difficult to borrow funds at all. Offering IP rights such as patents as security should ensure that the terms of the loan will be better than an unsecured loan.[86] However, the interaction between UK IP law, personal property security law, company law and insolvency will need to be improved if IP-backed debt finance is to flourish in an economically efficient manner. The author holds the view that to enhance access to corporate IP-backed finance, reforming secured transactions law to permit filing notice of a security interest in a patent via a *single* personal property security register cannot be underestimated. The "Principle of Least Effort" says that it is human nature to want the greatest outcome for the least amount of work (efficiency). In theory, lenders will choose their behaviour based on the minimisation of effort. This can be viewed as interactions between jobs needing to be done (registering security), and tools developed to accomplish them.[87] Preferably, in the author's view, the single register would be maintained by Companies House. This would simplify, streamline and ultimately make the system more efficient, accessible and less costly for all stakeholders in the patent-backed secured transaction. Innovating SMEs, their accountants, lenders and legal advisers are used to dealing with Companies House, as opposed to dealing with the UKIPO and its specialist registers and legislation. Streamlining the security registration process would not preclude the introduction of new or specialist rules

84 Tosato, A. 'Security Interests over Intellectual Property' (2011) 6(2) *Journal of Intellectual Property Law and Practice* 99.

85 Specialist registers also exist for registered trade marks and designs.

86 Phillips, J. 'Intellectual Property as Security for Debt Finance – A Time to Advance?' (1997) EIPR 276.

87 Zipf, G.K. *Human Behaviour and the Principle of Least Effort* (1949) Addison-Wesley.

to cover patents, trade marks or designs. The author agrees with Bezant[88] and Davies,[89] who advocate a single register "notice filing system" that embraces IPR for ease of use, reducing risk and enhancing certainty and argues further that these advantages reduce loan transaction costs (which are passed on to the borrower), outweighing the disadvantage of any loss of flexibility, whilst acknowledging that Personal Property Securities Act (PPSA) systems are not without difficulties. PPSA systems exist in Australia, the US and Canada and many other jurisdictions. Law reform in the UK in the field of security over IP assets is under consideration by the Secured Transactions Law Reform Committee.

However, other developments are underway that may assist SMEs. New finance options beyond traditional banking via online platforms such as Amazon, PayPal and Alibaba are beginning to take shape. These digital platforms assess lending risk differently, by reviewing e-commerce sales, or shipment timings, rather than collateral, which lenders emphasise is still problematic for innovation SMEs.[90]

3.8 The role of corporate governance in supporting access to IP finance

This chapter has focused on IP finance, using the difficulties faced by innovating SMEs face in accessing debt finance as an example to illustrate the corporate IP asset transparency problem. Corporate governance has a role to play in regulating the conduct of directors who act as stewards of corporate assets and make decisions regarding corporate finance alternatives. In managing accounting for innovation, we identified why it is crucial for start-ups and innovating SMEs to identify and record their corporate IP assets as an additional line item in the accountant's spreadsheet, even if accountants regard them as off-balance sheet items, as they will undoubtedly become more important and valuable to the enterprise as it matures. From a corporate governance point of view, ensuring the integrity of the traditional financial accounts is a key concern throughout the existence of the company (and not only when accounting standard IAS 38 for Intangibles recognises corporate IP as an asset on the balance sheet). It is important that the financial value of IP assets should be traced back to the day the company came into existence for traceability. Increasing and improving the use of "notes" to the accounts would also assist innovating firms to provide additional relevant corporate

88 Bezant, M. and Punt, R. 'The Use of Intellectual Property as Security for Debt Finance' (1997) *Intellectual Property Quarterly* 297; Henry, M. 'How Effective is Your Security over Intellectual Property?' (1991) *Journal Business Law* 507.

89 Davies, I.R. 'Secured Financing of Intellectual Property Assets and the Reform of English Personal Property Security Law' (Autumn 2006) 26(3) *Oxford Journal of Legal Studies* 559–583., .

90 Palma, S. 'Is technology enough to plug the SME financing gap?' (2 October 2017) *The Banker* at www.thebanker.com/Transactions-Technology/Is-technology-enough-to-plug-the-SME-financing-gap.

IP asset information. The history of the IP assets within the entity can then also be able to be tracked by the finance director. IAS 38 for Intangibles could be updated to include this approach to capturing corporate IP asset financial information. We illustrated why debt finance remains critically important to innovating firms, and especially SMEs, despite the availability of other finance options. We adopted a behavioural economics approach to identify that lenders need to develop more awareness and trust in corporate IP assets as a class, leading to a higher level of risk tolerance at the credit appraisal stage. We then examined two important barriers to the take up of IP-backed debt finance by lenders: (1) the problem of banking capital adequacy requirement for intangibles; and (2) the legal risks illustrated by the potential for competing interests in patents and registering security interests in them, a transparency issue. These are serious problems, but they are rooted in banking regulation and secured transaction law which can be improved and are not an inherent function of the usefulness, monopoly advantage or economic value of the inventions protected by the patents. No stakeholder appears to be seriously examining reform to the banking capital adequacy requirements and the negative impact on intangibles and IP rights assets such as patents in the lending environment. This is an area ripe for further research. Indeed, the author has advocated for systemic change and the development of a new global framework for IP finance. In particular, the evidence from a variety of countries points towards the need for banks to be IP asset and strategy "information demanders" as the first step in systematizing IP finance.[91] The UK and international community will need to collectively rethink the underemployed IP finance method and make it more viable as a finance alternative by integrating systemic thinking with the goal of reformatting it. As for registering security interests over IPR, a more general secured lending reform agenda is underway that will likely improve the situation for lenders. However, the author reiterates the need for the government to create a "Security over IPR Guide" for lenders which currently does not exist to facilitate innovation finance, IP and patent-backed lending.

In Chapter 4, the focus shifts to the accounting discipline and the problem of the uncertainty in valuing patents. This results in a lack of corporate transparency in traditional quantitative corporate reporting. However, it is crucial to highlight that the fact that patents are difficult to value does not mean they have no value. This is an accounting problem and, increasingly, the lack of transparency of IP assets is a corporate governance problem.

91 Kono, T. (Ed.) *Security Interests in Intellectual Property: Perspectives in Law, Business and Innovation* (2017) Springer Verlag Singapore. See Denoncourt, J. 'IP Debt Finance and SMEs: Revealing the Evolving Conceptual Framework Drawing on Initiatives from Around the World' in Kono, T. (Ed.) *Security Interests in Intellectual Property: Perspectives in Law, Business and Innovation* (2017) 1–38.

Part III

Accounting for IP: corporate IP assets and transparency

4 True and fair patent valuation

A corporate governance issue?

The debate about the purpose and significance of the "true and fair view" corporate reporting concept is associated with two well-known dichotomies in accounting: principles versus rules and substance over form.[1]

Introduction

This chapter examines the legal nature of "true and fair" intellectual property (IP) information disclosure in a corporate governance context in order to protect shareholders and assist company directors to meet existing obligations under UK company law. English law developed the "true and fair" concept which has been central to accounting and auditing practice in the UK for decades. It is a requirement of both UK and EU law.[2] Section 393 of the Companies Act 2006 (CA 2006) requires that the directors of a company must not approve accounts unless they are satisfied they give a true and fair view. However, there is no statutory definition of "true and fair". Nevertheless, the true and fair requirement remains of fundamental importance in the relevant UK accounting standards. The UK Financial Reporting Council (FRC) states that "Company directors must consider whether, taken in the round, the financial statements that they approve are appropriate. Similarly, auditors are required to exercise professional judgment before expressing and an audit opinion".[3] Accountancy dominates corporate IP asset valuation. As such, the accounting discipline is a macroeconomic instrument

1 Albu, C.N., Albu, N. and Alexander, D.J.A. 'The True and Fair View Concept: A Case Study of Concept Transferability' (14 April 2009) p 3 at SSRN: http://ssrn.com/abstract=177000.
2 The requirement that company and consolidated accounts give a true and fair view is recognised in Article 2 (3) of the 4th Company Law Directive and Article 16 (3) of the 7th Company Law Directive issued by the European Commission. Although these two Articles do not apply for accounts required to give a fair presentation in accordance with endorsed International Financial Reporting Standards (IFRS) under the International Accounting Standards (IAS) Regulation, the true and fair principle underlying them is expressly recognised in Article 3(2) of the IAS Regulation – no IFRS standard can be endorsed if it would conflict with the principles set out in those Articles.
3 True and Fair (2014) Financial Reporting Council.

of formidable proportions in terms of the integrity of corporate financial reporting. How the accounting standards treat corporate IP assets is, therefore, a corporate governance concern. Continuing our focus on patents, section 4.1 begins our analysis of the accounting principles and standards that apply to the financial recording and ultimately, the financial valuation of patent assets. The aim is to explain why corporate IP assets are unseen, underused and undervalued by companies, their shareholders, corporate regulators and other stakeholders.

To begin, accounting and financial statements act as a kind of internal control for investors, shareholders, financiers and suppliers who engage with the company. However, while the evolution of the credit and debit system that forms the basis of traditional accounting has been indispensable to the efficiency and material prosperity of the modern economy, financial innovation is needed in relation to accounting for intangibles, especially internally developed corporate IP assets that are "off-balance sheet". We analyse why traditional accounting methodology is in certain respects inadequate for dealing with such assets. For example, why is patent value seemingly unmeasurable and therefore largely invisible in the financial statements?

Section 4.2 critically analyses why the key methods for valuing intangibles are inadequate and unhelpful in the case of patents, as corporate assets. It has never been more necessary to be able to measure the *objective value* and *subjective quality* of IP and patent assets. Only when innovating firms have access to credit, granted by lending institutions who understand the full value and quality of patents as a form of currency, unit of account or as a store of value, will IP owners be able to access the funds they need to develop and commercialise their inventions and share them with the world. Valuing patents and commercialising inventions is a fundamental corporate governance issue for patent innovating firms.

Accounting standards, coupled with the rise and harmonisation of international accounting standards that affect the recording and valuation of patents and other IP rights, are a key factor inhibiting access to money for innovating businesses to grow. Section 4.3 explores the intersecting relationship between the requirements of International Accounting Standard for Intangibles (IAS 38), the characteristics of legal patent monopolies and the changing concept of corporate governance under the rubric of "shareholder value". In particular, a traditional legal analysis of whether there is scope to depart from IAS 38, in light of the UK's longstanding legal requirement that a company's financial accounts must provide a "true and fair" view, is carried out. A thorough exploration of these fundamental issues enables us to critically analyse possible measures to reduce the level of uncertainty inherent in recording, valuing and the corporate reporting of patent assets (applications and granted patents) to improve the quality of information available to debt financiers and other stakeholders.

4.1 The invisibility of IP and patent value on the balance sheet

Section 386 of CA 2006 requires every company to keep "adequate" accounting records. Adequate accounting records must be sufficient first, to show and explain the company's transactions; second, to disclose with reasonable accuracy, at any time, the financial position of the company at that time; and third, to enable the directors to ensure that the accounts they are required to prepare, comply with the relevant requirements of the law. In particular, the accounting records must contain entries from day-to-day of all sums of money received and spent by the company (and the matters to which they relate), and a record of the company's assets and liabilities.

Accounting statements provide information that shape a particular understanding of a business. However, accounting principles have traditionally relied on two inherent assumptions, first that tangibles rather than intangibles contribute to business performance and second, that business depends largely on an arm's length transaction between a willing buyer and a seller. Neither of these assumptions accommodates the nature of patents, an intangible time-limited monopoly legal right.[4] IP is not separately identified and valued for the purpose of incorporation into financial accounts within the UK.[5] This section explains how patent assets are presented in financial statements and highlights the problems involved when accounting for intangibles.

The fundamental problem is this. Despite the fact that the underlying value of patent assets has soared in the past decade, this increase in value remains largely *invisible* to the financial world if the patented invention has been developed "in house" as opposed to having been acquired (purchased) from a third party. By way of introduction, in the UK and many other countries, intangible assets such as patents, brands, customer relationships, information technology and know-how are accounted for in one way if they are created in-house (internally generated) and another if acquired (purchased).[6] Intangible assets have been variously defined, but the common thread of the definitions is that these assets provide future benefits but do not have physical embodiment. The "invisibility" of internally developed patented inventions and other intangible assets make them difficult to measure and helps to explain why their value is recorded off-balance sheet and does not form part of the financial statements. This means that if the patented invention is developed in-house by the innovating firm, it is not recorded on the company's balance sheet and is not evidenced in the company's financial statements. Rather it is immediately expensed, thus appearing as a cost, rather than as revenue. Further, these costs are reported only at a single point in time. Therefore internally generated patent assets are valued at little more than the patent attorney and patent

4 Ghafele, R. 'Accounting for Intangibles' (2010) 5(7) *Journal of Intellectual Property Law & Practice* 521–530.

5 Bezant, M. and Punt, R. 'The Use of Intellectual Property as Security for Debt Finance' (1997) *Intellectual Property Quarterly* 297; Henry, M. 'How Effective is Your Security over Intellectual Property?' (1991) *Journal Business Law* 507. Pre-1960s business assets mainly comprised tangible assets listed in the borrowers' financial statements. Verification was achieved by viewing the assets, checking receivables and reviewing debt instruments.

6 Conversely, for a bank, its loans are considered assets and are recorded on its balance sheet.

The iPhone demonstrates how the value of ideas and patented inventions is steadily increasing. Although the iPhone (a tangible item) is wholly assembled in China, this activity results in only 28% of the profits. Indeed, only 28% of the value of the iPhone is earned by materials and labour input. Seventy-two per cent (72%) of the value is earned by the technology and brand owners (intangible IP).

	Share of profits on iPhone sales
Technology and brand: Apple	58%
Technology inputs: US, European Union, Taiwan, Japan, South Korea, others	14%
Materials	22%
Labour, non-China	4%
Labour, China	2%

Figure 4.1 Distribution of value for the Apple iPhone in 2013

Sources: Kramer, G., Linden, G. and Dedrick, J. *Capturing Value in Global Networks: Apple's iPad and iPhone* (2011) and *Australian Intellectual Property Report* (2013)

filing fees, because the research is deducted as an expense, and not capitalised. In contrast, patent assets that are purchased are recorded at fair value using the purchase price and the assets are amortised accordingly.

With intangible patent assets dominating so much of our modern economy and the renewed drive to support and invest in new technology, surely it is appropriate to question why patent assets developed internally within a company are still largely off-balance sheet items in UK businesses, both small and large? As a matter of corporate governance, this issue warrants detailed examination. Figure 4.1 illustrates the increasing financial value attributable to IP.

It no longer makes sense that the intangibles a company develops itself are valued "at cost" because the research is deducted as an expense, whilst assets that are purchased at arm's length are recorded at "fair value". This accounting treatment results in inconsistency and makes it very difficult to compare the corporate finance of patent *developers* versus patent *acquirers*. For example, the different accounting treatment means that a patent developed by Company X and then sold to Company Y can change from a very low valuation to a high valuation, possibly worth hundreds of thousands or even millions of pounds, overnight. According to Professor Abraham Briloff,[7] this accounting difference could result in distorted market behaviour, tempting companies to buy patents rather than developing the inventions themselves.[8] Indeed, it could be this accounting practice that paves the way for the non-practising entities (the patent

7 Professor Emeritus of Accountancy at Baruch College, US.

8 This factor is largely driving the patent aggregating firms, also known as "patent trolls". Patent troll is a derogatory term for a company that obtains the rights to one or more patents in order to profit by means of licensing or litigation, rather than by producing its own goods or services.

trolls)? The author holds the view that if internally developed intangibles are not visible on the balance sheet they should be documented at an amount that more fully captures the costs of the R&D and the value of the patent portfolio to the business, ideally tracked from the date the company was incorporated as discussed in Chapter 3, section 3.3.1: "Managing accounting for innovation from the date of innovation". The object of financial reporting, which the detailed accounting standards are designed and assumed to achieve, is to present a "true and fair" view of the financial position of the entity at a particular point in time. Ultimately, *the law* evaluates what is "true and fair". However, neither of these approaches has yet to be accepted by the accounting standards bodies although there is increasing interest in intangibles accounting reform and several countries are permitting voluntary Intellectual Capital Statement (ICS) reporting. Accounting creates currency. This, in turn, will enable corporate patent assets to be more effectively and commonly used as loan security.

Firms that conduct R&D and file patents have significant intangible assets, yet these are substantially recorded as off-balance sheet assets and liabilities.[9] The reason for this lies in the formal accounting distinction between "on" and "off" balance sheet items. In general terms, an item should appear on the company's balance sheet if it is an asset or liability that the company owns or is legally responsible for. Patent ownership is a fairly straightforward matter to prove in legal terms by confirming the records held by the Patent Office. However, as the value of internally developed patent assets is regarded as "uncertain", traditional accounting principles provide that in order to be recorded on the balance sheet, the patent assets must *also* meet the tests of being:

(1) probable;
(2) measurable; and
(3) meaningful.

This is the crux of the difficulty in accounting for corporate patent assets. To date, internally generated patents have been regarded as complex to value and as such their value is inadequately financially recorded for modern purposes, resulting in a lack of financial transparency. From the lenders' point of view, this "invisibility" creates a key problem in that nothing exists on the financial statements (documents that they are familiar with) to quickly tell the lender *how* to value the firm's internally developed patent applications or patent portfolio. As a result, the undesirable level of uncertainty from the lenders' perspective is a formidable barrier which prevents favourable lending decisions being made. In order to lend

9 London-based 'Mediafinance Group' reported that banks refused to make a significant loan available for a film project because the driving factor, an intangible copyright, appeared as a loss on the profit and earnings statement – disclosed by the CEO of Mediafinance at the Association of Chartered Certified Accountants (ACCA), Roundtable Discussion on the Creative and Innovative Economy held in London, 12 March 2009 at ACCA.

appropriately, a lender needs relevant accurate information to value corporate patent portfolios as a form of security. In the UK, banks adhere to the *Lending Code*[10] which is monitored by the independent Lending Standards Board (LSB). Certain standards are expected in connection with the assessment of lending applications by "micro-enterprises"[11] i.e. very small innovating SMEs. The lender will assess whether the micro-enterprise can afford to repay the money borrowed and, according to the Code, this may include reviewing:

- why the applicant wants to borrow the money;
- the business plan and accounts;
- the business' cash flow, profitability, and existing financial commitments;
- any personal financial commitments which may affect the business;
- how the applicant has handled its finances in the past;
- information held by credit reference agencies, and possibly landlords.

The lender will also carry out credit assessment techniques such as credit scoring and consider any security provided. Unfortunately, for the lender to assess corporate patent assets as security, relevant useful financial information is lacking (or largely invisible) on a firm's balance sheet. Further details of the firm's patent strategy, surrounding IP and know-how are not a required feature of the borrower's company annual return and business review.[12] Currently, in the accounting field, the future value of a potential 20-year patent monopoly largely lies in the murky realm of ***uncertainty***, as opposed to ***calculable risk***. Uncertainty undermines value. However, presently the accounting profession has the power to define the currency of patents and other intangible IP assets in the accounting standards that apply to corporate financial statements. The next section examines how are valued and why this creates uncertainty for lenders.

4.2 Uncertainty, patent valuation and impact of corporate debt finance

Any uncertainty as to the borrower's ability to repay a loan is highly undesirable. For a lender, uncertainty is quite a different concept from that of risk because without some degree of certainty, one cannot begin to mathematically calculate risk. In 1921, Frank Knight argued that:

10 *Lending Code* (March 2011, revised 28th September 2015) available at www.lendingstandardsboard.org.uk/wp-content/uploads/2016/06/The-Lending-Code-Mar-2011-revised-2015-1.pdf

11 Micro-enterprises are small businesses with a turnover of no more than two million euros per annum and with fewer than ten employees.

12 Section 854 CA 2006 requires every company to submit an annual return to Companies House. This gives basic information about the company on a particular date, its return date, every year.

> Uncertainty must be taken in a sense radically distinct from the familiar notion of Risk, from which it has never been properly separated . . . A measurable uncertainty, or "risk" proper . . . is so far different from an un-measurable one that it is not in effect an uncertainty at all.[13]

In 1937, John Maynard Keynes[14] made a similar point to Ferguson. About "uncertain knowledge," Keynes wrote:

> The sense in which I am using the term is that in which the prospect of a European war is uncertain, or . . . the rate of interest twenty years hence . . . About these matters there is no scientific basis on which to form any calculable probability whatsoever. We simply do not know.[15]

Continuing our discourse on the concept of uncertainty, Peter Bernstein[16] explained:

> We pour in data from the past . . . but past data . . . constitutes a sequence of events rather than a set of independent observations, which is what the laws of probability demand. History provides us only with one sample of the . . . capital markets, not with thousands of separate and randomly distributed numbers.[17]

Is the present and future value of patents doomed to be unmeasurable and therefore uncertain? The "uncertainty" factor that still surrounds the techniques and practices of quantitative and qualitative patent valuation is the principal barrier to the development of IP and patent-backed lending. The core function of the lender is gathering information to reduce uncertainty about the borrower's ability to repay the loan. What financiers need is a reliable method of "measuring" and recording the value of the patent. Patent valuation is a complex task as there are many variables to consider. Thus the traditional view is that each patent is so entirely unique that there are no, or an insufficient number of, other similar patents to form a basis for any inference of value with any real probability.

13 Knight, Frank, H. (1911) as quoted in Ferguson, N. *The Ascent of Money: A Financial History of the World* (2012) Penguin Books p 344.

14 John Maynard Keynes, 1st Baron Keynes (5 June 1883–21 April 1946) was a British economist who is widely considered to be one of the founders of modern macroeconomics and the most influential economist of the 20th century.

15 Keynes, J. M. 'The General Theory of Employment' (1937) 51(2) *Economic Journal* 214.

16 Peter L Bernstein (22 January 1919–5 June 2009), a well-known American financial historian, economist and educator developed the efficient market hypothesis.

17 Bernstein, Peter, L. *Capital Ideas Evolving* (2007) John Wiley & Sons, New York.

4.2.1 Understand how we account for intangibles and the need to reform accounting practice

In 2005 the WIPO recognised that current accounting standards are ill-equipped to address the corporate IP asset dimension of business and issued the following statement:

> Clearly, the various challenges associated with determining the value of internally held intellectual property, paired with the inherent volatility associated with the value of some forms of IP, can be cited as major reasons why accounting has been reluctant to report on internally generated IP, which is seen as too subjective and risky. Furthermore, accounting has always been reluctant to anticipate future gains, overstate the value of assets or include assets on the balance sheet whose value is more volatile.[18]

Dr Roya Ghafele, a law and economics scholar, studied the language and terminology of accounting as it applies to IP and specifically intangibles. She concluded:

> Accounting constitutes a very specific form of language, which is highly standardized, mathematical in nature and seeks to uniformly and systematically describe events . . . On the balance sheet, IP experiences a specific form of authorisation. It is represented in the discourse of accounting by "intangibles", an imprecise term associated with the increasingly observed "gap between the market and book value", while current accounting systems are determined by a tangible assets' based perspective and offer little scope to document how IP relates to business performance. Accounting may thus be seen as a gate keeper of the status quo that poses significant challenges for IP-rich companies, confronted with the challenge to either communicate around the lingua franca of accounting or accept that under current accounting statements they cannot adequately document how IP relates to their business performance.[19]

A brief discussion of the history of double-entry bookkeeping will illustrate why the traditional accounting criteria are ill-adapted to recognising and valuing intangibles. This research provides a deeper understanding of the practical reasons that lead to uncertainty when accounting for intangible patent assets and IAS 38 Intangibles.

18 Ghafele, R. 'Getting a Grip on Accounting and Intellectual Property' (2005) *WIPO SME Newsletter* at www.wipo.int/sme.

19 Ghafele, R. 'Accounting for Intangibles' (2010) 5(7) *Journal of Intellectual Property Law & Practice* 521–530.

4.2.1.1 History of double-entry bookkeeping and its impact on accounting for intangibles

Ideas that revolutionised the way Europeans counted and accounted for their assets were introduced by Italian Renaissance mathematician, Leonardo of Fibonacci in his ground-breaking book *Liber Abaci*, "The Book of Calculation" published in 1202, in which he introduced Europe to the decimal system and showed how it could be applied to commercial bookkeeping. His ideas eventually led to the birth of banking in the late 13th century.[20] Fibonacci also introduced the concept of present value (the discounted value today of a future revenue stream).[21] Historically, the double-entry book keeping system, which forms the basis for modern accounting principles and is globally accepted, was simply a tool to track and document the exchange of tangible items and prevent embezzlement. The method of preparing and presenting financial business information used by accountants, the double entry book keeping system, is set out in Figure 4.2 and illustrates the debit and credit system of modern double-entry bookkeeping.

In double-entry bookkeeping all transactions in the accounts are entered *twice*: once as a debit and once as a credit. Debits increase balances in asset accounts and expense accounts, and decrease balances in liability accounts, revenue accounts, and capital accounts. Credits increase balances in liability accounts, revenue accounts, and capital accounts, and decrease balances in asset accounts and expense accounts. The *golden rule of accounting* is founded on the accounting equation:

Owner's Equity = Assets – Liabilities

If at any point the sum of debits for all accounts does not equal the corresponding sum of credits for all accounts, an error has occurred. It follows that the sum of debits and the sum of the credits must be equal in value. In essence, the accounting

Account Type	Debits	Credits
Assets	Increase	Decrease
Liabilities	Decrease	Increase
Income (revenue)	Decrease	Increase
Expenses	Increase	Decrease
Capital	Decrease	Increase

Figure 4.2 The double-entry bookkeeping system

Source: Adapted from Atrill, P. and McLaney, E. *Accounting & Finance for Non Specialists* (2012) Eighth Edition, Pearson

20 Modern fractional reserve banking allows the creation of credit and hence of money.
21 Goetzmann, W. N. *Fibonacci and the Financial Revolution* (March 2004) NBER Working Paper 10352.

equation serves as an "error detection tool" by making it a record of historical transactions. In case of error, each debit and credit can be traced back to a journal and transaction source document, thus preserving an audit trail. The double-entry bookkeeping system was originally designed to prevent fraud and misappropriation by employees of the *Renaissance* merchants of Venice.[22] Broadly speaking, the root of the problem is that modern accounting has difficulty dealing with intangibles because such assets do not fit the socio-historic evolution of accounting. This is because when a patent is applied for it becomes a form of property (an asset of the innovating firm and thus a form of currency). At this stage, there will be few, if any, historical market transactions to record in the accounts if the patent applications were developed internally as opposed to purchased from a third party. The patent applications are not recorded as a company asset in the balance sheet. However, the expenditure to internally develop the innovation to the patent filing stage is recorded. Thus, from an IP asset viewpoint, part of the equation appears to be missing in the balance sheet. Arguably, there is a basic question as to the integrity of the accounts. However, the double entry is debit expense, credit creditors (if credit was given) or cash at bank (if bought and paid for) so from the accounting standpoint, the balance sheet is affected by the transaction – just not in the desired way.

The next significant development in the history of accounting was the "accrual" method based on recording transactions. Income items are recorded when they are earned and deductions recorded when expenses are incurred. Therefore, modern accrual accounting still requires financial transactions to be recorded as they occur, creating an accurate record of all historic transactions. This historic information is then also largely used to confirm sales and cash flow trends. The nature of innovation leading to patents being filed and granted a few years later does not "map" well onto the accrual method of recording of transactions. Nevertheless, although patents are valuable business assets, this value is not gleaned from the company's financial statements. Again, this highlights another question as to the integrity of the accounts.

In essence, the accrual accounting system relies on a set of fundamental assumptions and principles which have become known as Generally Accepted Accounting Practice (GAAP). Fundamental accounting principles therefore shape a very particular perception of intangibles, which in turn shackles the fullest use of corporate IP and patent assets as security for loans. It is important for those working with patents in a commercial context to have an understanding of these accounting principles because financial terminology and practice permeates the exploitation and commercialisation of patented inventions (known as innovation in business parlance). A basic knowledge of GAAP provides both context and illumination for any transaction in which internally developed patents feature. Summarised briefly below are the main principles relevant to this discussion that

22 Ferguson, N. *The Ascent of Money: A Financial History of the World* (2012) Penguin Books.

underpin modern accounting rules, standards and practice and have been adopted by the Financial Accounting Standards Board (FASB) forming the basis for how intangible assets are treated in financial statements.[23]

First, the *revenue principle* or *realisation principle* provides that revenue (income) is earned when the sale is made, typically when goods or services are provided. A key element of the revenue principle in relation to the sale of tangible assets is that revenue is earned when legal ownership of the asset passes from seller to buyer.

Second, the *expense principle* provides that an expense occurs when the business uses goods or receives services. The business incurs an expense when goods or services are received.

Third, the *matching principle* correlates to the revenue and the expense principles. It provides that when revenue is recognised, one should match related expenses associated with the revenue. *Accrual-based accounting* is the application of the three principles. Basically, it means that one records revenue when a sale is made and records expenses when goods are used or services are received.

Fourth, the *cost principle* provides that figures recorded in the accounts should be quantified (measured) using historical cost. For example, if a firm owns a vehicle, the cost of the vehicle is the purchase price and not the current fair market value for the vehicle. The value of the vehicle as recorded in the accounts is not adjusted for changes in fair market value.

Fifth, the *objectivity principle* provides that accounting measurements and accounting reports should use objective, factual and verifiable data. This means that accountants, accounting systems and accounting reports should rely on objective data rather than subjective data. This is why an accountant always uses objective data (even if it poorly reflects the full commercial value of a patent) rather than subjective qualitative data relating to the future potential of the patent.[24]

Sixth, the *prudence principle* (also known as the conservative or neutral concept) ensures that assets and income are not overstated and liabilities and expenses are not understated. Accounting transactions and other events are often uncertain, however to report them in a timely manner, accountants need to make estimates applying their professional judgment to counter the uncertainty. Some liabilities will be contingent on a future occurrence or non-occurrence of an event (e.g. the grant of a patent, or the outcome of patent litigation). Accountants judge the probability of the occurrence of that event and if it is higher than 50 per cent, it should be recorded as a liability with a corresponding expense at the most likely amount. In this manner, the *prudence principle* which is embedded in IAS 38 intangibles operates to prevent liabilities and expenses from being understated. Periodic evaluations of assets should be made to ensure their carrying value does

23 Nelson, S.L Understanding the Basic Principles of Accounting (2011) *Quickbooks*.
24 www.qfinance.com/accountancy-checklists/the-ten-accounting-principles,

not exceed the expected benefits.[25] Over the past two centuries, the prudence concept has enabled accounting practice to diminish speculation by providing that quantitative results be conservatively stated in financial statements – which can be problematic for corporate IP assets. Maltby states:

> Prudent accounting represented the elaboration by the accounting profession of a distinctive competence (the determination of distributable profit) which enabled it to appear as the ally and advisor of large investors and management against "speculators", thereby ensuring an equal return for equal capital. Prudence was crucial to the accounting profession in regulating the social relations of capital.[26]

However, within the accounting profession there is "considerable debate about whether International Financial Reporting Standards (IFRS), as the key global standards, should include prudence and state its importance in their conceptual framework".[27] The key arguments against including the prudence principle in the IFRS related to the neutrality and comparability of the resulting financial statements. The author supports the view that appropriate narrative disclosures in the notes to the accounts of sensitivities of valuations (e.g. IP valuations) to changes in assumption should be viewed as the exercise of prudence. Further, the meaning of prudence is not fixed and immutable, but has altered progressively over the past two centuries[28]. Given the importance of IP assets to modern corporate balance sheets, the application of the prudence principle needs to evolve and could draw on the established Technology Readiness Level system (TRL)[29]

25 *Prudence and IFRS* (August 2014) The Association of Chartered Certified Accountants at www.accaglobal.com/content/dam/acca/global/PDF-technical/financial-reporting/tech-tp-prudence.pdf and Obaidullah (ACA, CFA) 'Prudence Concept' at http://accounting explained.com/financial/principles/prudence [Accessed 5 September 2017]

26 Maltby, Josephine, 'The Origins of Prudence in Accounting' (2000) *Critical Perspectives on Accounting* 11, 51–70 at p 1 DOI: 10.1006/cpac.1998.0283

27 The arguments for and against inclusion of the prudence principle in the IRFS are discussed in *Prudence and IFRS* (August 2014) The Association of Chartered Certified Accountants, beginning at p 3. The impact of increasingly common portfolios of potentially valuable IP assets on financial statements is an important factor that should be considered in the debate being evaluated by the standard setters.

28 Supra [26] at p 67.

29 Technology Readiness Levels (TRLs) were originally conceived at NASA in 1974 and formally defined in 1989. TRLs are a method of estimating the technological maturity of critical technology elements of a programme. They are determined during a Technology Readiness Assessment that examines programme concepts, technology requirements, and demonstrated technology capabilities. TRLs are based on a scale from one to nine with nine being the most mature technology. The use of TRLs enables consistent, uniform discussions of technical maturity across different types of technology. A comprehensive discussion of the TRL system has been published by the European Association of Research and Technology Organisations. Current TRL models tend to disregard negative and obsolescence factors and there have been suggestions made for incorporating such factors into assessments which would benefit judgments from an accounting perspective.

discussed in Chapter 2 as a barometer. Accounting is not simply a neutral technology for economic decision making; it sanctions particular distributions of wealth and legitimises particular social relationships.[30]

These six concepts provide a basic, but important understanding of aspects of the foundation on which accountants prepare financial statements that deal with assets, *both* tangible and intangible. The diverse range of stakeholders that have an interest in the financial position of an entity leads to a logical division in the discipline of accounting. "Financial accounting" is designed to enhance external reporting to third parties (such as lenders). In contrast, "managerial accounting" is concerned with collating information for internal management. Financial accounting more broadly targets a range of third parties, including shareholders and lenders, who do not control the actual preparation of financial statements and reports, nor do they have access to the underlying detail. The ability to understand and have confidence in the reports is directly dependent on the standardisation of accounting principles and practices that are used to prepare them. Without such standardisation, the financial statements of different companies would be difficult to understand and even more difficult to compare.

IP law is developing, but there are still large gaps in our understanding of the impact of IP rights on other disciplines, such as accounting and corporate governance, and vice versa. This is where the problems arise; we lack some understanding of the consequences of the rise of IP rights. If corporate finance and corporate governance are to be fit for the purpose of managing dynamic corporate IP assets, these disciplines may have to develop new expectations of accounting concepts applied to corporate IP assets. The question then is: how should corporate governance and accounting concepts evolve to accommodate intangible IP rights?

4.2.1.2 The credit appraiser's approach to the borrower's financial statements

Access to IP-backed debt finance relies on favourable credit appraisals. The credit appraiser uses the traditional corporate financial statements differently to the accountants. They want the entity's financial statements to help them assess the ability of the business to repay the principal sum borrowed with interest. The credit appraiser's approach to the potential borrower's traditional financial statements, the balance sheet and the profit and loss account, is explained below:

> The Balance Sheet is a stock concept, while the Profit and Loss Account is a flow concept. The former indicates the state of a business as on a particular date, while the latter tells us how the present state has come into being. The two together finally tell us how the *funds flowed through the business during a given period*. The accounting system first evolved the Balance Sheet,

30 Supra [26] at p 68.

> followed by the Profit and Loss Account at a much later date. In fact, the Balance Sheet of a business is never static, in spite of its being labelled as such. The Balance Sheet is a total concept, while the Profit and Loss Account is a partial concept . . . the reason why the Balance Sheet has received so much attention of lenders [is] not only to see whether the loan stands secured, but also to examine whether the value of the business is rising or not. The Profit and Loss Account tells us more about the operating management of the business, while the Balance Sheet indicates the efficiency of financial management. The ratios calculated between a stock variable (Balance Sheet) and a flow variable (Profit and Loss Account) enable us to estimate the overall efficiency of a business.[31]

Thus a credit appraiser's evaluation of the potential borrower's financial statements goes beyond checking to see if the loan stands secured; he also examines whether the value of the business is rising or not. Supplementary qualitative information about the firm's IP and patent assets will assist to answer the lender's second question. This is where corporate governance principles and an increased level of narrative reporting of corporate IP asset information and strategy have an important role to play. Further, there is a risk that funds loaned to a business will be used for purposes that have not been agreed. Accounting information is also used to check that the funds have been properly applied in the appropriate manner and that the terms of the loan agreement are being adhered to.[32] Information contained in financial statements should reduce uncertainty over the financial position and performance of the business. Having said that, accounting, like IP law, is also a developing discipline and we still have much to learn about user needs, specifically those of lenders. Under company law provisions, a qualifying SME need only submit "abbreviated accounts", namely a balance sheet but no profit and loss account, which immediately creates an enormous "information gap" for lenders.[33] An analysis of the legal requirements and accounting standards that apply to financial statements in the context of UK corporate reporting ensues.

4.3 The intersection of accounting and company law: bridging the gap between corporate finance and governance

In the 1970s, the EU initiated two directives on the harmonisation of rules of accounting, the Fourth and Seventh Directives[34] which made it clear that

31 Bhattacharya, H. *Banking Strategy, Credit Appraisal and Lending Decisions: A Risk-Return Framework* (2010) Oxford University Press p 256.

32 Atrill, P. and McLaney, E. *Accounting & Finance for Non Specialists* (2002) Third edition, Pearson,p 3.

33 s 447(1) CA 2006.

34 See Medhurst, D. *A Brief and Practical Guide to EC Law* (1994) 145–147 detailing the harmonisation directives.

accounting is at the centre of company law and thus a field of highest importance for corporate lawyers, regulators and company directors. However, a further impetus for harmonising accounting rules was the introduction of International Accounting Standards (IAS) including IAS 38 Intangibles which determines the accounting treatment of intangible IP assets, which includes patents. In sections 4.3.1–4.3.5 we introduce how the IAS operates within the UK corporate law system. In section 4.3.6 we examine the detailed provisions of IAS 38 and consider the impact on patents. Section 4.3.7 introduces UK company law financial reporting requirements and the "true and fair" view concept. Section 4.3.8 asks whether financial statements prepared according to IAS 38 provide a "true and fair" view as required by law and, if not, whether there is scope to depart from IAS 38.

4.3.1 European and UK rules of accounting

In the UK, Generally Accepted Accounting Practice (GAAP) is the body of umbrella regulation that establishes how company accounts must be prepared by UK companies. This includes accounting standards and UK company law. Indeed, "generally accepted accounting practice" is a defined statutory term in the UK's tax legislation. The main piece of legislation that governs financial reporting in the UK is the CA 2006 which incorporates the requirements of European law and sets out the minimum corporate reporting requirements for UK registered companies. For example, the Act requires limited companies to file their accounts with the Registrar of Companies, who then makes them available to the public (accessible to lenders). This means that every UK company (except very small companies which are exempt)[35] needs to prepare the accounts for submission to Companies House. Section 386 CA 2006 requires every company to keep adequate accounting records to show and explain the companies' transactions and the directors must prepare accounts for the company for each of its financial years.[36] Individual company accounts comprise a balance sheet (as at the last day of the financial year) and a profit and loss account. The annual accounts must give a "true and fair view" of the state of affairs as at the end of the financial year and of the profit and loss for the financial year of the company according to sections 396 and 494 CA 2006. In complying with the CA 2006, the accountants who prepare the accounts adhere to UK GAAP or practices which necessitate the basic accounting concepts briefly outlined in section 4.2. Accounting standards derive from a number of sources. In the UK, the chief standard-setter is the Accounting Standards Board (ASB), which issues standards called Financial Reporting Standards (FRS). The ASB is part of the Financial Reporting Council (FRC), an independent regulator.

35 Section 447(1) CA 2006.
36 Section 394 CA 2006.

4.3.2 IAS and the new UK GAAP: legal effect in the UK

Cross border commercial transactions make international accounting standards a necessity.[37] IAS are referred to as International Financial Reporting Standards (IFRS), although the term IAS is used in practice. Since 2005 it has been a legal requirement that all listed[38] European companies report under the IFRS.[39] In the UK, unlisted companies still have the option to report either under the IFRS or under UK GAAP. Section 50 of the Finance Act 2004 redefines "generally accepted practice" to include both EC-adopted IAS and UK GAAP for periods beginning on or after 1 January 2005 (the date in the EC Regulation). The vehicle for such introduction on a communitywide basis is Regulation 1606/2002 (the "IAS Regulation"), which provides for the procedure whereby IAS are to be adopted and sets out the financial statements to which they must be applied.[40] Broadly, the use of IAS is mandatory for the consolidated accounts of listed companies whose securities are admitted to trading on a regulated market. The IAS still make an impact as they are the basis for UK national standards. In recent years the differences between the two sets of standards (UK GAAP and IAS) have been streamlined.

In March 2013 the FRC (the body responsible for issuing UK accounting standards) issued FRS 102, the Financial Reporting Standard applicable in the UK. This followed the issue of FRS 100 Application of Financial Reporting Requirements and FRS 101 the Reduced Disclosure Framework, in November 2012. Together these standards comprise the "New UK GAAP", which take mandatory effect for accounting periods commencing on or after 1 January 2015.[41]

4.3.3 The IFRS for SMEs and micro-sized entities

At its September 2003 meeting, the International Accounting Standards Board (IASB) decided that it should develop accounting standards appropriate for SMEs and that development of IASB SME standards should start by extracting the fundamental concepts from the IASB *Conceptual Framework*[42] and the principles and related mandatory guidance from IFRS and related Interpretations. To that

37 Grossfeld, B. 'Global Accounting: Where Internet Meets Geography' (2000) 48(2) *The American Journal of Comparative Law* 268 (contemplating the effect that Internet globalisation will have on global accounting standards).

38 UK registered companies whose securities are admitted to trading on a regulated market in the EU.

39 Adopted by EC 1725/2003.

40 Moore QC, M. Opinion entitled, "True and Fair Requirement Revisited" for the FRC.

41 Crowe Clarke Whitehall LLP Corporate Business Newsletter FRS 102 'The New Accounting Standard for the UK'.

42 *Conceptual Framework for Financial Reporting: Summary of Tentative Decisions* (2017) IFRS Foundation at www.ifrs.org/-/media/project/conceptual-framework/current-stage/summary-of-tentative-decisions-june-2017.pdf.

Subject	IFRS	UK FRS
Goodwill and Intangible Assets	IAS 38	FRS 102

Figure 4.3 Financial Reporting Standards for intangible assets

end, on 9 July 2009, the IASB issued *IFRS for Small and Medium-sized Entities.*[43] On 26 July 2012, IASB announced that IASB staff, together with the SME Implementation Group, would develop guidance suitable for micro-sized entities that are applying the IFRS for SMEs. On 27 June 2013, IASB issued this guidance, which accompanies, but is not part of, the IFRS for SMEs. Essentially, the guide extracts from the IFRS for SMEs only those requirements that are likely to be necessary for a typical micro-sized entity, *without changing any of the principles for recognising and measuring assets, liabilities, income and expenses.* The IASB advises that compliance with this Guide will result in compliance with the IFRS for SMEs. The Guide will no doubt be very useful for micro-sized entities in preparing their accounts in an IFRS-compliant manner. But the issue of the different treatment of internally generated intangible assets remains, thereby continuing to inhibit innovating SME access to patent-backed finance. Figure 4.3 notes IAS 38 for intangible assets and the Equivalent UK Financial Reporting Standard (FRS) 102 which must be applied when preparing and presenting corporate financial statements.

Section 397 of the UK CA 2006 requires a limited company that submits individual accounts to Companies House[44] (this includes SMEs) to specifically state in the notes to the accounts that they have been prepared in accordance with IAS. Further, the audit report (if one is required under CA 2006) must also state clearly whether in the auditor's opinion, the annual accounts have been properly prepared in accordance with the Act and whether the accounts give a true and fair view of the company's financial position. In managing accounting for innovation, we identified in Chapter 3 why it is crucial for start-ups and innovating SMEs to identify and record their corporate IP assets as an additional line item in the accountant's spreadsheet, even if accountant regards them as off-balance sheet items. This is because they will undoubtedly become more important and valuable to the enterprise as it matures. From a corporate governance point of view, ensuring the integrity of the traditional financial accounts is a key concern. It is important that the financial value of IP assets should be capable of being traced

43 *International Financial Reporting Standard for Small and Medium-sized Entities* (IFRS for SMEs) (2015) IFRS Foundation at www.iacsa.co.za/wp-content/uploads/2016/11/IFRS-for-SMES-2015.pdf (effective 1 January 2017 with early application permitted).

44 All limited companies in England, Wales, Northern Ireland and Scotland are registered at Companies House, an Executive Agency of BEIS. There are more than three million limited companies registered in the UK and more than 400,000 new companies are incorporated each year.

back to the day the company came into existence. The IASB should consider whether it is appropriate to amend the *IFRS for Small and Medium-sized Entities* to include this approach to capturing key corporate IP asset financial information.

The "true and fair" requirements of the CA 2006 will be discussed in section 4.4 of this chapter. In the next section we discuss the legal status of accounting standards.

4.3.4 The legal status of accounting standards

Accounting standards are not, of themselves, law. IAS and GAAP are not enacted by parliaments, but by private organisations (usually with government support).[45] For example, the International Accounting Standards Committee (IASC) is an independent, private sector body, formed in 1973 and restructured in May 2000 with the objective of harmonising the accounting principles used by businesses around the world. IASC members currently number 143 professional accounting bodies in 104 countries representing over two million accountants worldwide. Accounting standards and principles can be equated with codes of conduct for corporations. However, their status as "law" is fragile because they are not formally enacted, are in a state of flux, and are simultaneously elusive and osmotic.[46] The reporting of intangible assets and the relationship between accounting principles, practice and standards has been the subject of intense discussion by accountants for many years. However, in terms of the potential of IP rights as corporate assets, how can we improve our fit?

4.3.5 IAS 38 Intangible Assets

IAS 38 Intangible Assets is at the heart of the issues faced by corporate IP owners who wish to ensure that their patent assets are financially recorded in a way that is both visible and useful to lenders and other stakeholders (e.g. shareholders, regulators). The first time accounting for intangibles was addressed in a thorough way was in IAS 38, promulgated in 1995 after a long and contentious gestation period that included the issue of two Exposure Drafts. IAS 38 is a comprehensive standard that superseded an earlier standard which dealt solely with R&D expenditures. In summary, IAS 38 outlines the accounting requirements for intangible assets, defined as non-monetary assets without physical substance but which are identifiable (either being separable or arising from contractual or other legal rights). Intangible assets meeting the relevant recognition criteria are initially measured at cost, subsequently measured at cost or using the revaluation model, and amortised on a systematic basis over their useful lives (unless the asset has an

45 Grossfeld, B. 'Lawyers and Accountants A Semiotic Competition' (2001) 36 *Wake Forest Law Review* 167–186 at http://wakeforestlawreview.com/.

46 Ebke, W. *Maerkte machen Rechtauch Gesellschafts-und Unternehmensrecht!* (2000) Festschrift Utter 12

indefinite useful life, in which case it is not amortised).[47] IAS 38 follows a conservative path in its treatment of intangibles along the lines of the US GAAP. It seems that no "potential future value" criterion exists and such information is not captured or evaluated. Is this a weakness or flaw in the accounting standard that needs to be addressed where corporate IP assets are concerned? There will not be a one-size-fits-all "potential future value" solution, as IP rights are used differently in different business sectors.

4.3.6 How does IAS 38 allow patent owners to communicate the financial value of intangibles and patents?

IAS 38 establishes recognition criteria, measurement bases, and disclosure requirements for intangible assets. Each of these elements is analysed in further detail. Additionally, IAS 38 sets out impairment testing[48] for intangible assets, to be undertaken on a regular basis. This is to ensure that only assets having recoverable values are capitalised and carried forward to future periods.

According to the IASC, the development of IAS 38 was controversial and gave rise to debate on two significant issues. First, should internally generated intangible assets be recognised in financial statements? The current IAS 38 confirms that they should be, but only when very strict criteria are met. Second, should there be an arbitrary upper limit on the useful life of intangible assets? In this regard, there is a presumption that the useful life of intangible assets will not exceed 20 years. In relation to patents, this is a non-issue. It is more of a concern in relation to other forms of intangibles such as trade marks, designs and copyright. Accordingly, in this book, we focus squarely on the first issue.

IAS 38 Intangible Assets was issued on 1 January 2012 by the IASB[49] and provides the basis for discussion of the relevant accounting requirements. We will embark on a critical analysis of the provisions from an IP or patent asset perspective:

> *IAS 38 Intangible Assets – Recognition and Measurement*
> The recognition of an item as an intangible asset requires an entity to demonstrate that the item meets the: (a) definition of an intangible asset; and (b) recognition criteria. This requirement applies to costs incurred initially to acquire or internally generate an intangible (patent) asset and those incurred subsequently to add to, replace part of, or service the asset.

Intangible assets are categorised by accountants as either identifiable or unidentifiable (e.g. goodwill) assets. An intangible asset is identifiable if it either:

47 Deloitte See www.iasplus.com/en/standards/ias/ias38.

48 Impairment testing of assets seeks to ensure that an entity's assets are not carried at more than their recoverable amount (i.e. the higher of fair value less costs of disposal and value in use).

49 www.ifrs.org/IFRSs/Pages/IFRS.aspx.

(a) is *separable*, i.e. is capable of being separated or divided from the entity and sold, transferred, licensed, rented or exchanged, either individually or together with a related contract, identifiable asset or liability, regardless of whether the entity intends to do so; or
(b) arises from contractual or other legal rights, regardless of whether those rights are transferable or separable from the entity or from other rights and obligations.

A patent is therefore recognised as an *identifiable* intangible asset. A patent may have some physical form as there may be tangible evidence of its existence, such as a certificate indicating that a patent has been granted or patent application documents, but this does not constitute the asset itself. Goodwill, on the other hand, cannot be meaningfully transferred to a new owner without also selling the other assets and/or the operations of the business.[50] Other identifiable assets can result from R&D activities e.g. a prototype or model, but this is secondary to the idea, knowledge or invention that is the primary result of the R&D activities. It is a fairly straight forward exercise to identify and classify inventions (patent assets), distinguishing them from goodwill. Next, the patent asset must be "recognised":

> *Recognition test*
> An intangible asset shall be recognised if, and only if:
>
> (a) it is probable that the expected future economic benefits that are attributable to the asset will flow to the entity; and
> (b) the cost of the asset can be measured reliably.

These two limbs of the IAS 38 recognition test comprise the challenging aspect of the standard in connection with internally generated inventions. When patent assets are purchased or acquired, there is no such difficulty as IAS 38 clearly states that:

> The probability recognition criterion is always considered to be satisfied for intangible assets that are acquired separately or in a business combination.

50 The UK FRS 10 takes the view that goodwill arising on an acquisition (i.e. the cost of acquisition less the aggregate of the fair value of the purchased entity's identifiable assets and liabilities) is neither an asset like other assets nor an immediate loss in value. Rather, it forms the bridge between the cost of an investment shown as an asset in the acquirer's own financial statements and the values attributed to the acquired assets and liabilities in the consolidated financial statements. Although purchased goodwill is not in itself an asset, its inclusion amongst the assets of the reporting entity, rather than as a deduction from shareholders' equity, recognises that goodwill part of a larger asset, the investment, for which management, remains accountable. See https://frc.org.uk/Our-Work/Codes-Standards/Accounting-and-Reporting-Policy/Standards-in-Issue/FRS-10-Goodwill-and-Intangible-Assets.aspx.

> An intangible asset shall be measured initially at cost.
>
> The cost of a separately acquired intangible asset comprises:
>
> (a) its purchase price, including import duties and non-refundable purchase taxes, after deducting trade discounts and rebates; and
> (b) any directly attributable cost of preparing the asset for its intended use.

In accordance with IFRS 3 Business Combinations, if an intangible asset is acquired in a business combination, the cost of that intangible asset is its fair value at the acquisition date. If an asset acquired in a business combination is separable or arises from contractual or other legal rights, sufficient information exists to measure reliably the fair value of the asset.

In accordance with this Standard and IFRS 3 (as revised in 2008), an acquirer recognises at the acquisition date, separately from goodwill, an intangible asset of the acquiree, irrespective of whether the asset had been recognised by the acquiree before the business combination. This means that the acquirer recognises as an asset separately from goodwill an in-process research and development project of the acquiree if the project meets the definition of an intangible asset.

Thus, acquired patent assets may be capitalised rather than expensed on the balance sheet, putting "patent acquirers" in a positive financial position relative to "internal patent developers". Reverting to internally generated patent assets, IAS 38 continues as follows:

> *Internally generated intangible assets*
>
> Internally generated goodwill shall not be recognised as an asset.
>
> No intangible asset arising from research (or from the research phase of an internal project) shall be recognised. Expenditure on research (or on the research phase of an internal project) shall be recognised as an expense when it is incurred.
>
> An intangible asset arising from development (or from the development phase of an internal project) shall be recognised if, and only if, an entity can demonstrate all of the following:
>
> (a) the technical feasibility of completing the intangible asset so that it will be available for use or sale.
> (b) its intention to complete the intangible asset and use or sell it.
> (c) its ability to use or sell the intangible asset.
> (d) how the intangible asset will generate probable future economic benefits. Among other things, the entity can demonstrate the existence of a market for the output of the intangible asset or the intangible asset itself or, if it is to be used internally, the usefulness of the intangible asset.
> (e) the availability of adequate technical, financial and other resources to complete the development and to use or sell the intangible asset.
> (f) its ability to measure reliably the expenditure attributable to the intangible asset during its development.

The TRL system could be used to meet the 'technical feasibility' requirement. The cost of an internally generated intangible asset according to IAS 38.51.67 Internally Generated Intangible Assets is the sum of expenditure incurred from the date when the intangible asset first meets the recognition criteria discussed above. IAS 38 prohibits reinstatement of expenditure previously recognised as an expense.

In other words, expenditure on an intangible item shall be recognised as an expense when it is incurred, unless it forms part of the cost of an intangible asset that meets the recognition criteria; or the item is acquired in a business combination and cannot be recognised as an intangible asset. If this is the case, it forms part of the amount recognised as goodwill at the acquisition date (see IFRS 3). Within the category of internally generated intangibles other than goodwill (such as patents), the patent(s) must demonstrate *each and every one* of the requirements set out in (a) to (f) above. There is no discretion to be exercised even if one element is lacking. A key issue is the future economic benefit requirement in (d) mandated by IAS 38. Under IAS 38 an intangible asset is only recognised if it is probable that future economic benefits specifically associated with it will flow to the reporting entity, and the cost of the asset can be measured reliably. The recognition criteria for intangible assets are derived from the IASC Framework and are similar to the recognition criteria for tangible assets (property, plant and equipment etc.). The "future economic benefit" envisaged by the standard may take the form of revenue from the sale of products and services, costs savings, or other benefits resulting from the use of the intangible asset by the firm. In the author's view if these types of future economic benefit are not available, then the inability to "recognise" such patent assets causes the firm's balance sheet to *under report* its economic resources – having a negative effect on any lending decision.

Another key element of the test for recognition of intangibles in (f) is also problematic in that the availability of "financial or other resources" to complete the development and to use or sell the intangible asset *must* be objectively shown. Very few start-ups and innovating SMEs will be in a financial position to do this, which is why they seek debt finance. This can only lead to a "Which comes first, the chicken or the egg?" type debate. In other words, the futility of identifying the first case (e.g. financial resources) of a circular cause and consequence. Meeting the requirements in (f) is a hurdle for innovating SMEs.

In a nutshell, IAS 38.51.67 Internally Generated Intangible Assets initially requires the application of a *cost approach* relating to the valuation of intangible internally generated patent assets. When an internally generated patent asset meets the recognition criteria, the cost is determined using the same principles as for an acquired tangible asset. The cost comprises all costs directly attributable to creating, producing and preparing the asset for its intended use. IAS 38 closely follows IAS 16 Property, Plant and Equipment with regard to elements of cost that may be considered as part of the asset. This means that the book value at initial recognition is the sum of expenditure incurred from the date when the development phase in relation to the patented invention began. Thus, internally developed patents will be recognised at the cost of creation, exclusive of costs which would be analogous to research. Under IAS 38, which must be applied by

UK companies, a patent valuation must adopt the cost approach for this valuation purpose. The next part of IAS 38 discusses the concept of financial measurement of the intangible asset, following the recognition process discussed above.

> *Measurement after recognition*
> An entity shall choose either the cost model or the revaluation model as its accounting policy. If an intangible asset is accounted for using the revaluation model, all the other assets in its class shall also be accounted for using the same model, unless there is no active market for those assets.
>
> Cost model: After initial recognition, an intangible asset shall be carried at its cost less any accumulated amortisation and any accumulated impairment losses.
>
> Revaluation model: After initial recognition, an intangible asset shall be carried at a revalued amount, being its fair value at the date of the revaluation less any subsequent accumulated amortisation and any subsequent accumulated impairment losses. For the purpose of revaluations under this Standard, fair value shall be measured by reference to an active market. Revaluations shall be made with such regularity that at the end of the reporting period the carrying amount of the asset does not differ materially from its fair value. An active market is a market in which all the following conditions exist:
>
> (a) the items traded in the market are homogeneous;
> (b) willing buyers and sellers can normally be found at any time; and
> (c) prices are available to the public.
>
> If an intangible asset's carrying amount is increased as a result of a revaluation, the increase shall be recognised in other comprehensive income and accumulated in equity under the heading of revaluation surplus. However, the increase shall be recognised in profit or loss to the extent that it reverses a revaluation decrease of the same asset previously recognised in profit or loss. If an intangible asset's carrying amount is decreased as a result of a revaluation, the decrease shall be recognised in profit or loss. However, the decrease shall be recognised in other comprehensive income to the extent of any credit balance in the revaluation surplus in respect of that asset.

After initial recognition of the intangible patent asset, it should be carried at its cost less any accumulated amortisation and any accumulated impairment losses. An allowed alternative treatment is "revaluation". As with tangible plant, property and equipment assets under IAS 16, the standard for intangibles permits revaluation subsequent to original acquisition, with the asset being written up to fair value. The requirement of an "active market" as defined in IAS 38 is highly problematic in the field of patents and other IP rights as there is no active regulated market (such as the London Stock Exchange for company shares). Such a market *does not yet exist*. The traditional accounting position is that a reporting entity will be unable to determine "reliably" (in the sense of objectively as opposed to subjectively) the fair value of a patent asset when comparable market transactions are infrequent or non-existent, and when alternative estimates of fair value cannot be calculated. This is a hole in the system as it pertains to patent and other IP assets and results in a lack of financial transparency in relation to the company's assets.

A further problem for innovating firms is that under IAS 38, if the intangible patent assets were not initially recognised (i.e. they were expensed rather than capitalised) it will not be possible to later recognise them at fair value. Accordingly, the revaluation option is unlikely to apply, especially to small businesses. While the IAS 38 comprises further requirements, a discussion of these aspects is unnecessary for the purpose of this book.

In the report of a workshop entitled *Manage and Account for Intangibles* held in February 1999 in Brussels, Gilbert Gélard, Chairman of the IASC Steering Committee on Intangible Assets, has stated that "IAS 38 is a step forward towards the separate recognition of intangible assets for the better understanding by users of financial statements of investments in intangible assets".[51] However, the IASC's former Secretary-General, Sir Bryan Carsberg,[52] has clarified that:

> Knowledge about intangible assets, particularly how to value them, is still in its early days. IAS 38 reflects the current limits of this knowledge, focusing on reporting the cost of intangible assets. There is growing demand for further information on the value of intangible assets using financial and non-financial indicators, maybe not as part of the financial statements. Debates on the subject are very much alive. IASC will watch the developments in this area and may do more work in the future when preparers and users have gained more experience on the value of intangible assets.[53]

Critics of IAS 38 hold that Sir Bryan Carsberg's statement delimits rather than extends the possibilities to capitalise intangibles and that the issue of intangibles is still being addressed in an overly conservative manner. According to accounting Professors Ulf Johanson, of the University of Lund, and Jan-Erik Grojer (deceased), of the Swedish University of Uppsala:

> It is important to note that IASC has never approached the issue of how to separate and label expenses on intangibles; nor has it dealt with the issue of qualitative information about intangibles . . . The conservative approach

51 Gröjer, J.-E. and Johansson, U. (1999) *Voluntary Guidelines on the Disclosure of Intangibles: A Bridge over Troubled Water?* (February, 1999) Working paper presented at the Workshop 'Manage and Account for Intangibles' 15–16, Brussels. Intellectual Capital Management Gathering (1999).

52 From 1995 to 2001, Sir Bryan Carsberg, former Professor of Accounting and Business Finance at the Victoria University of Manchester, served the IASC as Secretary-General.

53 /www.ll-a.fr/intangibles/international accoutningh.htm

> of the IASC and other national standard setting authorities is not very surprising. The standard setting bodies are not expected to take the lead in the issue of accounting for intangibles; in complex matters, they are supposed to take the position of codifying best practice.[54]

No best practice in corporate IP asset disclosure in the traditional corporate accounts from the point of view of corporate governance principle has yet emerged. However, the form of disclosure is less important than the content. More corporate IP asset and strategy information is needed. Disclosure and transparency will help to promote more widespread trust in the potentially valuable IP rights as corporate assets and how they can be deployed to support commercial objectives.

Dr Ghafele, critiquing IAS 38 and the language of accounting, states that the term "intangible asset" triggers the phrase of the "gap between the market and the book value", another expression that inadequately communicates about IP.[55]

Despite these views, it appears that the existing philosophy for the accounting treatment of intangible assets will essentially be continued and the problem of accounting for internally generated patent assets remains. Yet the IAS 38 standard is inappropriate from both a legal and a technological point of view. The author argues that there is no legal or technical difference in substance between a patent that has been internally generated as against that exact same patent which is purchased by a third party and they should not be treated differently in the accounts. In the case of an innovating SME, the value of its patents to the business model is greater than simply what someone else, *at this early point in the business life cycle*, will pay for it. In other words, IAS 38 has a greater negative impact on innovating SMEs in the early stage of their business, than on larger more established enterprises that have a strong trading history. The fragile balance sheets of innovating SMEs place them in a vulnerable position as confirmed in the 2014 "IP Valuation" report which states:

> The Expert Group reports that there are limitations on when and how it is possible to place the value of IP assets on the balance sheet of the company. The complexity of IP from an accounting perspective leads to problems in its reporting, which may result in the vulnerability of firms which base most of their performance on IP.[56]

They found a significant difference in the approach to lending to SMEs and start-ups compared with larger corporates that have a strong trading history.[57]

54 In their report of a workshop entitled, "To Manage and Account for Intangibles" held in February 1999, Brussels as quoted at www.ll-a.fr/intangibles/international accounting.htm.

55 Ghafele, R. 'Accounting for Intangibles' (2010) 5(7) *Journal of Intellectual Property Law & Practice* 521–530.

56 *Final Report from the Expert Group on Intellectual Property Valuation* (2014) p 6.

57 Ibid.

GB patent 123456 Internally generated by Company X Inventor: Steve Jones Claims: A, B & C Granted 5 September 2013	GB patent 123456 Acquired by Company Y from Company X for £100,000 on 6 September 2013 Inventor: Steve Jones Claims: A, B & C Granted 5 September 2013
Development costs £25,000	Purchase price £100,000
Patent value for financial reporting: £25,000	Patent value for financial reporting: £100,000

Figure 4.4 Internally generated GB patent 123456 vs acquired GB patent 123456

Figure 4.4 shows an example of the potential difference in the reported value of an internally generated patent as compared to an acquired (purchased) patent.

Patent GB123456 that is internally developed is the same, legally and technically, as Patent 123456 that is acquired the next day. The inventor, the claims that create the legal monopoly, the duration and the quality of the patent are all the same. Yet for accounting purposes, Patent 123456 is inconsistently valued. This is a simplistic illustration but it does show how this approach is irrational from both a legal and a technical point of view. There needs to be a way that the patent value for Company X is closer to the figure recorded for Company Y for the system to be fair to patent developers and patent acquirers.

Since 1999, it has been argued that there should be no difference between the requirements for: (a) intangible assets that are acquired externally; and (b) internally generated assets, whether they arise from development activities or other types of activities.[58] For patent-backed lending purposes, there are two main areas of inconsistency between the accounting for acquired versus internally generated patents. These are initial recognition at cost, and measuring fair value. Leo argues as follows:

> It may be strictly correct to state that acquired and internally generated intangibles are both treated the same in that both are being recognised at cost. However, even though the assets are in substance the same, initial recognition at fair value is allowed for acquired intangibles but not for internally generated intangibles. Acquirers are being given an advantage not available to those who generate their assets internally.[59]

IAS 38 recommends showing Intellectual Capital (IC) in the notes to the balance sheet. However, such notes are very brief and are only designed to clarify and explain specific individual line items in the financial statements and would not

58 Leo, K. *Intangible Assets: Seeking Consistency* (November 1999) *Australian CPA* p 31.
59 Ibid.

normally be comprehensive (see Chapter 7 for an illustration). It could become normalised accounting practice however, as recommended in Chapter 3, section 3.3.1 ("Managing accounting for innovation"), to expand the report of qualitative material concerning IP assets in the notes. While IAS has a high standing globally through policies designed to foster long-term agreement between domestic standards (as in the UK and other countries with well-developed accounting professions) and international standards, the flip side is that IAS 38 is now well-entrenched internationally. IAS 38, as it currently stands, continues to reinforce a lack of consistency between internally generated and purchased intangible assets as it appears to give precedence to historical cost. Further, it restricts the development of useful and relevant information for lenders and other stakeholders. Despite its shortcomings, this is the price of harmonising accounting standards.[60] Consequently, stakeholders involved in IP and patent-backed security transactions are likely to be in the progressive/reformist camp. This group holds the view that useful and relevant information is more important than information traditionally provided, which is high in terms of objectivity and reliability, but low in terms of relevance and usefulness. Can this problem be overcome? Higson argues that the difference between "progressives" and "traditionals" is the outcome of a lack of clear agreement, within the conceptual accounting framework, about what the financial statements are intended to achieve. If different groups are trying to achieve different things through the same medium, then conflict will be inevitable.[61] The *Banking on IP?* report largely adheres to the "traditionals" view. The authors state, ". . . this report does not advocate changes to . . . accounting standards. The steps required to unlock the business value of IP are pragmatic measures that build on principles and practices which exist today".[62] The authors therefore accepted the *status quo*; they did not consider recommending amendments to IAS 38 by way of introducing alternative (subjective and qualitative) valuation methodologies to measure patent value. Nor does the 2014 "IP Valuation" report directly consider the accounting standards or advocate any changes to them.

In June 2001, the US FASB unanimously approved *Statement 141 Business Combinations* and *Statement 142 Goodwill and Other Intangible Assets* which provide that every entity doing business in the US must determine the "fair market value" of its intangibles, rather than rely on "historic" values.[63] This important accounting policy development requires US companies to adopt a more

60 Mathews, M. R. and Higson, A.W. 'Potentially Dysfunctional Impacts of Harmonising Accounting Standards: The Case of Intangible Assets' (2000) Massey University.

61 Higson, A.W. *An Alternative Basis for the Construction of a Conceptual Framework Incorporating Financial Reporting*: Discussion Paper Series 192. Massey University: Department of Accountancy and Business Law.

62 Brassell, M. and King, K. *Banking on IP? The role of Intellectual Property and Intangible Assets in Facilitating Business Finance Final Report* (6 November 2013) Independent report commissioned by the UKIPO p 16.

63 See www.fasb.org/summary/stsum142.shtml.

rigorous and controlled method for tracking and valuing IP assets leading to increased corporate reporting of IP asset[64] is a potential solution for the UK and to be discussed further in Chapter 5.

From a legal perspective, company law goes a long way in prescribing the form and content of the accounting statements that companies must publish. UK financial statements are required to comply with sections 393–397 and 495 CA 2006. The ability to depart from accounting standards (whether domestic or international) is only available in cases where the result would be so *misleading* as to conflict with the objective of the relevant financial statements. In section 4.3.6 we critically examine the requirement under section 393(1) CA 2006 that a company's financial statements must provide a "true and fair" view. The requirement for accounts to show a "true and fair" view tends to override any other requirements.[65] We then attempt to answer the question whether the traditional accounting treatment of intangible patent assets (which includes IAS 38) meets this overarching legal requirement.

4.3.7 How UK and international accounting standard setters intersect with UK company law requirements

In the UK, Parts 15 and 16 of the CA 2006 drive the legal requirements for corporate accounts, financial reporting and the audit. As always, human actors have roles to play. It is of the highest importance to focus on the professional group that shapes the new company law. Who is the "standard setter"? Who is the *de facto* "company lawmaker"? In Germany, accountants have the upper hand through the German International Accounting Standards Committee (under § 342 of the German Commercial Code) which rules out the recognition of intangibles unless acquired.[66] In the US, we have seen that the Federal Accounting Standards Committee is the accounting standard setter. Powerful national groups such as these have much control over the rise and fall of accounting concepts and they participate heavily in the ongoing debate on the IAS. The Australian government's initiative to carry out further research on this intangible assets issue was not accepted by other members of the IFRS, primarily because certain associations were concerned with the tax implications for their members associated with addressing this inconsistency.[67] The global process of accounting standard setting and the UK standard setting process are intertwined. Nonetheless, the political struggle towards further recognition of intangible IP through accounting continues to evolve and is gaining momentum.

64 Neuhausen, B., Schlank, R. and Pippin, R. *Accounting for Business Combinations, Goodwill, and Other Intangible Assets* (2007) CCH Incorporated p 246.

65 Atrill, P. and McLaney, E. *Accounting & Finance for Non Specialists* (2002) Third edition, Pearson p 127.

66 German Commercial Code as translated by A.F. Schuster, Barrister of the Inner Temple.

67 'Considering the effects of accounting standards: An Australian Response to the European Financial Reporting Advisory Group' (2012) *Institute of Public Accountants* pp 15–16.

4.3.8 Assisting IP owners: a legal basis for departing from IAS 38?

There are ways to assist IP and patent owners who need to apply IAS 38 to value their corporate assets. One answer lies in solving the traditional accounting objective/quantitative "measurement" problem to overcome the obstacle created by the lack of an active patent market. A regulated market for patents would provide the information input necessary to meet the traditional (objective and quantitative) valuation methodology so that patent assets could be traded and then recognised under IAS 38. A patent market may come into existence in the future, and the EU is involved in developing an initiative to set up such a market,[68] however it is unlikely to assist innovating SMEs. As with regulated stock markets, only a small percentage of companies achieve a listing. This approach involves playing the accountants at their own game on their home field. Alternatively, one could establish legal authority to depart from IAS 38 altogether in order to reconfirm that the overarching legal policy with respect to financial statements is the substance of the information they contain, rather than the form.

As far as this author can see, no banking or lending association, nor any Law Society, corporate law association or patent attorney association is actively involved in the debate on IAS 38 and the accounting treatment of intangibles. Accountants continue to control the redirection and growth of the financial recognition of IP and patent assets in the corporate and financial world. Patents as financial assets "are" what accountants preparing the financial statements by following accounting standards tell us they "are". If patent assets are not reflected on the balance sheet and are fully expensed as they are undertaken, both the earning and book value of a company's equity will be understated by the accounting model. Thus, lenders will be provided with biased (conservative) estimates of the firm's patent values and of its capability for the creation of future wealth as a result of those patents. Accordingly, a key aim of this research is to inform the lawyers, patent attorneys and lenders as to the critical issues that arise directly as a result of IAS 38. These stakeholders need to more fully appreciate why IAS 38 is generally unhelpful in representing internally generated patent assets in UK and international company accounts, which results in them often being under-valued leading to potentially unfair or inaccurate credit risk evaluations. This causes the even more significant

68 *Creating a financial market for IPR Final report for EU Tender* No3/PP/ENT/CIP/10/A/N02S003, 5 December 2011. In the conclusions of its meeting on 4 February 2011, the European Council invited the Commission to explore the options for setting up an IPR valorisation instrument at the European level, in particular to ease SME access to the knowledge market, and to report back to the Council by the end of 2011. The Final report for EU Tender No 3/PP/ENT/CIP/10/A/NO2S003 "Creating a Financial Market for IPR" (6 December 2011) made policy recommendations to further evaluate the potential to create an IPR Market in Chapter 10. Policy Recommendation 10 states "The EC should not establish or support the IPR Financial Market before the underlying IPR Asset Market in Europe has been substantially improved and the rules of this underlying market are clear to the actors." The full report is available at www.breese.blogs.com/files/creating-financial-market-for-ipr-in-europe_en.pdf.

problem of limiting the growth of the domestic economy through lack of support for innovating firms – which are in a worse position than NPEs that purchase patents. Given the outcome, the importance of asking the following legal question should not be underestimated.

4.3.9 Do financial statements prepared according to IAS 38 provide a "true and fair view" as required by section 393(1) CA 2006?

A company's annual return includes its financial statements which are publicly available documents. Hypothetically, if those financial statements provide the public with biased (conservative) estimates of the firm's value (equity) and its capability to create wealth in the future (current earnings), this implies that current accounting statements fail to provide an unbiased (true and fair) view of the company's financial position. This is an important corporate governance issue because it is the board of directors that has primary responsibility for the corporation's external financial reporting functions. Section 393 CA 2006 states that the directors must not approve the accounts unless they are satisfied that they give a "true and fair" view of the assets, liabilities, financial position and profit or loss of the company.[69] Section 393 CA 2006 provides:

> (1) The directors of a company must not approve accounts for the purposes of this Chapter unless they are satisfied that they give a true and fair view of the assets, liabilities, financial position and profit or loss:-
>
> (a) in the case of the company's individual account, of the company;
> (b) in the case of the company's group accounts, of the undertakings included in the consolidation as a whole, so far as concerns members of the company.
>
> (2) The auditor of a company in carrying out his functions under this Act in relation to the company's annual account must have regard to the directors' duty under section (1).

Section 495(3) CA 2006 sets out the obligation of the auditors to prepare a report and clearly state whether, in the auditor's opinion, the annual accounts:

> (a) Give a true and fair view:-
>
> (i) in the case of an individual balance sheet, of the state of affairs of the company as at the end of the financial year,

69 The term *true and fair* was first used in the UK, where it originates, in legislation of 1948. However, prior legislation had used similar phrases. Companies legislation dated 1844 required UK companies to *present a full and fair balance sheet*, though the meaning of this phrase was never defined. A company was required to keep *full and true accounts*. By 1900, the auditor was required to state whether the balance sheet was *properly drawn up so as to exhibit a true and correct view*. This phrase was retained until 1948.

(ii) in the case of an individual profit and loss account, of the profit and loss of the company for the financial year,

(iii) in the case of group accounts, of the state of affairs as at the end of the financial year and of the profit or loss for the financial year of the undertakings included in the consolidation as a whole, so far as concerns members of the company

(b) have been properly prepared in accordance with the relevant financial reporting framework; and

(c) have been prepared in accordance with the requirements of this Act (and, where applicable, Article 4 of the IAS Regulation).

As the requirement to prepare accounts which show a "true and fair" view is a *legal* one, what is true is a question of fact and what is fair is a question of law for the courts to determine. The "true and fair" concept has been part of English company law for decades and is central to accounting and auditing practice. Despite this no statutory definition of the phrase exists in the CA 2006 or in other UK legislation. Nor is the expression "true and fair view" defined in the accounting literature. However, the phrase has been the subject of FRC research and case law which will be discussed.

The practical effect of section 393 is that all UK company directors have a duty to ensure that the financial statements are free from material misstatements and faithfully represent the financial performance and position of the company. In larger companies, the Managing Director and the Chief Financial Officer are crucial participants and boards usually have a high degree of reliance on these officers to ensure the integrity and supply of accounting information. These corporate officers oversee the internal accounting systems but they are dependent on accountants and auditors for the actual supply of information. In the UK, auditors must also consider and expressly state in their audit report whether or not company directors have fulfilled their responsibility for the preparation of "true and fair" financial statements.

Qualified UK accountants and auditors are members of accounting bodies which adopt codes of professional conduct and standards of ethical and technical conduct and competence. Accounting associations typically require their members to adhere to the accounting standards set by the IAS and the IFRS. This means that to avoid professional negligence, accountants must conform with IAS 38. Conversely, if they apply IAS 38 in carrying out their accounting duties, they will not be negligent even if the financial statements do not provide a "true and fair" view of the IP and patent assets.

In terms of corporate governance and company law, the supply of accounting information forms a crucial link in enabling the providers of finance and shareholders to monitor directors. Imperfections in the financial reporting process will cause imperfections in the effectiveness of corporate governance. The company law disclosure requirements have largely evolved to protect shareholders and creditors. The long-held public policy motive is that increased transparency will prevent fraud largely due to over-valuing corporate assets. Chapter 2 of Part 10 of the CA 2006 sets out directors' duties in sections 171–177 with the aim of amending and codifying the common law to bring it into line with the expectations of the modern business world. They also attempt to set out in whose interest a company should be run. Broadly speaking, the common law duties of directors were designed to prevent directors from being negligent and to make sure that they put the company's interests ahead of their own interests. The codified statutory duties have the same objectives. Section 172 includes the duty to promote the success of the company. It states that:

> (1) A director of a company must act in the way he considers, in good faith would be most likely to promote the success of the company for the benefit of the members of the who, and in doing so have regard (amongst other matters) to:-
>
> (a) the likely consequences of any decision in the long term;
> (b) the interests of the company's employees;
> (c) the need to foster the company's business relationships with suppliers, customers and others;
> (d) the impact of the company's operations on the community and the environment;
> (e) the desirability of the company maintaining a reputation for high standards of business conduct; and
> (f) the need to act fairly as between members of the company.

This section codifies the common law and is intended to promote the concept of "enlightened shareholder value" (ESV). The Rt Hon Margaret Hodge MP, Secretary of State for Trade and Industry, as she then was, made it clear in her Ministerial Statement on the reforms to directors' duties introduced by the CA 2006 that:

> There are two ways of looking at the statutory statement of directors' duties: on the one hand it simply codifies the existing common law obligations of company directors, on the other – especially in section 172: the duty to act in the interests of the company – it marks a radical departure in articulating the connection between what is good for a company and what is good for society at large.[70]

She was referring to the introduction into company law of the ESV concept whereby companies should pursue shareholder wealth in the long term, ensuring sustainable growth and profits based on a wider range of stakeholder interests.

70 McLaughlin, S. *Unlocking Company Law* (2013) Routledge p 320.

According to McLaughlin,[71] although the articulation of the connection between what is good for a company and what is good for society at large may be a radical step, ESV is not. She holds that it preserves the central role of the interests of shareholders in the structure of corporate governance. As directors are fiduciaries they are expected to act in good faith to promote the success of the company. A fiduciary is a person who holds a legal or ethical relationship of trust between himself or herself and one or more other parties (person or group of persons). Typically, a fiduciary prudently takes care of money for another person. A director is in a fiduciary relationship with shareholders who have invested funds in the company.

This challenging new duty has given company directors the most cause for concern because it has no obvious precursor, although it has clear links to the duty to act bona fide in the best interests of the company, which was the predominant and core fiduciary duty.[72] At this stage, the nature and extent of the duty is difficult to interpret as it not closely aligned to any previous duty when compared with other duties in Chapter 2 of Part 10 of the Act, and while informed by existing case law and academic opinion, any interpretation involves some speculation.[73]

However, turning to the list of matters to which the directors must have regard in promoting the success of the company, the most relevant provisions are: section 172(1)(a) the likely consequences of any decision in the long term; and section 172(1)(b) the interests of the company's employees. Directors need to ensure that the company is appropriately financed to carry out its operations. If a core activity of the company's operations involves internally generating IP and/or patents, then a central matter for the directors should be to endeavour to ensure their value is reflected in a true and fair way in the company's accounts to facilitate access to finance needed for commercialisation, generating a profit for shareholders. Inadequate finance will have a detrimental effect both on the long-term success of the company, profits and the job security of its employees (if any). The list of matters to which the directors must have regard, as set out in section 172(1), is not exhaustive.

Consider this: what if the problem is that internally generated patents have been systematically undervalued and as a result, a company's potential to succeed is hindered by an inability to finance its activities? Have the directors fulfilled their duty to the company? Have the directors acted in a way they consider in good faith would be most likely to promote the success of the company for the benefit

71 McLaughlin, S. *Unlocking Company Law* (2013) Routledge.

72 Keay, A. 'The Duty to Promote the Success of the Company: Is it Fit for Purpose?' at //www.law.leeds.ac.uk/assets/files/research/events/directors-duties/keay-the-duty-to-promote-the-success.pdf pp 3–4. This implies that to be successful, directors must manage risk. Directors are accountable for how they conduct the affairs of the company. The over-arching concept of good faith includes not simply the duty of care and loyalty, in the narrow sense, but promoting the welfare of the company must guide the fiduciary (director).

73 Ibid p 4.

of the members? For the director of a micro company with no other assets save a single internally generated patent, coupled with a duty to promote the success of the company, the question of the accounting treatment required by IAS 38 may play on his or her mind, especially in terms of accountability to shareholders and had employees. What if the directors of a company that internally generates patent assets, in carrying out their duty under section 172, genuinely believed that the company was being disadvantaged by adhering to IAS 38? In other words, that applying IAS 38 mandated accounting treatment to their patent assets would not result in a "true and fair" view? What if they refused to sign off the accounts under section 393 because they were unconvinced that the accounts gave a true and fair view of the company's intangible assets? To answer these questions requires a critical analysis as to whether there is a viable legal argument for directors of innovating SMEs to depart from IAS 38 and adopt a different accounting treatment for their internally generated patent assets (e.g. GSK's Internal Rate of Return as discussed in Chapter 6). This leads to an evaluation of the legal research undertaken in connection with judicial consideration of the concept of "true and fair" financial statements.

Prima facie, the word "true" in this context is taken to mean that the financial statements are factually correct and have been prepared according to applicable reporting frameworks such as the IFRS and do not contain any material misstatements that may mislead users. "Fair" value is primarily a legal concept and is intended to estimate a fair or reasonable or equitable (to use legal terminology) amount. It is not necessarily intended to reflect a likely cost, market or income approach to valuation. The essence of fair value, from a legal point of view, lies in the desire to be equitable to all parties. Fair valuation in respect of a patent or other IP right is the amount that will fairly compensate an owner who is deprived of the economic enjoyment of the patent where there is neither a willing buyer nor a willing seller. However in 2012, the UK FRC published its policy stance and clarification of the phrase "true and fair" view.

4.3.10 FRC research as to the meaning of "true and fair view"

The FRC announced that the most authoritative statements as to the meaning of "true and fair" have been legal opinions written by Lord Hoffmann and Dame Mary Arden in 1983 and 1984 and also by Dame Mary Arden in 1993 ("the Opinions"). Since then significant changes in accounting standards and company law have taken place leading some to query whether the views expressed in the Opinions still apply. The FRC commissioned a further legal opinion from Martin Moore (QC) (in 2008) to ascertain whether the approach to "true and fair" taken in the Opinions needed revision. The FRC reported:

> In his Opinion, Mr Moore has endorsed the analysis in the Opinions of Lord Hoffmann and Dame Mary Arden and confirmed the centrality of the true and fair requirement to the preparation of financial statements in the UK, whether they are prepared in accordance with international or UK accounting standards.

> Directors must consider whether, taken in the round, the financial statements that they approve are appropriate. Similarly, auditors are required to exercise professional judgment before expressing an audit opinion. As a result, the Opinion confirms *that it will not be sufficient for either directors or auditors to reach such conclusions solely because the financial statements were prepared in accordance with applicable accounting standards* [emphasis added].
>
> The FRC believes that this Opinion is an important confirmation of a key contributor to the integrity of financial reporting in the UK.[74]

The relevance of the "true and fair" concept has been squarely confirmed by the FRC in its short six page report, *True and Fair* published in July 2011.[75] Further, according to FRC Press Notice 338 the Accounting Standards Board and Auditing Practices Boards reaffirmed the importance of the "true and fair" view in both UK GAAP and IRFS. The first page of *True and Fair* (2011) states:

> In this note, we discuss the continuing primacy of the true and fair requirement and its relevance to preparers, those charged with governance and auditors.
>
> *Preparation of accounts*
>
> In his Opinion Martin Moore notes, in relation to the gradual shift over time to more detailed accounting standards, that "It does not follow . . . that the preparation of financial statements can now be reduced to a mechanistic process of following the relevant standards without the application of objective professional judgement applied to ensure that those statements give a true and fair view, or achieve a fair presentation."
>
> This professional judgement is all important.

The same page specifically mentions that this applies to "making judgements about valuation, aimed at giving a true and fair view" as well as "standing back at the end of the accounts process and making sure the accounts overall do give a true and fair view". The FRC then issued the following cautionary statement about "true and fair" and accounting standards, warning that a departure from the standards should only be taken in extremely rare circumstances:

> True and fair is not something that is merely a separate add-on to accounting standards. Rather the whole essence of standards is to provide for recognition,

74 The FRC at www.frc.org.uk/Our-Work/Codes-Standards/Accounting-and-Reporting-Policy/True-and-Fair.aspx.

75 See www.frc.org.uk/getattachment/55214e7d-6e34-4c11-af51-1b0533ec0c95/Paper-True-and-Fair1.pdf. The FRC has since published *True and Fair* (June 2014) available at www.frc.org.uk/getattachment/f08eecd2-6e3a-46d9-a3f8-73f82c09f624/True-and-fair-June-2014.pdf

measurement, presentation and disclosure for specific aspects of financial reporting in a way that reflects economic reality and hence that provides a true and fair view.

Accounting standards are arrived at after extensive consultation and after full due process. As a result, in the vast majority of cases compliance with accounting standards will result in a true and fair view, and disagreement with a particular standard does not, on its own, provide grounds for departing from it. Indeed under UK GAAP almost all true and fair overrides in the past were of law rather than of a standard.

Where the accounting standards clearly address an issue, but the answer does not seem to accord with "common sense" in a particular case, the solution is normally proper disclosure.

However, in those "extremely rare" circumstances where directors and auditors do not believe that following a particular accounting policy will give a true and fair view they are legally required to adopt a more appropriate policy, even if this requires a departure from the standard. As IAS 1 states, an entity cannot rectify inappropriate accounting policies by disclosure. These circumstances are more likely to arise where the precise circumstances are not covered by a relevant standard.

Where a company departs from a standard in order to give a true and fair view and a proper explanation is given of the reason for the departure and its effects, the Financial Reporting Review Panel will be reluctant to substitute its own judgement for that of the company's board unless it is not satisfied that the board has acted reasonably. There are a number of examples where the override has been used under IFRS, both inside and outside the UK.[76]

The *True and Fair* report (2011) relates to general principles and does not discuss any particular accounting standards nor does it mention intangibles assets or internally generated patent assets. Nor does Moore (QC)'s opinion,[77] from which the report is derived. At the conclusion of the Report, the following advice is made to preparers, directors and auditors to ensure that accounts in the UK continue to provide high-quality information:

- Always to stand back and ensure that the accounts as a whole do give a true and fair view;

76 *True and Fair*, FRC, July 2011 www.frc.org.uk/getattachment/55214e7d-6e34-4c11-af51-1b0533ec0c95/Paper-True-and-Fair1.pdf.

77 Moore QC, M. Opinion (2008) entitled 'The True and Fair Requirement Revisited' for the FRC. Moore QC, wrote a further opinion for the FRC entitled, "International Accounting Standards and the True and Fair View" dated 8 October 2013, available at www.frc.org.uk/getattachment/5d0b34be-5742-41d8-a442-6ad22d2b878e/Martin-Moore-QC-Opinion-3-October-2013-sig.pdf, in which he reiterated at paragraph 76 that accounts which are not useful to readers will not be true and fair.

- Be prepared, albeit in extremely rare circumstances, to consider using the true and fair override; and
- Ensure that the consideration they give to these matters is evident in their deliberations and documentation.[78]

On 3 October 2013, Baroness Hogg, FRC Chairman reported that stewardship reporting (holding management to account) should be included in the *Conceptual Framework* as a primary objective of financial reporting and not as a subset of the provision of decision-useful information.[79] In this legal analysis, the author submits that in the modern innovation economy, the existence of internally generated patent assets is not an "extremely rare occurrence", it is commonplace. In addition, IAS 38 clearly addresses the accounting treatment of intangible assets, but in the author's opinion the outcome of the application of IAS 38 (for the reasons detailed earlier in this chapter) does not seem to accord with "common sense". In such a case, according to the FRC, *the solution is proper disclosure*. This implies additional narrative disclosure. Companies that internally generate patents could voluntarily prepare the new ICS advocated by a significant proportion of the accounting profession, and which is already mandated in Denmark. Alternatively, another form of corporate narrative report could be used to supplement the company's traditional financial statements. The ICS format will be discussed in Chapter 5.

However, in his Opinion to the FRC, Moore (QC) clearly sets out that the "true and fair" requirement is an overarching concept, and is not the same as compliance with accounting standards. Thus, even where a company complies with an accounting standard, if the accounts fail to provide a "true and fair" view, then they are inadequate. Is this a question for accountants or for the corporate lawyers and the courts? Moore (QC) states that the scope for arguing that non-compliant financial statements nevertheless give a "true and fair" view, or a fair presentation, is very limited (paras 38–40). In determining whether a company's accounts show a "true and fair" view, the courts will rely heavily on the ordinary practices of professional accountants (para 8(c)). At this point, it would appear that the accountants are in the driver's seat on IAS 38. According to Moore (QC):

> 8(C) . . . That is because those practices reflect the accumulation of experience and good professional practice and mould the expectations of users of accounts as to the sufficiency and utility of the information in terms of quantity and quality.[80]

78 www.frc.org.uk/FRC-Documents/FRC/Paper-True-and-Fair.aspx at p 4.

79 *Accounting Standards are part of Legally Binding Corporate Reporting Framework* (3 October 2013) FRC available at: https://frc.org.uk/news/october-2013/accounting-standards-are-part-of-legally-binding-c

80 Moore QC, M. Opinion (2008) entitled, 'True and Fair Requirement Revisited' for the FRC p 38.

And further:

> (D) Compliance with generally accepted accounting principles as set out in relevant statements of standard accounting practice will be prima facie evidence of satisfaction of the true and fair standard and vice versa.
>
> (E) The application of the concept involves judgment on questions of degree. Reasonable business men and accountants may differ over the degree of accuracy or comprehensiveness, there may be differences over the method used to adopt a true and fair view and there may be more than one view of a financial position, any of which could be described as true and fair.

However, an important argument in favour of companies that internally generate patents, is what Moore (QC) goes on to say:

> (F) The concept is dynamic, evolving and subject to continuous rebirth. Accordingly, the detailed provisions of the Schedules to the Companies Act may have to yield to the overriding requirement to produce accounts which give a true and fair view.

There is little case law specifically on the question of whether accounts show a "true and fair" view and none that addresses the issues of inconsistent treatment of internally generated patent assets versus acquired patent assets (of which the author is aware). However, the case of *HMRC v William Grant & Sons Distillers Limited*[81] involved a revenue matter concerned with whether a profit or loss has been calculated in accordance with "the correct principles of commercial accountancy" and whether they did indeed show a true and fair view. In 2000, the Basel Committee on Banking Supervision concluded that in the absence of active markets it would be difficult to obtain or calculate a reliable fair value for certain non-marketable financial instruments held at cost. The Committee concluded that "it did not believe the time was right to prescribe full fair value accounting . . . for all financial assets and liabilities".[82] However, in the author's opinion, the time is now right. A test case would be welcome given the increasing interest and support from within the accounting community and others that IAS 38 should be amended to include and deal with qualitative information about intangibles. This would require the input of the legal profession and patent attorneys who possess the relevant legal and technical knowledge. The courts could evaluate the primacy of the overarching concept of financial statements providing true and fair information, rather than the current position – financial

81 [2007] UKHL 15. See also See *Balloon Promotions Limited v Wilson (Inspector of Taxes)* 3 March 2006 SPC00524; *Odeon Associated Theatres v Jones (Inspector of Taxes)* [1971] 1 WLR 442; *Gallagher v Jones (Inspector of Taxes)* [1994] Ch 107.

82 Basel Committee on Banking Supervision (2000). *Report to G7 Finance Ministers and Central Bank Governors on International Accounting Standards.*

statements providing objective but inconsistent and incomplete information regarding intangible patent assets.

The IASB Framework for the Preparation and Presentation of Financial Statements (the "Framework") sets out the concepts on which accounting practice is founded. It is similar in scope to the Statement of Principles of Financial Reporting made by the ASB in 1999. This Statement is explicit in reference to the "true and fair" requirement and provides:

> 12. It is inherent in the nature of the true and fair concept that financial statements will not give a true and fair view unless the information they contain is sufficient in quantity and quality to satisfy the reasonable expectations of the readers to whom they are addressed. Such expectations change over time and the Board seeks, through its accounting standards and other authoritative pronouncements, both to respond to those expectations and to influence them. The Statement of principles may therefore be expected to contribute to the development of the concept.
>
> 13. The Statement of Principle does not, however, define the meaning of true and fair – it is detailed legal requirements, accounting standards and, in their absence, other evidence of generally accepted accounting practice itself, that normally determine the content of financial statements. Nevertheless, as the Statement is a set of high-level accounting principles designed to help in setting standards, it has the true and fair view concept at its foundation. Its insistence on relevance and reliability as prime indicators of the quality of financial information is just one example of this.

As we know, the new UK GAAP which adopts IAS 38 will determine the method of recognising intangibles and measuring them for the financial reporting elements of the company's annual return commencing after 1 January 2015, resulting in the "mechanical application" of IAS to intangibles.

4.4 Achieving a true and fair view of internally generated intangibles

The time is ripe for a test case to obtain a judicial opinion focusing squarely on whether the application of IAS 38 provides a "true and fair" view of a company's internally generated intangibles. IAS 1 permits departure from IFRS if a particular IFRS (e.g. IAS 38) would be so misleading that it would conflict with the objective of the financial statements set out in the Framework. IAS 1 was adopted by EC 1725/2003 and thus the ability to depart from an IFRS is incorporated by reference.[83] A UK court may have regard to accounting standards such as IAS 38,

83 Moore QC, M. Opinion entitled, 'True and Fair Requirement Revisited' for the FRC p 38.

but is not legally bound by them in whether a company's financial statements give a "true and fair" view. The Court may take into account other evidence and expert evidence presented by accountants, lawyers, patent attorneys and lenders in arriving at their decision. Is there a special case to be made for a new bespoke financial standard for patent assets or intangibles generally, especially with respect to innovating SMEs?

In reply, accounting experts will likely argue that IAS 38 remains appropriate because in their opinion there is no way to reliably *measure the probability that the expected future economic benefits attributable to the asset will flow to the entity* using accepted accounting methodology. Further, they will point out that tangible assets and intangible assets should be treated the same. However, lawyers know that fair is not always equal and what is equal is not always fair. It can be fair to treat situations (or for our purpose, asset classes) differently. By way of analogy, imagine a teacher puts a chocolate bar on the top of a tall bookshelf and asks the tallest and the shortest students in the class to try to get it. That would be equal but unfair. If the shorter student got a boost up, that would be unequal, but fair.

If, hypothetically, the courts were to decide that the application of IAS 38 did not provide a "true and fair" view of the company's financial position and, accordingly, permitted a departure from IAS 38 in the treatment of internally generated intangibles (patent assets), what are the alternatives? How should the strict criteria set out in IAS 38 be relaxed? What new conceptual framework should the international accounting bodies adopt? The answers to these questions are important, but beyond the scope of this book.

Boards of directors need to engage with IP valuation to ensure that their portfolio of corporate IP assets represents value for shareholders. In order to assess the rate of return and make better-informed decisions regarding the portfolio, they need more relevant, accurate and timely information about their future value creating potential. IP valuations are undertaken for a variety of commercial reasons, usually event-driven, and not only to meet legal or regulatory corporate governance requirements.[84] In terms of IP valuation methodology, this will require that new IP factual and strategy information inputs form part of the IP valuation repertoire and go beyond established metrics, as the future value of corporate IP assets is context-driven. These inputs are typically available within the company or may be accessed from publicly available information sources. Valuation methodologies[85] need to effectively demonstrate that properly managed corporate IP assets will produce value are not simply "sunk costs" (past costs incurred that cannot be recovered). Sunk costs differ from future costs that a company may face because they are excluded from future business decisions, as the costs will be the

84 Brassell, M. and Maguire, J. *Hidden Value: A Study of the UK IP Valuation Market* (August 2017) independent report commissioned by the UKIPO p 64.

85 The *cost*, *market* and *income* approaches to IP valuation are currently embodied within the relevant industry standards. These could be revised to provide additional guidance on valuation of specific categories of IP rights.

same regardless of the outcome of a decision. Indeed, according to a recent study on the UK IP valuation market, the number of companies formally valuing their IP annually is likely to be less than 5,000 in total, although the fees involved in obtaining such valuations may be a barrier.[86] The figure is surprising given the high level of contemporary corporate investment in intangibles and is a concern from a corporate governance perspective.

Earlier in section 4.3.7 above, we noted that if the outcome of applying IAS 38 to internally generated patent assets did not accord with "common sense" then in such a case (according to the FRC) the proper solution is additional corporate and financial disclosure. In Chapter 5 we investigate the viability of additional narrative reporting (disclosure) of IP assets within the existing UK company law reporting framework, as well as the Intellectual Capital Report format.

86 Brassell, M. and Maguire, J. *Hidden Value: A Study of the UK IP Valuation Market* (August 2017) independent report commissioned by the UKIPO p 9. This report is invaluable for those seeking a more in depth knowledge of the variety of purposes that require IP valuation, methodologies, and professional practice.

Part IV

The corporate governance dimension: developing a normative practice in IP reporting

5 Transparency in corporate IP asset reporting

Accountability is impossible without transparency

Mary L. Schapiro, 29th Chair of the US Securities and Exchange Commission 2009–2012

Introduction

The corporate intellectual property (IP) asset disclosure culture and our understanding of corporate IP asset value in the UK is weak. This chapter aims to contribute a better understanding of how innovating companies could approach IP information and strategy reporting to enhance transparency and therefore, corporate accountability and responsible stewardship. In Chapter 4 we confirmed that current UK corporate reporting and disclosure laws, which hinge on IAS 38 in respect of intangible assets, arguably do not go far enough to give a "true and fair" view with respect to the internally generated patent assets on an innovating SME's balance sheet. It was argued that on the subject of corporate IP assets and strategies for value creation, existing corporate governance principles aimed at increasing shareholder value demand a higher level of transparency and disclosure. A true and fair view is a requirement of both UK and EU law and applies equally to accounts prepared in accordance with UK GAAP and IFRS. However, given the accounting methods currently used and likely to remain in place in the foreseeable future, enhanced ***voluntary*** disclosure of IP information and the business strategy to generate future value from its IP assets is recommended. Such disclosure would supplement and complement the traditional financial statements thereby reducing the information gap and increasing public trust in IP as an asset class over time. From a corporate governance perspective, shareholders and other outsiders need accurate, relevant and timely information to enable them to assess whether the company directors, who have the legal responsibility for managing corporate IP assets, are ensuring a reasonable return on those assets. In addition, disclosure of such information will assist stakeholders to identify pockets of corporate IP asset predictability and see whether directors are acting in the interests of the company rather than in their own self-interest. In *York Building Co v MacKenzie* (1795) it was held that:

> He that is entrusted with the interest of others cannot be allowed to make the business an object of interest to himself; because from the frailty of nature, one who has the power will be too readily seized with the inclination to use the opportunity for serving his own interest at the expense of those for whom he is entrusted. [1]

A further objective concerns the need for increased voluntary IP asset disclosure to support innovation finance. Financiers and other stakeholders are key users of financial statements. It is vitally important to enable positive, yet prudent, credit decisions being made in order to support innovation. Bhattacharya, formerly Professor of Finance at the Indian Institute of Management, confirms that in relation to credit appraisal, "[a]dditional information may be relevant to users in understanding the financial position and liquidity of an enterprise. Disclosure of this information, together with a commentary by the management is encouraged".[2] Credit appraisal involves evaluating a variety of information sources in order to arrive at a decision to lend. This includes Companies House records, credit history, automated tools and scoring systems. Richard Holden, Head of Manufacturing at Lloyds Banking Group, states that the current position within the SME debt finance market is that:

> At present, these seldom if ever include intangibles or IP; they don't get offered or asked for – they are just not on the agenda. As a result, it is unlikely in most cases, that the credit decision process considers IP to any degree. Paying much attention to IP at the moment would be a big leap in any event, but at least when it comes to understanding a company's overall position, it may provide comfort between doing something or not. It doesn't necessarily follow even at that point that lending will increased or be directly assigned to IP, but it might make the difference between lending and not lending.[3]

There is a disconnect between the entirety of the company's intangibles and the legal requirements of corporate reporting. Improving the quality of voluntary IP information made available to lenders and other financiers would currently involve a non-standard form or process with bespoke documentation, at least initially. This would have a cost attached to it which the bank would pass on in some way, unless standardised approaches were available.[4] It is essential to make IP asset information as easy as possible for lenders to understand, in particular, so that the

1 *York Building Co v MacKenzie* (1795) 3 Pat 378.

2 Bhattacharya, H. *Banking Strategy, Credit Appraisal and Lending Decisions: A Risk-Return Framework* (2010), Oxford University Press, Oxford p 464.

3 Brassell, M. and King, K. *Banking on IP? The role of Intellectual Property and Intangible Assets in Facilitating Business Finance Final Report* (6 November 2013) Independent report commissioned by the UK Intellectual Property Office, p61

4 Ibid p62

"invisible" IP and patent value can be "seen" to inform finance decisions. The goal of voluntary corporate narrative reports is to supplement and complement the financial statements, making the information as to corporate asset value more transparent, by aligning the figures with the narrative account signed off by the company's directors and independent auditors.

In this chapter, section 5.1 provides context with an overview of corporate reporting laws under the CA 2006. Section 5.2 examines the UK and European law on the level of corporate reporting required by firms (SMEs and plcs) to answer the questions: "Do corporate disclosure laws reach far enough to include intangible assets in the context of accounting methods currently used?"[5] and "What legal responsibility do company directors have for managing and ensuring a proper return on patent and other IP assets?". Identifying small pockets of predictability of even 5–10% would be a significant improvement and result in better outcomes for stakeholders. As long as there is no place for internally generated patents, IP and other intangibles on balance sheets, corporate law needs to ensure that such potentially value creating corporate assets, for which directors are responsible, are not ignored nor hidden from shareholders and the public. If traditional accounting of the value of IP rights is an ineffectual gatekeeper of the status quo because accounting statements cannot adequately document how patents and IP relate to business performance, then the law must step up and confront the challenge of communicating this crucial information. Section 5.3 considers the benefits of enhanced IP information disclosure, despite the increased regulatory burden and costs involved. Finally, section 5.4 analyses the format for making patent information disclosures.

5.1 Corporate reporting under the UK Companies Act 2006

Since 1844 when the registration and incorporation of companies first took place, public disclosure has been an important aspect of company law. The debate on how intangibles should be accounted for and reported in the financial statements has been present in the literature for over a century.[6] Today, private micro and SME companies, as well as the majority of non-listed UK companies, operate under a set annual financial disclosure requirement which may be accessed by the public. Section 854 CA 2006 requires every company to submit an annual return to Companies House. The annual return sets out basic information about the company on a particular date (its return date) every year. Such periodic annual reporting rarely takes the long-term nature of patents or other IP rights into account.[7] Companies must develop a method of reporting on their intangible

5 'The Perfect Storm: Corporate Disclosure, Shareholders, and the Importance of Intellectual Property' at www.ipprospective.com/portfolio-potential/the-perfect-storm-corporate-disclosure-shareholders-and-the-value-of-intellectual-property/.

6 Cañibano, L et al 'The Value Relevance and Managerial Implications of Intangibles: A Literature Review' (1998) OECD, Directorate for Science, Technology and Industry p 19.

7 Binctin, N. and Bonnet, G. *Le Capital Intellectuel* (2007) LexisNexis, France.

patent assets that is reflective of the value they provide to the business in the medium to long-term given that the sustainability of the organisation and the *long-term view* is now enshrined in the CA 2006 via the ESV concept and reform of the directors' duties under section 172 includes the duty to promote the success of the company. IP and patents, as corporate assets, have the potential to contribute to a company's profitability, long-term growth over the potential monopoly period, and ultimate success. Arguably, patents are an easier form of intangible to report on for two reasons: they require registration; and, as there is a cost involved, company directors will be aware of their existence. This level of awareness may even be higher when compared with other forms of intangibles such as know-how, confidential information and copyright, all of which are unregistered rights and thus incur no registration fees that must be accounted for. All companies, large and small, have corporate IP assets. The following sections discuss the UK corporate reporting requirements that apply whether the companies are SMEs or plcs.

5.2 SMEs, plcs and corporate IP asset disclosure

Every company is required to keep accounting records which must show with reasonable accuracy the financial position of the company at any particular moment in time.[8] A company's annual accounts consist of a balance sheet, a profit and loss account, the Directors' Report[9] and, if the company is not exempt from audit, the Auditor's Report.[10]

Currently, companies which are classified as small are permitted to submit abbreviated accounts to the Registrar of Companies, although full accounts will still have to be delivered to shareholders. Section 382 CA 2006 defines a company as "small" if it meets two out of the following three requirements: (1) the company's annual turnover is £5.6 million or less; (2) the total assets of the company are £2.8 million or less; (3) the company has 50 or fewer employees. This means that SMEs can submit shorter accounts, created from the statutory accounts, to Companies House – therefore even less information about the company will be publicly available.[11] The Financial Reporting Standard for Smaller Entities (effective

8 Section 386 CA 2006. Failure to keep accounting records may be punished by a fine and/or two years' in jail: section 389 CA 2006.

9 Section 415 CA 2006.

10 SMEs are typically exempt from the need to have their accounts formally audited.

11 'Accounts and Tax Returns for Smaller Companies' at www.gov.uk/prepare-file-annual-accounts-for-limited-company/prepare-annual-accounts. Further, the Small Business, Enterprise and Entities Act 2015 amended annual return and filing requirements when it came into force in 2016. Section 92 of the Act replaces Part 24 of the CA 2006 to remove the requirement to file an annual return. Instead, all companies are subject to a requirement to deliver to Companies House a confirmation statement stating that the company has delivered all the information it was required to provide in the period to which the confirmation statement relates (section 853A(1), CA 2006). This has resulted in even less disclosure by SMEs.

1 January 2015) provides detailed guidance to the legal requirements.[12] As discussed in Chapter 4, the directors must not approve the accounts unless they are satisfied that they give a "true and fair" view of the assets, liabilities, financial position and profit or loss of the company: section 393 CA 2006. Under the legal requirements, companies classified as small can choose not to submit a Directors' Report with their accounts. At the expense of transparency, small companies can lawfully reduce the regulatory corporate reporting burden disclosing less in their financial statements and choosing not to submit a Directors' Report.

5.2.1 The annual report and corporate IP asset information disclosure

Annual reports are longer and richer in content than ever before (making them more costly for companies to prepare) yet important IP information remains indiscernible. In 2012 the Association of Chartered Certified Accountants (ACCA), the global body for professional accountants, surveyed 500 annual report users in three common law jurisdictions: the UK, US and Canada. It reported that shareholders (equity investors) are the foremost audience of the annual report and that their needs must be placed at the heart of future developments in corporate reporting. Fifty per cent of the survey respondents confirmed that the annual report is their primary source of information; however, more than a quarter of the sample (26%) felt that it was difficult to assess a company's performance from the report.[13] Research by accounting firm Deloitte notes that the average 2014/2015 annual report in their sample was 135 pages long – yet 55% of investors responding to the 2015 Chartered Financial Analyst (CFA) UK annual survey on Financial Reporting and Analysis believed that the majority of annual reports omit important information about the company's financial performance and position.[14]

5.2.2 The Directors' Report and the former Business Review

In January 2006 the UK government introduced the "Business Review" [15] into the Directors' Report, based on best practice and not on mandatory Operating

12 'The Financial Reporting Standard for Smaller Entities' (July 2013) FRC at www.frc.org.uk/Our-Work/Publications/Accounting-and-Reporting-Policy/FRSSE-(effective-January-2015).aspx.

13 'Accountancy Futures, Re-assessing the Value of Corporate Reporting' (2012) Association of Chartered Certified Accountants, p 4 at www.accaglobal.com/content/dam/acca/global/PDF-technical/financial-reporting/reassessing-value.pdf accessed 10 October 2014.

14 CFA UK Annual Survey on Financial Reporting and Analysis (21 January 2015) CFA Society UK available at https://secure.cfauk.org/assets/1345/Analysis_of_FRAC_survey_2015.pdf. The CFA Institute is the global association for investment professionals. It has more than 100,000 members in 140 countries, of which more than 90,000 hold the Chartered Financial Analyst (CFA) designation.

15 Section 417 CA 2006.

and Financial Review (OFR) Reporting Standard (RS1),[16] to further inform shareholders.[17] The Business Review was aimed at presenting a fair review of the company's business and a description of the principal risks and uncertainties it faces, among other items.

Note that if the company's shares are publicly listed on a stock exchange within the European Union, or on the New York Stock Exchange or the American Nasdaq Stock Market, public disclosure under the Financial Services and Markets Act 2000 (FSMA)[18] requires the Business Review to report on additional matters including the main trends and factors likely to affect the future development, performance and position of the company's business. Thus, if patent rights are likely to have an impact on the business, relevant information concerning those rights must be disclosed. The FSMA also requires half-yearly financial reports as well as interim management statements.[19] For example, in a life science or technology company the value of a patent portfolio is likely to be central to appraising the value of the company. Obvious examples of key patent-related risks that must be disclosed are: (1) material litigation involving the patent portfolio; or (2) a revocation proceeding concerning a patent that is central to business operations. Another less obvious risk that should be disclosed is the expiry of a patent right owned by the company. Such disclosures are legally required if they have a potential financial impact and would assist the public to evaluate the future development, performance and position of the publicly listed company's business – in other words, if they are a material disclosure under the law.

5.2.3 UK company law: the Strategic Report

The reform of narrative reporting (i.e. the information that was formerly required in the Business Review) was one aspect of a wider reform agenda[20] aimed at modernising company law by making corporate reporting "simpler, clearer and more focused"[21] and to "improve corporate accountability and transparency".[22] In October 2012, a revised structure for narrative reporting in the form of the Companies Act 2006 (Strategic Report and Directors' Report) Regulations 2013

16 Yeoh, P. 'Narrative Reporting: The UK Experience' (2010) 52(3) *International Journal of Law and Management* 211.

17 Section 172 CA 2006.

18 Via the Disclosure and Transparency Rules promulgated by FSA pursuant to the FSMA 2000.

19 Disclosure and Transparency Rules (DTR) Rule 4.

20 'Encouraging Employers to Use Human Capital Reporting: A Literature Review of Implementation Options' (February 2013) Briefing Paper p 8.

21 Ibid p 17.

22 'The Coalition: Our Programme for Government' (May 2010) HM Government. The Small Business, Enterprise and Employment Act 2015 has simplified small companies' statutory filing requirements even further by replacing annual returns with a requirement to "check, notify changes if necessary and confirm" the statutory information at least once in a 12 month period.

(the “SR Regulations”) was enacted. The SR Regulations introduced a “Strategic Report” that applies to all companies and since October 2013 has replaced the previous Business Review described above pursuant to new sections 414A–D CA 2006. The requirements for the Strategic Report are similar to the Business Review (except for quoted companies which have to include qualitative information to provide an understanding of the development, performance and position in relation to their business model and strategy, gender diversity, human rights and greenhouse emissions). The reforms demonstrate the importance of narrative disclosures on diverse subject matter that the government believes are in the public interest (for companies not classed as “small”). The Strategic Report enables a company to tell its story, starting with the strategy, business model and the principle risks and challenges the company has faced.[23] Reporting on IC, intangibles or IP is not specifically mandated. This format could provide an opportunity for innovating SMEs to voluntarily express their patent strategy and business model. These reforms suggest that voluntary disclosure of patent information and strategy would be viewed positively as a powerful means for an innovating SME to communicate to its stakeholders. The FRC, in its December 2015 report entitled, *Clear & Concise: Developments in Narrative Reporting* confirmed that the overall quality of corporate reporting has improved since the introduction of the Strategic Report with a greater emphasis on materiality reporting, although opportunities for further improvement still exist and some companies are leading the way in developing best practice.[24]

5.2.4 European corporate reporting reform

In April 2013 the EC published a draft directive to require large and listed companies to include additional disclosures of non-financial information in their annual reports, similar to the disclosure requirements in the Strategic Report. The UK has implemented the new EU Non-Financial Disclosure Directive 2017. The Non-Financial Reporting Regulations insert sections 414CA and 414CB into the CA 2006, supplementing the existing strategic report requirements as set out in section 414C of the CA 2006. The regulations apply to companies and qualifying partnerships with financial years beginning on or after 1 January 2017. These new requirements have the potential to increase the reporting of non-financial information, diversity, better reporting in respect of section 172 CA 2006 and potentially strategic IP information through the requirement to report the company’s business model..[25] This EU-wide reform highlights the growing

23 ‘Better and Simpler Company Reporting’ (12 June 2013) at www.gov.uk/government/news/better-and-simpler-company-reporting.

24 *Clear & Concise: Developments in Narrative Reporting* (December 2015) Financial Reporting Council p 1.

25 ‘New UK Annual Report and Requirements to Disclose Human Rights, Diversity and Greenhouse Gas Emissions’ (20 June 2013) Linklaters UK Corporate Update.

importance of disclosure of non-financial information which will benefit patent owning entities.

With respect to SMEs, the European Parliament has adopted Directive 78/660/EEC on the annual accounts of certain types of companies as regards micro-entities, which consolidates EU accounting requirements into one directive, in particular relaxing the accounting rules for smaller companies.[26] The Directive took effect in 2013 and updates the EU's accounting framework, in particular, for our purposes: :

- permits micro-entities to prepare a very simple balance sheet and profit and loss account *with virtually no notes* (Directive 2012/6). Micro-entities are companies with less than 10 employees, a turnover of not more than €700,000 and/or a balance sheet total of not more than €350.000;[27]
- reduces the information to be provided by small companies in the notes to the accounts; and
- removes the EU requirement for small companies to be audited (though Member States can take a more proportionate approach).

The UK Government approved The Small Companies (Micro-Entities' Accounts) Regulations 2013 in November 2013 and introduced major (but optional) accounting exemptions for micro-entities. The recitals to the Directive expressly state the following:

> (10) The aim of this Directive is to enable Member States to create a simple financial reporting environment for micro-entities. The use of fair values can result in the need for detailed disclosures to explain the basis on which the fair value of certain items has been determined. Given that the micro-entity regime provides for very limited disclosure by way of notes on the accounts, the users of the accounts of micro-entities would not know whether the amounts presented in the balance sheet and the profit and loss account incorporate fair values. Accordingly, to provide certainty for such users in this regard, Member States should not permit or require micro-entities using any of the exemptions available to them under this Directive to use the fair valuation basis in drawing up their accounts. Micro-entities that wish or need to use fair value will still be able to do so by using other regimes under this Directive where a Member State permits or requires such use.[28]

26 Directive 2012/6/EU of the European Parliament and of the Council of 14 March 2012 amending Council Directive 78/660/EEC on the annual accounts of certain types of companies as regards micro-entities, (2012) *Official Journal of the EU* p L81/3.

27 Ibid.

28 Directive 2012/6/EU of the European Parliament and of the Council of 14 March 2012 amending Council Directive 78/660/EEC on the annual accounts of certain types of companies as regards micro-entities, (2012) *Official Journal of the EU* p L81/3.

This development echoes the current regulations and legislation applicable to small UK companies which have significantly reduced legal corporate reporting requirements. As such, it is uncommon for innovating SMEs in the UK and EU to report on patent information at all, not even in notes to the accounts.

5.2.5 The UK Directors' Report

The law deems the directors' duty to prepare the Directors' Report so important that the failure to do so is a criminal offence.[29] Corporate disclosure is a tool used to drive behaviours by company directors that are considered desirable. The board of directors, or individual directors, needs to make sure that the corporate management of the company's patent portfolio complies with CA 2006. Directors cannot ignore their duty to oversee these activities, even if the balance sheet obscures patent assets and other intangibles. Thus narrative reporting (e.g. in the Strategic Report) complements account reporting, setting out the directors' view of the future prospects and risks they must minimise. The "business judgment rule" [30] holds that business decisions are best left to the board of directors and the courts are reluctant to second-guess business decisions as they are not business people. While the "business judgment rule" is a relevant consideration, such business judgment must result from the directors being properly informed. As long as they do this they will not become liable merely because a decision turns out to have been a bad one. However, this section needs to be read in conjunction with section 174 CA 2006 which imposes a duty to exercise reasonable care, skill and diligence.[31] The paramount consideration is that the board ensures that it is appropriately informed and this requires it to be provided with accurate, relevant and timely information.[32] In relation to the company's IP assets, appropriate information should be disclosed in the Directors' Report and Strategic Review as legally required. Shareholders are in a vulnerable position and justifiably vest confidence, good faith, reliance and trust in the directors whose aid, advice or protection is sought to safeguard their investment.[33] As we saw in Chapter 4, each individual director on the board owes statutory duties to the company and must act in good faith to oversee the company's assets, including any IP and/or patent portfolio.[34] These provisions guide directors' management activities and determine

29 Sections 232–235 CA 2006.

30 As Lord Eldon stated in *Carlen v Drury* (1812) 1 Ves & B 149, 'The Court is not to be required on every occasion to take the management of every playhouse and brewhouse in the Kingdom'.

31 Keay, A. and Kosmin, L. *Directors' Duties* (2014) Second edition. Jordan Publishing, Bristol.

32 Marenberg, B. 'What Corporate Directors Need to Know About Intellectual Property' (9 March 2010) *Life Science Leader Magazine*.

33 *Hospital Products Ltd v US Surgical Corporation* (1984) 156 CLR 41, 68.

34 Sections 170(1) and 172 CA 2006. The directors do not owe duties to individual shareholders or to other stakeholders in the company: *Percival v Wright* [1902] 2 Ch 421.

whether they have acted properly.[35] However, from a corporate governance standpoint there are weaknesses in corporate reporting of IP assets that need to be addressed. Further, French legal scholar, Professor Nicolas Binctin is concerned about the anomaly of key patents treated as off-balance sheet assets that later may have to be disclosed in an annual report when they expire due to the detrimental impact on profitability. He also has concerns about corporate IP asset information disclosure in terms of the inadequacy of the annual reporting cycle, depreciation of IP assets (which conversely often increase in value over time) and the difficulty in revaluing IP assets under the accounting standards.[36] Failure to provide vital corporate IP asset and strategy disclosure may, it could be argued in some cases, even give third parties a misleading view (as opposed to a "true and fair") view of the reporting entity. The Enlightened Shareholder Value (ESV) concept requires directors to be more inclusive in their decision making, taking into account the relationships which the company has with stakeholders, such as financiers and lenders, in seeking to benefit the shareholders.[37] The independent auditors of the company have a duty to ensure that the narrative presented in the Directors' Report aligns with the financial accounts. Next, we consider why voluntarily reporting on patent information would be a positive step for innovating SMEs, even though they are not legally obliged to do so.

5.2.6 UK public companies: IP disclosure via the Strategic Report

The CA 2006 sets out different levels of reporting depending on the type of company. Although the level of corporate IP disclosure in the UK plc is higher than in SMEs, it is still weak. Section 414A requires all companies that are not small[38] to prepare a Strategic Report. For a financial year in which the company is a parent company, and the directors of the company prepare group accounts, the Strategic Report must be a group Strategic Report relating to the entities included in the consolidation.[39] The extent of disclosure required by a company will vary according to the type and size of company. However, the FRC's guidance does not differentiate on this basis. Material information that is necessary for an understanding of the development, performance, position or future prospects of the entity[40] should be disclosed in the Strategic Report, irrespective of the existence

35 Keay A. and Kosmin, L. *Directors' Duties* (2014) Second edition,Jordan Publishing, Bristol. Directors' duties may not be limited, waived or contracted out of, but companies may buy insurance to cover directors for costs in the event of breach.

36 Binctin, N. *Stratégie d entreprise et propriété intellectuelle* (2015) LGDJ, France.

37 McLaughlin, S. *Unlocking Company Law* (2015) Third edition, Routledge p 320.

38 Section 414B CA 2006.

39 Section 414A(3) CA 2006.

40 The FRC guidance uses the broader description "development, performance, position or future prospects of the entity" rather than the description "development, performance or position of the company's business" contained in the Act, unless the latter is more appropriate in a specific context.

or otherwise of an explicit statutory disclosure requirement. This is a mandatory requirement. With respect to intellectual capital (which comprises intangible IP assets) the FRC states the following:

> *Off-balance sheet resources*
> Most companies discuss their employees; given this is a now a requirement "to the extent necessary" this is not surprising. However, only 36% go beyond this to discuss other intangible assets such as brands, intellectual capital and natural resources. The off-balance sheet assets are often some of the most important to a company's future success; a comprehensive discussion of "performance and position" should include this aspect as well as the resources on the balance sheet.[41]

The FRC's guidance implicitly refers to IP assets. The Strategic Report is an integral part of the annual report therefore in relation to the directors' stewardship of the company's IP assets, disclosure made within the company law framework substantially increases the legitimacy and authority of the IP asset information disclosed. Further, filing a Strategic Report with Companies House will also assist directors to demonstrate how they have met their duty to promote the success of the company under section 172 CA 2006.

The Companies Act 2006 (Strategic Report and Directors' Report) Regulation 2013 requires quoted companies to make new disclosures about human rights, gender diversity and greenhouse gas emissions in their Strategic Report. This took effect for financial years ending on or after 30 September 2013. To date, IP information disclosure has not been specifically considered as a special topic for mandatory disclosure although in light of the issues raised in this book the author is of the view that there is a good case that it ought to be.

In addition to the Strategic Report, companies listed on the London Stock Exchange (LSE) for example must comply with even more onerous mandatory disclosure as they subscribe to the Disclosure and Transparency Rules (DTR).[42]

41 *Rising to the Challenge: A Review of Narrative Reporting by UK listed companies* (2009) Financial Reporting Council.

42 The UK Corporate Governance Code (September 2014) and the UK Stewardship Code (September 2012) also apply. The latter is directed in the first instance to institutional investors, by which is meant asset owners and asset managers with equity holdings in UK listed companies. It aims to enhance the quality of engagement between investors and companies to help improve long-term risk-adjusted returns to shareholders. The revised Stewardship Code was last published in September 2012 and will be next revised in 2018. The FRC sees the UK Stewardship Code as complementary to the UK Corporate Governance Code for listed companies. It should also be applied on a "comply or explain" basis. The Code sets out a number of areas of good practice to which the FRC believes institutional investors should aspire. UK Stewardship Code (September 2012) Financial Reporting Council at www.frc.org.uk/getattachment/d67933f9-ca38-4233-b603-3d24b2f62c5f/UK-Stewardship-Code-(September-2012).pdf. UK Corporate Governance Code (September 2014) at

The DTR are designed to promote prompt and fair disclosure of relevant information to the public investor market. According to the LSE, "[t]his helps to encourage investor confidence and maintain Europe's deepest pool of capital". In this respect, prospective investors in the company should have public information on the company's intangible IP assets which allow them to come to their own valuation judgments. Relevant information is "price-sensitive" information that would be likely to have a significant effect on the share price in the short term. While compliance with DTR is mandatory for listed companies, it is a matter for a company's board of directors to exercise its collective judgement to determine when to disclose significant inside IP asset information, typically applying the "reasonable investor test". The DTR are aimed at preventing market abuse, thus disclosure of appropriate IP asset information to the market could even be required daily if necessary to comply. It seems that while the traditional accounting system may not be coping with fluctuations in value inherent in intangible IP assets, the DTR mandate that listed companies must cope with disclosing "price sensitive information" in narrative form or risk their shares being suspended from trading. Even if the price sensitive information relates to corporate IP, then they must "comply or explain".[43] Do existing UK corporate disclosure laws reach far enough to include intangible IP assets where IP assets are material to the company's financial performance and position?

The following example involves an American listed company and is of interest because the high value corporate acquisition transaction was widely reported internationally. It serves to highlight the confusion surrounding corporate reporting and IP value (rather than for comparative law analysis purposes).

Motorola, Inc. was a multinational telecommunications company based in the United States. On 4 January 2011, after having lost $4.3 billion US from 2007 to 2009, the company was divided into two independent public companies, Motorola Mobility and Motorola Solutions.[44] On 22 May 2012 Google, Inc. announced that it would acquire Motorola Mobility's smartphone business and related IP assets for $12.4 billion US.[45] On 29 January 2014 Google announced that, pending closure of the deal, it would sell Motorola Mobility to Chinese technology company Lenovo for $2.91 billion US (subject to certain adjustments). Google retained ownership of the vast majority of the Motorola Mobility patent portfolio, including current patent applications and invention disclosures. Lenovo agreed to license the patent portfolio and other IP assets, further it acquired 2,000

www.frc.org.uk/directors/corporate-governance-and-stewardship/uk-corporate-governance-code/history-of-the-uk-corporate-governance-code.

43 Denoncourt, J. *Financial Reporting for Intangibles: Why Intangibles Remain Invisible* (17August 2014) at http://ipfinance.blogspot.co.uk/2014/08/financial-reporting-for-intangibles-why.html.

44 Ante, Spencer E. 'Motorola is split into two' (5 January 2011) *The Wall Street Journal*.

45 'We've acquired Motorola Mobility' *Google Official Blog* at https://googleblog.blogspot.co.uk/2012/05/weve-acquired-motorola-mobility.html.

patents outright as well as the Motorola Mobility brand and trade mark portfolio.[46] The $2.91 billion US was less than a quarter the amount Google, Inc. originally paid in 2012. The figure raised several important questions for shareholders. How did the directors arrive at $2.91 billion US? What strategic business considerations were involved? Was the transaction in the best interest of the company? According to US Generally Accepted Accounting Principles (GAAP), internally generated intangible IP assets are not reported as assets on the balance sheet of the company that created them (revisit our discussion in Chapter 4). Consequently, valuing the IP assets and evaluating the acquisition price was hampered by the lack of publicly disclosed corporate narrative IP information to complement the off-balance sheet figure. As a result, shareholders found it difficult to assess the impact on their shareholding of the licensing and sale of the former Motorola Mobility IP assets to Lenovo.[47]

This mini-case study clarifies why the IP information gap is problematic from a corporate governance point of view – the shareholders' need for corporate IP asset information was not being met. It demonstrates the need to apply corporate governance principles to corporate IP assets and shows why enhanced narrative IP asset disclosure in jurisdictions with IP-rich publicly listed companies is needed. Next we examine the issue of director accountability.

5.2.7 Directors' accountability for IP information disclosures

As a part of the effort to strengthen the markets generally and ward off a recurrence of problems that led to the global financial crisis in 2008, corporate accountability and the shareholder powers that ensure it (e.g. director elections) need a new emphasis, bringing accountability and transparency to the disclosure of corporate IP asset information. While directors have a perceived fear of losing competitiveness, the IP information gap is festering and needs attention from the corporate regulators. The Motorola acquisition mini-case study echoes the ACCA's finding as it demonstrates the tension between the value of corporate intangible IP assets and the inadequate way companies report such assets in their mandatory traditional financial statements. As a minimum, shareholders should have information about the directors' stewardship and management of the company's valuable intangibles and IP assets to allow them to make informed decisions regarding their investment. Corporate regulators need to acknowledge and promote the importance of high-quality corporate IP asset disclosure to empower shareholders, investors and other stakeholders. Strengthening the ability of shareholders to identify issues and for example, to ask questions at annual general meetings with a view to holding

46 'Lenovo to Acquire Motorola Mobility from Google' (29 January 2014) Google Investor Relations Press Announcement at https://investor.google.com/releases/2014/0129.html.

47 Kasznik, E. 'Financial reporting for intangibles: the Case of the Invisible Assets' at http://ipfinance.blogspot.co.uk/2014/08/financial-reporting-for-intangibles.html.

boards of directors accountable, should further empower shareholders and lift the awareness of how corporate IP assets and financing patterns shape business strategy. Economic theory suggests that increased transparency should promote greater trust in the intangible economy.

However, a key reason why directors are reluctant to disclose additional qualitative narrative information regarding corporate IP assets is that they will then be held accountable for that information. There are severe legal consequences for any failure to report "fairly" so as not to mislead under the CA 2006. On the other hand, remaining silent on the issue of corporate IP assets is also problematic as directors are also liable for material omissions. A director is liable to compensate the company for any loss it suffers as a result of the omission of anything legislatively required to be disclosed.[48] Consequently, directors have difficult decisions to make regarding the scope of the company's IP asset disclosure. As a starting point, one needs to ensure that the narrative disclosure aligns with the numeric intangible figure in the financial statements in order to make the value of the IP assets to the business more transparent. If the intangibles figure on the balance sheet has increased or decreased significantly from the previous year or reporting period, this is material information and the company needs to explain why. Basically, directors always need to "explain the money".[49] Both the directors and the independent auditors should consider whether the figures for intangibles in the accounts and the corporate narrative in the Strategic Report are in alignment.

5.2.8 The cost of compiling and disclosing corporate IP asset information

Directors will also be concerned about the cost to gather, verify and substantiate the IP information, as well as specialist advisor fees. The costs tend to grow with increased disclosure. Typically, this is a greater problem for smaller companies with fewer resources than for large listed companies. However, small innovative companies have a greater incentive to reduce uncertainty through disclosure as demonstrated by the information asymmetry caused by IAS 38 and IP assets being off-balance sheet and thus invisible to the financial world.[50] In modern corporate markets, greater transparency and non-financial indicator disclosure are central to increasing shareholder value.

48 Section 463(2) Companies Act 2006

49 Denoncourt, J. *Financial Reporting for Intangibles: Why Intangibles Remain Invisible* (17August 2014) at http://ipfinance.blogspot.co.uk/2014/08/financial-reporting-for-intangibles-why.html.

50 This implication has been supported in a study by Ahmed, K. and Courtis, J.K., 'Associations between Corporate Characteristics and Disclosure Levels in Annual Reports: A Meta-Analysis' (March 1999) 31(1) *The British Accounting Review* 35–61.

5.2.9 Corporate disclosure mini-case study to illustrate the IP information gap in an annual report: Royal Philips (Netherlands)

The following example illustrates a global company's approach to the stewardship and strategic management of its valuable IP assets. Frans van Houten, CEO of Philips, one of Europe's biggest and most successful global technology companies, gave the keynote speech at the IP Business Conference in Amsterdam in June 2014, explaining how the company's IP assets create shareholder value:

> So today I want to talk about the close relationship at Philips between our businesses and Philips Intellectual Property & Standards, or IP&S for short. As they say, a business strategy without an IP strategy is no strategy. This is certainly true for Philips, a company which has innovation and R&D written into its DNA. That's why IP&S is involved in our entire process of value creation . . . Gerard Philips filed our company's first patent in 1905, on an invention to extend the lifetime of the incandescent light bulb. Ever since, IP has been intimately linked to our innovation . . . Our total portfolio now consists of 64,000 patents, 46,000 trade marks, 93,000 design rights and 4,700 domain names . . . So it's clear that we have got some high-quality IP. But why have we got it, how did we get it and what do we do with it? That depends on our business strategy and especially on our strategy for innovation and R&D. For each business, it is all about the alignment of business strategy, R&D strategy and IP strategy.[51]

This type of narrative qualitative IP information absolutely complements the quantitative financial figure assigned to intangible assets on the company's group accounts. However the 2013 Royal Philips' annual report governed by the law of the Netherlands does not set out intangibles or IP assets as a separate item in the table of contents. Group Financial Statement note 12 to the accounts deals with intangible assets excluding goodwill on page 160 and Company financial statement Note A Intangible assets on page 193.[52] Apart from the notes to the accounts, there is a short narrative report on page 90 under the heading "Philips IP & Standards" which states:

> Philips IP&S proactively pursues the creation of new intellectual property in close co-operation with Philips' operating businesses and Philips Group Innovation.
>
> IP&S is a leading industrial IP organization providing world-class IP solutions to Philips' businesses to support their growth, competitiveness and profitability.

51 Speech by Frans van Houten at IP Business Conference, 23 June 2014 at www.newscenter.philips.com/main/standard/news/speeches/20140624-speech-by-frans-van-houten-at-ip-business-conference.wpd

52 Royal Philips Annual Report 2013 at www.philips.com/philips/shared/assets/Investor_relations/pdf/PhilipsFullAnnualReport2013_English.pdf.

> Philips' IP portfolio currently consists of approximately 13,200 patent families, 2,680 trade mark families, 3,930 design families, and 2,150 domain name families.
>
> Philips filed approximately 1,550 patent applications in 2013, with a strong focus on the growth areas in health and well-being.
>
> IP&S participates in the setting of standards to create new business opportunities for the Healthcare, Consumer Lifestyle and Lighting sectors. A substantial portion of revenue and costs is allocated to the operating sectors. Philips believes its business as a whole is not materially dependent on any particular patent or license, or any particular group of patents and licenses.[53]

As a result of the last sentence quoted above, arguably a shareholder has no express IP asset information on which to assess Royal Philips' IP asset value story, strategy, management or stewardship of those assets in the medium to long term. Whilst it may be true and fair for Philips to say that its business as a whole is not materially dependent on any particular IP asset or licence or groups thereof, in the author's opinion the magnitude of the substantial value residing in the company's IP portfolio merits additional disclosure for corporate governance stewardship purposes. Further, Philips' claim that it is not materially dependent on any particular IP or licence would be much more difficult for less substantial businesses or for companies in other sectors such as pharmaceuticals (whose business model is more reliant on valid patent protection) to sustain. No IP asset risk or enforcement or infringement litigation is reported. Even so, the Royal Philips demonstrates how narrative disclosure concerning IP assets, to complement the financial statements, is largely absent in corporate reports. Royal Philips' largest shareholders are sophisticated enough and have the resources to undertake registered patent, trade mark and design searches and monitor stock exchange announcements to arrive at a reasonable understanding of the strategic value of Philips' IP assets. But many other smaller shareholders are not so able. On the other hand, the author is not suggesting a company report on every single patent, trade mark or design family or licence. Clearly this would be excessive. However, a more appropriate level of information regarding Royal Philips' IP management and strategy could be disclosed given that what is reported to shareholders is less than that provided by the CEO in his speech to the IP Business Congress 2014. In the author's opinion, a level of disclosure in line with the extent of information disclosed in relation to Philips' employees, for example, would be a minimum level to aim for.

Nevertheless, credit where credit is due, Philips has a dedicated Executive Vice President & Chief Strategy and Innovation Officer on its board of directors, whose corporate responsibilities include strategy, innovation, design and sustainability.

53 Ibid.

> The head of IP&S, Brian Hinman . . . at least once a quarter, talks to the company's Board. Brian reports to Jim Andre, who is my Chief Strategy and Innovation Office in our Executive Committee. He's not reporting to the Chief Legal Officer or General Counsel, no, I have my CIPO[54] report directly to my head of Strategy and Innovation, at the very heart of our company's business . . . Philips IP&S has developed great valuation models, so we can put a financial value on all those benefits of IP that are not directly monetary. IP&S has five main remits: IP Creation, IP Value Capturing, IP Value Contribution, IP Counselling and representing Philips in IP matters in the public domain, including work on technical and public standards.[55]

This is positive in terms of demonstrating effective overall IP asset management and stewardship. The Royal Philips example has simply been used to illustrate the point regarding the need to further enhance IP asset, strategy and risk information disclosed generally from the point of view of investor protection and corporate governance, rather than a strict comparative law approach. It likely highlights the tip of the iceberg. In the author's opinion, the type of IP information expressed by Philips' CEO to the IP Business Conference would be a material disclosure to shareholders in a publicly listed UK Strategic Report. A UK public company, whose business model is based on exploiting IP assets (e.g. pharmaceutical products protected by patents and trade marks) should provide narrative information about its IP portfolio in its Strategic Report. If this type of information is lacking, then it could well be argued that the company should not be soliciting investment from the public on investor protection grounds. Rather, it might consider changing its corporate status and revert to a private company status with reduced corporate reporting obligations.

5.3 Materiality and public companies' IP disclosures

When applying the UK disclosure requirements, both company law and accounting standards include concepts of materiality. Corporate narrative reporting takes the same approach to materiality as set out in the accounting standards or regulation and only disclosures that are material or relevant should be made. In terms of the Strategic Report, the CA 2006 uses language such as "to the extent necessary", "key" (e.g. key performance indicators) and "principal" (e.g. principal risks and uncertainties), so only information that is material to shareholders should be included in the Strategic Report. The concept of materiality set out in ISA (UK and Ireland) 320, which is based on the accounting standards, guides the auditor's view of the application of materiality to disclosures in the company's financial statements. Arriving at a judgement as to what information is material is largely

54 Chief Intellectual Property Officer.
55 Deloitte at www.iasplus.com/en/standards/ias/ias38.

qualitative so it is helpful to indicate the purpose of the disclosure. For example, a business model disclosure will focus on how the company captures and creates value, while a strategy disclosure will help to show the board's plans for developing the business and benefiting from its existing corporate assets now and in the future. A solid articulation of the business model and principal risks gives valuable insights such as how the company generates cash, how it operates more broadly and the prevailing corporate culture.

In fairness to company directors, more guidance is needed to identify the types of disclosures that need to be made to ensure transparency of intangibles and IP assets. What is a material disclosure in an IP business context? How, what, when, where and how much should a particular company disclose with respect to intangible assets? In other words, corporate governance disclosure theory and principles need to be applied to a new class of assets, namely, IP assets and strategy. Presently, there is minimal if any bespoke guidance on corporate intangibles' reporting published by the regulators, the professional or academic communities. So, despite the existence in the UK and elsewhere of mandatory legal disclosure requirements relevant to corporate intangible IP assets, the lack of guidance and enforcement by the regulators perpetuate the gap in publicly available information. A broad understanding of an appropriate level of intangible asset reporting and disclosure has not yet emerged.[56] Factors such as materiality of IP assets to the success of the company, industry disclosure norms, company size, managerial ownership, company age and business and technology life cycle will impact on the extent of the need for corporate IP asset disclosure. For example, company age has often been seen as a proxy for risk in the sense that established companies are less risky. Kim and Ritter (1999) provide evidence that non-financial information is of greater importance in the valuation of younger companies because forecast earnings work better for assessing younger companies than historical earnings do.[57]

The status quo is that non-financial narrative qualitative and strategic IP information has a lower priority than traditional quantitative financial information. However, with respect to IP assets and the modern creative and information economy, this may be shifting as shareholders and others consider that the existing degree of corporate disclosure of IP assets, strategy, management, stewardship and risk factors is insufficient. The ability to evaluate the quality of intangible IP asset disclosures and then assess whether a company has fallen below the standard, in breach of its disclosure obligations and/or directors' duties, is highly specialised and a murky area even for the regulators.[58] From the perspective of corporate

56 Denoncourt, J. *Financial Reporting for Intangibles: Why Intangibles Remain Invisible* (17August 2014) at http://ipfinance.blogspot.co.uk/2014/08/financial-reporting-for-intangibles-why.html.

57 Beatty, R. et al 'IPO Pricing with Accounting and Comparable Firm Information' (2000) Working paper, Southern Methodist University.

58 Denoncourt, J. *Financial Reporting for Intangibles: Wwhy Intangibles Remain Invisible* (17August 2014) at http://ipfinance.blogspot.co.uk/2014/08/financial-reporting-for-intangibles-why.html

governance it is an issue that merits additional attention. Even so, the UK has some of the highest standards of corporate governance in the world, which makes the jurisdiction attractive to new investment – but there is room for improvement. Companies regularly report on non-financial indicators such as employees, health and safety, environmental impact and corporate social responsibility; it is time to ensure they report on their IP not only to protect shareholders, but to promote the success of the company as well.

The two mini-case studies have enabled us to reflect on what appears to be an IP information gap evident in even highly successful publicly listed companies. There is no suggestion of fraud or furnishing misleading information. Yet, consider other IP-rich companies that prove to be less successful or even fail. The lack of corporate IP asset transparency would be viewed more severely. In the 18th century there were no safeguards against fraud or furnishing misleading information. The price of the shares of the infamous South Sea company bore no relation to the actual value of the company – it collapsed, not in isolation, and created a domino effect which led to a deep suspicion of joint stock companies for the rest of the 18th century.[59] This led the UK Parliament to promptly pass the Bubble Act 1720 prohibiting joint stock companies. This piece of legislation is thought to have forged the beginning of the strong connection between lawyers and business people. Business people wanted to know what the Bubble Act meant in the context of their business ventures. In order to finance the business, a company creates and issues shares (an intangible just like the company that issues it). The creation and issue of shares to raise money from other people is a major concern of company and securities law. The distinction between loan capital (as discussed in Chapter 3) and share capital is the distinction between borrowing and selling. The power to raise money by issuing shares is in itself an incredible privilege society grants to business people. A stock exchange offers two major facilities. It puts buyers and sellers in contact with each other and it provides access to the capital resources of the public at large when companies seek to raise money by making new share issues. If a person is buying a share in a company, modern company law provides a framework to ensure that potential buyers are fully informed about the issuing company and the legal rights attached to shares. The information provided to buyers/investors cannot be relied on forever, after a certain period investors may no longer rely on it. Arguably, the two most influential stock exchanges are London Stock Exchange (LSE) and New York Exchange, known as Wall Street. The scale of modern securities markets and internationalization mean that a lack a transparency of corporate value would have a far greater impact than the South Sea Bubble, the Great Crash of 1929 or the Dot-com bubble of 2000. Over the centuries the business of regulating the trading of shares on offer to the public has been given effect through mandatory legislation which enshrines

59 Howard, C. *Companies, What They Are and How They Work* (1989) Oxford University Press p 5.

that material disclosures be made to the market. However, while the integrity of the regulated stock markets is a prime global concern, there are also many benefits to be had from increased corporate disclosure of IP assets by non-listed companies, as discussed below.

5.4 The benefits of communication and increased corporate IP asset disclosure

In 1750 the Italian economist Ferdinando Galiani stated that "value is a relation between persons". A critical source of value for IP-rich firms is the ability to communicate how its IP contributes value, contributes to corporate financial performance, creates successful business relationships and supports medium and long term goals of the firm. IP assets are complex and heavily dependent on individuals, communities and organisations who do not behave rationally. No one should take successfully commercialising innovation for granted as complex dynamics are a work. IP-rich firms are all players in the global attraction game, and each firm seeks to attract high-calibre employees, collaborative partners as well as investors and financiers. Value does not necessarily lie where it is assumed to lie as a number in a corporate balance sheet. Firms need to be able to demonstrate their intangible qualities and value to shareholders and other stakeholders in order to build successful commercial relationships. To be taken seriously by potential investors, shareholders and financial institutions an IP-rich firm needs to create a compelling explanation of how its IP creates value and gives it competitive monopoly advantages in the marketplace. The firm will reap the benefits later when, for example, attracting finance and new shareholders. A talent for communicating with its shareholders and stakeholders can be a "trump card". Firms that accurately communicate the value of their corporate IP assets in a timely manner will have a distinct competitive advantage. On the other hand, a reluctance to disclose timely, relevant and useful information about corporate IP assets, preferring to keep them invisible and less vulnerable to scrutiny, is in the author's opinion, a poor strategy. An "angel investor" may only review the company's documentation for a matter of minutes before moving on to the next one. Financiers may make lending decisions based on very limited contact with the company – so transparency about how its IP creates value will be critical to communicating how the business will develop revenue streams and future cash flow.

An IP-rich firm needs to communicate its future goals accurately and take steps to execute the business plan. This will build the relationship and trust. As part of the business life cycle, the firm is continually seeking to attract core employees, customers, strategic partners, investors and lenders. Growing innovation firms need to find the right people, and they need to keep them. Communication barriers make the valuation of corporate IP assets more complicated than necessary. One approach that adds to trust is to increase the transparency and visibility of intangibles. Firms should be proactive in communicating their qualitative and strategic worth, in addition to the quantum recorded in the traditional balance sheet. As we know from our analysis in earlier chapters, intangible IP assets are usually recorded off-balance sheet in traditional financial accounts so their value to those outside the firm is obscured and needs to be revealed. Sustainable value for an IP-rich firm rests on its ability to communicate the firm's brand and how its IP creates value, which will foster a valuable network of relationships, giving rise to future opportunities. What is valuable changes over time – some of the SMEs of today will become the plcs of tomorrow. According to Dr Chris Donegan, an intangible asset specialist:

> Investors can tell a lot about a company from how it files and manages its patent portfolio. Patent demographics provide investors with an instant snapshot of a company's innovative trajectory. Overlaying this picture against that of a competitor, firms can provide a unique view of corporate competitiveness that, when combined with industry and financial analysis, is a lot more revealing than your usual Wall Street reporting. Unhappily, the conversation around IP value remains heavily siloed. Legal, tax and R&D "own" the conversation on patents, marketing own brands and trade marks, human resources own culture. The greatest value for IP professionals working with the investment community therefore is to tie these elements of organisational intellectual property together with traditional metrics of value into a single analytical framework. When that is done routinely, the contribution of intellectual property will become evident in the C-suite and IP professionals will be elevated to board level. Until then, IP will remain the worst-communicated secret in corporate value creation.[60]

Prudent voluntary corporate disclosure by innovating firms is recommended to rectify the invisibility of intangible assets on a company's balance sheet. This would help a firm overcome the deficiencies that result from applying IAS 38 to internally generated patent assets. In 2002 a Canadian study analysed the content of the annual reports of 10,000 Canadian companies searching for a list of intellectual capital (IC)-related terms and reported that only a very small number of IC disclosures actually took place.[61] As a common law country, the Canadian corporate reporting regime is generally similar to that required in the UK. In both Canada and the UK, the legal corporate reporting requirements drive the level of information that is available to the public (including lenders). Little information related to IP, patents or other IC is publicly available via corporate reporting in either jurisdiction in the SME field.

60 Donegan, C. 'Intellectual property: the worst-communicated secret in value creation' (5 August 2015) Fraserburgh, UK available at www.lexology.com/library/detail.aspx?g=2a49ce37-f1e0-46b6-acc4-ea1d874d7e45.

61 Bontis, N. 'Intellectual Capital Disclosure in Canadian Corporations' (2003) 7(1/2) *Journal of Human Resource Costing and Accounting* 9–20.

In relation to debt finance, there is also evidence that increased disclosure is positively correlated with lower effective interest costs.[62] Companies with additional informative disclosure policies have more accurate earnings forecasts, reduced estimated risks and reduced information asymmetry. The reduced risk that results from the greater disclosure of information leads to lower borrowing costs. Equally, lower borrowing costs provide organisations with an incentive to disclose greater amounts of information.[63] This outcome is directly relevant to IP-backed finance. In truth, lenders can never know precisely how much value will be realised at a future point in time for any given asset, however they need to develop the skills to become better at predicting the future value of a borrowers' IP assets in the age of the knowledge economy. Certainly, there is a cost involved in compiling the IP information. However, once the required IP information and reporting format is standardised, the cost of collecting and reporting is likely to be outweighed by the increased access to debt finance.

Company annual reports are a key communication tool to legitimise corporate activity.[64] Accuracy is positively associated with market value (because it reduces uncertainty) and improved forecasts of future value.[65] Borrower-provided disclosure via the legally mandated company annual return (which must be signed off by the directors as giving a "true and fair view") is information that is already required by the lender at no cost to it. Lenders would incur costs if they had to actively acquire the information independently from other sources. Such due diligence costs will be passed on to the borrower in any event by way of arrangement fees, disbursement and/or the interest rate applied to the loan. Voluntary disclosure would also help directors document how they have carried out their duty to promote the success of the company, a legal requirement for which there is minimal guidance from the case law. The ICS, an alternative corporate disclosure format, will be discussed in the next chapter.

5.5 The importance of non-financial corporate IP information

This chapter has illustrated the conceptual differences between accounting presentation and corporate disclosure law. We discussed the underlying theory for the existence of corporate reporting regimes and why reporting on corporate IP assets should be reflective of the value they provide to the business in the medium to long term.[66] It is crucial to make IP information as easy as possible for shareholders

62 Lang, M. and Lundholm, R. 'Corporate Disclosure Policy and Analyst Behaviour' (October 1996) 71(4) *The Accounting Review* 467–492.

63 Ibid.

64 Guthrie, J. and Petty. R. 'Intellectual Capital Literature Review: Measurement, Reporting and Management' (2000) 1(2) *Journal of Intellectual Capital* 155.

65 Ibid.

66 International Integrated Reporting *Towards Integrated Reporting: Communicating Value in the 21st Century* (2011) Discussion Paper at http://theiirc.org/wp-content/uploads/2011/09/IR-Discussion-Paper-2011_spreads.pdf

to understand so that the "invisible" value of IP assets can be "seen" to inform decision making. Improving the quality of non-financial corporate IP information available to shareholders and external stakeholders is one way to assist companies to overcome the distortion of the IAS 38 related financial calculations concerning the fiscal value of their IP assets. The information in the Strategic Report and the annual report will also assist shareholders to determine whether directors have ensured a proper return on the corporate IP assets. Corporate reporting could be significantly improved by recognising that IP assets can be simultaneously quantified (using the market approach where historical transactions exist), quality assessed, compared and evaluated with additional disclosure of relevant, timely and accurate qualitative narrative information. However, directors need more detailed guidance on how to present the information (e.g. models) as well as the scope and extent of disclosure required to meet minimum corporate disclosure obligations. Chapter 6 addresses this question at three levels, namely the form, style and substance of legal rules pertaining to corporate disclosure of intangibles and IP rights. This entails an evaluation of the nature and content of the respective corporate disclosure rules in four jurisdictions: Denmark, Germany, the US and Japan, all of which have explicit rules pertaining to corporate intangibles and IP asset disclosure. This approach will enable us to identify the similarities and differences, with the aim of discussing normative policy recommendations.

6 International initiatives in corporate narrative IP asset disclosure

Read a useful prospectus lately? How about an informative annual report? How come few of these traditional reports offer a clue about which emerging young company is about to take over the world, about which established blue-chip company is about to fall into a competitive black hole?[1]

Professor Leif Edvinnson, the world's first adjunct
Professor of IC at Lund University, Sweden

One of the aims of this book is to identify and understand possible differences and similarities between legal systems in relation to achieving greater transparency of corporate IP asset and strategy. This chapter presents a comparative functional analysis of the status of narrative corporate IP asset disclosure in four legal systems, all advanced economies, describing the conceptual frameworks and evaluating relevant principles. With respect to countries in the European Union, the Intellectual Capital Statement (ICS) approach in Denmark and Germany is examined. The theory of IC (Intellectual Capital) reporting is that financial information informs as to past performance but indicates little about the firm's future potential. The future potential of an enterprise lies not within its financial capital, but in its IC. Creating transparency about the firm's IC will enable it to manage its intangible resources (such as IP assets) better, imparting greater certainty to shareholders, investors and other stakeholders about its future earnings potential. In addition, the legal systems of two of the world's largest economies, the US and Japan, are included for the purposes of wider comparison of the national approach to corporate IP information disclosure given their status as top patent filers in the world.[2] On the basis of this scrutiny, we observe that although the legal systems fundamentally differ, the rationale for these corporate

1 Edvinsson, L. am]nd Malone, M. *Intellectual Capital Realizing Your Company's True Value by Finding Its Hidden Brainpower* (1997) Harper Collins Publishers, USA p 1.

2 *World Intellectual Property Indicators 2016* Economics and Statistics Series, World Intellectual Property Organization, p 7 available at www.wipo.int/edocs/pubdocs/en/wipo_pub_941_2016.pdf.

governance rules share a common foundation of transparency and shareholder protection. In the 21st century, legal differences, in particular the distinction between civil law and common law countries, have become less marked.[3] This chapter contributes to the literature by identifying a type of embryonic normative functional convergence. "Functional" in this context means that a comparable result is produced, with more corporate IP asset and strategy information being disclosed, but along different paths. Functional convergence is likelier at this stage in the development of corporate IP information and strategy disclosure than formal convergence.[4] In each of the legal systems examined, various mechanisms to enhance the corporate IP reporting culture interpenetrate. In terms of comparative law methodology, while "convergence" is a controversial topic, in the author's view the conclusions reached here do not depend on whether the jurisdiction has a common law or civil law tradition. Rather, the national mentality toward IP rights, the level of development of a national IP law framework (as evidenced by the country's ranking on the Intellectual Property Rights Index 2016[5]), reliance on IP rights within firms and the emergence of "thought-leaders" to inform responses to the gaps in traditional accounting transparency are key. Although no "best practice" has emerged, all jurisdictions studied are seeking a higher level of transparency of corporate IP assets and strategy to inform decision making and protect shareholders. As a result of intensified international competition, law-makers in other countries may be keen to improve the potential of their companies by learning how enhance shareholder value through corporate reporting and disclosure of IP value creation. Concepts from Denmark, Germany, Japan and the US could be adopted.

In section 6.1 we review the impact of the ICS, a corporate disclosure format. In section 6.2 we study international policy initiatives regarding corporate reporting of IC, intangibles and IP in Denmark, Germany, Japan and the US.

6.1 The Intellectual Capital Statement (ICS)

The theory underpinning IC asset reporting is that while accountants report numbers in the common language of monetary value, there is no logical reason why decision makers, directors or other stakeholders such as financial institutions and lenders should restrict themselves to such an information set. A modern format for the increased disclosure of intangible assets (including IP rights) originated in the 1990s led by a handful of Scandinavian companies including

3 Markesinis, B.G. (Ed.) *The Gradual Convergence: Foreign Ideas, Foreign Influences, and English Law on the Eve of the 21st Century* (1994) Clarenden Press, Oxford; Siems, M. 'Legal Origins: Reconciling Law and Finance and Comparative Law' (2007) 52 *McGill Law Journal* 55.

4 Gilson, R.J. 'Globalizing Corporate Governance: Convergence of Form or Function' (2001) 49 *American Journal of Corporate Law* 329, 337–345.

5 *Intellectual Property Rights Index 2016* TenthEdition, Property Rights Alliance at http://internationalpropertyrightsindex.org/blog.

Skandia, Carl-Bro and Celemi. Sveiby argued that these companies sharply illustrate the differences in managerial attitude between the industrial and post-industrial ages with respect to corporate reporting.[6] The ICS has now existed for over two decades, led by Denmark. It is a non-financial indicator type of narrative report focusing on intangibles and lends itself to disclosure of IP rights as corporate assets. It is an important corporate governance initiative to re-visit that has insights to offer the UK. This is because the way in which the intrinsic corporate value of a business is judged is now evolving beyond the traditional metrics such as: price to earnings (p/e) ratio, the share price divided by the earnings per share; dividend yield, the annual income distributed by a company expressed as a percentage of the share price; sales, margins, profitability and balance sheets. Companies, especially technology or digital companies, will have intrinsic value only if they produce genuine financial returns and deliver some form of utility to society, otherwise markets risk socio-economic phenomena echoing "tulip mania" in 17th century Holland, in which tulip prices deviated from their intrinsic value. Non-financial metrics are increasingly important because they can be better indicators of long term, sustainable financial performance. An analysis of the ICS theory and literature is set out below.

Professor Leif Edvinsson,[7] regarded as a pioneering contributor to the theory of IC, instigated the creation of the world's first public corporate IC Annual Report in 1994. In March 1997, he and co-author Michael S. Malone *published Intellectual Capital: Realizing your Company's True Value by Finding Its Hidden Brainpower.*[8] This work defined the meaning of IC, how it is classified and how it could be measured. They offer guidance (in Chapter 3 of the book) on how to build an IC report. Edvinsson was the first director of IC at Skandia, a Swedish financial services company and is a Professor (adjunct) of IC at Lund University, Sweden. The aim of his work is to integrate the role of knowledge and intangible assets into accounting procedures and financial practices. His research began with the following questions and answer:

> Read a useful prospectus lately? How about an informative annual report?
>
> How come few of these traditional reports offer a clue about which emerging young company is about to take over the world, about which established blue-chip company is about to fall into a competitive black hole?
>
> And even when these reports do manage to capture a glimmer of reality, how come those clues lie between the lines of the accompanying, barely

6 Sveiby K.E. *The New Organisational Wealth: Managing and Measuring Knowledge-Based Assets* (1997) Berrett-Koehler, San Fransisco.

7 Edvinsson received an MBA from the University of California, Berkeley, USA, and the qualification of '*civilekonom*' from Lund University, Sweden. He is the author of numerous articles on IC. In January 1998, Edvinsson received the prestigious Brain Trust "*Brain of the Year*" award, UK. He is the world's first Professor (adjunct) of IC at Lund University.

8 Edvinsson, L. and Malone, M. *Intellectual Capital: Realizing your Company's True Value by Finding Its Hidden Brainpower* (1997) Harper Business, USA.

> legible text[9] and not in bold type in the balance sheet? . . . The answer to that is in the traditional model of "accounting," which so beautifully described the operations of companies for half a millennium, is now failing to keep up with the revolution taking place in business.[10]

Edvinsson concluded that, "[i]t has become obvious that the real value of companies cannot be determined *only* by traditional accounting measures".[11] Gary Hamel, Professor at the London School of Business, argues further that "an asset is really only a perception of an opportunity about which a majority of people have agreed".[12] Keith Bradley of the Open Business School (UK) asked: "Do we have the tools to manage these hidden assets? The simple answer is 'no, we don't'".[13] Chapter 4 of this book has added to this thinking by examining the historical development of accounting practice to show why this discipline is ill-designed to deal with intangible IP rights, especially those that are internally developed by a firm. However, the ICS provides an accepted methodology for enhancing the narrative corporate disclosure of intangibles, supplementing the information available in the traditional financial accounts and to be further discussed as the chapter unfolds. From a critical standpoint however, the ICS literature provides very little specific guidance on the reporting of IP rights, a weakness upon which this book sheds light. In 2001, the first IC World Congress took place at McMaster University, Canada. Since then Austria[14] and Denmark have introduced regulatory reporting of IC. The Danish Financial Statements Act (DFSA)[15] requires reporting on IC resources and environmental aspects in the management report if it is material to providing a true and fair view of the company's financial position.[16] In particular, the DFSA 2001 states in Chapter 11, section 99(2) that the management's review "shall describe the enterprise's knowledge and know-how resources if they are of special importance to its future performance". Other countries, including Germany, Norway, Hong Kong, Japan[17] and Australia[18] also have voluntary reporting guidelines.

9 Edvinsson is referring to the footnotes to the accounts.
10 Edvinsson, L. and Malone, M. supra n [8] p 1.
11 Ibid p 3.
12 Ibid p 4, ensues from Edvinsson's interview with Hamel in July 1996.
13 Bradley, K. *Intellectual Capital and the New Wealth of Nations* (21 October 2006) Lecture given at the Royal Society of Arts, London p 6.
14 See The Austria University Act 2002.
15 Danish Act on Commercial Enterprises' Presentation of Financial Statements, etc. Danish Act no 448 of 7 June 2001. See http://csrgov.dk/legislation.
16 DFSA Chapter 3, section 11(1).
17 See 'Japanese Guidelines for Disclosure of Intellectual Assets Based Management', No English reference.
18 Johanson, U., Koga, C., Skoog, M. and Henningsson, J. 'The Japanese Government's Intellectual Capital Reporting Guideline: What are the Challenges for Firms and Capital Market Agents?' (2006) 17(4) *Journal of Intellectual Capital* 474–491.

In 2007, the Research Committee of the Institute of Chartered Accountants of Scotland commissioned a 134-page rigorously refereed report, *Intellectual Capital Reporting: Lessons from Hong Kong and Australia* which confirmed the limitations of traditional accounting and examined IC reporting in various nations.[19] The study investigated the voluntary IC disclosure of Australian and Hong Kong companies observing:

> The fact that traditional financial practice does not include non-financial performance adversely impacts knowledge-based organisations. Those that are looking to raise capital in the debt and/or equity markets are particularly affected.[20]

The research, although it did not address IP and patent assets specifically, concluded that IC is expressed in narrative rather than numerical terms; the current IC policy vacuum results in a lack of standardisation of corporate reporting and there is a need for a level of international standardisation; the level of IC disclosure is relatively low and linked to company size; and finally, the voluntary reporting of IC information indicate that *the data has a value*.[21]

Accordingly, it is confirmed that there is a need to report IC information. The IC literature has continued to expand via dedicated outlets including the *Journal of Intellectual Capital* and the *International Journal of Learning and Intellectual Capital*.[22] Next, the enhanced corporate disclosure regime adopted by Denmark in 2000 is examined. This regime requires Danish companies to increase the level of corporate reporting of all company assets, bothtangible and intangible.

6.2 International policy initiatives regarding IC reporting

6.2.1 Denmark

Denmark[23] is a key system of interest given its mandatory narrative IC reporting regime. It is also noteworthy that there is a strong voluntary component in the

19 Guthrie, J, Petty, R and Ricceri, F. *IC Reporting: Lessons from Hong Kong and Australia* (2007) at http://icas.org.uk/guthrie/ pp 29, 46.

20 Ibid Executive Summary p *v*.

21 Guthrie, J. and Petty. R. 'Intellectual Capital Literature Review: Measurement, Reporting and Management' (2000) 1(2) *Journal of Intellectual Capital* 155–176, i and ii.

22 Alcaniz, L., Gomez-Bezares, F., Roslender, R. 'Theoretical perspectives on intellectual capital: a backward look and a proposal for going forward' (June 2010).

23 Denmark became a member of the European Economic Community (now the EU) in 1973, maintaining certain opt-outs; it retains its own currency, the krone. Denmark has developed a mixed economy that is classed as a high-income economy by the World Bank. The IP Rights Index 2016 showed Denmark ranked 11th out of 128 countries with an overall score of 8.2 (with scores of 7.7 in IP Protection, 7.7 in Copyright Piracy Level, and 9.3 in Patent Protection). See http://internationalpropertyrightsindex.org/country?c=DENMARK.

reporting procedure and culture.[24] According to the Danish Ministry of Science, Technology and Innovation (DMSTI), "an IC statement is an integrated part of company knowledge management".[25] Constructing an ICS is based on four types of knowledge resource (as commonly applied in the IC field): employees, customers, processes and technologies. These are evidenced by a statement representing the organisation's knowledge management work through:

(1) a knowledge narrative;
(2) a set of managerial challenges;
(3) a number of initiatives; and
(4) relevant indicators.[26]

The Danish Intellectual Capital guideline initiative between 1997 and 2000 and the Danish Agency for Trade and Industry (DATI) pursued a project on IC reporting. This ICS project laid the foundation for the development of the Danish ICS guidelines based on the experience of 17 companies who participated in a Danish Agency for Trade and Industry ICS Project.[27] Prior to the initiative's launch, many Danish companies had already begun to undertake their own initiatives with the objective of successfully managing knowledge. The Danish guidelines sought to systematize and produce a better understanding of these different initiatives and design an educational tool for firms. In 2000, the DMSTI published the first ICS guidelines in the world, *A Guideline for Intellectual Capital Statements: A Key to Knowledge Management.* These guidelines demonstrate that the corporate reporting approach is built on the same principles as financial statements which ask questions relating to the same issues. The difference lies in how the questions are asked and that the answers are provided in narrative form, rather than numerical form. Figure 6.1 presents a comparison of the questions that underpin financial statement and ICS questions.

The ICS is not a balance sheet in the classical financial sense. It gives a detailed account of a firm's IC (which may include information about IP rights such as granted patents and patent applications) and balances this with achieving targets. Following implementation by approximately 100 Danish companies and public organisations, in 2003 DMSTI produced a revised document entitled *Intellectual Capital Statements – The New Guideline* on how to prepare an ICS.[28] It provides

24 *Encouraging Employers to use Human Capital Reporting* (2013) Briefing Paper, UK Commission of Employment and Skills p 21.
25 *A Guideline for Intellectual Capital Statements* (2000) Danish Agency for Trade and Industry, Ministry for Trade and Industry p 7.
26 Ibid.
27 *Analysing Intellectual Capital Statements* (2003a) Danish Ministry of Science, Technology and Innovation at https://pure.au.dk/ws/files/217/analyse_uk.pdf.
28 *ICS – The New Guideline* (February 2003b) Danish Ministry of Science, Technology and Innovation ISBN: 87-91258-52-9 at https://pure.au.dk/ws/files/217/analyse_uk.pdf.

Financial statements	Intellectual Capital Statements
What are the organisation's resources in terms of assets and liabilities, cash flow, profit and loss.	What does the organisation's knowledge resource encompass?
How has the organisation invested its working capital (calculated as current assets minus the current liabilities)?	How has the organisation enhanced its knowledge resource?
What is the organisation's return on investment (profitability ratio known as the "ROI"), typically calculated by dividing net profit by total assets.	What are the outputs derived from the organisation's knowledge capability?

Figure 6.1 Comparing financial statements and Intellectual Capital Statements

a specific methodology and incorporates examples of non-financial indicators that can be reported. Ideally, the statement should include all the relevant information that reflects the reality of the company, including both numerical data and a range of complementary visualisations. From a corporate governance standpoint, the information in an ICS should be readily accessible to all stakeholders, in contrast to complex traditional accounting statements which many struggle to understand. However, for the purpose of this book, the DMSTI guidance is limited as it does not give specific information on the disclosure IP rights information and strategy which is a weakness this research addresses.

A study published in the *British Accounting Review* in 2008 found no evidence of use in the UK of the ICS, in the form of a separate statement produced by a company that focuses exclusively on the reporting of aspects of their IC, management and resources.[29]

Another study found that while no UK publicly listed company in its sample had published a stand-alone ICS, on average 10.6% of each annual report was devoted to disclosing IP information.[30]

Nevertheless, the adoption of an ICS format is potentially one way to assist innovating firms to overcome the distortion of the IAS 38-related financial calculations concerning the fiscal value of their patent portfolios, improving the quality of non-financial patent information available to external stakeholders. Producing an ICS is likely to be an expensive exercise for the innovating firms whether they are private SMEs or public limited companies due to the costs of collating and verifying the information. Further, dedicated IP and especially patent information disclosure guidance is needed as the evidence shows that UK companies generally have very little experience with this category of IC subject matter. The Danish Guideline Project and its principal output, the ICS, have attracted only a very limited extent of empirical attention since the conclusion of

29 Striukova, L. et al 'Corporate Reporting of IC: Evidence from UK Companies' (2008) 40 *The British Accounting Review 297–313,* 298–301.

30 Ibid p 308–309.

the initiative in December 2002 and the implementation and evolution of the disclosure of IP asset information as part of the ICS also remains embryonic.[31]

In 2001–202, the United States introduced legislation to increase transparency as to the value of corporate assets aimed at increasing the level of investor protection, with certain specific guidance for corporate intangible assets and IP rights. However, the US experience differs markedly as its enhanced corporate intangibles and IP disclosure laws were largely the result of a wave of corporate collapses that resulted in a deep lack of trust in companies, their corporate governance procedures and financial accounting policies, which will be discussed in paragraph 6.2.4. However, Germany has advanced the budget, as discussed below.

6.2.2 Germany

Germany[32] has world-leading capability in terms of adapting inventions to industry and spreading them throughout the business sector, supported by a network of public institutions that help companies recombine and improve ideas. The Fraunhofer Institutes, partially supported by the government, move radical ideas into the marketplace in novel ways. They facilitate the use of research by SMEs across Germany's entire industrial sector.[33] German innovation results in corporate productivity gains that are widespread, rather than concentrated in high-tech sectors. As such, Germany has been receptive to its neighbour Denmark's IC guidelines and has developed its own.

This section explores and compares the German ICS reporting system to identify the effectiveness, limitations and solutions as regards narrative corporate reporting of patent assets. A 51-page document entitled *Intellectual Capital Statement – Made in Germany Guideline 1.0 on the Preparation of an ICS*, (the "*Guide*" published in 2004 by the Federal Ministry Economics and Labour is evaluated.[34] ICS reporting in Germany (known as *Wissenbilanz)* is voluntary and the *Guide* is highly relevant as it targets SMEs – indeed the opening paragraph states:

> ICSs can be used for external communication in order for instance to acquire funding for future investments . . . The ICS is an aid here to SMEs. It offers

31 Nielsen, C., Roslender, R. and Schaper, S. 'Continuities in the use of the Intellectual Capital Statement Approach: Elements of an Institutional Theory Analysis' (March 2016) 40(1) *Accounting Forum*16–28.

32 Germany's IP Rights Index 2016 ranking increased by 0.1 to 7.7 placing it 9th in Western Europe and 16th in the world. Germany is classified by the IMF as part of the Advanced Economies group and by the World Bank as a high income OECD nation. Germany is a member of the European Union. The IP Rights Subindex increased by 0.1 to 8.2 with scores of 7.8 in IP Protection, 7.6 in Copyright Piracy Level, and 9.3 in Patent Protection.

33 Breznitz, D. 'Why Germany Dominates the US in Innovation' (27 May 2014) *Harvard Business Review* available at https://hbr.org/2014/05/why-germany-dominates-the-u-s-in-innovation Dan Breznitz Professor Breznitz holds the Munk Chair of Innovation Studies and is a co-director of the Innovation Policy Lab at the Munk School of Global Affairs, University of Toronto.

34 www.akwissensbilanz.org/Infoservice/Infomaterial/Leitfaden_english.pdf.

> a structure for the presentation and evaluation of competences that are critical to success and the innovative potential of the enterprise. The ICS portrays the intangible assets, and hence supplements the traditional balance sheet with the criteria missing today . . . [35]

This statement comprehensively acknowledges the reasons for the German government's support of the use of ICS to close the information gap, improve transparency, facilitate access to debt finance and standardise the capture and processing of IC information.

The *Guide* is the result of a project supported by the Federal Ministry of Economics and Labour whereby prototype ICSs were drafted by 14 representative SMEs. Encouragingly, all the SMEs involved unanimously agreed that drafting their ICS was beneficial. The German model builds on and further develops the Danish ICS method and the drafting mechanics are discussed below.

The German ICS model begins with a corporate "Fitness Check" as set out in Figure 6.2. A company answers 11 questions in the middle column of the table with yes (1) or no (0). The ratio between the positive and negative answers shows the degree to which the requirements are met. The more questions that are answered positively, the easier it will be to draft the ICS. Conversely, if the majority of the answers are negative, this highlights the need to give particular attention to these areas when drafting the ICS. The 14 SMEs in the pilot study completed the Fitness Check.

The *Guide* then sets out six steps for drafting an ICS with four milestones.[36] This is simple, non-technical approach that would be straightforward for any firm to carry out, as summarised in Figure 6.3.

The *Guide* does not provide a sample report as completed by one of the SMEs in the pilot study, which would have enhanced its usefulness. Nor does it address IP or patents specifically or give any example of the narrative style of IP asset reporting, which is a weakness. Rather, the *Guide* adopts a more general approach and this limits its utility, from a corporate narrative IP reporting perspective. However, the author assumes that an innovating firm with an IP portfolio would address each of the seven items with an IP focus. Corporate IP portfolio owners still need additional bespoke guidance, for disclosing IP information in a standardised format or model. The ICS offers an opportunity for increasing the level of transparency, however within the IC community there has been little direct focus on IP assets per se. Like Denmark, on the other side of the globe, high tech nation Japan has also recognised the corporate IP information gap. Japan has made key policy to overcome the lack of transparency through mandatory disclosure requirements, as explained below.

35 ICS – Made In Germany Guide 1.0 pp 8–9.

36 ICS – Made In Germany Guide 1.0, p 16.

Fitness Check on preparation of an Intellectual Capital Statement	Yes/No	Comparative Value
Q1 Are many of your employees engaged in intellectually challenging tasks?		6 out of 14
Q2 Have we already dealt with controlling and management systems (such as quality management process optimisation, BSC, etc)?		10 out of 4
Q3 Does our management want and support Intellectual Capital Statements?		12 out of 14
Q4 Is our organisation willing to devote time and resources to intellectual capital statements?		12 out of 14
Q5 Do the employees regard intellectual capital statements as an important project?		6 out of 14
Q6 Can we involve employees from various areas of our enterprise in intellectual capital statements?		13 out of 14
Q7 Are we willing to discuss our strengths and weaknesses openly and constructively?		12 out of 14
Q8 Is management open to proposals and change?		10 out of 14
Q9 Do we recognise "soft factors" as important success factors?		14 out of 14
Q10 Are future topics already touched upon and broadly discussed?		12 out of 14
Q11 Do we have a documented, communicated business strategy?		10 out of 14
RESULT		

Figure 6.2 The ICS Fitness Check

Source: ICS – Made In Germany Guide 1.0 p 14

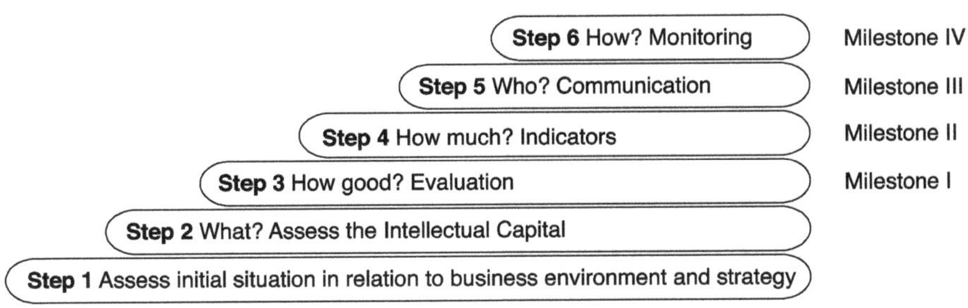

Figure 6.3 Six steps to drafting an Intellectual Capital Statement

Source: ICS – Made In Germany Guide 1.0 p 16

6.2.3 Japan

Japan is an interesting country renowned for its innovativeness in bringing to market new technologies and is largely a nation built on the effective use of IP to offset the low level of natural resources. The country has a robust and sophisticated national IP framework in place[37] and its company law is comprised of a mixture of different legal traditions having had a number of legal transplants over time.[38] Over the past decade, the Japanese government has introduced initiatives regarding the disclosure of IC which as we have seen comprises IP rights among other non-financial indicators. Following business research in the field of knowledge management that began in earnest in the 1980s, in 2004 Japan's Ministry of Economy, Trade and Industry (METI) introduced the *Guideline for Intellectual Property Information Disclosure* (GIPID)[39] to increase the acknowledgement of IP assets through the voluntary extension of corporate reporting.[40] The Guideline states that the rationale for implementing an IP disclosure regime is that:

> Becoming a nation that quests for sustained growth of its economy and society through vigorous promotion of creation, protection and exploitation of intellectual property, in short a "nation built on intellectual property," is an urgent goal for Japan to strengthen its industrial competitiveness . . . the METI also established a "Pilot Model for Disclosing Patent and Technical Information" with the hope that those companies that practice "intellectual property-backed management" will disclose information concerning their intellectual property and gain fair market valuation.[41]

Japanese corporate regulators, shareholders and other stakeholders presently have a greater awareness of the nature of IP assets and a more detailed understanding of firms' IP strategies for value creation than those in other most other countries. This makes it easier for Japanese shareholders, investors and financial institutions to link the corporate IP asset and strategy information to corporate value andthe

37 Japan's IP Rights Index score increased by 0.1 to 8.1 placing it 3rd in Asia and Oceania and 8th in the world. Japan is classified by the IMF as a part of the Advanced Economies group and by the World Bank as a high income OECD nation. The IP Rights Sub-index remained the same at 8.6 with scores of 8.4 in IP Protection, 8.1 in Copyright Piracy Level, and 9.3 in Patent Protection. See http://internationalpropertyrightsindex.org/country?c=JAPAN.

38 Siems, M. and Cabrelli, D. *Comparative Company Law A Case-Based Approach* (2013) Hart Publishing Limited, Oxford p 19.

39 *Reference Guideline for Intellectual Property Information Disclosure in the Pursuit of Mutual Understanding between Companies and Capital Markets through Voluntary Disclosures of Information on Patent and Technology* (January 2004) Ministry of Economy, Trade and Industry, Japan.

40 Johansen, U. et al, 'The Japanese Government's Intellectual Capital Reporting Guideline: What are the Challenges for Firms and Capital Market Agents?' (2006) 7(4) *Journal of Intellectual Capital* 474–491.

41 'A revolution postponed' (May/June 2014) *IAM Magazine* 5–6, 3 at www.iam-media.com/ctredir.ashx?g=cc6edf40-3f31-4157-b1aa-0cb886775091.

cost of finance. The Japanese Government shifted its IC and IP disclosure target from plc investor communications to non-listed SME communications with a view to adjusting the perceptions of lenders to IC and IP assets when contemplating loans to SMEs.[42] This shift occurred precisely for the reasons outlined earlier in Chapter 2 of this book, namely that young Japanese SMEs (in common with young SMEs around the world) still rely heavily on debt finance (loans) from financial institutions. Consequently, they benefit from increasing the level of their corporate narrative IP reporting. During the shift, Japanese lenders were under the "Action Program Concerning the Enhancement of Relationship Banking Functions".[43] As a consequence of these government-led initiatives, Japanese financial institutions have become "information demanders". More timely, relevant and useful IP asset information serves to better inform investment as well as credit appraisal with the aim of increasing the amount of positive lending decisions to young IP-rich Japanese SMEs. In Japan as in Denmark, there already appears to be a different mindset towards the corporate disclosure of IP asset and strategy information. Next, we consider the experience of mandatory corporate IP asset reporting in the United States, the home of Wall Street[44], the original home of the New York Stock Exchange and the historic headquarters of the largest American brokerages and investment banks.

6.2.4 United States

Over the centuries, the United States[45] has been very successful at developing and financing radical ideas, especially in relation to the digital economy (e.g. Google, Facebook and Twitter). It has strong entrepreneurial ecosystems in the Silicon Valley and Boston. The US approach to corporate reporting for listed companies mirrors that of the UK and is of comparative system interest for three reasons: (1) it has the largest economy in the world; (2) it is an important "exporter" of corporate governance theories and ideas;[46] and (3) it has express reference to corporate IP and intangibles as part of its mandatory disclosure requirements.

42 Ordonez de Pablos, P. and Edvinsson, L. *Intellectual Capital in Organizations: Non-Financial Reports and Accounts* (2015) Routledge pp187–191.
43 *Action Program concerning enhancement of Relationship Banking Functions (Background and Basic Policy Concept)* (28 March 2003) Japanese Financial Services Agency, English version at www.fsa.go.jp/news/newse/e20030328-1a.pdf.
44 The term Wall Street is also used as a collective name for the financial and investment community.
45 The United States' IP Rights Index 2016 score increased by 0.1 to 7.7 placing it 2nd in the North America and 15th in the world. The US is classified by the IMF as part of the Advanced Economies group and the World Bank as a high income OECD country. The Sub-index for IP Rights Increased by 0.2 to 8.6 with scores of 7.9 in IP Protection, 9.8 in Patent Protection, and 8.2 in Copyright Piracy Level. See http://internationalpropertyrightsindex.org/country?c=UNITED+STATES.
46 Siems, M. and Cabrelli, D. *Comparative Company Law A Case-Based Approach* (2013) Hart Publishing Limited, Oxford p 19.

This has resulted in a higher level of corporate IP asset and strategy disclosure than in the UK, and the application of established corporate governance "materiality" principles to IP disclosures in the interest of investor protection.

By way of background, the US re-evaluated various aspects of its corporate disclosure requirements in light of the shockwaves produced from the 2001 fraudulent accounting scandal that led to the collapse of one of the world's largest energy traders, the Enron Corporation. The external auditor, accounting firm Arthur Anderson (now dissolved), was investigated for approving Enron's financial statements and reports when they contained false information as to profit and loss and poor financial reporting. Enron's complex financial statements were confusing to shareholders and analysts. In addition, its complex business model and unethical practices required that the company use accounting limitations to misrepresent earnings and modify the balance sheet to indicate favourable performance.[47] The US Securities and Exchange Commission (SEC) investigated the publicly listed company and it was proven that Enron had essentially managed to breach *basic* accounting procedures. In terms of corporate governance, this was a shock because on paper, Enron had a model board of directors comprised predominantly of outsiders with significant ownership stakes and a well-qualified audit committee. Yet, the company's true financial performance was concealed through a series of accounting and financing manoeuvres. Between December 2001 and April 2002, the Senate Committee on Banking, House and Urban Affairs and the House Committee of Financial Services held multiple hearings about the Enron scandal and related accounting and investor protection issues. These hearings and other corporate scandals that followed Enron, led US Congress to reevaluate its corporate reporting and disclosure legal requirements culminating with the passage of the Sarbanes-Oxley Act on 30 July 2002 (SOX 2002) to address corporate governance failings.[48]

SOX 2002 was the most significant US federal legislation to emerge in response to the corporate governance failures.[49] It set new or expanded requirements for all US public company boards, management and public accounting firms. A number of provisions also apply to privately held companies. In terms of intangibles and IP rights, SOX 2002 mandates increased corporate reporting of all company assets (tangible and intangible).[50] The Act requires publicly listed companies (not

47 Healy, P.M. and Krishna G. P. 'The Fall of Enron' (Spring 2003) 17(2) *Journal of Economic Perspectives* 9.

48 Chhaochharia, V., Grinstein, Y. 'Corporate Governance and Firm Value: The Impact of the 2002 Governance Rules' (March 2007) *Johnson School Research Paper Series* No. 23-06. Johnson School of Management pp 7–9. Other corporate scandals in the US included Tyco International, Adelphia, Peregrine Systems and WorldCom which collectively cost investors billions of US dollars when the share prices of the affected companies collapsed and shook public confidence in the US Securities markets.

49 SOX 2002 was named after was named after sponsors US Senator Paul Sarbanes and US Representative Michael G. Oxley.

50 (Pub, L. 107û204, Stt.745 Pub .L. enacted July 30, 2002), also known as the "Public Company Accounting Reform and Investor Protection Act" (in the Senate) and "Corporate

SMEs) to increase their reporting on internal control structures and procedures for financial reporting.[51] Title III comprises eight sections that mandate senior executives take individual responsibility for the accuracy and completeness of corporate financial reports.[52] Thus, US public companies (as with UK listed companies) have a legal obligation to effectively measure, closely monitor and disclose the relationship between the IP rights and their financial performance. They translate changes in the scope and strength of those rights into reportable indicators of financial performance.[53] SOX 2002 and the US securities laws generally require that processes be in place to ensure that financial statements and reporting are reliable under GAAP standards. IP rights that have a "material" effect on financial performance must be disclosed, including off-balance sheet instruments.[54]

Essentially, a greater emphasis on the accurate valuation of all assets is prescribed by SOX 2002 even though, as in the UK CA 2006, there is no statutory language that refers specifically to IP (with one exception). Thus, in the US as in the UK, IP is also largely invisible or hidden, not only in the financial accounts but also more generally in corporate law. SOX 2002 requires documentation of the "fair value" and not the "value in use" of corporate assets. It adheres to the generally accepted definitions of intangibles.[55] However, there is one clear express acknowledgement of IP assets. Item 101(c)(1)(iv) of Regulation S-K clarifies that the Act requires a public company to disclose in its annual report:

> the importance to the industry segment of the company, and the duration and effect of all patents, trademarks, licenses, franchises and concessions held by the company to the extent the foregoing is "material."

This US regulation expressly refers to disclosure of IP rights. In relation to patents, it is taken to mean that any material information regarding patents and the licensing of such patents is required to be disclosed in a publicly listed US company's annual report. Commentators have pointed out that some of the important IP issues raised by this Item are not only what is material, but what is meant by the phrase "importance to the industry segment" of the company being

and Auditing Accountability and Responsibility Act" (in the House), is a US federal law that set new or enhanced standards for all US public boards, management and public accounting firms.

51 Sections 302 (Disclosure Controls), 401 (Off-balance sheet items), 404(Assessment of Internal Control) SOX 2002

52 Enron and Worldcom. The bankruptcy of Enron highlighted how off-balance instruments were fraudulently used.

53 Manickavasagam, V. 'IP Best Practices in the Post Sarbanes-Oxley Act Era' (February 2011).

54 Kote, L. et al (2005); *Report and Recommendations Pursuant to Section 401(c) SOX 2002. On Arrangements with Off-Balance Sheet Implications, Special Purpose Entities, and Transparency of Filings by Issuers* at www.sec.gov/news/studies/soxoffbalancerpt.pdf

55 Gallagher & Cawsey Co. 'Wading Through the Intellectual Property Requirements of the Sarbanes-Oxley Act of 2002' (2005).

reported on, and the "effect of" the IP?[56] Ultimately, disclosure of a patent asset for example is required if it assists the public (e.g. potential investors or lenders) in evaluating the company or has a potential financial impact.

The materiality standard in the US requires that all material information must be disclosed on a continuous basis by publicly listed companies (who sell their shares to the public).[57] From a legal analysis, this is a mixed question of fact and law. Materiality requires an assessment of the inferences that a reasonable shareholder would draw from a given set of facts.[58] This is a subjective legal standard, so there is no express legal rule for what is material, as each situation is different (fact specific). Making a distinction between material and non-material information can initially be bewildering. The corporate governance materiality standard is relevant for determining which IP asset and strategy information is to be prioritised. In both the US and the UK, the materiality threshold provides an effective filter for corporate narrative information IP asset and strategy disclosure, allowing major trends and significant events to be identified without being buried under an avalanche of information or "clutter" as referred to by the UK Financial Reporting Council (FRC).

Under the US Securities and Exchange Act 1934, material information is defined as information "to which there is a substantial likelihood that a reasonable investor would attach importance in deciding to buy or sell the securities registered". The US Supreme Court has determined that materiality refers to something that has "significantly altered" the "total mix" of information available to an investor. To clarify further, the SEC has explicitly stated that both "qualitative" and "quantitative" factors must be used in arriving at a materiality determination. This legal reasoning is persuasive in the UK. When the qualitative analysis called for in a materiality determination is combined with a quantitative report on the value of corporate intangibles, it can fairly be argued that a company's position and prospects relating to corporate IP assets and strategy should be among the preeminent issues considered for disclosure by the company's board of directors. The legal concept of material disclosure also requires publicly listed company directors to view the materiality of corporate IP assets from a broader perspective than in the past and then make carefully considered fact-specific judgements. In the UK, to guide a company in making full and fair disclosures in capital markets, the materiality concept ultimately depends on the answer to the question, "what would investors find important and will it affect the share price?". The answer to this question will be assisted by asking questions such as: Are the company's IP assets directly related to the business? Is it relevant to judging business performance? How are the corporate IP assets being managed and who is responsible? How do we know they are being well managed in the interest of the company and to promote the success of the company? Has any official IP

56 Ibid p 7.

57 This standard does not apply to non-listed companies.

58 *Marksman Partners L.P. v. Chantal Pharm.*, 927 F. Supp. 1297, 1305–06.

infringement allegation been made? There is empirical evidence that the interpretation and the effectiveness of forward-looking information (e.g. IP strategy) depends on the reputation of a company.[59] The subjective legal materiality standard also allows directors and their advisors to argue that something is immaterial as it was insufficiently certain or important to significantly affect the share price of the company.

The US has developed various doctrines to further clarify the materiality concept, which can assist with making material IP disclosures. These include the "reasonable investor" standard, the "hidden facts" doctrine, the "bespeaks caution" doctrine, the "simple math rule" and the emerging "reasonably available data" rule.[60] The "simple math rule" means that a failure to disclose the bottom line is immaterial as a matter of law where the data necessary to calculate the bottom line has been disclosed. Under the "buried facts" doctrine, a disclosure is deemed inadequate if it is presented in a way that conceals or obscures the information sought to be disclosed. The doctrine applies when the fact in question is hidden in a voluminous document or is disclosed in a piecemeal fashion which prevents a reasonable shareholder from realizing the "correlation and overall import of the various facts interspersed throughout" the document.[61] US courts also look to market reaction to assist them in making their materiality determination.[62] Accordingly, corporate governance legal theory and doctrines already exist for disclosure on a real-time basis, but there is little guidance or examples specifically of IP-related disclosures except in the IT, pharma and biotechnology publicly listed companies.

Company directors face a significant challenge in balancing the disclosure obligations against the fiduciary duty to preserve asset value, magnified when that asset value may be destroyed by premature disclosure or diminished by excessive disclosure, especially where patent rights are concerned. However, even where disclosure of a patent licence or other sensitive disclosure might otherwise be required, the SEC has a confidential treatment procedure which may be followed for certain information otherwise subject to disclosure.[63] The author is unaware of a similar procedure under CA 2006. In the UK, section 414C(14) CA 2006 makes clear that the disclosure of information about impending developments or matters in the course of negotiation is not necessary if the disclosure would, in

59 Bravo, F. 'Forward-looking Disclosure and Corporate Reputation as Mechanisms to Reduce Stock Return Volatility' (2016) (19)1 *Spanish Accounting Review* 122–131.

60 Padfield, S.J. 'Who Should do the Math? Materiality Issues in Disclosures that Require Investors to Calculate the Bottom Line (15 May 2007) 34(4) *Pepperdine Law Review* 4–5 at https://papers.ssrn.com/sol3/papers.cfm?abstract_id=928630.

61 *Werner v. Werner*, 267 F.3d 288, 297 (3d Cir. 2001) (quoting *Kas v. Financial General Bankshares, Inc.*, 796 F.2d 508, 516 (D.C.Cir.1986)).

62 Thomas, R.S. 'The Materiality Standard for Intellectual Property Disclosures' (2002) 42(2) *IDEA The Journal of Law and Technology* 205–226.

63 The SEC has set forth substantive and procedural guidelines for Rule 24b-2 confidential treatment requests in 'Confidential Treatment Requests' (28 February 1997, addendum 11 July 2001) SEC Division of Corporation Finance Staff Legal Bulletin No. 1.

the opinion of the directors, be seriously prejudicial to the interests of the company. This is the case even if that information is considered material.

In the US, SOX 2002 has reaffirmed the need to meticulously value and monitor all assets, and there is a specific reference to IP assets from a corporate disclosure compliance perspective. These requirements ensure that more internal corporate information about all IP is communicated and translated into external financial reports.

However, critics argue the onerous corporate reporting requirements have negatively impacted the system. A significant body of academic research exists regarding the costs and benefits of SOX 2002, which arrive at different conclusions.[64] This is due in part to the difficulty of isolating the impact of SOX from other variables affecting the stock market and corporate earnings. It has been mooted that the average cost for a publicly listed US company to comply with the SOX 2002 legal disclosure requirements is circa $4 million US per annum.[65] A Foley and Lardner Survey in 2007 analysed the change in the total costs of being a US public company (e.g. external auditor fees, directors and officers insurance, board compensation, lost productivity, and legal costs). They found they were significantly affected by SOX 2002 legal requirements. Nearly 70% of survey respondents indicated public companies with revenues under $251 million US should be exempt from SOX section 404.[66] While the rationale for the stricter level of corporate reporting for publicly listed companies is sound, the practical cost of compliance is clearly very high. Nevertheless, as the Chief Executive Officer and the Chief Financial Officer are required to unequivocally take ownership of their financial statements under section 302, SOX 2002 requirements have enhanced corporate transparency (based on the accuracy of analyst forecasts) significantly improving investor confidence and more accurate, reliable financial statements.[67] This shows that in the US the principle of increased disclosure of corporate IP assets is sound, what is needed are appropriate tools to achieve cost efficiencies by systematizing the level of IP asset and strategy disclosure.

6.3 An evolving conceptual framework for corporate IP asset disclosure

In this chapter we have compared certain national solutions to the corporate intangibles and IP asset information and strategy gap. In Chapter 4 we saw that

64 Shakespeare, C. 'SOX 2002 Five Years On: What Have We Learned?' (2008) *Journal of Business & Technology Law*: 333; 'Five years of Sarbanes-Oxley' (26 July 2007) *The Economist*.

65 Halling, D. B. *The Decline and Fall of the American Entrepreneur: How little known laws and regulations are killing innovation* (2009). Mr Halling is a US patent attorney. His Chapter 6 discusses the effect of SOX on the US technology start-up ecosystem.

66 'Foley Study Reveals Continued High Cost of Being Public' (2 August 2007) www.foleyandlardner.com.

67 Arping, S. and Sautner, Z. 'Did SOX Section 404 Make Firms Less Opaque? Evidence from Cross-Listed Firms' (2013) 30 *Contemporary Accounting Research* 1133–1165.

the corporate disclosure requirements for SMEs are minimal under the CA 2006 given the availability of using the "abbreviated" reporting format so that astonishingly, no corporate IP information or strategy may be publicly available at all. Corporate IP assets are largely invisible or hidden, not only in the financial accounts but also more generally in corporate law. The ICS is not a legal requirement under UK or EU company law. In 2002 Edvinsson warned:

> There have always been occasional and temporary gaps between market perception and accounting reality. But now that gap is turning into a chasm. And that suggests that we are not looking at aberration but a systemic flaw in the way we measure value.[68]

There is a need to integrate corporate IP assets into accounting and corporate governance procedures. Presently however, only Denmark, Germany, Japan and the US provide their own national IC and IP corporate reporting guidelines. However, the OECD, the EC and the World Bank are supporters.[69] The contribution of IC reporting is the process of creating a narrative that shows how a firm creates value for its shareholders and stakeholders by developing and using its intangibles, including corporate IP. Moreover, although identified as a component of IC, more emphasis on corporate reporting of IP assets and strategy is needed as it has been largely overlooked. An improved narrative reporting format needs to ensure that it identifies, measures and constructs a coherent presentation of how the firm uses its corporate IP assets in the company's best interests. However, to date, only Japan and the US have succeeded in developing a culture of narrative intangibles reporting, whereas in most regions a similar culture has yet to be encouraged and fostered.

Cost is the one important reason why, in the author's opinion, corporate narrative reporting of IC, IP and off-balance sheet items such as internally generated patent assets is controversial. In some cases, the costs involved in formally disclosing IP asset information and strategy will be warranted given the potential benefit that information will bring to enhance the prospect of securing a line of credit. A lender does not need to know the exact value of the patent rights. Rather, it simply needs to know that the value of the IP rights is *sufficient* to cover monthly repayments and any unpaid amounts if the debtor defaults on the loan.[70] The ICS supplements the traditional accounts and in the UK could be

68 Edvinsson, L. *Intellectual Capital Realizing Your Company's True Value by Finding Its Hidden Brainpower* (1997) Harper Collins Publishers p 2.

69 In 2002 the EC funded the MERITUM (1999–2003) project which led to the Guidelines for the Management and Reporting of Intangibles (2002) classifying IC into categories of human, structural and relational capital. The EC's RICARDIS (2006) project adopted the MERITUM (2002) classification of IC.

70 Murphy et al *Patent Valuation Improving Decision Making through Analysis* (5 April 2012) Wiley.

voluntarily made in addition to statutory reports. In the author's view, in time it would be sensible to include IC and IP expressly in mandated statutory reports. However, firms require more guidance on *how* they should make material and non-material IP disclosures in order to avoid directors' liability for misleading information, a topic which will be discussed in the next chapter.

6.4 Final remarks on corporate IP asset transparency and disclosure

The preceding pages show that during the past 15 years or so we have come to better understand why corporate intangibles such as IC and IP are presently such an important category of business asset. Earlier in Chapter 4, we saw that it is unlikely that traditional financial accounting on its own is capable of meeting these new corporate governance disclosure challenges. Denmark, Germany, Japan and the United States are all countries that rank in the top 20 countries in the Intellectual Property Rights Index 2016. The national corporate narrative reporting approaches, reviewed above, evidence a distinctly normative quality with respect to the disclosure of intangibles such as corporate IC and IP. However, in this chapter we identified that within the various ICS guidelines, there is a lack of critical (theoretical) consideration of how specifically corporate IP assets are best disclosed to ensure transparency and protection of shareholders and other stakeholders. At the very least, it is appropriate that corporate disclosures contain a combination of numbers and narrative to triangulate IP asset information and generally devote more critical thought and space to reporting corporate IP assets. The current corporate IP asset reporting policy vacuum results in a lack of standardisation of the type and level of disclosure. There is a need for a level of international standardisation. Currently, the level of IP disclosure is relatively low and generally linked to company size (as shown in Chapter 5). Finally, the reporting of IC and IP information in Denmark, Japan and the US indicates that the data has a value and is a becoming a normative corporate governance regulatory requirement in those jurisdictions, all advanced economies with robust IP legal frameworks. However, widespread buy-in and uptake from the corporates to increase the level of IP asset and strategy reporting has yet to lead to any significant step change in practice.

In the remaining chapters, we will consider how it might be possible to approach corporate IP asset information and strategy disclosures in a more progressive way. A shift from traditional financial reporting to corporate narrative disclosures will have a consequent impact on the primacy of the accounting profession in determining IP value via IAS 38 intangibles, and multidisciplinary input will be needed from IP and legal professionals, national IP offices and corporate regulators. We have real regulatory advances in a handful of jurisdictions which were examined in a critical manner, highlighting that the rationale for the supplementary narrative disclosure mechanisms share a common foundation of transparency and shareholder protection. Although the analysis did not elicit any standard approach, Denmark, the US and Japan are examples of jurisdictions that actively provide a more robust corporate governance legal framework and are becoming the standard setters. Companies operating in those jurisdictions receive guidance to assist them to report on IP asset and strategy information to create a more transparent business environment. The functional corporate governance system in each comparator country has introduce guidance and the US and Japan have both enacted laws that expressly embed the obligation to report narrative report corporate IP information.

In Chapter 7 we continue our focus on corporate patent assets and consider the content and structure for both mandatory and voluntary disclosure of IP and patent information.

7 Substance and form

Developing a normative practice for corporate narrative IP asset disclosures

A true and fair view implies that all statutory and other information is not only available but is presented in a form in which it can be properly and readily appreciated.

Sir Russell Kettle (1887–1968) Chartered Accountant and Author[1]

Introduction

In this chapter we address the question "How should innovating firms report their corporate IP assets?" It is vital for them to provide a coherent shape for identifying and reporting how corporate IP assets create value for shareholders, investors, lenders and other stakeholders interested in the future growth prospects of the firm. We focus on patent assets to illustrate the concepts. The "corporate patent value story" should aim to show "how the money is made" in a consistent, clear and uncluttered manner.[2] In addition, the innovating firm should demonstrate the role the patent assets play within the business, whilst adopting a balanced perspective, with a view to increasing transparency and reducing asymmetric information regarding the financial accounting metric currently used to value its patent portfolio. The aim of this chapter is to consider the content and structure for voluntary disclosure of patent information. In the UK, this could be integrated into the Strategic Report (a form of corporate narrative reporting) contained in the firm's annual report. In section 7.1 we introduce the views of the Financial Reporting Council (FRC) on the subject of intangibles, intellectual capital reporting and the relevant literature. Section 7.2 presents a mini-case study that qualitatively analyses the specific narrative "patent disclosures" made in a publicly listed corporation's annual report.

1 Kettle, R. 'Balance Sheets and Accounts under the Companies Act, 1948' in Baxter, W.T. (Ed.) *Studies in Accounting* (1950) Sweet & Maxwell p 17.

2 Cowley, A. and Swaffield, A. 'The Strategic Report A Practical Guide to the New Regulations' (2014) Deloitte.

Section 7.3 discusses current thinking by EU and UK multidisciplinary subject matter experts to derive a basis on which to build a guide for UK innovating SME voluntary patent information and strategy disclosure.

7.1 The UK FRC's guidance on the Strategic Report

In August 2013 the UK Parliament approved the Companies Act 2006 (Strategic Report and Directors' Report) Regulations 2013. The purpose of the Strategic Report is to inform shareholders and help them to assess how the directors have performed their duty to promote the success of the company.[3] It is separate to the Directors' Report and must be separately approved by the board of directors. The FRC is the UK's independent regulator responsible for promoting confidence in corporate reporting and governance mandated by the CA 2006 to foster investment.[4] It seeks to ensure that "[c]orporate reports contain information which is relevant, reliable, understandable and comparable, and are useful for decision making, including stewardship decisions".[5] It encourages entities to prepare a high quality Strategic Report which provides a "holistic and meaningful picture of an entity's business model, strategy, development, performance, position and future prospects".[6] According to the FRC:

> In practice, an annual report comprises three distinct components – narrative reports; corporate governance statements; and financial statements. The information contained in these components has different objectives which should guide preparers to where disclosures could be located. The aim is to promote cohesiveness and enable related information to be linked together.[7]

And further:

> The overriding objective of narrative [company] reporting is to provide information on an entity, insight into its main objectives and strategies, the principal risks it faces; and to complement, supplement and provide context for the related financial statements.[8]

This statement perfectly expresses why an innovating SME with little else than off-balance intangible patent assets should consider voluntarily supplementing and providing context for the related financial statements – which do not identify

3 Section 414(C)1) CA 2006.

4 www.frc.org.uk/Our-Work/our-key-activities.aspx.

5 *Rising to the Challenge: A Review of Narrative Reporting by UK Listed Companies* (2009) Accounting Standards Board p 1. The FRC reviewed the annual reports of 50 UK listed companies focussing on content, communication and clutter.

6 *FRC Exposure Draft: Guidance on the Strategic Report* (2013) at p 7.

7 Ibid p 10.

8 Ibid.

or reflect their value – via the submission of a Strategic Report. The Strategic Report should contain a fair and balanced review, consistent with the size and complexity of the business of:

(a) the development and performance of the company's business during the financial year;
(b) the position of the company at the end of the year; and
(c) a description of the principal risks and uncertainties facing the company.

Large companies must include financial and non-financial key performance indicators (KPIs) although medium-size companies are exempt from disclosing non-financial KPIs. Corporate IP and patent information is a non-financial KPI that innovating firms should consider voluntarily disclosing in their annual return. An annual report, tailored to meet an innovating firm's business objectives, should provide the information necessary for shareholders and other stakeholders to assess the firm's:

(a) development, performance and position;
(b) future prospects;
(c) strategy for achieving its objectives;
(d) business model; and
(e) governance.[9]

As early as 2008, the FRC recommended that listed companies needed *to improve the inclusion non-financial KPIs* (such as IC and IP) to explain how the key drivers of the business are monitored and that "quality supplemental information is never clutter".[10] Crucially, the FRC expressly states that it welcomes "enhancement" to narrative reporting:

> Preparing a good quality annual report that communicates effectively all the important information is a major intellectual and logistical challenge. Many companies continue to devote significant time and effort to improving their narrative reporting, but there are always opportunities for further enhancement as experience and best practice develop.[11]

However, with respect to IC specifically, the FRC has stated the following:

> *Off-balance sheet resources*
> Most companies discuss their employees; given this is a now a requirement "to the extent necessary" this is not surprising. However, only 36% go

9 *Guidance on the Strategic Report* (June 2014) FRC p15 at www.frc.org.uk/getattachment/2168919d-398a-41f1-b493-0749cf6f63e8/Guidance-on-the-Strategic-Report.pdf; and section 417 CA 2006.

10 Supra n [6] p 20.

11 Supra n [6] p 3.

> beyond this to discuss other intangible assets such as brands, intellectual capital and natural resources. The off-balance sheet assets are often some of the most important to a company's future success; a comprehensive discussion of "performance and position" should include this aspect as well as the resources on the balance sheet.[12]

In other words, the FRC recommends that all company narrative reports contain *more* information and focus on the area of IC. By definition, IC includes corporate IP information. In terms of level of information, the FRC non-mandatory guidance is:

> 3.19 The Strategic report should be considered as the top layer of information for shareholders. Some users may requires a greater level of detail. In this case, the strategic report can be used to signpost to other complementary information.
>
> 3.20 Signposting enables shareholders to "drill down" to detailed complementary information that is related to a matter addressed in a particular component but that is not necessary to effectively communicate the information that is required by law or regulation in respect of that component. This more detailed complementary information should be placed elsewhere in the annual report, or published separately.[13]

Information is material if its omission or misrepresentation could influence the economic decisions shareholders take on the basis of the annual report as a whole. Only information that is material in the context of the Strategic Report should be included within it.[14] This will very much depend on the entity in question. Materiality is an entity-specific aspect of relevance based on the nature or magnitude (or both) of the actual or potential effect of the matter to which the information relates in the context of an entity's annual report. It requires directors to apply judgement based on their assessment of the relative importance of the matter to the entity's development, performance, position or future prospects and was discussed in detail earlier in Chapter 6. Finally, qualitative factors (such as corporate IP asset information and strategy) may have a greater influence on the determination of materiality in the context of the Strategic Report than in respect of items in the financial statements. Both financial and non-financial information could be material.[15]

12 Section 417(4)(a) and (b) CA 2006.
13 Supra *Guidance on the Strategic Report* n [9] p 12.
14 Ibid para 5.1 p 15.
15 Note however, that the CA 2006 does not use the term "material", the concept is implied by many of its requirements.

7.1.1 Reducing uncertainty through voluntary IP asset corporate reporting

Almost two decades ago, Ernst[16] found that patent active firms with a narrow technological focus outperform other companies according to various profitability and productivity measurements. In later studies, he also found that two to three years after a firm files patent applications its sales increase, showing a causal relationship.[17] Ramb and Reitzig concluded that European patent applications tend to have a stronger correlation with a firm's market value than its investment in R&D as set out in the balance sheet.[18] This study supports the need for enhanced IP information and especially patent information disclosure. In 2013, Dr Carl Frey of Oxford University said:

> That patent information explains the market value of firm better than information being published in firms' annual financial statements is also evident from studies conducted by Hirschey and Richardson (2004) in relation to US firms, but it is also found to be true for Japanese firms (Hirschey and Richardson, 2001) and as well as a German one (Trautwein 2007). Accordingly, it has been suggested that patents can be used to signal future economic benefits to capital markets (see for example, Blind et al, 2006) a view that has received empirical support.[19]

Dr Frey's research explores reducing patent and trade mark information asymmetry by enhanced corporate disclosure by listed companies concentrating on disclosure in capital markets (not voluntary patent information disclosure by private SMEs). Dr Frey concludes that reporting IP information assists listed companies to overcome stock market uncertainties due to asymmetric information, reducing the costs of capital. We can infer that an innovating SME seeking debt finance will have an interest in ensuring that its IP information is captured, presented and made available to lenders. The legally mandated UK annual corporate reporting requirements provide an opportunity to do this, however, IP information corporate reporting is still at its infancy.[20] In the author's view capturing the "corporate IP asset value" story at an early stage of the firm's business life cycle will have the added benefit of ensuring that the firm systematically reports the

16 Ernst, H. 'Patenting Strategies in the German Mechanical Engineering Industry and their Relationship to Company Performance' (1995) 15(4) *Technovation* 225–240.

17 Ibid.

18 Ramb, F. and Reitzig *A Comparative Analysis of the Explanatory Power of Balance Sheet and Patent Information for Market Values of German Firms* (2004) Working paper, Copenhagen Business School.

19 Frey, C.B. *Intellectual Property Rights and the Financing of Technology Innovation* (2013) Edward Elgar Publishing Limited p 19.

20 Lev, B. *Intangibles Management, Measurement, and Reporting* (2001) Brookings Institution Press; Blair, M.M. and Wallman, S.M.H. *Unseen Wealth: Report of the Brookings Task force on Intangibles* (2001) Brookings Institution Press, Washington D.C.

progress and growth of its patent portfolio throughout the business life cycle. For example, historical patent information will also eventually be highly useful (and much less costly to collate at a later date) if the firm decides to raise equity finance in the future. Therefore, in order to further develop IP asset disclosure, we narrow our focus specifically to patent information corporate reporting. The GSK mini-case study in the next section critically examines the patent information disclosures made by GSK in its 2012 annual report, demonstrating this global pharmaceutical company's approach to informing its shareholders and other stakeholders as to the value of its patent portfolio as a key corporate asset.

7.2 Mini-case study: GlaxoSmithKline plc 2012 Annual Report

The patent-related information disclosed by the global pharmaceutical company GSK in its 2012 annual report[21] was selected as an example of "best practice" in respect of patent information disclosure. The pharmaceutical sector business model is heavily reliant on the validity of patents to protect the active ingredient of key medicinal products (in contrast with the Royal Philips' business model). A case study methodology was chosen because the detailed examination of an individual substantial corporate disclosure should provide realistic insight into a coherent model for presenting a variety of patent information. It is an exploratory form of empirical inquiry which investigates a contemporary phenomenon within its real-life context.[22] For our purposes, the mini-case study is useful for demonstrating theoretical legal concepts in an applied setting and bridging the gap between black letter law and practice: descriptive (how) and explanatory (why). The GSK 2012 annual report was carefully combed for specific narrative patent information disclosures and the commentary weaves in a critical analysis as to the significance of the disclosures. A key assumption underlying the analysis is that the amount of space in the report devoted to a subject indicates the relative importance of the subject matter from the perspective of those who have written it.[23] Although GSK has more onerous narrative corporate reporting obligations as a quoted company than a typical innovation SME, the aim is to critically analyse:

- the type of patent information GSK selected to disclose;
- how that information is drafted and presented;
- what type of information GSK has not disclosed; and
- whether the selection of patent information disclosure can be used as the foundation for a guide to voluntary patent information disclosure (adopting a more streamlined format).

21 See GSK Annual Report 2012 at www.gsk.com/media/2694/annual-report-2012.pdf.

22 Yin, R.K. *Case Study Research: Design and Methods* (1984) Sage Publications, Newbury Park p 23.

23 Striukova, L. et al 'Corporate Reporting of IC: Evidence from UK Companies (2008) 40 *The British Accounting Review* 297–313, 298–301, 304.

7.2.1 GSK corporate history

GSK plc was incorporated as an English public limited company on 6 December 1999, formed by a merger of two listed companies: Glaxo Welcome plc and SmithKline Beecham plc. It is the parent company of the GSK group, a major global healthcare group involved in the creation, discovery, development, manufacture and marketing of pharmaceutical products and health-related consumer products. GSK's shares are listed on both the London and the New York Stock Exchanges.[24] The company's commercial success depends on the creation of patent-protected innovative new medicines, vaccines and healthcare products. As we have seen, UK company law requires directors to prepare financial statements for each financial year and GSK's directors are required to prepare group financial statements in accordance with IFRS as adopted by the EU. In preparing the GSK financial group statements the directors have also elected to comply with IFRS,[25] as issued by the IASB. GSK's directors are well aware of their legal obligations and the fact that the annual report will be heavily scrutinised by numerous experts, including accountants, lawyers and many others. They take great care in preparing it to ensure its accuracy before it is released. GSK make a substantial investment in their patent portfolio which is of critical importance to its shareholders. Therefore, as a listed company, information pertaining to the company's valuable patent portfolio is required by law to be disclosed in alignment with the UK Corporate Governance Code.[26] The patent information selected for disclosure and the way that GSK discloses it should therefore be of a high standard. All references to "patents" in GSK's annual report are underlined to highlight where they appear in the text.

7.2.2 Structure of GSK's 2012 Annual Report

GSK's 2012 Annual Report[27] ("the Report") is lengthy, at 252 pages and is divided into five parts as set out in Figure 7.1.

The Report does not contain a stand-alone section reporting on the company's IP or patent portfolio. However, it contains a "Products, competition and IP" section in "Part 5 Investor information" on pages 229–231 towards the very end of the Report. This structure in itself underscores the IP and patent information visibility and transparency problem. The reader's attention is not specifically

24 GSK 2012 supra n [21] p 251.

25 The International Financial Reporting Standards, usually called the IFRS Standards are standards issued by the IFRS Foundation and the International Accounting Standards Board (IASB) to provide a common global language for business affairs so that company accounts are understandable and comparable across international boundaries.

26 UK Corporate Governance Code, Financial Reporting Council at www.frc.org.uk/directors/corporate-governance-and-stewardship/uk-corporate-governance-code/history-of-the-uk-corporate-governance-code.

27 Supra n [21].

Part 1 Strategic review Chairman's statement CEO's review Strategic review How we performed What we do, Where we do it Our market How we deliver Responsible business	**Part 4 Financial statements** Directors' statement of responsibilities Independent Auditor's report Financial statements Notes to the financial statements Financial statements of GlaxoSmithKline plc prepared under UK GAAP
Part 2 Financial review & risk Financial review Financial position and resources Financial review 2011	**Part 5 Investor information** Product development pipeline Products, competition and intellectual property Quarterly trends Five year record Share capital and share price Dividends Annual General Meeting 2013 US law and regulation Tax information for shareholders Analysis of shareholdings Shareholder services and contacts Glossary of terms and index
Part 3 Governance & remuneration Our Board Our Corporate Executive Team Chairman's letter Board report to shareholders Committee reports Remunerations Committee Chairman's letter Total remuneration for 2012 Pay performance for 2012 Remuneration Policy for 2013 Directors' emoluments and total remuneration Directors and Senior Management	

Figure 7.1 Structure of the GSK Annual Report 2012

1. Fair review: business description and strategy (CA417(3)(a))
2. Principal risks and uncertainties (CA 417(3)(b))
3. Financial review: performance and position (CA 417(4)(a)&(b))
4. Trends and factors (CA 417(5)(a))
5. CSR: environment, employees, social & community (CA 417(5)(b))
6. Relationships: contractual and other arrangements (CA 417(5)(c))
7. Financial Key Performance Indicators (KPIs) (CA 417(6)(a))
8. Non-financial Key Performance Indicators (KPIs) (CA 417(6)(b))

Figure 7.2 CA 2006 requirements for listed company disclosures

Source: *Rising to the Challenge: A Review of Narrative Reporting by UK Listed Companies in 2008/2009* Accounting Standards Board pp 5–17

drawn to the patent information in the Report at any point. Rather, one has to analyse the whole report very carefully to find the relevant patent information disclosed (other than in Part 5, much of which forms short notes to the accounts). The Report was drafted to comply with legal requirements for listed company's disclosures using the former Business Review format as set out in Figure 7.2.

In summary, GSK's IP and patent information disclosures are embedded throughout the Report as the company proceeds to address the disclosure requirements mandated by the CA 2006. This is not problematic for our purposes as we are interested in analysing the nature and content of the patent information disclosures which can be adapted to provide guidance for firms to report their patent information using the ICS or Strategic Report format (discussed in section 7.1 above).

7.2.3 GSK's financial statements

In order to contextualise our discussion of GSK's narrative patent disclosures, we first consider the consolidated financial statements in Part 4 of the Report, namely, the traditional financial reports. The Report discloses that as at 31 December 2012 GSK's intangible assets were worth £10,161 million (see Figure 7.3). Note 19 elaborates on these intangible assets.[28] GSK's balance sheet was prepared using the historical cost convention and complies with application of UK GAAP accounting standards. The figures and the accounting treatment were independently audited by PricewaterhouseCoopers LLP [29] who confirmed that in their opinion "the Group financial statements give a true and fair view of the state of the Group's affairs".

Note that "other intangible assets" are of by far the greatest value in this balance sheet. They appear to have increased in value by £2,359 million, the greatest proportion between the two years of any of the company's asset categories – a

28 Supra n [21].

29 Chartered Accountants and Statutory Auditors based in London.

Non-current assets	**Notes**	**2012£m**	**2011£m**
Property, plant and equipment	17	**8,776**	8,748
Goodwill	18		
Other intangible assets	19	**10,161**	7,802
Investments in associates and joint ventures	20	**579**	560
Other investments	21	**787**	590
Deferred tax assets	14	**2,385**	2,849
Derivative financial instruments	41	**54**	85
Other non-current assets	22	**682**	525
Total non-current assets		**23,424**	21,159

Figure 7.3 GSK consolidated balance sheet as at 31 December 2012 and intangible assets

whopping 30% increase. The accounting treatment in respect of "other intangible assets", (including patent assets) is set out in Note 19 at page 146 of the Report and is reproduced below:

> *Other Intangible Assets*
> Intangible assets are stated at cost less provisions for amortisation and impairments.
>
> Licences, *patents*, know-how and marketing rights separately acquired or acquired as part of a business combination are amortised over their estimated useful lives, generally not exceeding 20 years, using the straight-line basis, from the time they are available for use. The estimated useful lives for determining the amortisation charge take into account *patent* lives, where applicable, as well as the value obtained from periods of non-exclusivity. Asset lives are reviewed, and where appropriate adjusted, annually. Contingent milestone payments are recognised at the point that the contingent event becomes certain. Any development costs incurred by the Group and associated with acquired licences, *patents*, know-how or marketing rights are written off to the income statement when incurred, unless the criteria for recognition of an internally generated intangible asset are met, usually when a regulatory filing has been made in a major market and approval is considered highly probable.

Note 19 adopts the language of accountants and focuses on amortisation issues for intangibles which are affected by patent expiry dates. This is entirely appropriate, but a shareholder or an external stakeholder would need to look further into the Report to find out more relevant information to identify the composition of the patent portfolio and GSK's IP management strategy ("the patent value story") for deriving value and cash flow from those assets and the reason for the significant positive change in the value of intangibles between

2011 and 2012. A 30% change in intangible asset value is a material fact warranting additional explanation to shareholders, in the author's opinion (even more so if the value had decreased by a similar percentage). However, intangibles ratios are not yet an established category of financial information in the accounting literature. Capital market analysts and shareholders are not regularly demanding additional public information on business performance and rates of return in relation to IP and intangibles. However, with further insight into the world of intangibles as corporate assets, this will change. Another type of ratio that the author believes will increasingly be of interest to shareholders, potential investors and other stakeholders such as governments is the ***intangible to tangible asset ratio.***

Accounting information is used to answer a key question about the business: Is it making a profit? Financial statements are used to assess various aspects of a business' performance and progress. Various ratios are calculated to make comparisons easier and more meaningful (with other businesses or for the same business over a period of time), the results are expressed as percentages, e.g. the percentage of gross profit to sales, or the working capital ratio. The results of analysis are used to judge a business' performance. This is done by making comparisons with other similar businesses, usually within the same year e.g. was the gross profit to sales percentage last year better or worse than the average for the trade or industry? Has the trend of the gross profit percentage to sales over the last five years been up or down over a number of years? Similarly, ratios involving the intangibles figures reported in a company's financial statement will be a useful tool for shareholders and others in assessing business decisions made by the board of directors where intangibles and IP assets are involved.

As we know, accounting rules distinguish between two types of intangible assets, acquired and self-created. The IAS 38 accounting standard which leads to intangible assets being included or excluded from the reported intangibles figure will make a huge difference to their value. Lim, Macias and Moeller have demonstrated that intangibles (which includes IP assets) have a robust positive relationship with leverage even though these intangible assets are not reported in firms' financial statements or regulatory filings (in the US).[30] Further, they find that intangible assets are a primary determinant of capital structure.[31] In other words, owning intangible assets provides significant benefits for companies.[32] Capital structure is directly relevant to corporate governance and the decisions

30 Lim, S.C., Macias, A.J. and Moeller, T. 'Intangible Assets and Capital Structure' (August 2014) *Baylor University research paper* p 14 at www.baylor.edu/business/finance/doc.php/231371.pdf..

31 Ibid pp17–18.

32 Companies with intangible assets typically generate 29% higher revenues per employee according to OHIM' s 2013 EU-wide study of 2.3 million European firms to analyse the contribution of IPR-intensive industries to economic performance and employment in Europe. Further, according to *Intellectual Property and the U.S. Economy: 2016 Update* (26 September 2016) US Department of Commerce, IP-intensive industries support at least 45 million US jobs and contribute more than $6 trillion US, or 38.2% of US gross domestic product.

taken by the board of directors. To systematically monitor performance in the medium to long term, the ratio of reported intangibles to tangible assets can be calculated to compare the company against the intangibles ratios generated by similar companies or even to calculate an industry average intangible assets ratio. Such value changes can even be the reason to invest or acquire the company. If material, rather than lump all intangibles together in one figure in a financial statement, the intangibles figures could be reported in components e.g. innovation (technology related), brands (market related) and others to provide further transparency.[33]

There is more work needed in the field of financial statement analysis with respect to intangibles and IP assets. The market consistently puts a higher value on shareholder equity than the value appearing on corporate balance sheets. The price-to-book gap is too large to be attributed solely to the mismeasurement of conventional equity or to the vicissitudes of the stock market. Numerous observers have pointed to absence of intangible assets from corporate balance sheets as an important source of the puzzle.[34] A broader financial statement analysis inclusive of intangibles is needed to assess business performance and good corporate governance. Developing metrics for a more elaborate analysis of business performance requires a parallel development in the way a company's financial and narrative data are organised and presented. Using intangibles ratios as an assessment tool will be an important step in this direction.

7.2.4 GSK's CEO Review and Business Review[35]

The CEO Review and Business Review are the critical sections of interest in terms of the content and level of IP and patent information disclosure. Sir Andrew Witty's CEO's Review on page 3 does not specifically mention either IP or patents, although it discusses R&D. The Strategic Review is covered in pages 1–49 of the Report. On page 10 under the heading "Innovation" GSK reports that:

> At the core of our business model is the use of knowledge and the development of IP. We create value by researching, manufacturing and making available products that improve people's health and well-being.

33 Supra n [29] p 14.

34 Hulten, C.R. and Hao, J. 'What is a Company Really Worth? Intangible Capital and the "Market to Book Value"' *Puzzle* (November 2008) p 2 at http://econweb.umd.edu/~hulten/WebPageFiles/Intangible%20Capital%20and%20the%20%60Market%20to%20Book%20Value%27%20Puzzle.pdf Note that at page 16 the authors state that intangible assets do not explain the entire price-to-book gap. Some part of the remaining gap may reflect the volatility of the stock market, with its episodes of exuberance and pessimism.

35 In future GSK annual reports this type of information will be required in the new Strategic Report format.

This statement is highly significant as it accentuates the value the board ascribes to GSK's IP which implies legal monopoly protection using patent rights. This theme is echoed under the heading "Sustainability" also on p 10 of the Report where GSK reports:

> Sustainability in our business performance is critically important if we are to deliver continued innovation and access to our products. We must produce profitable performance to ensure we remain competitive and have the funds to invest in our people and assets. A key element of this is an environment that appropriately rewards innovation across both *patent-protected* and branded products.

Patents are specifically mentioned for the first time on page 10. In a diagram on page 11, GSK confirms that its assets include its "IP, people and infrastructure", a phrase that implies patents. Information on GSK's approach to IP is set out on page 15 under the specific heading "IP and trade marks" and is the second time GSK directly refers to patents and the following issues are disclosed:

- patent protection;
- challenges to the validity of granted patents and legal proceedings;
- patent life (duration and expiration of the legal monopoly);
- generic medicine pressures; and
- competitors.

GSK's substantial patent portfolio protects its investment in the development of pharmaceuticals by giving it the exclusive right to sell the medicine while its patent is in force. A generic medicine contains chemically identical active ingredients (or within an acceptable bioequivalent range) as the original (usually patent-protected) GSK formula. However, a generic medicine is one that is manufactured and distributed in a jurisdiction in which GSK has no patent protection. Sometimes the formulation of the generic medicine may be patent-protected, but not the active ingredient. When a generic medicine is put on the market, market competition typically leads to substantially lower prices for both the original brand and the generic forms. Lower market price would negatively impact GSK's profits from sales. GSK's patent information disclosure states:

> The process of discovering and developing a new medicine or vaccine takes many years and can cost up to £1 billion. IP and the effective legal protection of our IP – via patents, trademarks, registered designs, copyrights and domain name registrations – is critical in ensuring a reasonable reward for innovation and to fund R&D. (See pp33 to 38 for the pharmaceutical and vaccines development process.) Patent protection for new active ingredients is available in major markets, and patents can often be obtained for new drug formulations, manufacturing processes, medical uses and devices for administering products.

Emerging markets are not all aligned on their approach to recognising patent-protected medicines.[36]

Although we may obtain patents for our products, this does not prevent them from being challenged before they expire. Further, the grant of a patent does not mean that it will be held valid and enforceable by a court. If a court determines that a patent we hold is invalid, non-infringed or unenforceable, it will not protect our innovation in that legal jurisdiction. Significant litigation concerning such patent challenges is summarised in Note 44 to the Financial Statements, "Legal proceedings". The life of a patent in most countries is 20 years from the filing date. However, the long development time for new medicines can mean that a substantial amount of this patent life has been eroded before launch. In some markets it is possible to have some of this lost time restored and this leads to variations in the amount of patent life available for each product we market.

In addition all of our commercial products are protected by registered trademarks in major markets, and our trademarks are important for maintaining the brand identity of our products. There may be local variations. For example, in the US the trademark Advair covers the same product sold in the EU as Seretide. Trademark protection may generally be extended as long as the trademark is used by renewing it when necessary. We enforce our trademark rights to prevent infringements.

Generic Pressures

When patents expire on medicines, these medicines can be subject to competition from generic products.[37] The effect of this is particularly acute in Western markets, where generic products can rapidly capture a large share of the market. As generic manufacturers typically do not incur significant costs for R&D, education or market development, they are able to offer their products at considerably lower prices than branded competitors. The same pressures do not apply as significantly to vaccines, or to products where patents exist on both active ingredients and the delivery device, such as inhaled respiratory medicines.

Competition

Within the pharmaceutical industry, competition can come from other companies making patent-protected medicines with indications to treat similar diseases to our medicines, or from manufacturers making generic copies of

36 Certain countries in emerging markets, India is one example, have excluded pharmaceuticals from patentability on public policy grounds to enable local manufacturers to make generic formulations that are sold at more affordable price points.

37 When patents or other periods of exclusivity expire, manufacturers can apply to regulatory bodies to sell generic versions of GSK's original formulations.

> our medicines following patent expiration. Our principal pharmaceutical and vaccines competitors include: Abbott Laboratories, Amgen, AstraZeneca, Bristol-Myers Squibb, Eli Lilly, Johnson & Johnson, Merck, Novartis, Pfizer, Roche Holdings, Sanofi and Takeda. The Consumer Healthcare market has become more challenging. Consumers are demanding better quality and better value. Retailers have consolidated and globalised, which has strengthened their negotiation power. Our principle competitors in these markets include: Colgate-Palmolive, Johnson & Johnson, Procter & Gamble, Unilever, Pfizer and Novartis. In addition, many other smaller companies compete with GSK in certain markets.

Highly important information regarding the use of patents and how they affect GSK's business model is "signposted" in narrative form in the Business Review. However, the information is general in nature and would apply to other pharmaceutical firms. Despite its generality, the disclosure is important because it contextualises how patent assets impact GSK's business strategy and, crucially, highlights the critical *value of patent monopolies* to the pharmaceutical business as a whole. This information acts as an introduction signalling the importance of patents in value creation for GSK. It contextualises the firm's "patent value story". This "signposting" aspect of patent information and strategy disclosure will be further developed in Chapter 8.

7.2.5 GSK's investment in R&D

Information relating to R&D is regularly disclosed by innovative quoted firms and GSK is no exception. This is the heading under which one would most likely look for information about patents, given that patents flow from inventions created during the R&D stage of the product development cycle. At page 32 of the Report, GSK describes its "Investment in R&D".

> In 2010, GSK became the first major pharmaceutical company to publish an internal rate of return (IRR) on our R&D investment, to indicate the positive value being realised from our choices within the R&D organisation. IRR provides a measurement offering an insight into how we manage our R&D business. This is based on a complex methodology that weighs the R&D costs incurred to discover and develop our late stage pipeline projects against the profits of new medicines and vaccines as they achieve regulatory approval and are made available to patients. It incorporates actual and predicted sales figures on probabilities of success for medicines in the pipeline. We also take into account an estimate of attributable R&D costs, estimated profit margins, capital investment and working capital requirements.

GSK uses the Internal Rate of Return (IRR) valuation methodology in order to fill the gap that traditional accounting for intangibles creates (as discussed in Chapter 4). The IRR figures, used only for internal management purposes, enables

GSK to demonstrate to external information users the "positive (financial) value being realised from our choices within the R&D organisation" which would not otherwise be visible in the traditional style of accounts that are published. Publication of the IRR assists GSK to overcome the information asymmetry that arises from only publishing traditional financial accounts. GSK's IRR valuation methodology is helpful, and of course if an innovating SME is in the position to devote sufficient financial and human resources to calculate its IRR, this would be a positive disclosure from a debt finance point of view. However, the IRR valuation methodology is complex (therefore expensive). Further research is warranted to provide guidance as to standardised IRR-type methodologies.

7.2.6 GSK's Strategic Review, Outlook, Risk Management Strategy and Global Patents Group (GPG)

This section of the Report provides a directional map for where GSK is headed and how it intends to get there. This involves the process of thinking about GSK and its related environment and internal business strategies as an integrated whole. Although not expressly stated, patent-protected products will be a key component in how GSK will achieve the aims stated in its "Outlook". The following paragraphs analyse the patent information disclosures made by GSK.

The concept of "risk management" is introduced on page 47 of the Business Review. Risk factors alert shareholders, potential investors and financiers to those issues that could materially alter a company's performance and financial outlook. GSK discloses "protecting IP rights" as a key risk of the group.[38] One's attention is not immediately drawn to patent information subject matter. However, the "risk factors" disclosure that follows on pages 78–86 is substantial, detailed and informative and provides specific information about GSK's patent strategy. Certain aspects of how GSK manages its patent assets are described, supplementing the general information provided earlier on page 15 of the Report. GSK introduces the principal risk factors and uncertainties it faces on page 78, namely:

(1) securing and protecting IP rights in products;
(2) loss of patent monopoly rights, either due to expiry or as a result of successful legal challenge;
(3) patent enforcement;
(4) the potential impact of the differing strength of legal protection for patent monopolies of developed countries versus lesser developed countries;
(5) competition (e.g. from generic pharmaceutical manufacturers, such as those markets in which GSK does not have patent protection for its products); and
(6) protecting confidential information.

38 This specific "risk factor" is reported in more detail following the Financial Review in a separate section of the Annual Report entitled "Investor Information" on pp 78–79 of the GSK Annual Report 2012.

These types of IP-related disclosures are directly relevant to innovating firms and are transferable to the ICS or Strategic Report. It is the lengthiest patent information disclosure in the Business Review and this section has likely been prepared with the input of GSK's GPG mentioned on page 79. The narrative patent information is still quite general and applies to any large pharmaceutical company that operates internationally. Nevertheless, it concisely highlights key risks associated with GSK's patent rights. This type of patent information disclosure could be emulated by innovating firms.

The corporate reporting regulations for listed companies, set out in the FSA's Disclosure and Transparency Rules[39] and the UK Corporate Governance Code,[40] require a discussion of the "mitigating activities" a company takes to address the risks and uncertainties identified above. The "Mitigating Activities" section on page 79 is the first time the GPG, a key part of GSK's internal patent management strategy, is mentioned and demonstrates that GSK recognises the need to coordinate patent management strategy.

> *Mitigating activities include*
> The Group is supported by a global patents organisation within the legal group whose focus is to seek to ensure and protect the intellectual property rights of the Group. Beginning in 2011 and continuing through 2012, the GPG sought to implement improvements to certain time-driven processes and controls in order to better manage its ability to obtain and maintain patent protection for the Group's key assets and to minimise risk of invalidity or unenforceability of its patents. These processes relate to (1) implementing a new review process designed to help with obtaining and maintaining appropriate patent protection for key assets; (2) identifying opportunities for and obtaining patent term extensions; (3) ensuring timely payment of required renewal fees; and (4) ensuring appropriate listing of patents in the Orange Book[41]. The enhanced processes seek to ensure that all key patent applications are reviewed by senior management prior to worldwide filing and prior to grant and that senior management approval is obtained prior to listing of patents in the Orange Book or the initiation of Abbreviated New Drug Application litigation. In addition, the Group has initiated a post approval patent review process to ensure ongoing review of the quality of patents after grant. The GPG maintains internal litigation processes designed to ensure successful enforcement and defence of patent with the goal of maintaining exclusive rights to market major products. The GPG monitors

39 http://fshandbook.info/FS/html/handbook/DTR.

40 www.frc.org.uk/Our-Work/Publications/Corporate-Governance/UK-Corporate-Governance-Code-September-2012.pdf.

41 The Orange Book is the US Food and Drug Administration's publication which sets out Approved Drug Products with Therapeutic Equivalence Evaluations.

> new developments in patent law in the major markets in which the Group operates to seek to ensure appropriate protection of the Group's assets. The Group (sometimes acting through trade associations) works with local governments to seek to secure effective and balanced IP protection designed to meet the needs of patients and payers while supporting long-term investment in innovation.

This disclosure signposts that the GPG is actively responsible for coordinating GSK's global patent management strategy including obtaining and maintaining patent protection for the Group's key assets and to minimise risk of invalidity or unenforceability of its patents. The existence of the GPG is noteworthy from a corporate governance perspective in terms of internal accountability and leadership. However, this disclosure really only hints at how GSK manages is patent assets. For example, there is no disclosure of:

- representation within the GPG;
- local patent strategy for key regions including the UK;
- the designation of a Chief IP Officer or a key manager responsible for the global or regional patent portfolio(s); or
- whether responsibility for patent strategy is divided by product or otherwise.

To demonstrate leadership and accountability, a company should consider disclosing who is responsible for coordinating and managing the firm's IP strategy and whether external advisors' advice and expertise is obtained (e.g. patent attorneys or IP solicitors).

7.2.7 GSK's patent litigation (actual and potential)

In the Financial Review, GSK mentions "Legal and other disputes" (Notes 29 and 44) at page 64 which refers to patent litigation. Patent litigation presents a *financial risk* for GSK as significant company revenue is endangered when a patent is challenged. This is so even if the legal proceeding is brought to enforce the patent against an infringer, because the defendant's response usually includes a bare denial of infringement and a counterclaim to revoke the GSK patent on the ground that it is invalid. A typical patent case will last for over a year with the associated legal costs and the possibility of an appeal to extend the proceeding. It is not unusual for a pharmaceutical company to be involved in a number of legal proceedings at any one time. Thus, the validity of key corporate assets, namely patent rights, that are the result of substantial investment in R&D over the years, is at stake. In Chapter 4 we saw that patents have the status of a cost centre for a company (a liability on the balance sheet) and as a minimum have an economic replacement value. Patent litigation involves assessing a large number of uncertainties some of which are common to all litigation while others are unique to patent rights. On page 65 GSK disclosed the following legal risks:

> Like many pharmaceutical companies, we are faced with various complex product liability, anti-trust and patent litigation, as well as investigations of our operations conducted by various governmental regulatory agencies. Throughout the year, the General Counsel of the Group, as head of the Group's legal function, and the Senior Vice President and Head of Global Litigation for the Group, who is responsible for all litigation and government investigations, routinely brief the Chief Executive Officer, the Chief Financial Officer and the board of directors on the significant litigation pending against the Group and governmental investigations of the Group.
>
> These meetings, as appropriate, detail the status of significant litigation and governmental investigations and review matters such as the number of claims notified to us, information on potential claims not yet notified, assessment of the validity of claims, progress made in settling claims, recent settlement levels and potential reimbursement by insurers.
>
> The meetings also include an assessment of whether or not there is sufficient information available for us to be able to make a reliable estimate of the potential outcomes of the disputes. Often, external counsel assisting us with various litigation matters and investigations will also assist in the briefing of the Board and senior management. Following these discussions, for those matters where it is possible to make a reliable estimate of the amount of a provision, if any, that may be required, the level of provision for legal and other disputes is reviewed and adjusted as appropriate.

Note 44 Legal Proceedings on pages 210–217 under the heading 'IP' discloses several patent litigation proceedings and the outcome to date. The patent litigation disclosed relates to ten of GSK's pharmaceutical products. In brief, the litigation involving GSK mainly concerns: (1) enforcement of patent rights against infringers; and (2) defending the validity of its patents. This disclosure is the most detailed patent information in the Report, yet is succinct and informative. In the main, GSK states its involvement in the patent or licence-related litigation and provides a brief background and description of each proceeding in a lengthy table with the following headings: "product affected", "type of litigation"; and "disclosure". Litigation is fraught with uncertainty, which is inherent in situations where there is more than one possible outcome.[42] A company must take care to ensure that their corporate disclosure of the risks involved in patent litigation provides a "fair summary" of the material information relied on by the board of directors in their decision making. The first step is to identify the uncertainties and be aware of what can happen. Next, the company should assess the associated risks as to the likelihood or probability of each possible outcome occurring.[43] A company should also consider the settlement value of the litigation so that it can assess risk and

42 Poltorak, A. and Lerner, P. 'Introducing Litigation Risks Analysis' (May 2001) Issue 109 *Managing Intellectual Property* p 1.

43 Ibid p 2.

cost of pursuing or defending an action weighed against the cost to settle the action. Is the patent litigation worth the expense? If patent rights are uncertain, pursuing settlement and negotiating a licence with the alleged infringer may be the best option in order to avoid the patent being invalidated. Note that GSK does not specifically disclose how much it spends on legal fees nor do they quantify the potential damage in relation to each case.

Nelson and Pritchard in their 2007 study concerning firms' voluntary disclosure of litigation risk examine the characteristics of narrative corporate disclosures. They found that firms subject to greater litigation risk (such as GSK and its patent litigation) disclose more cautionary language, update the language more from year to year, and use more readable language.[44] However, they also found that firms should take care to remove cautionary language in their narrative disclosure when litigation risk decreases.[45]

In formulating a patent litigation risk disclosure strategy, an innovating firm must contend with uncertainty regarding the future. *Actual* patent litigation should be voluntarily disclosed to provide a fair view. However, if there is no actual litigation, the firm could carefully consider whether there is any need to disclose potential litigation and if so, use cautionary language in doing so. Innovating firms should draft the disclosure using plain English and minimise the use of technical language and legal terms.[46]

Evaluating patent litigation risk inevitably leads a company to consider the quality of its patent portfolio. Poor-quality patents, perhaps due to inadequacies in patent examination and issuance quality from patent offices (discussed in Chapter 2) leads to those patents being prone to litigation risk. Shareholders and other stakeholders need to understand that poor-quality patents and careless patent-granting contributes to increased financial and legal risk.[47]

In summary, patent litigation risk has important implications for the corporate disclosure policies of innovating firms.[48] Making decisions about patent litigation is about managing legal risk. The costs of patent litigation can be disruptive and adversely impact normal business operations.[49] As the cost of patent litigation is high and the outcome will have a financial impact on the business, firms should seriously consider all the effects of legal proceedings. On the other hand, the rewards for well-organised and financed patent enforcement action can be substantial. In the long term, the strategic benefits of strong patent enforcement

44 Nelson. K. and Pritchard, A. *Litigation Risk and Voluntary Disclosure: The Use of Meaningful Cautionary Language* (August 2007) Second Annual Conference on Empirical Legal Studies p 1.

45 Ibid.

46 Ibid p 7.

47 Martin, D. and Beling, P. 'Patent Litigation Risk Characterization: Prospective identification of Financial Risk in Patent Holdings' (2004) M-Cam draft pp 4–5.

48 Ibid p 3.

49 'Patent Litigation: Is it Worth the Expense?' (1 April 2006) 26(7) *Genetic Engineering & Biotechnology News*.

include a deterrent effect on other potential infringers of the patent in question and increase the likelihood that future patent disputes are settled out of court.[50] An innovating firm should be sensitive to changes to their litigation risks. Disclosure must be current and firms must update their disclosed litigation risks annually. The innovating firm should avoid "boilerplate" litigation risk disclosure which is a concern to corporate regulators and should strive to disclose information that is relevant to financial risk. Ultimately, what is important for the innovating firm is to make the effort to disclose and demonstrate to the potential investors and stakeholders the company's appreciation of the legal risks that may arise in connection with patents and that it is actively managing those risks.

7.2.8 GSK's confidential information

The possible disclosure of confidential information is a hidden risk of patent litigation. As part of the discovery process, the parties may be required to divulge sensitive product development, manufacturing, marketing or pricing information to defendants and potentially to the public, although court procedures may be implemented to preserve confidentiality. Whereas GSK discloses *actual* litigation to which it is a party, it also reports two further specific business risks, including "Potential Litigation" and "Protecting our Information" on pages 84 and 85 respectively. The latter focuses on how GSK protects its confidential information. This is an important component of patent strategy, as in order to be patentable, the legal requirement under the PA 1977 is that the invention must be "new". Section 2(1) PA 1977 provides that an invention shall be taken to be "new" if it does not form part of the state of the art. An invention lacks novelty if the specified combination of features has already been anticipated in a disclosure. In *SmithKline Beecham Plc's (Paroxetine Methanesulfonate) Patent,*[51] the House of Lords held there were two requirements for anticipation: prior disclosure and enablement. These are distinct concepts each of which has to be satisfied and each of which has its own rules. If any features of GSK's potentially patentable inventions are made public before a patent application has been filed, the opportunity to be granted a patent will be lost. This is a serious risk for a company that relies on patent-protected products. GSK's disclosure regarding its confidential information on page 85 is set out below:

> *Protecting our information*
> Risk description: Risk of exposing business critical or sensitive data due to inadequate data governance or information systems security.
>
> The Group relies on critical and sensitive data, such as corporate strategic plans, personally identifiable information, trade secrets and IP, to drive

50 Martin, D. and Beling, P. 'Patent Litigation Risk Characterization: Prospective Identification of Financial Risk in Patent Holdings' (2004) M-Cam draft pp 4–5 at p 3.

51 *SmithKline Beecham Plc's (Paroxetine Methanesulfonate) Patent* [2006] RPC 10.

planning and operations. Security of this type of data is exposed to escalating external threats that are increasing in sophistication and changing from a goal of disruption to being financially or politically motivated. Failure to implement appropriate safeguards to adequately protect against any unauthorised or unintentional access, acquisition, use, modification, loss or disclosure of this critical or sensitive data may adversely impact the Group's ability to maintain patent rights and competitive advantages and may result in legal non-compliance resulting in fines and penalties or inability to sell product in a particular market.

Mitigating activities include
The Group assesses changes in our risk environment through briefings by government agencies, subscription to commercial threat intelligence services and security information sharing with other companies – both in our industry and beyond. The Group's policies and controls on information protection are regularly reviewed and employees are routinely trained. The Group has dedicated information security expertise and resources. In response to the changing external risk environment, the Group has implemented a global programme to further increase business awareness of information protection requirements, further define minimum information security expectations for third-party agreements, implement additional technical controls to protect data, and improve its security event monitoring . . .

GSK's disclosure is general and concise, signifying that the company recognises the issue and has a programme in place. However, it does not disclose who is responsible for managing its confidential information.

7.2.9 GSK's information for investors: products, competition and IP

GSK provides an Investor Information section on pages 224–247 entitled "Products, Competition and IP", beginning at page 229 with a table containing 42 entries setting out the relevant patent expiry dates in the US and EU. A sample of the first entries of patent expiry information is set out in Figure 7.4.

The impact of patent expiry on GSK's pharmaceutical business is critical information for investors. Once a pharmaceutical enters the market, patent protection can result in high profits, with gross profit margins exceeding 90%. When a patent that covers a product expires, generic manufacturers offer the products at prices reported to average about 30% of the price of the brand-name originals. Once a pharmaceutical product loses patent protection, lower-price generics quickly siphon off as much as 90% of sales.[52] The pharmaceutical industry

52 DeRuiter, J. and Holston, P. 'Drug Patent Expirations and the "Patent Cliff"' (20 June 2012) *US Pharmacist*, Jobson Publications.

Products	Compounds	Indicator(s)	Major Competitor Brands	Patent Expiry Dates USA	Patent Expiry Dates EU
Respiratory Veramist	fluticansone propionate	rhinitis	Nasonex	2021	2023
Flixotide/ Flovent	fluticansone propionate	asthma/ COPD	Qvar, Singulair	Expired compound (2016) (*Diskus* device) 2013–2025 (HFA-device/ formulation)	Expired (compound) (*Diskus* device) 2017 (HFS-device/ formulation)

Figure 7.4 Extract from GSK Investor Information, Products, Competition & IP table

is now experiencing the long-expected and much-discussed patent cliff.[53] A notable 2012 patent expiration for GSK is the patent covering the diabetes drug Avandia (rosiglitazone). Further, as a result of GSK's past corporate disclosures, industry analysts confirm that over the next few years GSK will lose patent protection on its anti-triglyceride product Lovaza (omega-3-acid esters), the benign prostatic hyperplasia drug Avodart (dutasteride), the HIV/AIDS product Combivir and asthma medication Advair. In 2010 these drugs combined accounted for over $1 billion US in earnings in the United States alone. A generic form of Combivir is already available in the United States.[54] This is a significant "patent cliff" that will result in additional generic competition for GSK, potentially eroding millions of pounds of turnover in the near future. Disclosure of patent expiry dates is *critically important* for GSK shareholders and potential investors (equity financiers). In terms of the type of information contained in Figure 7.4, GSK's disclosure could have provided more detailed information as to how they planned to optimise earnings before a significant patent expires (e.g. through raising prices, enhanced advertising, a complementary pipeline product or out-sourcing to lower cost regions of the world). However, a lengthy "Pharmaceuticals and Vaccines product development pipeline" table is set out in pages 225–288. This discloses investment in new pharmaceutical inventions that GSK believes will

53 A "patent cliff" signifies the potential sharp fall in revenues when a patent expires on one or more important company products – a company's revenues may "fall off a cliff" because these products can be reproduced and sold at much lower prices by competitors. While the term applies to any industry, recently a "patent cliff" has come to be linked with the pharmaceutical industry.

54 Supra DeRuiter n [51].

Compound	Type	Indication	Phase	Marketing Authorisation Application (Europe)	Achieved Regulatory Review Progress New Drug Application (NDA) USA/ Biological Licence Application (BLA)

Figure 7.5 Pipeline Pharmaceuticals and Vaccines

address unmet pharmaceutical needs and that are also profitable and represents GSK's strategy for minimising the impact of the revenue loss attributable to patent expiry in the near future and to maintain profitability. The table headings and column structure is set out in Figure 7.5.

There is no additional narrative disclosure apart from the "Pipeline table" which provides certain limited information concerning future actions, prospective products or product approvals which are intended to enhance future performance. Nor is there any narrative disclosure of pipeline pharmaceuticals with the profit potential of Lovaza, Avodart, Combivir and Advair emerging in the near future. There is no discussion of patent applications at all. The facts show that although GSK's board of directors has invested £4 billion in its R&D pipeline they have not made any express forward-looking statement regarding its pipeline in this section.[55] However, much earlier, on page 3 in the CEO's Review, Sir Andrew Witty summarises the GSK R&D pipeline as follows:

> In R&D, the Group made significant progress in 2012. We now have six key new products under regulatory review and expect Phase III data on 14 assets in 2013 and 2014. In total, over the next three years, GSK has the potential to launch around 15 new medicines and vaccines globally.

Further on page 10 under the heading "Innovation" GSK discloses:

> In 2012, we invested £3.5 billion in core research and development of new medicines, vaccines and consumer products, and we are currently evaluating around 50 investigational medicines for diseases such as cancer, diabetes, heart disease and respiratory illnesses. Over the next three years, we have the potential to bring around 15 new medicines to patients.

One has to carefully analyse the table and then draw inferences and make independent conclusions from the information presented at either end of the Report. For shareholders and investors, this is time consuming and unhelpful. "Joining the dots" for the annual report reader and expressly explaining with

55 GSK reports on p 8 of the Report that in 2012 the company spent £3.5 billion before non-core items and £4.0 billion in total on their search to develop new medicines, vaccines and innovative consumer products.

specificity how, for example, it will replace blockbuster pharmaceuticals whose patents are expiring with new pharmaceutical products that have the potential to become big sellers, would improve the disclosure. This weakness in narrative patent information disclosure is echoed by auditing firm KPMG International which confirms that in general, "[d]isclosure of R&D pipelines remains relatively limited, influenced by the problems and lack of success of recent years, and competitive pressure" and, "[w]e do not see the issue of scientific risk yet being embraced: companies' disclosure is, in general, limited and the governance of R&D merits a higher profile".[56] Further, according to Ed Giniat, Global Chair of KPMG's Pharmaceutical Practice US, as significant revenue is at risk when a patent is litigated or expired, replacing these revenue streams magnifies the need for successful R&D.[57] For instance, GSK could make it more explicit that its strategy is to focus on growth in emerging markets to mitigate patent losses in developed markets or to acquire new patent portfolios with earlier product launch schedules from other companies.[58] On the other hand, adopting a selective or restrictive approach to R&D pipeline disclosure, by limiting detailed discussion of early stage R&D, arguably is sensible given the high failure rate. Nevertheless, many shareholders, investors and financiers hold the view that increased transparency is useful for assessing the relative attractiveness and competitive positioning of the R&D pipeline.[59] Ultimately, from a corporate governance point of view, additional relevant and genuinely useful information would assist with an assessment of the directors' stewardship of corporate IP assets.

GSK does not disclose information about discontinued R&D projects or patents it has let lapse. According to KPMG, disclosure of discontinued projects remains rare and that in a highly scrutinised industry, success and failure will be readily apparent to interested investors and financiers; it should enhance the reputation of companies to disclose failures.[60] Bearing in mind that R&D is crucial to the future of the business and accounts for a high percentage of a company's annual expenditure, more detailed, "joined up" disclosure of R&D, relevant IP and patent information would be beneficial from a corporate governance perspective.

7.2.10 GSK's board of directors

The board of directors is collectively responsible for the long-term success of the company.[61] GSK has a competent and well-qualified board, and while Moncrief

56 KPMG *An Overview of Risk and Disclosure* (15 May 2012) at www.kpmg-institutes.com/institutes/healthcare-life-sciences-institute/articles/2012/05/risk-and-disclosure-in-the-global-pharmaceutical-industry.html, pp 2–3.

57 Ibid p 7.

58 'Glaxosmithkline undervalued say analysts' (11 December 2013) p 16 at www.morningstar.co.uk/uk/news/114764/glaxosmithkline-undervalued-say-analysts.aspx.

59 Ibid.

60 Ibid p 18.

61 UK Corporate Governance Code p 8.

Slaoui is GSK's Chairman of R&D[62], there does not appear to be a director (executive or non-executive) who is a qualified patent attorney or IP law specialist. According to the International IP Strategists' Association (INTIPSA) it is no longer adequate to simply rely on the traditional role of the Chief Legal Officer or Chief Technology Officer (CTO) to assume leadership and responsibility for IP and patent matters. In certain medium and large companies, especially in the US, responsibility for IP matters now rests with the Chief IP Officer (CIPO) or the Director of IP operating at the intersection of IP, technology and business. The IP Director needs to understand where IP fits into the business and overall commercial reality.[63] INTIPSA advises that:

> There is a direct parallel between the CIPO role and that of the CTO, both having a strong emphasis on advising and influencing. The CIPO must be able to identify strategic IP issues, trends, and industry sector issues plus be able to lobby internally and externally if and when required. The CIPO should be a leader in IP strategic thinking, including in such key areas as the acquisition of IP, IP portfolio optimisation, setting goals for IP exploitation and understanding IP risk mitigation. This will include litigation and settlements. Understanding the business environment from an IP perspective, interpreting that for the business and providing foresight is also crucial. Being able to communicate IP thinking to the company's other executives as well as externally is a key responsibility.[64]

GSK, or any firm with a business model that relies heavily on patent protection, should consider appointing a director with patent expertise (e.g. either a patent attorney or an IP solicitor or ideally both) to support the board's decision making with respect to these valuable corporate intangible assets. A cost-benefit analys is would be helpful here in relation to innovating firms with limited resources who could engage the services of competent IP professionals or consultants as needed.

7.2.11 Increased transparency

In addition to the matters discussed above, in the author's opinion increased transparency is needed in the following areas.

7.2.11.1 Depth of patent portfolio

Despite its patent assets having growing strategic importance, GSK does not report specifically on the depth of its patent portfolio (number of patents, patents

62 As at 2012.

63 'The Role of the Chief Intellectual Property Officer' (2013) INTIPSA p 2 at www.intipsa.com/wp-content/uploads/2013/01/INTIPSA-Tips-The-role-of-the-CIPO1.pdf

64 Ibid p 3.

per jurisdiction etc.), patent families, the strength of particular patent pools or sales and acquisitions of patents. A search of *Esp@cenet*, the EPO's worldwide patent database, confirms that 6,147 results were found for GSK as the applicant.[65] Patents have also been filed by several of GSK's international subsidiaries within the corporate group. The size and quality of a company's patent portfolio will have a direct impact on its reputation, return on investments and access to the market. All patents are not equal in value or importance and shareholders, potential investors or financiers will need to use additional qualitative information to rank the expected value of the patents. But the narrative corporative reporting provides little insight into the "big picture" of GSK's patent portfolio. With respect to innovation, patent assets are seen as a clear signal of a company's competitiveness and more transparency in this area would be welcome. Indeed, reports suggest that GSK is undervalued.[66]

7.2.11.2 Key researchers, teams and inventor's rights

GSK does not present any information about the expertise and performance of key prolific and influential R&D employees and/or those named as inventors in GSK patents. The IC of this important group of GSK staff does not feature. The role of key R&D personnel is critical not only to innovation but they may also act as witnesses in patent litigation. A risk to GSK's financial results is potentially that personnel named as inventors or co-inventors may be entitled to compensation under section 40 PA 1977 (as amended) if the patent was of "outstanding benefit" to GSK (the employer). In *Kelly & Chiu v GE Healthcare Ltd*[67] two employee medical researcher/inventors were awarded "air share" compensation, namely a combined amount of 3% of GE's £50 million profit. Whether or not this type of issue is a reportable "principal" risk warranting disclosure is an issue for GSK's board. In the UK post-*Kelly*, the board may also need to consider whether and how it should implement an appropriate inventor compensation scheme.

7.2.12 How GSK IP and patent portfolios create value

As a listed pharmaceutical company, GSK's patent disclosure is extensive when compared to companies in most non-pharma business sectors. However, one must comb through the whole of the Report in order to collate patent-related information. The "IP value story" is not assembled into one section for ease of reference, largely because GSK follows the Business Review structure and must report on a myriad of matters in addition to patent information, thus the structure

65 Search carried out on 11 February 2014.
66 Supra n [57].
67 [2009] EWHC 191 (Pat).

could be improved in this regard. In several instances detailed patent information e.g. expiry and litigation is presented in simple tables that arrange patent information in rows and columns with a prominent header row and typically using a wide format (as opposed to a narrow format). As a communication tool a table enables a form of generalisation of patent information whilst providing a familiar way to communicate data. GSK does not appear to use any other visuals to illustrate or disclose its patent information. Although the Index to the Report lists IP, one suggestion is to simply include a "Patent Information" heading and reference to the relevant page numbers in which disclosures occur. Another suggestion is to have a standalone "Patent Information" section in the "Investor Information" part of the report.

From a corporate governance point of view, it is not unreasonable to suggest that more narrative information is needed on the effect of patent expiry on GSK and what the company plans to do to escape the patent cliff and potential declining revenue. This is needed to assess the current board of directors stewardship of its patent assets and strategy that support its pharmaceutical business model. The Strategic Report should enable GSK and other patent-owning firms to present their business models, strategy and objectives, principle risks and future outlook more reliably, less generally and more completely, together with a higher degree of detailed patent information.

Is the IP asset and strategy information in the Report representative?

How can what we have learned in the mini-case study translate to other firms? The long gestation periods for the R&D programmes in the pharmaceutical industry lead invariably to the conclusion that patented medicines should be regarded as capital investments, and that this conclusion is reinforced by the body of evidence linking intangibles to company valuation and productivity.[68] From a corporate governance standpoint, key questions involve "agency" issues by shareholders and other interested parties seeking to monitor the actions of managers and this has inclined accounting principles toward a conservatism that stresses accuracy in valuation and relies on data generated by arms-length market transactions.[69] One consequence of this conservatism is that hard-to-value assets like intangibles are excluded from the accounts and therefore further information is needed in narrative form to ensure corporate transparency.

68 This literature includes studies relating financial market value to R&D (e.g. Hall, R. 'A Framework Linking Intangible Resources and Capabiliites to Sustainable Competitive Advantage' (Nov 1993) *Strategic Management Journal* at http://onlinelibrary.wiley.com/doi/10.1002/smj.4250140804/abstract; Lev, B. *Intangibles Management, Measurement, and Reporting* (2001) Brookings Institution Press, Washington D.C.).

69 Ibid pp 25–26.

7.3 Corporate IP disclosures: evaluating the findings of the *Banking on IP?* report and the *Final Report from the Expert Group on Intellectual Property Valuation*

The *Banking on IP?* report only briefly touches on corporate disclosure of IP or patents under the CA 2006 stating, "[c]alculation of estimates [of value] for micro, SMEs is further complicated by the filing of abbreviated accounts".[70] This point is not developed further in the remainder of the report. Recommendation five does however suggest a more transparent marketplace will transform IP and intangibles as an asset class. The EC "IP Valuation" report published in March 2014[71] takes up the point of corporate narrative reporting more directly in section 4.4 "Possibilities for complementary reporting of IP and IPRs". It suggests that disclosure might include:

> Examples of useful information on IP/IPRs can be the number of patents, the description and the number of patents actively employed in firm activities, the time to expiration for the major IPRs, the description and number of patent submissions and the associated degree of success and the like. Sometimes non-financial indicators are mixed with financial data to create new insightful information. Examples of such indicators for the IPO/IPRs and research area are sales per patent (or family of patents) or revenue from the products/services introduced from R&D in the last 3–5 years.[72]

The "IP Valuation" report also acknowledges the poor situation as to the recognition, measures and disclosure of IP and concludes that the present reporting and information frameworks are in urgent need of updating[73] and that the filing of a "management report", detailing IP and IP value in addition to financial statements, is recommended.[74] The Expert Panel proposes:

> the introduction of an additional IP reporting section in corporate information and data about IP and IPRs as a section of a company's financial statement. The enrichment of the management report by more information about IP and/or a separate statement about IP are other possible actions . . . Yet we need to consider the fact that small companies (small in terms of Article 3 paragraph 2 of the EU Accounting Directive) are not required to publish a Management Report. However it could be seen as a first move in

70 Brassell, M. and King, K. *Banking on IP?* (6 November 2013) Independent report commissioned by the UKIPO p 25.

71 *Final Report form the Expert Group on Intellectual Property Valuation* (March 2014) European Union (referred to as the "IP Valuation" report). This report does not reference the 2013 *Banking on IP?* report or refer to it in the bibliography.

72 Ibid p 41.

73 Ibid p 44.

74 Ibid pp 45 and 65.

the right direction for collecting more and better information about IP/IPR in Europe.[75]

These conclusions and recommendations directly support the approach taken in this book with respect to corporate governance, disclosure, transparency and innovating firms – disclosure of their patent information and strategy is recommended to supplement and triangulate the quantitative information presented in the traditional financial statements. The Expert Panel did not, however, fully considered in detail how companies (especially SMEs who are typically exempt from corporate narrative reporting) should make such disclosure. It is hoped that the GSK mini-case study corporate IP information and strategy analysis assists to fill this space.

7.4 Corporate IP disclosure: breadth, depth and scope

The corporate financial reporting space has been dominated by a focus on a company's tangible assets, to such an extent that equity investors focus on a single metric – the "earnings-per-share" number. The narrow and incomplete focus on short-term financial performance is only of interest to short-term equity investors who focus on the regulatory disclosure requirements for shareholders, as opposed to the type of information of interest to other stakeholders such as financiers and lenders. There is a new and more holistic view, as well as an unmistakable movement for companies to disclose IP and patent information, that escapes the accounting lens, but can be captured by the corporate governance lens. This is why company law should take the lead to provide a "true and fair" view of a company's IP assets.

Relatively little research has been done in the field of narrative corporate reporting and specifically, intangibles, IP and patent information and strategy disclosure. There is a great demand for high-quality interpretative research which is able to build knowledge from observation of phenomenawithin a contextually rich environment.[76] The GSK case study considered the content and structure of GSK's disclosures including the value of intangibles in the financial statements which led to a discussion as to the potential for intangibles ratio analysis to enhance assessment of business performance. We also considered GSK's disclosures related to patent information and strategy in its 2012 annual report, designed as an inductive qualitative research to provide insight into narrative corporate reporting practice. This does not entail a claim for "applicability" that would warrant courts to apply the results directly in litigation.[77] GSK was selected to

75 Ibid pp 65–66.

76 Schell, C. 'The Value of the Case Study as a Research Strategy' (1992) *Manchester Business School* p 14 at www.finance-mba.com/Case%20Method.pdf.

77 Hwaidi, M. *Why and How Empirical Study in Commercial Law?* (2014) Annual Conference of Socio Legal Study Association at Robert Gordon University p 3.

enable us to analyse a high level of "material" patent information disclosures in terms of breadth, depth and scope. As GSK's patent information disclosure is thought to be of a very high standard, given the company's access to best expert advice in preparing its annual report, it provides us with some knowledge as to current best practice in terms of disclosure in the UK typical in the pharma sector. Relevant aspects of GSK's patent information disclosure could be emulated by innovating firms on a voluntary corporate reporting basis, dependant on their IP business model and the cost to produce such information as discussed in Chapter 5. The case study found that GSK disclosed the following types of patent information in narrative form:

- generalised patent information contextualised to signpost the value of patent protection and patent monopolies to the pharmaceutical business;
- a summary of how the Internal Rate of Return on R&D investment is calculated;
- key risks arising in connection with GSK's patent rights:
    - (i) securing and protection patent rights;
    - (ii) patent life (duration and expiration of the legal monopoly);
    - (iii) challenges to the validity of granted patents and legal proceedings;
    - (iv) patent enforcement activities;
    - (v) competition from generic medicine manufacturers;
    - (vi) confidential information; and
- patent management information including its GPG.

As a form of research, the case study is unparalleled for its ability to consider a single research question within an environment rich with contextual variables.[78] The GSK 2012 Annual Report mini-case study serves as exploratory research, but the scope for application of the evidence-based material patent information disclosures is much greater as the findings are transferable to innovating firms and other corporates. This research helps provide a new understanding of how narrative corporate disclosure of certain types of patent information may increase transparency and reduce asymmetric information regarding the financial accounting metric currently used to value key corporate patent assets and investment in R&D. The knowledge gained from the exploratory case study and other literature in earlier chapters will be applied in Chapter 8, where such knowledge is comprehensively used as the foundation for constructing a streamlined (or simplified) materiality evaluation narrative patent information disclosure model for innovating UK firms. Chapter 8 considers whether such disclosure should be legally mandatory or voluntary.

78 Schell, C. 'The Value of the Case Study as a Research Strategy' (1992) *Manchester Business School* p 14 at www.finance-mba.com/Case%20Method.pdf.

8 A triage-style "materiality evaluation model" for IP and patent disclosures

The common wisdom is that "you manage what you measure". The corollary is, of course, "out of sight, out of mind".[1]

Mr W. Richard Frederick, Principal Administrator, Organization of Economic Cooperation and Development (OECD)

Introduction

In Chapter 2 we saw that the IP and patent ecosystem, both globally and in the UK, has undergone important changes in the past few years. Changes have been set in motion by the advent of ever-increasing technological innovation, resulting in more granted patents and the ensuing economic value attributed to intangible corporate IP assets which remain largely hidden in traditional accounting statement formats and company law. Applying for and being granted patents, for example, positively affects perceptions of innovating firms and improves valuation estimates in early financing rounds (for example, the more patents owned, the higher the likelihood of attracting finance).[2] Large publicly listed firms are also shedding some light via their corporate IP asset information disclosure in their statutory corporate narrative reports. Chapter 7 presented a mini-case study involving GlaxoSmithKline (GSK), a global firm with a sizeable patent portfolio, that critically analysed the nature and content of the narrative patent information disclosures made in the company's 2012 annual report. The goal of this chapter is to build on the narrative content and style of the Danish and German ICS method and drafting mechanics, the GSK patent information disclosure and other relevant literature, to derive a new model and specific guidance for innovating firms as to the type of patent information they may wish to voluntarily report in

1 Frederick, W.R. (2009) '*Recent Developments in IC Reporting and their Policy Implications*' *OECD* Education Working Papers, No. 17, OCED Publishing, Paris, p 8.

2 Hsu, D. and Ziedonis, R. *Patents as Quality Signals for Entrepreneurial Ventures* (2007) Paper presented at DRUID Summer Conference.

an ICS or in the Strategic Report of the company's annual return.[3] The book puts forward that disclosing narrative qualitative (non-financial) IP and patent information ensures that the value of the innovating firm's IP portfolio is neither "out sight" nor "out of mind" and this will assist shareholders and stakeholders such as lenders to identify IP assets and link them to the value and growth of the business. However, as explained in Chapter 5, if a company is entitled to rely on the small companies' exemption, delivery of a Directors' Report to Companies House is optional.[4] In many private SMEs, the only member is a sole director[5] and to date, from a corporate governance perspective, it has been seen as a completely unnecessary administrative burden to require such directors to prepare a Directors' Report for themselves which no one else sees. As we also know, from an innovation perspective, a significant problem for shareholders, investors and financiers is that internally generated patent assets lack transparency in the company's annual accounts under IAS 38 Intangibles and without relevant useful information investment and finance decisions falter. On a positive note, according to Frederick:

> There appears to be a trend to report beyond the limits of what traditional accounting standards require, and include a broader set of important value drivers. The question has moved from whether this information is important and whether it needs to be reported, to how to best report it.[6]

In the modern IP ecosystem, the need for increased voluntary disclosure of IP and patent information by SMEs and innovation firms is acute. What is less clear is how and patent information innovating firms should voluntarily disclose. Chapter 8 examines how to uniformly, succinctly and cost-efficiently disclose relevant patent information and strategy that has been subject to director-level review. This requires the development of a conceptual framework leading to a new model for voluntary information reporting. Section 8.1 summarises the views on solving the intangibles reporting problem addressed in earlier chapters and sets out the rationale for the author's preferred approach. Arguments are made in favour of voluntary patent information and strategy disclosure as opposed to mandatory disclosure, at this point in time. Section 8.2 presents an original user-friendly "triage-style" *Essential, Desirable & Optional Patent Information and Strategy* disclosure model, the foundation for a coherent shape for innovating firms to voluntarily report how corporate patent assets create value for the firm in

3 Once every year, every company must deliver a return (now known as a confirmation statement) to Companies House containing relevant information about legally mandated features of the company's affairs: section 854(1) CA 2006. Refer also Chapters 5 & 6.

4 Sections 444(1) and 444(a) CA 2006.

5 The "one-man" company. Alternatively, the sole member of the company may be the nominee of the director.

6 Supra Frederick n [1]. This chapter touches on the UK Operating and Business Review on [see pages 000] and predates the new Strategic Review.

narrative form using key qualitative (non-financial) patent information indicators. The new "business triage style"[7] three-tier model is compared and contrasted with the Danish and German ICS models, the GSK patent disclosures and other literature. Section 8.3 considers potential criticism of enhanced voluntary patent information disclosures by innovating firms. Finally, while the new disclosure model is a starting point, it begs the question: How should patent information and strategy disclosure be facilitated? In section 8.4 we identify the relevant stakeholders that need to be involved in assisting and advising innovating SMEs to prepare their corporate narrative disclosures.

8.1 Views on solving the corporate IP transparency problem

This book, over the course of the seven previous chapters, has explored the three approaches to solving the hidden intangibles, corporate reporting and governance problems.

8.1.1 Overhauling the fundamental accounting treatment of intangibles

Chapter 4 argued that traditional financial statements do not reveal what drives IP and patent value due to requirements of IAS 38 accounting standard for intangibles. This approach situates the problem and the solution within the domain of traditional *financial* reporting, and specifically, as a task for the accounting and valuing professions. However, we have seen in Chapters 4 and 5 that reform of IAS 38 Intangibles is unlikely to take place in the short-to-medium term due to the need for a regulated IP and patent markets to provide accountants with historical transaction financial data which has not yet emerged.

Further, until recently there has been relatively little attention paid to IP, tax and corporate governance. IP and patent owning firms are often unfamiliar with the specific tax issues applicable. Income generated by corporate IP assets can significantly affect the firm's tax liability. The recognition of income and deductions related to intellectual property depends on factors including the ownership of the property created, whether ownership is transferred properly, and the nature of the taxpaying company's activities when the property was created. More transparent corporate reporting of IP assets will facilitate tax planning. For example, schemes that give preferential tax treatment to income arising from patents are likely to have significant effects on the location of ownership of new IP and could

7 Using the same triage categories employed by military medical and disaster medical services, business processes are categorised as essential/critical (red) important/urgent (yellow), or optional/supportive (green). See Zich, J. 'Business 911: Triage for Trying Times' (June 1994) *Stanford Business School Magazine*.

lead to substantial reductions in tax revenue.[8] Or, a disposition of IP may produce income, capital gain or loss or a charitable contribution deduction, or may enable income generated by the IP to be assigned to another party.[9] The tax law for corporate IP assets is complex and comprises a labyrinth of general principles and specific provisions. As IP continues to supplant tangible property so as to generate corporate wealth, interpreting and applying these rules can be a daunting task for corporate finance directors, internal and external accountants and their tax advisers. Corporate governance measures to enhance disclosure and transparency of IP assets will also moderate tax related information asymmetry between shareholders and the board of directors. As the primary purpose of the corporate tax system is to raise revenue, this has policy relevance for tax administrations in monitoring corporate tax planning activities (as well as the standard setting bodies in relation to IAS 12 Income Taxes).[10] Recent tax scandals in the UK and EU involving global companies Starbucks and Amazon underscore the significance of tax management by the board and corporate social responsibility.

8.1.2 Supplemental reporting outside of the existing accounting framework via the ICS or other reporting formats

The second approach holds that fundamentally changing the IAS 38 accounting standard is not feasible. It is undesirable because the existing system of accounting and financial reporting functions with relative certainty internationally. It provides a certain group of users with adequate information. As a result, this view holds that an entirely new form of corporate reporting is needed, designed specifically for the needs of new/other users and should be separate from traditional accounts.[11] As discussed in Chapters 5 and 6, other forms of reporting are emerging such as the ICS, a separate management report, which covers a broader range of corporate intangibles as well as IC and IP information and strategy. In relation to IP-backed lending, since 2010, five Hong Kong banks[12] have offered more favourable financial and/or service privileges to successful business loan applicants who have voluntarily prepared their own ICS.[13] The Hong Kong IP Department

8 Griffith, R., Miller, H. and O'Connell, M. 'Ownership of Intellectual Property and Corporate Taxation' (April 2014) 112 *Journal of Public Economics* 12–23 at www.sciencedirect.com/science/article/pii/S0047272714000103.

9 IP-owning tax payers should ensure consistency in the tax treatment of a sale or licence between the parties.

10 Nor Shaipah Abdul Wahab and Holland, K. 'Tax Planning, Corporate Governance and Equity Value' (June 2012) 44(2) *The British Accounting Review* 111–124 at www.sciencedirect.com/science/article/pii/S0890838912000212.

11 Supra Frederick n [1] p 21.

12 Bank of China (Hong Kong) Limited, Chon Hing Bank Limited, Citi Commercial Bank, Hang Seng Bank Limited and the Bank of East Asia.

13 'Hong Kong banks sign up to ground-breaking IC initiative' (April 2010) *Intellectual Asset Magazine blog* at www.iam-magazine.com/blog/Detail.aspx?g=3d6fc595-6202-40f0-ba82-6d5ee1b05def.

(HKIPD) worked closely with the banks to facilitate this. HKIPD have also produced a helpful Guide to IC Management.[14] In 2013, Frey recommended the introduction of a new type of "Growth Report".[15] In 2014, the *Final Report from the Expert Group on IP Valuation* recommended supplementary reporting of non-financial information on IP suggesting that companies file a mandatory separate "management IP report" detailing IP and IP value.[16] However, in Chapter 6 we noted that the ICS is in decline, remains the exception rather than the rule and has generally not been embraced by corporates, who may prefer the "integrated reporting" approach discussed below.

8.1.3 Better disclosure via the existing UK corporate reporting framework

The third approach recommends that accounting standards for intangible assets should be *supplemented* through the narrative disclosure of better and more detailed information. This additional information can appear in traditional financial statements as notes to the accounts, or, as recommended in this book, in existing corporate annual narrative reporting. As such, additional voluntary qualitative disclosures concerning intangible assets integrated into the annual report would have to comply with existing corporate reporting regulations. Therefore, the limitations of IAS 38 are overcome within the traditional financial statements and corporate reports. However, the question is: What type of disclosure and where? The author contacted Jackie Maguire, a UK representative of the EC Expert Group via LinkedIn, to elucidate the decision to recommend mandatory over voluntary corporate reporting. She advised that a mandatory versus voluntary corporate reporting obligation was:

> a subtle point, but companies have a tendency to follow the hard rules when it comes to financial reporting and do little more than is necessary. For instance, there is nothing stopping plcs from making an IP statement in their annual report now – however very few do! We wanted to see a step change in encouraging companies to think regularly about their intangible assets and the value that they provide for their business.[17]

The Expert Group's report does not articulate any further consideration of the dilemma between voluntary or mandatory reporting from a company law or corporate governance perspective.

14 See www.ipd.gov.hk/eng/ICM.

15 Frey, C.B. *IP Rights and the Financing of Technology Innovation* (2013) Edward Elgar Publishing Limited, Chapter 5.

16 *Final Report form the Expert Group on Intellectual Property Valuation* (March 2014) European Union.

17 The exchange took place via a Linked in discussion at www.linkedin.com/groups?gid=2991669&goback=%2Ebzo_*1_*1_*1_*1_*1_*1_*1_intipsa&trk=rr_grp_name.

In any event, all three approaches are being advanced. Imperative changes are occurring in the accounting field in the treatment of certain intangibles, namely, the financial valuation of trade marks via the adoption of the new ISO 10668 Monetary Brand Valuation.[18] An ISO standard for patent valuation does not yet exist. In summary, while there is a convergence to a line of thinking that more information on patents, IP and intangibles is generally warranted, there is not yet a consensus as to *how* and *where* to report such information and whether reporting should be *voluntary* or *mandatory*. In this book, we argue that ideally the appropriate method for supplementary corporate IP asset and strategy information is via the company's annual corporate narrative reporting as this streamlines the number of reports companies need to make. As part of their lending policy, if more favourable financial and/or service privileges were offered to innovating firms who voluntarily prepared and filed their own Strategic Report integrating material IP disclosures, then this is a pragmatic win-win situation. Filing with Companies House renders the report public. Lenders would have access to important non-financial information to help them to identify solid borrowers that in theory, should meet legal corporate reporting standards. The next section advances further legal arguments as to why disclosure of patent information and strategy by non-listed companies should remain voluntary in the UK in the short to medium term.

8.1.4 Voluntary or mandatory IP disclosure and directors' liability

Making IP reporting mandatory for non-listed companies is equivalent to requiring accountability. This is a difficult issue, politically as much as technically. The author's view is that it is premature to impose a legal duty on company directors to report on IP and strategy without providing them with more detailed guidance on how to do so appropriately. This is due to the severe legal consequences under the CA 2006 for failure to report "fairly" so as not to mislead.[19] The "true and fair" view concept remains pivotal in the corporate reporting of accounting information and central to accounting practice.[20] As such, any narrative IP information disclosed as part of a company's annual corporate reporting will need to be verifiable and capable of substantiation to ensure the information disclosed

18 International Organization for Standardization released ISO 10668 in 2010 setting out principles to be used when valuing a brand and may be used for the purpose of corporate finance and fundraising. ISO 10668 requires three types of analysis before arriving at a valuation: legal, behavioural and financial.

19 Under section 414A a person is guilty of a criminal offence and liable for a fine of up to £5,000 for failure to comply with the legal requirement to prepare a Strategic Report or to take all reasonable steps for securing compliance with the requirement. CA 20006 (Strategic Report and Directors' Report) Regulations 2013 No. 1970.

20 Parker, R. H. and Nobes, C. *An International View of True and Fair Accounting (International Accounting)* (1994) Cengage Learning EMEA.

is not false or misleading. This is the price companies pay in return for the benefits of separate corporate personality and especially, limited liability.[21]

Equally, material disclosures of IP information and strategy, whether voluntarily or mandated within the legal framework of the CA 2006, substantially increases its legitimacy and authority.[22] This is so because section 463 CA 2006 sets out a strong statement of the liability of company directors who make false and misleading statements in their corporate reports. A director is liable to compensate the company for any loss it suffers as a result of:

(a) any untrue or misleading statement; or
(b) the omission of anything legislatively required to be included in it.[23]

This provision may worry inexperienced directors, however, crucially, to reassure them there is a safe harbour (this is a legal provision of a statute to reduce or eliminate liability in respect of certain conduct as long as one, in this case the company director, is able to demonstrate good faith). A director will only be liable under section 463 if he *knew* that the statement was untrue or misleading, or was *reckless* as to whether it was untrue or misleading, or knew the omission was a *dishonest concealment of material fact*: section 463(3). The safe harbour provisions were included in the CA 2006 as the government felt that too strict a liability would encourage directors to make heavily qualified statements in their narrative reports which would reduce their usefulness. Therefore directors' liability is limited to the company itself and does not extend to shareholders, investors or other third parties such as lenders. This does not affect any civil penalty or criminal liability, but should reassure company directors as their exposure is limited and in particular, negligence claims cannot be brought against them.

Thus a combination of factors has hindered company directors (even in large, well-resourced publicly listed companies) from reporting on their intangible assets, especially IP and patents, in their narrative corporate reports: (1) the hidden value of intangibles in traditional financial statements; (2) a lack of corporate leadership to identify and manage intangibles internally; and (3) and the knowledge of how to report.

Corporate reporting standards enhance the quality and reliability of the information presented because directors need to be satisfied that their disclosures are both "material" and show a "true and fair" view. Thus bearing in mind consequences of non-compliance with section 463 CA 2006, an innovating firm's director must make an informed decision as to whether or not to voluntarily

21 Mason, S. French, D. and Ryan C. *Company Law* (2013–2014) Oxford University Press p 108.

22 If the report was prepared under the small companies regime, that fact must be stated in a prominent position above the directors' signatures: section 419(2) CA 2006.

23 Section 463(2) CA 2006.

disclose IP information and strategy. Non-listed company directors will have to carefully consider the benefits of disclosure, balanced against the risks, costs and administrative burden of doing so. For these reasons, the author holds the view that corporate IP assets information and strategy disclosure, should be voluntary – to be decided on a case-by-case basis by directors who are in a position to evaluate the company's specific circumstances, its size, complexity, the nature of the risks and challenges it faces, coupled with the human and financial resources available for making disclosure that meets the legal standard required by the CA 2006.

After systematically considering and comparing the benefits and costs of preparing IP disclosures, the director should consider whether doing so would promote the success of the company under section 172 CA 2006. If the answer to this question is in the affirmative, the director(s) may determine to optionally file a Strategic Report (from which they are otherwise exempt). In other words, the need to obtain finance may justify the voluntary disclosure. Moreover, if the company's directors elect to disclose, the benefits to the innovating firm are twofold:

(1) disclosure will improve corporate governance with respect to the transparency of the directors' stewardship of valuable IP assets; and
(2) disclosure raises awareness of the availability of those assets as potential security in debt finance transactions as well as to potential equity investors and others who may become interested in the innovating firm's business.

In Chapter 3 in our discussion of corporate finance we saw that lenders typically require copies of a corporate borrower's annual returns when appraising commercial loan applications. The availability of corporate IP asset information and strategy, designed to meet the "true and fair" corporate governance standard, would be helpful for commercial lenders who evaluate the innovating firm as a potential borrower using both quantitative (traditional accounting statements) and qualitative (narrative corporate reports) measures. This would assist them to triangulate intangibles financial data through cross verification with corporate narrative disclosure. To educate and promote voluntary disclosure integrated into the company's annual report should be the first "step change" in encouraging companies to think regularly about their IP assets and the value they provide to the business in the longer term. The first tier of the original model is introduced below.

8.2 A new triage style IP disclosure materiality evaluation model

The original *Essential, Desirable & Optional Patent Information and Strategy* corporate narrative disclosure model has been devised as a new bespoke model to facilitate disclosure by firms, small or large, listed or non-listed. It will help to answer the question, "what is a material IP disclosure?" in the context of the company and its business model. The model builds on the narrative content and style of the Danish and German ICS method and draws on the GSK patent information disclosure, and other relevant literature, as a foundation adopting "business triage style" approach to provide innovating firms with specific guidance as to the type of patent information they may wish to voluntarily report in the Strategic Report of the company's annual return. Although this model focuses on patent information and strategy disclosure similar "business triage style" models could be developed for other types of IP rights. To begin, at the early stage of the innovating firm's patent innovation life cycle, a firm is trying to achieve several things, including to:

- ensure that R&D staff have "freedom to operate";[24]
- generate quality patents for their portfolio;
- ensure that their core business is adequately protected; and
- initiate managerial processes to facilitate patent generation, maintenance, monitoring, competition and enforcement.

Non-financial qualitative patent information value indicators address the relevance of patents to the firm's business largely by determining the overall context and strategy of the patent portfolio. These factors, or "value indicators", may influence the value of the patent(s) both positively and negatively. Similarly, by way of analogy, consider the example of a retail store on any UK high street. Factors such as location, frontage, size and retail traffic etc. affect the financial value of a building used as a retail shop. But what of the threat of online shopping? How does this impact on the valuation of the store? It may not – it probably affects the value of the business carried out in the shop, but the effect of the online shopping may have little effect on the freehold value. In the same way, the combination of patent-related qualitative factors determines the value of the patent portfolio and needs to be undertaken before contemplating the mathematical or financial valuation, which is why the narrative needs to highlight and evaluate the patent assets. Patent protection will provide a business with multiple qualitative patent value indicators that directly and indirectly relate to cash flow, information directly relevant to lenders.

Narrative qualitative patent information aims to capture more of the value that *indirectly* contributes to cash flow. The starting point is the relevant patent specifications.[25] Internal management should evaluate the portfolio to categorise, rank and compare the individual patents or vis-à-vis competitors' portfolios, assessing

24 Reilly, R.F. 'Attributes That Influence IP Value' (Spring 2015) *Forensic Analysis Insights* 3.

25 This is a written description of the invention with drawings and "claims". The "abstract" summarises the patent specification. Most successful patent applications have detailed descriptions in the specification that are several pages long, describe different versions of the invention and refer to a set of drawings showing these different versions. The exact style and content varies according to the subject matter. For instance, complicated machinery, electronic equipment and chemical processes need many more pages of description and drawings than a straightforward item with few parts. See the UK IPO's *Patent Applications Guide* at www.ipo.gov.uk/p-apply.pdf.

the risks and opportunities created by the portfolio to formulate and document strategy to maximise the future value creation. This is commonly known in the management discipline as a SWOT analysis (Strengths Weaknesses Opportunities and Threats).[26]

8.2.1 Formulating and documenting patent information and strategy

Making a material or voluntary corporate disclosure, regardless of the format, forces a company to formulate and document its patent information. This is an important step for an innovating firm as the process harnesses the "power of focus" that can lead to critical management decisions in the short, medium and long-term. For example, documenting patent strategy assists firms to focus on filing patents in the most important areas, or drop or license innovative projects in more marginal areas so that the quality of work in its core area of business increases.

The first step is to identify, define and describe the patent (or IP) portfolio. This is akin to carrying out "due diligence", a process that primarily assesses three essential attributes: (1) the legal monopoly rights exist i.e the patent is properly registered and is still in force; (2) that good legal title (ownership) of the patent can be established; and (3) the patent rights can be enforced to prevent third parties from using the invention without permission (in order to sustain cash flows derived from using or licensing the patent). These attributes relate directly to the financial potential the patent(s) for the company.

8.2.2 Devising the three-tier *model*

A model is a simplification of the chosen part of reality that helps us to master a large and complex system, which cannot be easily understood in its entirety. A model is intended to be easier to use for certain purposes than the complete system observed. One of the main issues considered before devising the original *three-tier* patent disclosure model was how it would fit into the existing legal corporate reporting framework, taking into account the guidance and consensus with respect to corporate governance and reporting contained in the UK Corporate Governance Code ("the Code") published by the FRC to facilitate effective, entrepreneurial and prudent management that can deliver the long-term success of a company.[27] The Code is not a rigid set of rules, rather it consists of principles of good disclosure as follows:

- Leadership (Section A);
- Effectiveness (Section B);

26 Humphrey, A. 'SWOT Analysis for Management Consulting' (December 2005) *SRI Alumni Newsletter*.

27 September (2012) and applies to the reporting periods beginning on 1 October 2012 at www.frc.org.uk/Our-Work/Publications/Corporate-Governance/UK-Corporate-Governance-Code-September-2012.pdf p 1.

- Accountability (Section C);
- Remunerations (Section D); and
- Relations with shareholders (Section E).

The standards of good practice with respect to corporate narrative disclosure apply to listed companies[28] and are based on the underlying principles of good corporate governance: accountability, transparency, probity and focus on the sustainable success of an entity over the longer term.[29] For the sake of simplicity and to reduce the administrative burden on innovating firms, the proposed model is envisaged to operate within the existing company law reporting regime with the principles espoused in sections A–C of the Code.[30]

The first tier, *Essential Voluntary Patent Information and Strategy* disclosure model ("the *Essential* disclosure model"), is designed to act as a "meta standard" which succinctly identifies the specific patent-related information and strategy indicators that are potentially material and should be disclosed in the Strategic Report. The model adopts a simple ten step process. The *Essential* disclosure model draws on the Danish and German ICS question method and intentionally avoids detailed methodological work steps and requirements. However, in contrast to the Danish ICS which is based on four types of knowledge resources, namely employees, customers, process and technologies and the German ICS Fitness Check comprising 11 questions followed by six steps for drafting an ICS, the *Essential* disclosure model is streamlined and tailored to facilitate an evaluation of whether patent information and strategy is material and should be disclosed. Neither the Danish ICS, German ICS nor the FRC provide bespoke corporate IP asset disclosure guidance; they tend to provide more general guidance on intangibles disclosure, a broader category of asset. The *Essential* disclosure model and the comprehensive *Essential, Desirable & Optional Patent Information and Strategy* business triage style disclosure model address this gap in the literature.

The *Essential* disclosure model is conceptualised for use by any innovating firm regardless of industry sector and promotes uniformity and comparability. It makes use of the existing UK company law reporting principles espoused in sections A–C of the Code relating to leadership, effectiveness and accountability and the views of the FRC (see Figure 8.1). In Chapter 7, we found that GSK's narrative disclosures were embedded throughout the entire 252 page 2012 annual report and one had to piece together the "patent value story". In contrast, both the *Essential* and the *Essential, Desirable & Optional Patent Information and Strategy* disclosure models contemplate a stand-alone patent information and strategy section with the report.

The *Essential* disclosure model acts as a starting point to initiate discussion on the formulation and documentation of voluntary patent information disclosure

28 Disclosure and Transparency Rules promulgated by FSA pursuant to the FSMA 2000 p 2.

29 Ibid p 1.

30 Supra n [27].

to raise awareness of the company's hidden intangible patent assets. This model addresses the lack of patent and other information concerning intangibles arising as a result of the shortcomings of traditional financial accounting statements prepared in accordance with IAS 38 Intangibles and enhances corporate governance disclosure theory. It does so by providing a set of qualitative non-financial patent information indicators to make visible the invisible and concurrently assist directors of innovating firms comply with their duty under section 172 CA 2006 in the spirit of the Code. The qualitative patent indicators are informed by the GSK case study, other reports and literature and the narrative format is inspired by the ICS concept discussed in Chapter 6.

8.2.3 Material non-financial qualitative patent indicators for disclosure

A useful and reliable patent information disclosure needs to be firmly anchored in fundamental qualitative non-financial indicators, accepted and endorsed by the relevant stakeholders. The first issue to be addressed is to signpost the existence of potentially valuable patents and patent applications and their central role within the firm's business strategy: "the patent value story". This is not the same as carrying out a patent due diligence exercise (however material disclosures will assist with patent due diligence when the need arises). Innovating firms need to become effective at translating their research and inventions into profits. Although shareholders have the power to elect company directors who set business strategy, other stakeholders such as lenders have no legal authority to tell an innovating firm borrower what to do to commercialise its patented innovations. An equity financier will have more say depending on its percentage of equity and whether it holds a managerial role in the business. Lenders, however, can only observe and evaluate the choices and outcomes made by the innovating firm.

8.2.4 The Essential *disclosure model*

A Strategic Report, tailored to meet a UK innovating SME's business objectives, should provide the information necessary for shareholders and other stakeholders to assess an innovating firm's:

(a) development, performance and position;
(b) future prospects;
(c) strategy for achieving its objectives;
(d) business model; and
(e) governance.

The following qualitative non-financial indicators are regarded as IP disclosures that assist to provide a "true and fair" view of on an IP-rich business. These are the recommended minimum level of disclosure, if material, for companies with small patent portfolios.

1. **The Patent Value Story** – the business model as the platform for structuring the ensuing disclosure
2. **The Patent Portfolio** – development, performance and position, growth opportunities and time frame
3. **The Patent Strategy** – strategy for achieving set objectives
4. **IPR & Patent Management** – governance, stewardship and leadership
5. **Patent licensing and agreements (if any)** – commercial relationships and responsibilities if sufficiently certain
6. **Cost to commercialise** – finance requirements and objectives
7. **Patent life of key patents** – freedom to operate and duration of monopoly advantage
8. **Principal risks and uncertainties associated with key patents** – financier and investor information
9. **Financial status of the patent asset** – currently or previously used as security for debt
10. **Annual comparison of key patent asset performance indicators** – track performance over time

Figure 8.1 Essential disclosure model

Figure 8.1 depicts the first tier of the disclosure model. The *Essential* disclosure model is not used to give a detailed description of all possible real or theoretically real pieces of patent information and strategy; instead, it illustrates types of IP information that are potentially material.

One should not overlook the importance of *simplicity* in terms of the application of the model. The model attempts to elaborate clearly and unambiguously the minimum material patent information indicators to be prioritised for disclosure. The information can be presented in a relatively short form, a two-to-three page narrative report in a streamlined, succinct narrative style. Those who rely on the disclosure need to have confidence that information about the patent assets disclosed is "true and fair". Further, the consequences of any risks involved should be disclosed. The disclosure should be made in a consistent and uniform format, contributing to certainty and objectivity. Nonetheless, there will be wide variation in what is a material IP disclosure for a particular company and how companies choose to disclose the patent information and strategy indicators pertaining to their business. The *Essential* disclosure model headings provide a useful materiality evaluation framework for the disclosure and permit a free-form approach to the narrative style to enhance flexibility. The FRC report entitled, *Louder than Words,* provides general principles with respect to effective communication in corporate narrative reporting.[31] These are reproduced in Figure 8.2.

31 *Louder than Words: Principles and Actions for Making CorporateRreports Less Complex and More Relevant* (June 2009) FRC.

1	**Focused**	Highlight important messages, transactions and accounting policies and avoid distracting readers with immaterial clutter.
2	**Open & Honest**	Provide a balanced explanation of the results – the good news and the bad.
3	**Clear & Understandable**	Use plain language, only well-defined technical terms, consistent terminology and an easy-to-follow structure.
4	**Interesting & Engaging**	Get the point across with a report that holds the readers' attention.

Figure 8.2 Principles for effective communication in narrative corporate reporting

At the election of the innovating firm, the *Essential* disclosure model can be further elaborated upon to provide more detailed and comprehensive material patent information and strategy disclosure as the company grows and acquires more resources. Figure 8.3 sets out the original three-tier *Essential, Desirable & Optional Patent Information and Strategy* disclosure model. This comprehensive materiality evaluation model includes additional optional (voluntary) qualitative patent indicators that flow directly from the *Essential* indicators.

The model provides a straightforward yet flexible approach for a company to evaluate additional material and non-material patent information and strategy disclosure. Beyond the *Essential* patent indicators, innovating firms' company directors should consider whether to report the additional *Desirable* and *Optional* information on a cost-benefit or "low cost to collate and produce" basis. This is a crucial decision for financially-challenged innovating firms, especially start-ups and SMEs. Thus the model accommodates the "growth" of the company enabling it to upgrade the patent information and strategy disclosed as it progresses through the business life cycle without losing uniformity, reliability or comparability over time. The model does not adopt the language of accountants and could be further enhanced through the use of visuals or graphics to complement the narrative. The majority of the patent indicators in the model are self-explanatory and were discussed in Chapter 7 in the GSK mini-case study, or with respect to the Technology Readiness Level system (Chapter 2). However, those requiring further elaboration are discussed below.

8.2.5 Patent indicators used in the models

8.2.5.1 The EPO's IPscore® 2.2 patent valuation software

IPscore® 2.2 is a tool created by the European Patent Office to help companies evaluate and manage patents and development projects. The tool provides a financial forecast that shows the net present value of the technology project being

NARRATIVE DICLOSURE	**Essential Tier 1** ① →	**Desirable Tier 2 (consider on a cost – benefit basis)** ② →	**Optional Tier 3 (if low in cost to collate and produce)** ③
1. **The "patent value story"** – the business model	Describe the most value-creating patents in the reporting year and how those patents have created such a value for the business. One paragraph setting out business model.	Contextualise how patent assets impact business strategy and highlight the critical value of patent monopolies to the business as a whole. Technology complexities (especially "displacement" technology) Technology Readiness Level. Activities performed by the entity to maintain the value capacity. Sustainability of the business model and patent value. Internally generated patent assets. Acquired patent assets. Sale of patents.	Independent valuation or European Patent Office IPScore. Internally estimated value of the patents (e.g. GSK Internal Rate of Return methodology). Depth of its patent portfolio (number of patents, patents per jurisdiction), patent families, the strength of particular patent pools.
2. **The patent portfolio** – development, performance and position – growth opportunities	Link patents granted or pending to key products Confirm "freedom to operate" in key countries or regions. Note any material blocking patents. Whether the patent assets are in the R&D process or in the product development cycle. Product characteristics. Future economic benefits to be derived from the patent assets and estimated timeframe. Future outlook.	Patent pools.	Patent citations.

Figure 8.3 Essential, Desirable & Optional Patent Information and Strategy disclosure model

NARRATIVE DICLOSURE	Essential Tier 1 1 →	Desirable Tier 2 (consider on a cost – benefit basis) 2 →	Optional Tier 3 (if low in cost to collate and produce) 3
3. **Patent strategy** – strategy for achieving its objectives	Set out objectives for achieving invention commercialisation.	Information about potential uses of the patent assets. Information about the markets in which the patent assets might be used. Investment in R&D.	Further development, R&D pipeline. Abandoned patents. Abandoned projects. Research and innovation management strategy – structure for optimally progressing research and debt or equity finance raised. Patent renewal management and strategy.
4. **IPR & patent management** – governance	Patent management policy to confirm corporate governance, stewardship and leadership of Patent Assets. Corporate group structure – is there a subsidiary company that owns the patent assets to isolate risk?	Managerial responsibility for co-ordinating and managing the firm's patent strategy. Patent or IP related qualifications of Board of Directors (executive and non-executive). Chief IP Officer (CIPO) or IP Management Team. Professional advisors – patent attorneys, legal, accounting etc.	Detailed patent portfolio management strategy. Education and training. Patent searching. Staff briefings (e.g. obligations owed to employer in respect of IP). Staff newsletters. Profile key inventors/researchers. Invention disclosure policy. Employee incentives and reward schemes. Awards and prizes to demonstrate peer recognition, Staff publications. Business premises located within a technology park or the like.

Figure 8.3 (*continued*)

NARRATIVE DICLOSURE	Essential Tier 1 1 →	Desirable Tier 2 (consider on a cost – benefit basis) 2 →	Optional Tier 3 (if low in cost to collate and produce) 3
5. **Patent licensing and agreements** – commercial relationships and responsibilities (if sufficiently certain to disclose)	Principal patent licence agreements (licence-in or licence-out). Exclusivity. Product distribution agreements. Patent pool licences.	Sales information relating to patented products (actual and predicted). Collaboration agreements (e.g. with a university or technology institute).	Market size (existing and expected). Market share (existing and expected). Trademark and other marketing rights. Know-how.
6. **Cost to commercialise** – finance requirements and objectives	Costs incurred to develop the patent assets.	Estimated R&D costs, and development phases. Costs envisaged to complete commercialisation of the patented invention. Financial resources available to apply for and renew patents.	Patent Box or other tax incentives or tax relief.
7. **Patent life of key patents**	Expiration and duration of key legal patent monopolies.		Discontinued patents. Discontinued R&D projects.

Figure 8.3 (continued)

NARRATIVE DICLOSURE	Essential Tier 1 1 →	Desirable Tier 2 (consider on a cost – benefit basis) 2 →	Optional Tier 3 (if low in cost to collate and produce) 3
8. **Principal risks and uncertainties associated with key patents** – investor and financier information	Securing and protecting patent rights and confidential information. Loss of patent monopoly rights either due to expiry or successful challenges to the validity of granted patents, patent revocation, patent lapse due to non-payment of renewal fee. Legal proceedings: patent validity; patent enforcement; patent infringement litigation; breach of confidence; inventor's remuneration rights (actual and potential). Competitors and competitive landscape (products, competition and patents), availability of product substitutes.	Risk management processes. Consequences of failure to secure freedom to operate. "Mitigating activities" the company takes to address the risks and uncertainties. Standard of patent protection and enforcement in relevant international jurisdictions outside the UK and EU. General contextual information about the industry Monitoring the competition for patent infringement Monitoring competitor's patents and patent applications	
9. **Financial status of the patent asset**	Is or has the patent asset been used as security against debt?		
10. **Annual comparison of key patent asset performance indicators**	Systematically track and report the progress and growth of the patent portfolio throughout the business lifecycle. Milestone achieved.	Performance and value-creation metrics.	

Figure 8.3 (continued)

evaluated so that companies can better assess the projects and better integrate them into their management strategy.[32] The Item 1 Patent Value Story Optional Tier 3 column refers to an indicator described as *IPScore*.[33] The EPO's *IPScore* patent valuation software is neither well-known nor widely used in the UK at present. It is a useful online publicly available patent value assessment tool that can guide users to carry out their own free patent or patent portfolio valuation. The EPO acquired, adopted and distributed the *IPScore* software to the national patent offices in its member states.[34] The software enables users to carry out a basic qualitative patent evaluation for internal company management and provides a qualitative valuation of a single patent or development project and has a built-in financial model which, by producing a financial forecast, presents an order of magnitude for the value of the patented technology when put to use in the company. *IPScore* creates a financial model that is able to provide a forecast of the patented technology's foreseeable contribution to liquidity over a 10-year period which is relevant to a lender's evaluation of growth and future cash flowing through the business. The calculation period is governed by the pre-determined life of the patented technology. The net present value is a discounted foreseeable liquidity flow.[35] Thus although *IPScore* does not evaluate the patent as a legal document, legal protection is the foundation of value which is why disclosure of the *IPScore* is optional, supplementing traditional financial statements. It is comparable to GSK's disclosure of its Internal Rate of Return methodology discussed in Chapter 7. The *IPScore* report is only as accurate as the information inputs and a lender could insist any such report be prepared by an independent valuer. However, *IPscore* could be useful for innovating SMEs as it is a free online resource hosted by the EPO.

8.2.5.2 Patent citations

The Item 2 Patent Portfolio Optionalal Tier 3 column sets out patent citations as an indicator. There is evidence to suggest that there is a strong correlation between patent value and patent citations observable in patent information documents.[36] For example, the number of references to prior patents generated during the patent registrar's search and examination process, and the number of citations a patent has received indicate its importance scientifically and therefore

32 EPO at www.epo.org/searching-for-patents/business/ipscore.html#tab-1.
33 IPScore®2.2 Manual (2009) p 9.
34 The author conducted a search of the UK IPO website at www.ipo.gov.uk and did not find any link to the IPScore webpage.
35 For a detailed explanation of the assumptions in the financial calculations, see *IPScore 2.2.Manual* (2009) Chapter 6.
36 Hall, B.H., Jaffe, A. and Trajtenberg, M. 'Market Value and Patent Citations' JEL Classification: O31, O38 UC Berkeley at http://eml.berkeley.edu/~bhhall/papers/HallJaffeTrajtenberg_RJEjan04.pdf p 1.

its relative value. Further, certain patents will have many forward "non-self" citations. A forward citation is a reference to the patent to be evaluated in a later document. Such citations are objective evidence that the patent has high value and is a seminal patent that protects major technical innovations within the particular field. The number of citations can be empirically calculated and investigated, which is helpful and reliable as an information input. The observable result is a network of links called a "patent citations network" which is a useful qualitative evaluation tool.[37] In summary, the number of times a patent is cited tends to convey its scientific importance and therefore its value. Notwithstanding a simple citation count, it is important to consider how and why citations arise and the information they suggest. Using a patent citation count as indicator of value is only as useful as the level of expertise of those who understand its significance. This may be difficult for a lender to assess without the assistance of an experienced patent attorney.

8.2.5.3 Freedom to operate: the impact of neighbouring patent rights

Item 2 The Patent Portfolio Tier 1 Essential requires that freedom to operate be confirmed. "Freedom to operate" is a patent law phrase. Patent value is heavily influenced by the property rights that surround the patent monopoly. However, a single patent operating in isolation is rare, except for start-ups and micro-firms. In patent portfolios there may be blocking patents held by third parties that could significantly detract from the value of a company's patent rights. A blocking patent is one that relates to a particular area of technology which prevents another patent from being used (without a licence from the first) because that other patent relies on technology covered by the first.[38] Therefore owning a patent does not automatically provide the owner with a "freedom to operate". Another patent may block the desired use. Where there are many separately owned blocking patents covering a particular product or process, a "patent thicket"[39] is said to exist (discussed in Chapter 2). It is recommended that the company (via a patent attorney) undertake a patent search to confirm whether blocking patents exist and make any appropriate disclosure on their impact. This may be required to provide a "true and fair" view. Dealing with any blocking patent incurs costs, either to license it or to work around it and such costs will need to be deducted from the future economic benefits that are projected from the blocked patent.

37 Hand, J. and Lev, B. *Intangible Assets: Values, Measures, and Risks* (2003) Oxford University Press pp 208–213; Michel, J. and Bettels B. 'Patent Citation Analysis' (2001) 51(1) *Scientometrics* 85–201.

38 Guellec, D., Martinez, C. and Zuniga, P. 'Blocking Patents: What They Are and What They Do' (5 June 2008) Preliminary Paper.

39 *Patent Thickets – An Overview* (25 November 2011) UK Intellectual Property Office Informatics Team.

8.2.5.4 Patent pools and synergistic patents

A patent pool is a consortium of two or more companies that agree to cross-license patents relating to a particular technology.[40] In other words, companies join together to create a resource for their collective benefit. Thus, the creation of a patent pool can save the innovating firm time and financial resources, and in the case of blocking patents, it may be the only reasonable way to commercialise the invention. Within a portfolio there could also be synergistic patents that could enhance the value of the company's patent rights. The mirror image of a blocking patent is a synergistic patent portfolio comprising a group of related patent rights.[41] These may be worth more in the aggregate when held in a single portfolio (or controlled in a single patent pool) than if held separately by different owners. This strategy may also have the effect of overcoming blocking patent problems and lead to an increase in value for each of the patents. A patent forming part of a synergistic portfolio may have a higher value than if it is held in isolation. In such a case, it will be important to consider the strength of the patent family.[42]

8.2.5.5 Licences: revenue that improves cash flow

A patent can be licensed for use by several licensees simultaneously without decreasing its value. This stands in sharp contrast to intangibles such as goodwill. As such, there is a potential multiplying effect on future potential income streams which innovating firms need to highlight and information that potential lenders need to take on board.

8.2.5.6 Financial resources to apply for and renew patents

The total cost of applying for and maintaining a UK patent over its lifetime, not including any enforcement of the patent rights, is made up of professional fees, official fees payable to the UK Patent Office and fees payable for professionally prepared patent drawings. As discussed in Chapter 2, the lifetime cost of a typical patent over its complete 20 year monopoly is of the order of £10,000–£20,000, (plus value added tax for UK companies and individuals).[43] This cost range needs to be multiplied by the number of UK patents held by the company as well as similar figures for applying and maintaining patents in other countries which may be higher due to translation costs.

40 *Patent Pools and Antitrust – A Comparative Analysis* (March 0214) Prepared by the WIPO Secretariat a p 3.

41 Murphy, W., Orcutt, J. and Remus, P. *Patent Valuation Improving Decision Making through Analysis* (2012) Wiley p 103.

42 A patent family is a set of patent applications or publications taken in multiple countries to protect a single invention by a common inventor(s). For example, an application is made in the UK and then extended to other offices.

43 Franks & Co. '36% Increase in Official UKIPO Patent Fees' (27 May 2010) at www.franksco.com/news/2010/5/36-increase-in-official-ukipo-patent-fees.

8.2.5.7 Monitoring competition

Innovating firms, especially SMEs, generally do not have significant financial resources to monitor competition or to detect potential patent infringement.[44] The concept of policing one's property is well-known in trade mark law and trade mark owners must patrol the marketplace for infringers or risk the dilution or loss of their trade marks, especially if the mark becomes generic.[45] The duty of patent owners to police their patents is less clear-cut. Innovating firm directors have stewardship of the company's patent assets and in the author's view, as a matter of good practice, there should be management procedures in place to patrol the marketplace for patent infringement appropriate to the company's circumstances. If significant competition exists then this is "material" information that should be disclosed in order to provide a "true and fair" view of the business. The innovating firm then needs to create a strategy to deal with the competition or to the avert infringement in order to preserve its place in the market.

The UKIPO provides training[46] in patent searching and detecting infringement using publicly available patent databases and online resources, which could be accessed by innovating firms to police potential infringement. Staff could be trained to be alert to infringing products and have policies in place for dealing with infringement or to carry out the watching briefs internally. This function could also be outsourced to a firm with a "watching brief" on the key patent journals published by patent granting offices.

8.2.5.8 IP management

In many innovating firms, responsibility and accountability to shareholders for IP and patent matters is vague, often falling on the shoulders of the R&D director, chief technology executive, the company secretary or in-house lawyer if there is one. In addition, corporate IP professionals are being asked to participate in internal IP management processes. However, in the evolving corporate environment to enhance good corporate governance there is a need for the board of directors to show leadership with respect to IP and patent management. Increasingly, IP-rich large companies appoint a Chief IP Officer (CIPO).[47] Innovating firms should report who within the organisation is responsible and accountable for material decisions made about IP and patent assets. If the board of directors is advised by external IP professionals to assist with such decisions, this is important information to disclose as it demonstrates prudent controls are

44 Rabinowitz, A. 'Keep Your Eye on Your Ball: Patent Holders' Evolving Duty to Patrol the Marketplace for Infringement' (Spring 2007) 5 Art. 1 *Northwestern Journal of Technology and IP*.

45 Ibid p 192.

46 www.ipo.gov.uk/ipenforce/ipenforce-resources.htm.

47 Harrison, S. and Sullivan, P. H. *Einstein in the Boardroom: Moving beyond Intellectual Capital to I-stuff* (2006) Wiley, Chapter 2.

in place to manage corporate patent assets and that the directors have effectively discharged their duties.

Further, the innovating firm may optionally disclose key innovation staff and inventors who have responsibility for driving the technical aspects of the innovation and patent strategy. Staff with contributions to successful inventions, notable qualifications or other esteem factors such as academic or professional publications will enhance the perception that the innovating firm has the ability to achieve its innovation objectives. New highly qualified staff may be attracted to work with the innovating firm. IP management and leadership is important information for lenders who need reassurance that the patent assets over which they may take security are being looked after.

8.2.5.9 Incentives and/or reward schemes

In the model, it is optional to report whether incentives and/or reward schemes are offered to key researchers and inventors to align their interest with the company's commercial goals. Research shows that monetary rewards are by far the most effective way to motivate employees who choose these by more than three to one over non-monetary recognitions.[48]

8.2.5.10 Awards and prizes

The significance and impact on the innovating firm of winning industry awards and prizes should not be underestimated. A company begins with a commercial purpose. But not all that strive succeed. An award or prize recognises excellence in the field and may carry a monetary award or other benefits and provides public and peer recognition which the company can use to distinguish itself and translate into support, financial and otherwise. The more prestigious the award, the more positive reputational impact it has on the innovating firm's ability to successfully achieve its innovation and commercial objectives.

8.2.5.11 Best practice in material IP disclosures: how much?

The assumption that a "true and fair" Strategic Report implies full comprehensive disclosure is unrealistic. The real purpose of a narrative Strategic Report on patent information and strategy is to ensure fairness across the spectrum of information recipients. The Strategic Report should disclose real-time insight on non-financial performance measures that could potentially inform decision making by users of the information. As a matter of good practice, the company should hold documentary evidence to prove its patent information and strategy disclosures

48 'Inventor Reward and Recognition Programs Benchmark' (2011) *ipPerformance Group*, Napierville, Illinois.

(whether direct or implied) that are capable of objective substantiation. It is only if this standard is met that external stakeholders are likely to have confidence in the narrative disclosures. In the absence of adequate substantiation the courts may regard the disclosures as misleading.

Boilerplate and generic statements like "our goal is deliver value from our patent portfolio to our shareholders" should be avoided unless they are an introduction to company-specific content setting out how this will be achieved. Companies should not be over optimistic or exaggerate the value, accuracy, scientific validity or practical usefulness of the patents and patented products or processes. If a comparison or comparative statement is made, companies must hold evidence that relates to their own and the competitors' patents that are the implicit or explicit subject of the comparison.

By definition, patents are only granted for "new" inventions: section 1(1)(a) PA 1977. The claims section of the patent provides the description of the property rights in the invention that are conveyed by the patent. Section 14 PA 1977 provides that every application shall contain a patent specification containing a description, a claim and an abstract. Section 14(5) requires a high degree of particularity in that the claims must define the matter for which patent protection is sought, be clear and precise, be supported by the description and relate either to the invention or to a related group of inventions which are linked to form a single inventive concept. The patent specification and the specific claims delimit the scope of the patent monopoly. Any subsequent litigation, whether in relation to patentability, infringement or revocation, will be very closely concerned with what is the true basis of the invention as set out in the claims. According to Lord Russell in *Electric & Musical Industries Ltd v Lissen Ltd*: [49]

> The function of the claims is to define clearly and with precision the monopoly claimed so that others may know the exact boundaries of the area in which, if they venture therein, they will be trespassers.

Therefore, companies who wish to make "new" and especially "breakthrough" claims are advised to collate sound research data to form a body of evidence to substantiate the strategic impact of the patent claims (e.g. properly controlled experimental studies).

Opinions expressed regarding the future value creation of the patent portfolio or individual patents should be supported with independent evidence of their accuracy. An experienced patent attorney's opinion as to the quality of a patent claim is a fundamental information input that feeds into the qualitative assessment of patent value. If opinion on the future value creation of the patent assets is divided, the disclosure should not portray the future outlook as generally agreed. The board of directors has a duty to ensure that its patent information and strategy

49 (1939) 56 RPC 23.

disclosures provide a "true and fair" view. In particular, if such disclosures have not been independently substantiated, the board will need to determine that any patent information or strategy disclosure it makes is not untrue, unfair or misleading.

In summary, the "business triage style" *Essential, Desirable & Optional Patent Information and Strategy* disclosure model creates a simple framework to collate and present the "patent value story". The qualitative patent information value indicators used involve data that in many instances is already publicly available or capable of substantiation, but is drafted to construct a narrative. Once the relevant information has been researched it is relatively easy for a shareholder, potential investor or lender to instruct an appropriately qualified patent attorney or patent lawyer to classify and evaluate the disclosure. We have seen that a quantitative traditional financial valuation only gives an indication of the estimated monetary value of an innovating firm's patent portfolio and to date this approach has been insufficient in terms of the very limited number of patent-backed financing decisions made by lenders. There is no logical reason why stakeholders should restrict themselves to the financial statements. The new corporate narrative disclosure model also facilitates a SWOT analysis of the firm's patents and strategy. For example, the outcome of a review of the firm's financial statements, corporate annual report and Strategic Review (based on the model) may or may not be that the innovating firm's

> patent portfolio protects a technology of strategic importance for an attractive market; it can be enforced efficiently, but significant investment is still needed to progress the development of product X. The company will not be able to generate the projected sales and hence profit, unless full finance is made available to it at the beginning of the projected period.[50]

In another example, a lender may appraise the borrower's position by concluding:

> It appears that the Xcel Innovation Company Ltd is an innovating SME in the process of consolidation. It has made substantial investment in its biotechnology patents and renewal fees during the last three years as growth of assets during the period will reveal. These investments are principally supported by a government research grant and the company is now seeking a long-term loan. It might take a few more years to fully reap the benefits of these investments. During this consolidation period, Xcel Innovation has projected a moderate sales growth of approximately 7.5% per annum which is conservative but reasonable. The operating structure of XcelInnovation is strong. It has a stable growth-to-profit ratio. Loan approved.

50 Bhattacharya, H. *Banking Strategy, Credit Appraisal and Lending Decisions: A Risk-Return Framework* (2010), Oxford University Press, Oxford pp 386–388.

External reporting can influence internal decision making by virtue of the fact that the company tracks the performance of its corporate IP asset performance externally, and perhaps even committing to targets, as many companies do.

8.3 Criticism of narrative IP disclosures

Despite the fact that they have been in existence for decades, the usefulness of corporate narrative disclosures generally has been subject to criticism. Malone recognises the potential pitfalls of intangibles narrative reporting:

> There are some good reasons for not attempting to measure the intangible assets, the intellectual capital, of companies and other organizations. Such a measurement will be difficult, imprecise, and it will open the Pandora's Box of politicization and hype, fad and fraud.[51]

There is no doubt that a high degree of judgement is necessary in assessing what and how to disclose. This is the aim of the *Essential, Desirable & Optional Patent Information and Strategy* disclosure model – to provide guidance for company directors and a basis for users to assess comparability. Malone states further, however, that an attempt *must nevertheless be made* to describe intangibles. Countries that have ICS regimes clearly accord the ICS the same level of official recognition as the traditional financial statements. Similarly, in the UK, as the patent information and strategy disclosure will be presented in the Strategic Report, it also has official recognition. Nielsen studied the trends and issues in management commentary over the previous two decades of attempts to create guidelines and regulation for corporate strategy narratives, concluding that:

> A solution to making management commentary matter to the investment community is to emphasise the interconnectedness between parts of the narrative sections according to the logic of the business model. Furthermore, regulation should be concerned with creating guidance on how to structure management commentary and strengthen such narrative statements through relevant performance measures.[52]

This is precisely what the business triage style disclosure model attempts to do, create a framework to demonstrate the role the patents (or other IP) assets play in future value creation for the business. It is this interconnectedness that is key to providers of capital and debt finance. Therefore, to address criticisms, voluntary disclosure of patent information should have a strategic focus and be communicated

51 Malone, S. 'Quantifying the Brave New World' (1999) *Hoover Digest* 1999 No. 1.

52 Nielsen, C. 'Dilemmas in the Usefulness of Business Reporting Narratives towards Investors and other Professional Decision-makers' Department of Business Studies, Aarlborg Universitet p 1.

clearly, truthfully, fairly and unambiguously in compliance with the legal requirements of the CA 2006. Reporting IP and patent information and strategy should be balanced and objective and enable comparisons over time by building on commonly accepted indicators, which fall outside obligatory disclosure by GAAP, and provide a better understanding of the company's key financial drivers beyond the figure for intangibles as recorded in the traditional financial statements. The new model will assist users to evaluate management performance with respect to patent assets enabling them to differentiate between good, bad and ugly corporate stewardship, a central part of corporate governance. A variety of problems that stem from the lack of transparency about material IP and patent assets may be overcome including accountability, directors' acting in their own interests, selective disclosures and insider dealing.[53] Integrated reporting and integrated thinking are a self-reinforcing cycle aimed at supporting "efficient and productive capital allocation" and also "act as a force for financial stability and sustainability".[54]

An important issue for directors is accountability versus confidentiality. Although there may be concerns about disclosure of confidential IP and patent information, one needs to weigh this against the need for improved awareness of lenders and other stakeholders of patent asset value as a core part of the business. Companies should be alert to avoid public disclosure of information that may be conveyed in confidence directly to the lender. A proper balance can be struck between the public interest of transparency, accountability and the private interest of confidentiality.

In conclusion, we have studied innovating firms whose competitive advantage rests largely on their ability to manage their strategic resources, which for our purposes are intangible IP assets, rather than tangible in shape and character. We saw in Chapter 3 that the signalling effect of patent value is not being received by UK lenders contemplating making loans to innovating SME firms. The value of an innovating SME's patent portfolio value will change once applications are granted, and will change again, if and when a legal challenge, either offensive or defensive, has been successful. The strength of the *Essential, Desirable and Optional Patent Information and Strategy* disclosure model for narrative corporate disclosure is its simplicity and that it provides a concrete solution for the lack of transparent patent information in traditional accounting statements and abbreviated corporate reports. One can argue that if the patent information and strategy is important for the management of the company, then it is also relevant for shareholders and external stakeholders to piece together sufficient relevant information to put the financial numbers with respect to intangibles in context.

53 The latter applies only to publicly listed companies. Section 52 Criminal Justice Act 1993 creates three kinds of insider dealing offences involving the use of inside information and dealing in securities.

54 'The International IR Framework' by the International Integrated Reporting Council, December 2013.

Further, the model facilitates access to debt finance by providing an effective method of communicating useful patent information and strategy that meets the "true and fair" standard required by corporate disclosure laws to lenders and provides essential forward-looking information, crucial for lenders to estimate growth prospects. The model directly supports and furthers the implementation of three key recommendations made in the *Banking on IP?* report and could be included in a UKIPO resource toolkit and supporting services which when integrated will:

- help old and new economy businesses identify and communicate their IP and its relationships to cash flows;
- help companies and lenders understand the business value of IP; and
- improve efficiency in due diligence on IP assets.[55]

Providing stakeholders with corporate IP asset information will enable them to provide the company with useful insights about matters that are important to them, including economic, social, technology, tax and governance issues and trends in the short, medium and long term that affect the company's ability to create value. This will also assist innovation companies to identify material risks and opportunities and provide useful feedback for the board into the development and implementation of the company's strategy as they acquire a better understanding how stakeholders perceive value.

8.4 Implementation

The "business triage-style" *Essential, Desirable & Optional Patent Information and Strategy* disclosure model initiates a new discourse and its reception depends on political consensus and wide acceptance by the innovating firms themselves. Creating confidence in new types of patent information is a question of *normalising* company disclosure practice, being consistent so as to create user experience in understanding such performance measures.

The success of the IP disclosure "materiality evaluation" model needs government endorsement and support to encourage and promote its use by providing resources to educate innovating SMEs and commercial lenders. At present, bespoke advice to innovating SMEs or companies about IPR and patent information and strategy corporate narrative disclosure is lacking. No official bespoke guidance exists to encourage innovating SMEs, who are otherwise exempt from providing a Strategic Report (formerly the Business Review) in their annual return, of the benefits of doing so.

55 Brassell, M. and King, K. *Banking on IP? The role of Intellectual Property and Intangible Assets in Facilitating Business Finance Final Report* (6 November 2013) Independent report commissioned by the UKIPO p 2.

Taking into account these points, adoption of the model would benefit from being recommended by BEIS and UKIPO who could interact with the FRC and Companies House in terms of promotion and guidance to innovating firms. A multi-agency approach is needed to coordinate the IP law and corporate governance advice contemplated by the model.

In addition, within the private sector there is clearly an important role for both the accounting and IP professions to play. Turning first to the accounting profession, innovating SMEs at the early stage of their business life cycle typically contact an accountant to establish the corporate entity and assist with filing of tax returns with HMRC and file corporate reports with Companies House. Accountants are therefore the first port of call. The UKIPO's IP Finance toolkit can help to raise the level of awareness of accountants of the need to consider IP as corporate assets. They should identify any internally generated patent assets, for example, that should be accounted for from the date the company is created in addition to recording a figure for intangibles in traditional financial statements applying IAS 38 Intangibles. Accountants should also advise that intangible corporate assets potentially warrant additional voluntary narrative corporate disclosure in accordance with the model presented. Similarly, the patent attorney who files the patent application on behalf of the innovating SME should be in a position to highlight the benefits of voluntary disclosure of patent information and strategy in the firm's annual return to facilitate access to finance. The actual preparation of the narrative disclosure could follow the three-tier business triage style model which may involve the input of the innovating firm's accountants, patent attorneys and legal advisors, as determined by the company directors following a cost-benefit analysis.

In the future, it is predicted that multidisciplinary accounting practices will need to employ or subcontract to IP or patent specialists to assist with preparation of patent information and strategy disclosures and the independent auditing of these. Sophisticated accounting firms looking to the future will need more than just accounting, tax, consultancy and audit services to service their clients whether innovating SMEs or larger corporate entities. A form of multidisciplinary legal practice is already possible with the introduction of the Legal Services Act (2011) which introduced the Alternative Business Structure (ABS). This enables non-lawyer groups such as accountants to share the management and control and bring together lawyers and other professionals, potentially patent attorneys, to provide services requiring a multidisciplinary approach. Similarly, commercial lenders will increasingly need to access IP and patent analysts to evaluate the assets of its IP-rich clients.

8.5 Modern corporate governance and IP assets

IP-rich companies must comply with corporate governance principles to meet the 21st century society's expectations. We saw in Chapter 2 that the political, economic, social, technological and legal context is certainly vastly different from that of the 19th century when the limited company was first invented. The scale and significance of corporate IP assets to value creation are of a different order. Chapter 5 concluded that company directors need more detailed guidance on how to present the corporate IP information (e.g. models) as well as the scope and extent of disclosure required to meet minimum corporate disclosure obligations. The *Essential, Desirable and Optional Patent Information & Strategy* disclosure model is a material evaluation tool for the new class of corporate assets that dominates the modern economy. The model provides guidance for a specialised type of narrative report to meet the needs of a group of stakeholders that is broader than shareholders and investors, but which contemplates other capital providers such as commercial lenders and banks. The innovating firm will then have a well-considered, coherent basis for ensuring connectivity between the various media and the message it communicates concerning its patent monopoly-based business model from the date the company was created. This will help to align the "How IP creates value" plan across its company website, social media, brochures and product and services information. A new disclosure structure will initiate an IP value revelation process, whilst recognising that change is inevitable and that it is challenging to manage a dynamic IP portfolio that evolves but needs to be conserved. Nevertheless, it is crucial to make IP information as easy as possible for shareholders to understand so that the "invisible" value of IP assets can be "seen" to inform decision making. Improving the quality of non-financial corporate IP information available to shareholders and external stakeholders is one way to assist companies to overcome the distortion of the IAS 38 related financial calculations concerning the fiscal value of IP assets. It has taken the accounting discipline over 400 years to develop its guiding principles. Contrast the current modern level of accounting information companies must disclose with what is currently reported in terms of corporate IP asset and strategy information. Does corporate disclosure of IP assets and strategy diminish the existing legal framework or complement it? In the author's view the answer is the latter. Who are our allies in trying to address this corporate governance agenda? Key actors to promote accountability of the board of directors for managing corporate IP assets include the IP media, company shareholders, stock exchanges, corporate analysts, national IP offices, WIPO, corporate regulators, financiers, IAS, CIPA, FRC, IRC, the Institute of Directors and academics. Members of these groups and institutions are the key actors in the IP ecosystem to promote change. In the UK, we have not experienced the strong public reaction to the Enron accounting scandal that occurred in the US, which led to public interest and demands for an appropriate response and the SOX legislation. However, there are other modern ways, such as the power of multimedia to raise awareness and change behaviour. The 1993 film *Free Willy* led to increased public awareness and support for the International Whaling Commission's moratorium on whaling. Along these lines, but with less impact, the award-winning financial crime thriller *Follow the Money*[56] is about wind

56 Known as *Bedraget* in Danish.

farm innovation firm Energreen, a leading player in the renewable energies market whose business model depends on new technology and hopes to float on the Danish exchange. However, the Ministry of Climate and Energy is contemplating reducing subsidies to the wind turbine industry, potentially deleterious to the business. Energreen's chief scientist is pressured to overstate technological outcomes in the prospectus. First broadcast in Denmark in January 2016, *Follow the Money* plays up the differences between what the company wants its stakeholders to see and the bleaker reality. It is a soft learning example that demonstrates the need for corporate governance practice to address a weak corporate IP disclosure and transparency culture.

I am optimistic that the new model will be considered by innovating start-ups and SMEs with consensus among stakeholders in the field because those with good news will begin to disclose material IP and patent information and strategy, motivating others to join ranks – as financiers, investors and other stakeholders penalise silence. Early innovating SME adopters who file a voluntary narrative corporate report as part of their corporate communication strategy drawing on the model could potentially build impetus and momentum for future mandatory IP management reporting regulation, not to mention commercial success.

Chapter 9 provides final reflections, recommendations and conclusions to renew our understanding of corporate governance, transparency and disclosure of corporate IP assets and strategy. One of the practical problems faced in this book and by company law, is to distinguish between large companies and small ones. Nevertheless, the more important unofficial class of company is the IP-rich company, small or large, public or private.

9 Corporate governance and IP value creation reporting

Reflections, conclusions and recommendations

According to Darwin's Origin of Species, it is not the most intellectual of the species that survives; it is not the strongest that survives; but the species that survives is the one that is able best to adapt and adjust to the changing environment in which it finds itself.[1]

Leon C. Megginson, 'Lessons from Europe for American Business' (1963)

Introduction

The emergence of IP rich companies is the new corporate governance challenge. This is because IP is largely invisible, not only in the financial accounts, but also more generally in corporate law theory and the legal framework. The insights shared in this book demonstrate that corporate governance theory has to respond to the new order of contemporary corporate dependency on intangibles and IP assets. The reliability of traditional financial statements for reporting the value of increasingly IP-rich companies and their role in value creation for the business continues to be questioned by academic and professional communities, activist shareholders and the banking and finance community. Corporate governance, transparency and disclosure principles have an important role to play in demystifying intangible IP assets. Good corporate governance will ensure that intangible IP assets are more transparent for shareholders and other stakeholders; regulate the conduct of firms who manage them on behalf of members; and finally, enable more effective scrutiny by corporate regulators in the public interest.

Over the course of eight chapters we have dealt with a variety of topics. It would not be feasible to consider all of the evaluations of the findings, therefore in this concluding chapter we will focus on the impact of corporate governance on corporate IP assets. We used associative thinking to combine concepts and materials and use them in a new way to develop the literature in this emerging

1 Leon C. Megginson, 'Lessons from Europe for American Business' (1963) 44(1) *Southwestern Social Science Quarterly* 3–13, 4.

field of corporate IP transparency and disclosure. We began with an introduction in *Part 1 The corporate IP landscape,* setting out the political, economic, social, technological and legal (PESTLE) environment in which IP monopolies operate in the UK. This provided an IP ecosystem context and a foundation for the corporate finance and corporate governance issues arising.

Part 2 The IP finance dimension: corporate governance and transparency illustrated why reliance on debt finance (borrowing), as compared with other types of funding (selling shares), is critically important for innovation firms at the early stage of the business life cycle. We identified the negative impact of the lack of public corporate IP asset and strategy information, especially in relation to securing loans to raise finance to support business objectives and bring the innovations we all benefit from to market.

> *First Woman:* "What is the value of your company's IP?"
> *Second Woman:* "Compared to what?"

In Chapter 2, we identified the Technology Readiness Level (TRL) system which is widely used in the technology sector. The TRL system is a credible, well-established system for estimating technological maturity based on a scale from one to nine. The TRL system could be immediately used by companies and financial institutions to facilitate communication about innovation and technology and to make comparative evaluations. In Chapter 3 the need for financial institutions to have a better IP awareness and develop more institutional trust in corporate IP assets was explored. The combination of traditional legal research with an evaluative socio-legal framework adds to the literature concerning behavioral finance and corporate IP assets is quite novel.

Part 3 Accounting for IP: corporate IP assets and transparency explored the debt financing difficulties experienced by innovation firms and exposed the unintended, yet considerable adverse impact of International Accounting Standard (IAS) 38 Intangibles with respect to internally generated IP, and patents in particular. We saw that contemporary corporate wealth is commonly quantified and is typically understood financially. As a corporate governance theorist, this led us to review UK corporate governance rules exempting SMEs from certain public reporting requirements (to reduce the administrative burden). We found that these rules have had the unintended policy consequence of creating a deep void resulting in a lack of transparency of information about corporate SME IP assets. We learned why, in relation to IP assets the numbers "don't always add up" or even worse are "missing" with respect to internally generated patent assets and SMEs exempt from certain aspects of corporate reporting. Numbers are seductive because they make comparisons easy, but when corporate IP assets are added to the mix, we have seen that numbers alone cannot quantify the company's real value.

We took this approach, namely a preliminary in depth analysis of corporate IP finance, in order to lay the groundwork and provide a platform for analysing how core accounting principles are applied to intangibles and IP assets. Accordingly, in Chapter 4 we identified precisely why core accounting principles have their limitations – they were never designed to account for the future value creation power of IP rights (the property rights which underpin contemporary corporate wealth creation business models). Rather, the core accounting principles were designed to prevent embezzlement and have been a product of their history ever since the Renaissance. This analysis enabled us to compellingly demonstrate why traditional accounting practice, on its own, suffers from important weaknesses when communicating a "true and fair" view of the future value creation potential of corporate IP assets to a company. This is squarely a topic that must be addressed by the corporate governance legal framework, relevant transparency, materiality and disclosure principles. We are in an age that highly values innovation and creativity. IP rights are an intangible version of wealth that are as – or even more – important than numbers in a balance sheet. The research in this book is the author's attempt to shed some light on this problem. It is crucial to see things clearly for what they are if we are to understand what is needed to shape the future. The accounting profession continues to explore the issues arising as a result of the mechanical application of IAS 38 Intangibles, but there is no movement to amend the standard and as such the status quo remains.[2] Yet, there is empirical evidence that the scale and significance of corporate IP assets to value creation are now of a different order and a more holistic approach is needed. In the meantime, economies, companies and regulators are deeply embedded in traditional thinking which has become a straightjacket, especially for SME innovation firms.

Next, in *Part 4 The corporate governance dimension: developing a normative practice in IP reporting* we considered that corporate disclosure theory predicts that an increase in the level of disclosure of IP asset and strategy information should reduce information asymmetries, leading to potential benefits such as a decrease in the cost of capital, increased access to finance, lower interest rates etc. and foster trust in IP-rich companies. High quality dialogue relies on robust information. We studied the qualitative (as opposed to quantitative) side of corporate IP assets and strategy to overcome the lack of transparency of these intangible assets and reveal greater predictability of IP value over time. However, before a satisfactory corporate governance standard can be developed, a fundamental issue still needs to be resolved: what level of IP asset information does society believe companies should publicly disclose? What is best practice? Corporate governance egalitarianism is, as we shall construe it, the doctrine that

2 A new development in the field of transparency related to non-financial indicator reporting took place in July 2017 when the European Financial Reporting Advisory Group (EFRAG) and the FRC met to discuss the IASB Discussion Paper *Disclosure Initiative – Principles of Disclosure.* This initiative aims to suggest principles governing, what, how and where information should be disclosed in the financial statements to improve information provided to users of financial statements. The comment period ended on 2 October and on13 December 2017 the Board began considering the high-level feedback on its Discussion Paper. There is no particular feedback reported in relation to intangibles or IP asset reporting. An overview of the feedback is available at www.iasplus.com/en/meeting-notes/iasb/2017/december/disclosure-initiative.

it is desirable for everyone to have a standard level of information about a company's corporate IP assets and strategy. Companies need to consider reporting how their directors have discharged their duty to non-shareholder stakeholders as required by section 172 CA 2006. Although the main focus is on the common law tradition of corporate governance in England and Wales, the corporate disclosure of IP assets in other jurisdictions was studied by way of comparison to discover best practice in high ranking IP-driven economies. We examined certain aspects of disclosure and accountability principles evolving in Denmark, Germany, Japan and the US. We comparatively analysed the emerging response in those jurisdictions elucidate how to address the IP information gap in the UK. In Chapter 5 we discussed the Intellectual Capital (IC) reporting approach that has its origins in Denmark. We noted that IC reporting is still light on guidance specifically related to IP asset and strategy disclosures. We then analysed the strict legal obligations on Japanese companies generally and US publicly listed companies to disclose corporate IP asset information and strategy as part of their existing corporate reporting frameworks, noting the advantages and disadvantages of each. Although the comparative analysis did not elicit any normative standard approach, Denmark, Japan and the US are examples of jurisdictions that are actively striving to create a more robust corporate governance legal framework and leading the way in best practice in corporate IP asset reporting. Companies operating in those jurisdictions make more transparent corporate IP strategy and assets reports. Substance trumps form. In other words, the functional corporate governance system in each comparator country has company laws or regulations that expressly embed obligations to report narrative corporate IP information. Equally, the UK Companies Act 2006 could be amended to include specific references to corporate IP assets and strategy alongside the requirements to report on the environment, employees, the impact on society and community, human rights and gender diversity. Why are such steps needed? To be blunt, the purpose of transparency in corporate governance is to "keep the bastards honest".

> There cannot be honest markets without honest publicity. Manipulation and dishonest practices of the market place thrive upon mystery and secrecy.[3]
>
> The United States Congress on adoption of the Securities Exchange Act in 1934.

In laymen's terms, corporate governance is concerned with "following the money" and weeding out "humbug" and "bullshit".[4] In anecdotal discussions over the

3 H.R.Rep. No. 1383, 73d Cong., 2d Sess., 11 (1934). The US Supreme Court has "repeatedly described the 'fundamental purpose' of the [Exchange] Act as implementing a 'philosophy of full disclosure.'" *Santa Fe Industries, Inc. v. Green*, 430 U.S. 462, 477–478 (1977), quoting *SEC v. Capital Gains Research Bureau, Inc.*, 375 U.S. 180, 186 (1963).

4 Frankfurt, H.G. *The Importance of What We Care About* (2007) Fourteenth edition, Cambridge University Press pp 117–120. On page 118, "humbug" is defined to include "deceptive misrepresentation, short of lying".

past years, the author has met with resistance to her view that corporate IP asset and strategy should be more transparent to the public through the provision of material, timely, relevant and accurate qualitative information. Accountants and company directors, whilst acknowledging the "IP information gap" that pervades in the UK argued that: shareholders would not understand such complex information; listed companies already make informal disclosure to market analysts who disseminate the information; free public registers of granted IP rights exist which the public can access; or, if the company does not depend on any one IP right, there is no need to formally disclose as it is not material. These attitudes should ring alarm bells. The shareholder, investor or financier is not in a position to "do the math"[5] or carry out a comprehensive review of a company's IP portfolio to determine what information is material. From a legal perspective, the corporate transparency doctrine is much more than simple honesty – it does not depend on the degree and timeliness of the disclosure. For example, if a company engages in a transaction that costs its shareholders money, but does not admit its responsibility for the loss until years later, that is not transparent corporate conduct, regardless of how comprehensively the company disclosed the details of the transaction. The law must respond to stimulate the narrative reporting that will complement and give context to the numbers published in traditional financial accounts under the "Intangibles" column. The company itself should be the primary source of its own IP information and strategy disclosure (and not secondary sources such as market analysis), otherwise the company cannot be held accountable. Over the last few years the FRC in the UK has seen an increased emphasis on narrative reporting with the introduction of the Strategic Report. However, neither common principles nor best practice in corporate narrative IP disclosure have emerged to assist company directors carry out their duty to disclose.

How the normative standards for corporate narrative reporting of IP information and strategy could develop was the subject of Chapters 6, 7 and 8. We found that a more rigorous approach needs to be applied to IP-rich companies (large and small, public and private) in order to ensure that the principle of full and fair disclosure is upheld. Shareholders, potential investors and other stakeholders such as financiers may suffer from the lack or inaccuracy of information needed to form a judgment of the intrinsic merits of shares. They may also be misled as to relative values of the shares by, for example, distorted impressions gained from the intangibles figure reported in the balance sheet or a figure for an intangible that suddenly appears on a balance sheet when a business is sold. Public listed companies are required to disclose how their IP adds value to the business and accordingly they have much more experience in doing so as is evidenced in the three mini-case studies (Motorola Inc, Royal Philips and GlaxoSmithKline)

5 Padfield, S.J. 'Who Should Do the Math? Materiality Issues in Disclosures that Require Investors to Calculate the Bottom Line' (2006) 34 *Pepperdine Law Review*, University of Akron Legal Studies Research Papers No. 6-11 at https://papers.ssrn.com/sol3/papers.cfm?abstract_id=928630.

involving American, Dutch and UK companies. Listed companies regularly report on issues such as freedom to operate (ownership of IP) and identify IP-related risks in their strategic reports and risk registers (e.g. litigation risk: infringement and enforcement). This good practice should be applauded. It can also have a wide impact in the non-listed and SME sectors, because it is fundamentally about communication, improving transparency and accountability within the existing corporate governance system.

But, are corporate IP assets and strategy really such a "special" category of asset within the existing legal disclosure framework? Corporate IP is simply less visible leading to an "out of sight out of mind" mentality. Corporate IP assets and strategy are not the only complex, abstract and future-oriented issues in the modern corporate environment. Consider entities that have mandatory legal obligations to report on the environment and the impact of climate change (as well as those who have decided to report *voluntarily* to enhance their reputations).[6] Investor groups in both Canada and the US have petitioned the Ontario Securities Commission and the Securities and Exchange Commission to issue statements clarifying the application of existing disclosure requirements to climate change-related risks.[7] True and fair disclosure is essential to the integrity of the securities markets. However, some opine that shareholders and other stakeholders will not be able to understand corporate IP issues and that it would simply complicate disclosures to include it. In the *Basic* case[8] the US Supreme Court offers a different view, stating:

> Disclosure, and not paternalistic withholding of accurate information, is the policy chosen and expressed by Congress . . . The role of the materiality requirement is not to attribute to investors a child-like simplicity, an inability to grasp the probabilistic significance of negotiations, but to filter out essentially useless information that a reasonable investor would not consider significant, even as part of a larger mix of factors to consider in making his investment decision.

Nevertheless, it has to be acknowledged that innovation firms perceive a downside to increased communication about their IP assets which they see as another costly administrative burden. More detailed guidance from a credible source such as the FRC about the standard for appropriate IP asset and strategy disclosures (whether mandatorily or voluntarily) would help shift this mindset.

As discussed in Chapters 6 and 7, the key factor for determining disclosure by public companies is the "materiality" principle, which essentially acts as a filtering

6 This will include companies whose operations are greenhouse gas emissions intensive, or whose facilities or real estate are particularly vulnerable to climate-related hazards.

7 Hendersen, G.E. 'The Materiality of Climate Change and the role of Voluntary Disclosure' (2009) *Osgoode Hall Law School Legal Studies Research Paper Series (CLPE) Research Paper No. 47* at https://papers.ssrn.com/sol3/papers.cfm?abstract_id=1515955## .

8 *Basic Inc. et al v Levinson et al* 485 U.S. 224 (1988) at 234 at https://h2o.law.harvard.edu/collages/7204.

standard, and is integral to our modern corporate governance regime. Materiality requires an assessment of the inferences that a reasonable shareholder would draw from a given set of facts.[9] The corporate governance "materiality" standard is relevant for determining which IP asset and strategy information is to be prioritised. In both the US and the UK, the "materiality" threshold provides an effective filter for corporate narrative information IP asset and strategy disclosure, allowing major trends and significant events to be identified without being buried under an avalanche of information or "clutter" as referred to by the UK FRC. In the US we saw that the concept of "materiality" is embedded into disclosure obligations under Regulation S-K, which expressly refers to IP (noted in Chapter 5) so IP is not invisible in corporate law in the US as it is in the UK.[10] We discussed the Sarbanes-Oxley Act of 2002 and noted the tension between the desire to protect shareholders and investors from fraud via full and fair disclosure and the desire to avoid the negative consequences of excessive litigation and overly burdensome disclosure requirements. We cited academic studies that have concluded that well-governed companies perform better in commercial terms and that corporate reputation represents the market's perception of the quality of the company's management and board of directors. Consequently, a company (itself protected against risk by the legal privileges of limited liability and separate legal personality) that is governed to benefit the well-being of all that its business operations affect, will have minimal difficulty in being truly transparent.[11]

In conclusion, the corporate IP asset and strategy information gap is not consistent with the corporate governance philosophy of full and fair disclosure. As a result, there is a heightened need for corporate governance policy to react and respond. The way in which corporate value is judged is evolving. Traditional methods of appraisal, measures and ratios have worked well with classic asset categories, but are less than optimal in valuing intangible corporate IP assets. We suggest that the sheer "magnitude" of a company's corporate IP asset portfolio may be material as an independent fact. In terms of timely, relevant and accurate narrative disclosures, the more material the facts, the more they should be brought to the attention of shareholders and other stakeholders. Having determined materiality, directors should consider: (1) whether all the relevant pieces of data necessary were disclosed proximately to one another and in the place where a reasonable investor would expect to find them; (2) whether the data was appropriately cross-referenced; and (3) whether the import of the data was sufficiently highlighted to alert the reasonable investor.[12] These issues were examined in the best practice in corporate IP asset and strategy disclosure mini-case study involving

9 *Marksman Partners L.P. v. Chantal Pharm.*, 927 F. Supp. 1297, 1305–1306 (US).

10 Thomas, R.S 'The Materiality Standard for Intellectual Property Disclosures' (2002) 42(2) *IDEA The Journal of Law and Technology* 205 at www.buscalegis.ufsc.br/revistas/files/anexos/4068-4062-1-PB.pdf.

11 With the exception of lawful confidential information and trade secrets.

12 Padfield, S.J supra n [5] at p 3.

GSK's 2012 annual report in Chapter 7. The idea of studying the content of narrative disclosures in corporate annual reports is not new; what is new is considering corporate narrative, specifically of *IP information and strategy disclosures,* within the context of the UK's IP ecosystem and corporate regulation.

Looking ahead, the American SEC is currently proposing changes to corporate disclosure requirements and these are likely to be more onerous with respect to intangibles and IP assets.[13] In early 2016, the author made a submission to the UK's Law Reform Commission to highlight the need for more express references to corporate IP assets and strategy in the Companies Act 2006 which is currently under consideration. There are also the implications of Brexit for corporate reporting in the UK to consider. How the framework for accounting and corporate narrative reporting will change depends on the UK Government's negotiations to exit the EU. The UK may decide to adopt international standards over EU standards. New transparency and disclosure requirements will arise either in law or through voluntary guidelines to address specific public policy objectives, for example, greater accountability to stakeholders other than shareholders. New digital communications channels will continue to shape and change the form and content of corporate reporting in annual reports in the future, especially in terms of the provision of corporate IP asset information and data via company companion websites which will be able to communicate more timely, searchable and downloadable information.

9.1 IP in the boardroom

What about the boardroom and the level of IP knowledge? Assessing materiality requires a deep understanding of the IP legal framework. Many large private and public companies have created the role of the Chief IP Officer (CIPO). Indeed, the author has had personal experience of similar roles in Australia and in the UK, which led her to this field of research. We saw that certain countries at the top of global IP rankings such as Denmark, Germany, the US and Japan are actively increasing the amount of corporate IP asset and strategy disclosure required by firms to improve transparency. As yet, however, there is no international consensus as to best practice or standards. Rapid and disjointed developments in the law are combining to create substantial corporate disclosure issues, particularly for publicly listed multinational companies. At the same time, stakeholder activism on IP issues is emerging with shareholders demanding transparency, or at least substantive disclosure, on matters ranging from financial estimates of corporate IP assets to information about the company's positioning and IP strategy. In the author's experience, those responsible for compiling, verifying and publishing the narrative reports need refined expertise in relation to the law of IP rights generally,

13 'SEC Proposes Amendments to Update and Simplify Disclosure Requirements as Part of Overall Disclosure Effectiveness Review' US Securities and Exchange Commission press release (6 April 2016) at www.sec.gov/news/pressrelease/2016-141.html.

as well as more targeted bespoke guidance on corporate IP asset and strategy reporting.

This unmet need for guidance led the author to create the flexible three-tier business triage style corporate narrative model set out in Chapter **8.** To assist with a materiality assessment, the original model draws on developments in IC reporting originating in Denmark (as further developed in Germany) but, uniquely, also on the medical and military triage concept. The triage-style model implicitly embeds the principles for narrative corporate reporting espoused by the FRC, the UK's independent audit regulator. In the UK, the Strategic Report format must comply with the requirements of the CA 2006, even if made voluntarily, substantially increasing the legitimacy and authority of the information disclosed.

Although this model uses patents as the basis for illustration, it could be adapted to other forms of IP and used as a guide for innovation firms small and large, private and public, in the UK and other countries with respect to deciding what is a "material" IP disclosure. On 20 July 2016, the FRC's Culture Coalition published a report exploring the relationship between corporate governance and long-term economic success in the UK.[14] A key finding of the study in terms of corporate governance and reporting is that in order to foster the conditions for sustainable long-term investment, it is vital that the market has confidence in the quality of corporate governance and reporting. The corporate collapses of the 1980s and the global financial crisis in 2008 renewed the world's focus on the need for effective corporate governance as poor practice has enormous impact on confidence in companies. This book recommends an enhanced and more active role for corporate governance with respect to corporate intangible IP rights, which it is argued, should be treated as at least as important as other reporting themes such as: remuneration; gender balance and diversity on the board of directors; environment; climate change and most recently Brexit. At the same time, within the IP ecosystem, the topic of corporate governance is the subject of intense debate. It is significant that at the recent IPBC Global 2017 Conference, the major theme of the keynote speech by Laura Quatela, CIPO at Lenovo, was "IP in the boardroom". The issue of corporate governance and IP assets will not easily disappear. A failure to act here may lead to increasing distrust of IP rights monopolies by an already wary public.

We started this journey by exploring the challenges faced by IP-rich SMEs; what actions could they take? Early growth stage SMEs who internally generate IP, integral to future value creation, often have fragile balance sheets. The following recommendations are aimed at enhancing transparency of their corporate IP assets, business strategy and their role in value creation.

14 The report is the culmination of the FRC's Culture Coalition, a collaboration with the Chartered Institute of Management Accountants (CIMA), Institute of Business Ethics (IBE), Chartered Institute of Internal Auditors (IIA), Chartered Institute of Personnel and Development (CIPD) and the City Values Forum, as well as interviews with more than 250 chairmen, CEOs and leading industry experts, from the UK's largest companies. See www.frc.org.uk/News-and-Events/FRC-Press/Press/2016/July/Corporate-culture-key-to-sustainable-growth.aspx.

Recommendation 1
UK SMEs should ensure they benefit from the existing UKIPO and BEIS freely available resources as set out in Chapter 2 to identify and manage their IP (beyond their financial statements of expenditure). This will enable them to build their narrative qualitative disclosure.

Recommendation 2
It is crucial for the company to identify and record IP assets even if they are regarded as are "off-balance sheet" items under relevant accounting standards. Corporate IP assets will undoubtedly become more important and valuable to the enterprise as it matures. Early stage IP asset financial information from the *date of incorporation* is needed for traceability and integrity of financial accounting information. This in turn will support the contextual narrative information to provide a true and fair view of the financial position of an enterprise. The traditional financial report of the quantitative value of the company's intangibles should be enhanced through the use of detailed "notes" to the accounts.

Recommendation 3
Innovating SMES should designate a director or company officer to manage the company's IP from the outset and lead ongoing IP management as the company grows. In a one-person company, the director should be aware of this aspect of his or her responsibility to promote the success of the company under section 172 CA 2006 (as seen in Chapter 8).

Recommendation 4
Innovating SMEs should consider making voluntary narrative disclosure of corporate IP asset and strategy information in the Strategic Report of the annual return to enhance access to finance. They can use the *Essential, Desirable & Optional* business triage-style model presented in Chapter 8 to assess the materiality of any voluntary IP disclosures. This should be updated annually to demonstrate reliably and repeatedly, how their corporate IP assets deliver value beyond the balance sheet (which inadequately documents internally generated IP as an expense). By using the corporate regulator's reporting format, SMEs will avoid having to generate multiple sets of information e.g. management reports, ICS, growth statements.

9.2 The great IP education challenge

> One of the greatest problems we face today is how to adjust our way of thinking to meet the challenge of an increasingly complex, rapidly changing, unpredictable world. We must rethink our way of organising knowledge.
>
> Edgar Morin (8 July 1921)[15]

15 French philosopher and sociologist, UNESCO Chair of Complex Thought, Morin is known as a founder of transdisciplinarity.

The findings in this book inform our understanding of the extent to which corporate IP assets have had a thorny impact on diverse disciplines such as corporate finance, accounting and company law and corporate governance. The UK, home to the City of London, a leading global financial centre, needs to join the elite group of corporate IP disclosure standard setters. But how can a responsible corporate culture of IP transparency be stimulated to create a rosy future to connect corporate communication with the desires of shareholders, investors and other stakeholders? The answer lies in education that embeds IP awareness in the curricula, especially university programmes outside the law school. A national higher education learning and teaching IP Excellence Framework would advance this objective. However, it is also important to focus specifically on company director education, such as that offered by the Institute of Directors (IoD)[16] and other accredited providers. As with chartered company secretary qualifications[17], there is a need for the modern CIPO profession to be similarly qualified to an appropriate standard to support the board's governance objectives and to ensure that a company's IP strategy and decision making, how it achieves its aims and all IP-related activities undertaken comply with legal, ethical and regulatory requirements. Accountability through monitoring and control is a solution to the problem of trust in IP rights as a form of corporate value. In the words of Marianne Levin, LLD, PhD, *honoris causa*, Professor of Private Law, Stockholm University, IP law has evolved from being "a little island to a big ocean".[18] While the traditional approaches might solve the complexity of other governance issues such as gender balance, corporate social responsibility etc. there is a need to adopt a new way of thinking in order to deal with corporate IP. Good corporate IP governance is a new way of thinking that needs to be supported by policy and decision makers. It is, therefore, necessary to examine whether the idea of good corporate IP governance exists within the international legal system. A number of examples provided from Denmark, Germany, Japan and the United States and several mini-case studies helped to demonstrate the broad picture.

16 The IoD is the UK's longest running organisation for professional leaders, founded in 1903 and incorporated by Royal Charter in 1906. The IoD's mission statement states that it stands for "free enterprise, entrepreneurialism, wealth creation and good corporate governance" and represents "the views of businesses and IoD members in the media and with government". The IoD has just over 30,000 full members which come from companies of all sizes and from all industries. The author is a graduate of the Institute of Australian Company Directors (IACD).

17 In the UK, the Chartered Secretaries Qualifying Scheme (CSQS) is the main qualification needed to achieve chartered status and become a full member of ICSA. Candidates must complete an ICSA accredited university programme that awards the GradICSA status, as well as a postgraduate qualification.

18 Professor Levin was the key note speaker at the 10th Anniversary European Intellectual Property Teachers' Network Conference 2017 convened by the author and hosted by Lund University, Sweden on 28–30 June.

Ultimately, this book teases out more new ideas and discussions on corporate IP governance issues, demonstrating the close relationship between academic research and professional practice.

9.3 Is there a case for doing nothing?

It is well known the UK has some of the highest corporate governance standards in the world. Does that mean there a case for doing nothing? Should companies simply be left to their own devices? The difficulty with this argument is that the corporate IP information gap will simply become even more ingrained. In theory, if all listed companies stepped up their level of corporate IP disclosures, the improved level of transparency should begin to bolster IP asset values and support investment in innovation and the economy.

To achieve this, companies and their boards of directors need to change the way they think and work. They need to think differently about corporate governance and the transparency of corporate IP assets and strategy. Better and more efficient techniques of making material IP disclosures must be embraced. If more IP-rich companies take the initiative, following frontrunners (e.g. publicly listed companies), this will lead to financial sector reform. This will require progress through "all four stages of acceptance" identified by the British biologist, IBS Haldane:

(1) this is worthless nonsense;
(2) this is an interesting, but perverse, point of view;
(3) this is true, but quite unimportant;
(4) I always said so.[19]

Haldane was referring to reactions to new ideas in science and not about corporate governance or the law, but his words resonate in today's corporate environment. This will be achieved by a legal solution to the transparency problem advocating thatcorporate governance take the lead. Lord Denning said:

> If we never do anything which has not been done before, we shall never get anywhere. The law will stand still whilst the rest of the world goes on and that will be bad for both.[20]

The came to study this interdisciplinary topic because she is an anomaly, a person with corporate, IP and some accounting knowledge. The growing level of investment in corporate intangible IP assets demands that corporate governance law

19 Haldane, IBS, 'The Truth about Death' (1963) 58 *Journal of Genetics* 463–4.
20 *Packer v Packer* [1953] 2 All ER at p 22.

responds. I hope this book adds to the body of knowledge related to corporate governance and IP generally with a view to application within the UK and maybe further afield. While the work may stimulate academic discourse, if the research helps to promote the success of innovation companies in the long term, it will have served an equally important purpose.

Bibliography

Books and articles

A Guide to Funding Innovation (2013–2014) Oxford Innovation Ltd https://innovation.ox.ac.uk/

'A Revolution Postponed' (May/June 2014) *Intellectual Asset Management*

'Accounts and Tax Returns for Smaller Companies' at www.gov.uk/prepare-file-annual-accounts-for-limited-company/prepare-annual-accounts

'Accountancy Futures, Re-assessing the Value of Corporate Reporting' (2012) Association of Chartered Certified Accountants at www.accaglobal.com/content/dam/acca/global/PDF-technical/financial-reporting/reassessing-value.pdf

Adams, M. and Oleksak, M. 'Fitting the Intangibles Pieces Together: A Call to Arms' (30 September 2010) *Intellectual Asset Magazine*

Admati, A. and Hellwig, M. *The Bankers' New Clothes: What's Wrong with Banking and What to Do about It* (2013) Princeton University Press, Princeton NJ

Aguilar, F. *Scanning the Business Environment* (1967) Macmillan, USA

Ahmed, K. and Courtis, J.K. 'Associations between Corporate Characteristics and Disclosure Levels in Annual Reports: A Meta-Analysis' (March 1999) 31(1) *The British Accounting Review*

Alcaniz, L., Gomez-Bezares, F. and Roslender, R. 'Theoretical Perspectives on Intellectual Capital: A Backward Look and a Proposal for Going Forward' (June 2010) 35 Accounting Forum 104–117 at http://dx.doi.org/10.1016/j.accfor.2011.03.004.

Albu, C.N., Albu, N. and Alexander, D. 'The True and Fair View concept in Romania: A Case Study of Concept Transferability' in Albu, C.N. and Răzvan V.M. (Ed.) *Accounting in Central and Eastern Europe (Research in Accounting in Emerging Economies, Volume 13)* Emerald Group Publishing Limited

Allsebrook, D. and Maestre, S. *Intellectual Property as a Security Device* (1996) Meredith Lectures, McGill University

Ante, Spencer E. 'Motorola is split into two' (5 January 2011) *The Wall Street Journal*

Arnold, J.A. and Moizer, P. 'A Survey of the Methods used by UK Investment Analysts to Appraise Investment in Ordinary Shares' (1984) 14(55) Summer *Accounting and Business Research* 195–207

Arnold, R., Bently, LA.F., Derclaye, E. and Dinwoodie, G.B. 'The Legal Consequences of Brexit Through the Lens of IP Law' (15 February 2017) 101(2) *Judicature*

Arping, S. and Sautner, Z. 'Did SOX Section 404 Make Firms Less Opaque? Evidence from Cross-Listed Firms' (2013) 30 *Contemporary Accounting Research* 1133–1165

Arundel, A. and Kabla, I. 'What Percentage of Innovations are Patented? Empirical Estimates for European Firms' (1998) 27(2) *Research Policy* 127–141

Atrill, P. and McLaney, E. *Accounting & Finance for Non Specialists* (2002) Third edition, Pearson Education Ltd.

Baddeley, M. *Behavioural Economics: A Very Short Introduction* (2017) Oxford University Press, Oxford

Baltussen, G. 'Behavioural Finance: An Introduction' (13 Jan 2009) at SSRN: http://ssrn.com/abstract=1488110 or http://dx.doi.org/10.2139/ssrn.1488110 accessed 9 March 2015

Bannerjee, A. V. 'A Simple Model of Herd Behaviour' (1992) 107 *Quarterly Journal of Economics* 797–817

Barkley Rosser, J. 'A Nobel Prize for Asymmetric Information: The Economic Contributions of George Akerlof, Michael Spence, and Joseph Stiglitz' (2003) 15(1) *Review of Political Economy*

Basel III: A Global Regulatory Framework for More Resilient Banks and Banking Systems (December 2010, Revised June 2011) Basel Committee for Banking Supervision, Bank for International Settlements pp 6–23 at www.bis.org/publ/bcbs189.pdf accessed 21 November 2014

Beatty, R. et al *IPO Pricing with Accounting and Comparable Firm Information* (April 2000) Working Paper, Southern Methodist University

Beck, T., Demirguc-Kunt, A. and Levine, R. 'Legal Theories of Financial Development' (2000) 17(4) *Oxford Review of Economic Policy*

Bennett, P., Holzman, L., Hanlon, R., and Sobel, D. 'Security Interests – Less Than Secure?' (2006) *Managing Intellectual Property*

Berger, A.N., Frame, W.S. and Miller, N.H. 'Credit Scoring and the Availability, Price, and Risk of Small Business Credit' (2005) 37(2) *Journal of Money, Credit, and Banking* 191–222

Berger, A.N. and Udell, G.F. 'A More Conceptual Framework for SME Finance' (2006) 30(11) *Journal of Banking & Finance* 2945–2966

Berges, A., Guillen, M.F., Moreno, J.P. and Ontiveros, E. *A New Era in Banking: The Landscape After the Battle* (2014) Bibliomotion, Inc. Kindle Edition

Bernstein, P.L. *Capital Ideas Evolving* (2007) John Wiley & Sons, New York

Bezant, M. and Punt, R. 'The Use of Intellectual Property as Security for Debt Finance' (1997) *Intellectual Property Quarterly* 297

Bhattacharya, H. *Banking Strategy, Credit Appraisal and Lending Decisions: A Risk-Return Framework* (2010), Oxford University Press, Oxford

Biggs, S.F., Bedard, J.C., Gaber, B.G. and Linsmeier, T.J. 'The Effects of Task Size and Similarity on the Decision Behaviour of Bank Loan Officers' (1985) 31(8) *Management Science* 970–986

Binctin, N. and Bonnet, G. *Le Capital Intellectuel* (2007) LexisNexis, France

Binctin, N. *Stratégie D'entreprise et Propriété Intellectuelle* (2015) LGDJ, France

Blair, M.M. and Wallman, S.M.H. *Unseen Wealth: Report of the Brookings Task force on Intangibles* (2001) Brookings Institution Press, Washington D.C.

Bontis, N. 'Intellectual Capital Disclosure in Canadian Corporations' (2003) 7(1/2) *Journal of Human Resource Costing and Accounting* 9–20

Bootle, R. *The Trouble with Markets: Saving Capitalism from Itself* (2009) Nicholas Brealey Publishing, London

Bornstein, D. *How to Change the World: Social Entrepreneurs and the Power of New Ideas* (20 Sept 2007) Second Edition, Oxford University Press, USA

Bradley, K. *Intellectual Capital and the New Wealth of Nations* (21 October 2006) Lecture given at the Royal Society of Arts, London

Bravo, F. 'Forward-looking Disclosure and Corporate Reputation as Mechanisms to Reduce Stock Return Volatility' (2016) 19(1) *Spanish Accounting Review* 122–131

Breznitz, D. 'Why Germany Dominates the US in Innovation' (27 May 2014) *Harvard Business Review* at https://hbr.org/2014/05/why-germany-dominates-the-u-s-in-innovation

Brookings, A. *Intellectual Capital: Core Asset for the Third Millenium Enterprise* (1996) Cengage Learning EMEA, USA

Bunn, M.D., Savage G.T. and Holloway B.B. 'Stakeholder Analysis for Multi-sector Innovations' *Journal of Business and Industrial Marketing* (2002) 17(2/3) 181–203

Burr, V. *An Introduction to Social Constructionism* (1995) Routledge, London, UK

Cain, B. and Marshall, J. 'Taking Security over Patents' (March 2014) *Taylor Wessing* at www.taylorwessing.com/synapse/march14.html accessed 11 November 2014

Canibano, L., Covarsi, M. and Sanchez, M. 'The Value Relevance and Managerial Implications of Intangibles: A Literature Review' (1998) OECD, Directorate for Science, Technology and Industry

Chhaochharia, V. and Grinstein, Y. 'Corporate Governance and Firm Value: The Impact of the 2002 Governance Rules' (March 2007) *Johnson School Research Paper Series* No. 23-06 Johnson School of Management p 7–9

'Chinese company's $1.3 billion patent and trademark loan enters the IP deal Pantheon' (4 April 2014) *Intellectual Asset Management Blog* at www.iam-magazine.com/blog

'Chinese companies have secured over $10 million in patent-backed loans since 2008' (6 March 2014) *Intellectual Asset Management blog* at www.iam-magazine.com/blog/detail.aspx?g=7fd84e0c-af7a-4d28-ba91-746bbb44e318&q=china#search=%22china%22

Clarkson, D. 'Britain avoids triple-dip recession' (16 April 2013) *MSN Money* at http://money.uk.msn.com/features/britain-avoids-triple-dip-recession

Cohen, M. 'China to provide financial incentives for filing patent applications abroad' (12 June 2012) *ChinaIPR blog* at http://chinaipr.com/2012/06/12/china-to-provide-financial-incentives-for-filing-patent-applications-abroad/#more-427

Coren, G. *James Dyson Against the Odds: An Autobiography* (1997) Orion Business, Great Britain

Cowley, A. and Swaffield, A. 'The Strategic Report A Practical Guide to the New Regulations' (2014) Deloitte at www.ukaccoutningplus.co.uk

Crompton, S. 'Patent Litigation Funding on the Rise in the UK' (29 August 2012) *Managing IP* at www.managingip.com/Article/3081518/Patent-litigation-funding-on-the-rise-in-UK.html

Crosse, H. D. *Management Policies for Commercial Banks* (1962) Prentice-Hall Inc., Englewood, New Jersey

Cull, R., Lance E., Davis, N. R. and Lamoreaux-Rosenthal, J. 'Historical Financing of Small-and Medium-size Enterprises' (2006) 30(11) *Journal of Banking & Finance* 3017–3042.

Dalgano, S, *Technology Valuations – The Whys and Wherefores and Why Nots* (2003) Paper presented at LEZANZ Conference in Adelaide

Das, S. 'Protecting ideas is crucial for eco-technology to succeed' (4 June 2010) *The Financial Times*, The Environmental and Intellectual Property Special Report

Davis, A. *Seeds of Change: Emerging Sources of Non-bank Funding for Britain's* SMEs (2012) Centre for the Study of Financial Innovation p 1 at www.csfi.org/files/Seeds_of_Change_by_Andy_Davis_PDF.pdf accessed 21 November 2014

Denoncourt, J. 'Hanging on Every Word' (May 2002) *Managing Intellectual Property*

Denoncourt, J. 'Intellectual property and venture capital: the secrets to building innovation ecosystems: A special report' (9 Sept 2014) *IP Finance blogspot* at http://ipfinance.blogspot.co.uk/search?q=Denoncourt accessed 14 November 2014

Denoncourt, J. 'Reform to the UK Company Registration of Charges Scheme, The Companies Act 2006 (amendment of Part 25) Regulations 2013 (SI 2013/600)' (2013) 22 *Nottingham Law Journal* 138–140

Denoncourt, J. 'Financial reporting for intangibles: why intangibles remain invisible (17August 2014) *IP Finance blogspot* at http://ipfinance.blogspot.co.uk/2014/08/financial-reporting-for-intangibles-why.html

Denoncourt, J. *Patent-backed Debt Finance: Should Company Law Take the Lead to Provide a "true and fair" View of SME Patent Assets?* (2015) PhD thesis, University of Nottingham

Denoncourt, J. 'IP Debt Finance and SMEs: Revealing the Evolving Conceptual Framework Drawing on Initiatives from Around the World' in Kono, T. (Ed.) *Security Interests in Intellectual Property: Perspectives in Law, Business and Innovation* (2017) Springer Verlag, Singapore

DeRuiter, J. and Holston, P. 'Drug Patent Expirations and the "Patent Cliff"' (20 June 2012) *US Pharmacist*, Jobson Publications at www.uspharmacist.com/content/s/216/c/35249/

Deszo, L. and Loewenstein, G. 'Lenders' Blind Trust and Borrowers' Blind Spots: A Descriptive Investigation of Personal Loans' (2012) 33(5) *Journal of Economic Psychology* 996–1011

Di Giantomasso, F. 'The Tangible Problem of Intangibles' (1 December 2001) *AICD Review* 23

Directive 2012/6/EU of the European Parliament and of the Council of 14 March 2012 amending Council Directive 78/660/EEC on the annual accounts of certain types of companies as regards micro-entities (2012) *Official Journal of the European Union* L81/3 at http://ec.europa.eu/internal_market/accounting/legal_framework/annual_accounts/original_text_en.htm

Disclosures of Information on Patent and Technology (January 2004) Ministry of Economy, Trade and Industry, Japan.

Donaldson, T. and Preston, L.E. 'The Stakeholder Theory of the Corporation: Concepts, Evidence, and Implications' (1995) 20(1) *Academy of Management Review* 70–71

Donegan, C. 'Intellectual Property: The Worst-communicated Secret in Value Creation' (5 August 2015) Fraserburgh, UK at: www.lexology.com/library/detail.aspx?g=2a49ce37-f1e0-46b6-acc4-ea1d874d7e45

Dutton, W. and Helsper, E. *The Internet in Britain* (2007) Oxford Institute, Oxford

Ebke, W. *Maerkte machen Rechtauch Gesellschafts-und Unternehmensrecht!* (2000) Festschrift Utter 12

Eccles, L. 'How bank lending fell by £365 billion in five years' (7 September 2014) *Daily Mail* at www.dailymail.co.uk/news/article-2747042/How-bank-lending-fell-365-BILLION-five-years-delight-controversial-payday-loan-firms.html accessed 21 November 2014

Edvinsson, L. *Accounting for Minds* (1997) out of print

Edvinsson, L. and Malone, M. *Intellectual Capital: Realizing your Company's True Value by Finding Its Hidden Brainpower* (1997) Harper Business, USA.

Edwards, D. 'Patent Backed Securitization: Blueprint for a New Asset Class' (2000) Gerling NCM Credit Insurance

'Ensuring Creditor Protection is Asia-Pacific Construction Projects Part II: Property Securities Law in the Asia-Pacific Region' (2013) *DLA Piper* at www.dlapiper.com/~/media/Files/Insights/Publications/2013/02/Ensuring%20creditor%20protection%20in%20construction%20pro__/Files/propertysecuritieslawasiapacific/FileAttachment/propertysecuritieslawasiapacific.pdf accessed on 14 November 2014

Ernst, H. 'Patenting Strategies in the German Mechanical Engineering Industry and their Relationship to Company Performance' (1995) 15(4) *Technovation* 225–240

Ernst. H. 'Patent Information for Strategic Technology Management' (2003) 25(3) *World Patent Information* 233–242

'Europe 3Q 2014' (2014) *Dow Jones Venture Source*, p 2 at http://images.dowjones.com/company/wp-content/uploads/sites/15/2014/10/Dow-Jones-Europe-VentureSource-Report-3Q-2014.pdf accessed 21 November 2014

Ferguson, N. *The Ascent of Money: A Financial History of the World* (2012) Penguin Books, London

Fink, C. 'Introduction' Chief Economist WIPO (26 March 2010) Document Code WIPO/IP/ECON/GE/10/REF/A/ROUNDTABLE/INTRO at www.wipo.int/meetings/en/doc_details.jsp?doc_id=137479

'Five years of Sarbanes-Oxley' (26 July 2007) *The Economist*

Flack, J.H. 'Secured Transactions: Practical Things Every Business Law Should Know About UCC Article 9' (March 2011) *American Bar Association Newsletter* at http://apps.americanbar.org/buslaw/committees/CL983500pub/newsletter/201103/flack.pdf

Forsythe, M. and Sanderson, H. 'Financing China Costs Poised to Rise with CDB Losing Sovereign-Debt Status' (June 2011) *Bloomberg Market Magazine*

Frankfurt, H.G. *The Importance of What We Care About* (2007) Fourteenth edition, Cambridge University Press, Cambridge

Franks & Co. '36% Increase in Official UKIPO Patent Fees' (27 May 2010) at *www.franksco.com/news/2010/5/36-increase-in-official-ukipo-patent-fees*

Frederick, W.R. *Recent Developments in Intellectual Capital Reporting and their Policy Implications* (2009) OECD Education Working Papers, No. 17, OCED Publishing at www.oecd-ilibrary.org/education/recent-developments-in-intellectual-capital-reporting-and-their-policy-implications_227362757626

Frey, C.B. *Intellectual Property Rights and the Financing of Technology Innovation* (2013) Edward Elgar Publishing Limited, Cheltenham UK

'From Ideas to Assets: Singapore's IP Financing Scheme' (1 September 2014) Managing IP at www.managingip.com/Article/3382687/From-idea-to-asset-Singapores-IP-financing-scheme.html

'Fulbright's 9th Annual Litigation Trends Survey: Litigation Bounces Back' (26 February 2013) at www.nortonrosefulbright.com/news/93066/fulbrights-9th-annual-litigation-trends-survey-litigation-bounces-back-regulation-hits-high-us-release

Fulcher, James *Capitalism: A Very Short Introduction* (2004) Oxford University Press, Oxford

Furneaux, R., Kaye, R., Holah, M. and Bicknall, P. 'IP in Business Transactions: UK (England and Wales) Overview' *Thomson Reuters* at http://uk.practicallaw.com/0-501-8472#a799071

'G20 Leaders' Statement The Pittsburgh Summit' (2009) Pittburgh, Illinois at www.g20.org/official_resources/leaders%E2%80%99_statement_pittsburgh_summit

Gallagher & Cawsey Co. 'Wading through the Intellectual Property Requirements of the Sarbanes-Oxley Act of 2002' (June 2005) at www.invention-protection.com

Garrett J. F. *Banks and Their Customers* (1995) Oceana Publications, Dobbs Ferry NY

Garvey, S. 'Strategies to improve patenting and enforcement' (29 May 2008) *IPkat blog* at http://ipkitten.blogspot.co.uk/2008/05/strategies-to-improve-patenting-and.html

Ghafele, R. 'Accounting for Intangibles' (2010) 5(7) *Journal of Intellectual Property Law & Practice* 521–530

Ghafele, R. 'Getting a Grip on Accounting and Intellectual Property' (2005) *WIPO SME Newsletter* at www.wipo.int/sme.

Gilson, R.J. 'Globalizing Corporate Governance: Convergence of Form or Function' (2001) 49 *American Journal of Corporate Law* 329

Gitomer, J. *Little Teal Book of Trust* (2008) Pearson Education Inc. Publishing as FT Press

'GlaxoSmithKline undervalued say analysts' (11 December 2013) at www.morningstar.co.uk/uk/news/114764/glaxosmithkline-undervalued-say-analysts.aspx

Goetzmann, W. N. *Fibonacci and the Financial Revolution* (March 2004) NBER Working Paper 10352

Graham, P. 'Registration of Company Charges' (2014) *Journal of Business Law* 175

Griffith, R., Miller, H. and O'Connell, M. 'Ownership of Intellectual Property and Corporate Taxation' (April 2014) 112 *Journal of Public Economics* 12–23 at www.sciencedirect.com/science/article/pii/S0047272714000103

Gröjer, J.-E. and Johansson, U. (1999) *Voluntary Guidelines on the Disclosure of Intangibles: A Bridge over Troubled Water?* (February 1999) Working paper presented at the Workshop 'Manage and Account for Intangibles' p 15–16, Brussels. Intellectual Capital Management Gathering (1999).

Grossfeld, B. 'Global Accounting: Where Internet Meets Geography' (2000) 48(2) *The American Journal of Comparative Law*

Grossfeld, B. 'Lawyers and Accountants A Semiotic Competition' (2001) 36 *Wake Forest Law Review* 167–186 at http://wakeforestlawreview.com/

Guellec, D., Martinez, C. and Zuniga, P. *Blocking Patents: What They Are and What They Do* (5 June 2008) Preliminary Paper Directorate for Science, Technology and Industry, OECD at ftp://zinc.zew.de/pub/zew-docs/veranstaltungen/innovationpatenting2008/papers/GuellecMartinezZuniga.pdf

Gullifer, L. 'Personal Property Security Law: Where Next?' (2012) *Butterworths Journal of International Banking and Financial Law* 465 and 541

Guthrie, J. and Petty, R. 'Intellectual Capital Literature Review: Measurement, Reporting and Management' (2000) 1(2) *Journal of Intellectual Capital* 155–176

Haapio, H. 'Visualizing Contracts and Legal Rules for Greater Clarity' (2010) 44(3) *The Law Teacher*

Haldane, I.B.S. 'The Truth about Death' (1963) 58 *Journal of Genetics* 463–4

Hall, B. H. 'Patents and Patent Policy' (2007) 23(4) *Oxford Review of Economic Policy* 568–587

Hall, B.H., Jaffe, A. and Trajtenberg, M. 'Market Value and Patent Citations' (May 2001) JEL Classification: O31, O38 UC Berkeley at http://eml.berkeley.edu/~bhhall/papers/HallJaffeTrajtenberg_RJEjan04.pdf

Hall, B., Helmers, C., Rogers, M. and Vana, S. 'The Importance (or not) of Patents to UK Firms'at Oxford Economic Papers (12 April 2013), 1 of 27 doi:10.1093/oep/gpt012

Hall, R. 'A Framework Linking Intangible Resources and Capabiliites to Sustainable Competitive Advantage' (Nov 1993) *Strategic Management Journal* at http://onlinelibrary.wiley.com/doi/10.1002/smj.4250140804/abstract

Halling, D.B. *The Decline and Fall of the American Entrepreneur: How Little Known Laws and Regulations are Killing Innovation* (2009) Self-published and available on www.amazon.co.uk

Hand, J. and Lev, B. *Intangible Assets: Values, Measures, and Risks* (2003) Oxford University Press, Oxford

Harrison, S. and Sullivan, P. H. *Einstein in the Boardroom: Moving beyond Intellectual Capital to I-stuff* (2006) Wiley, Hoboken USA

Harvey, F. 'Scramble for funds in a harsh climate' (4 June 2010) *The Financial Times Environmental and Intellectual Property Special Report*

Hatzikiriakos, K. *Secured Transactions in Intellectual Property Software as Collateral* (2006) LexisNexis Butterworths, London

Hatzikiriakos, K. *Secured Lending in Intellectual Property* (2017) Second edition, LexisNexis, Canada

Healy, P.M. and Krishna G. P. 'The Fall of Enron' (Spring 2003) 17(2) *Journal of Economic Perspectives* 9

Hedelin, E. and Sjo'berg, L. *Risk Assessments – Loan Officers' Assessment of New Entrepreneurs' Personal Characteristics* (1993) NUTEK, Stockholm

Hendersen, G.E. 'The Materiality of Climate Change and the role of Voluntary Disclosure' (2009) *Osgoode Hall Law School Legal Studies Research Paper Series (CLPE)* Research Paper No. 47 at https://papers.ssrn.com/sol3/papers.cfm?abstract_id=1515955##

Henry, M. 'How Effective is Your Security over Intellectual Property?' (1991) *Journal Business Law* 507

Higson, A.W. *An Alternative Basis for the Construction of a Conceptual Framework Incorporating Financial Reporting* Discussion Paper Series 192, Massey University, Department of Accountancy and Business Law

Hilson, J.F. *Asset-Based Lending: A Practical Guide to Secured Financing* (August 2014, Banking and Commercial Law Library) Fourteenth edition, Practising Law Institute, New York

'Hong Kong Banks sign up to ground-breaking intellectual capital initiative' (April 2010) *Intellectual Asset Magazine blog* at www.iam-magazine.com/blog/Detail.aspx?g=3d6fc595-6202-40f0-ba82-6d5ee1b05def

Horrigan, B. *Corporate Social Responsibility in the 21st Century: Debates, Models and Practices Across Government, Law and Business* (2010) Edward Elgar Publishing, Cheltenham UK

Howard, C. *Companies, What They Are and How They Work* (1989) Oxford University Press, Oxford

Hsu, D. and Ziedonis, R. *Patents as Quality Signals for Entrepreneurial Ventures* (2007) paper presented at DRUID Summer Conference

Hulten, C.R. and Hao, J. 'What is a Company Really Worth? Intangible Capital and the "Market to Book Value"' *Puzzle* (November 2008) at http://econweb.umd.edu/~hulten/WebPageFiles/Intangible%20Capital%20and%20the%20%60Market%20to%20Book%20Value%27%20Puzzle.pdf

Humphrey, A. 'SWOT Analysis for Management Consulting' (December 2005) *SRI Alumni Newsletter*

Hwaidi, M. *Why and How Empirical Study in Commercial Law?* (2014) Annual Conference of Socio Legal Study Association at Robert Gordon University

'Income Contingent Repayment Plan 2 – Interest Rates' Student Loans Company at wwwstudentloanrepayment.co.uk/portal/page?_pageid=93,6678715&_dad=portal&_schema=PORTAL

Inman, Philip, 'Vince Cable hits out at Bank of England over loans to small business: Business secretary angered by blocking of regulatory reforms that favour mortgages rather than lending to private companies (19 June 2014) *The Guardian* at www.theguardian.com/business/2014/jun/18/vince-cable-bank-england-loan-small-business

Instefjord, N. and Nakata, H. 'Loan Monitoring and Bank Risk' (17 April 2014) First Draft available at SSRN: http://ssrn.com/abstract=2426149 or http://dx.doi.org/10.2139/ssrn.2426149

'Intellectual Property Financing Scheme' (14 November 2014) IPOS see www.ipos.gov.sg/IPforYou/IPforBusinesses/IPFinancingScheme.aspx

International Integrated Reporting Committee *Towards Integrated Reporting: Communicating Value in the 21st Century* (2011) Discussion Paper at http://theiirc.org/wp-content/uploads/2011/09/IR-Discussion-Paper-2011_spreads.pdf

'*International Regulatory Framework for Banks (Basel III): Capital*' (June 2011) Basel Committee for Banking Supervision, Bank for International Settlements at www.bis.org/bcbs/basel3.htm accessed 21 November 2014

International Financial Reporting Standard for Small and Medium-sized Entities (IFRS for SMEs) (2015) IFRS Foundation at www.iacsa.co.za/wp-content/uploads/2016/11/IFRS-for-SMES-2015.pdf (effective 1 January 2017 with early application permitted).

Inventor Reward and Recognition Programs Benchmark (2011) ipPerformance Group, Napierville, Illinois

'Inventor Sir James Dyson still the region's richest' (9 May 2011) *This is Somerset* (Bristol)

IPScore®2.2 Manual (2009) European Patent Office at www.epo.org/searching/free/ipscore.html

Jacob, R. *Patents and Pharmaceuticals* (29 November 2008) Paper given at the Presentation of the Directorate-General of Competition's Preliminary Report of the Pharma-sector Inquiry

'Japanese Guidelines for Disclosure of Intellectual Assets Based Management', no English language reference available

Johanson, U., Koga, C., Skoog, M. and Henningsson, J. 'The Japanese Governement's Intellectual Capital Reporting Guideline: What are the Challenges for Firms and Capital Market Agents?' (2006) 17(4) *Journal of Intellectual Capital* 474–491

Josef Ackermann im Gesprach: 'Ohne Gewinn ist alles nichts' (20 November 2009) interview in Suddeutsche Zeitung www.suddeutsche.de/geld/josef-ackermann-im-gespraech-ohnegewinn-ist-alles-nichts-1.144881

Kahnemann, D., Slovic, P. and Tversky, A. *Judgment under Uncertainty: Heuristics and Biases* (1982) Cambridge University Press, Cambridge, MA

Kasznik, E. 'Financial reporting for intangibles: the Case of the Invisible Assets' at http://ipfinance.blogspot.co.uk/2014/08/financial-reporting-for-intangibles.html

Keay, A. 'The Duty to Promote the Success of the Company: Is it Fit for Purpose?' p 3 at www.law.leeds.ac.uk/assets/files/research/events/directors-duties/keay-the-duty-to-promote-the-success.pdf

Keay, A. *The Enlightened Shareholder Value Principle and Corporate Governance* (2013) Routledge Research in Corporate Law, Routledge, Abingdon and New York

Keay, A. and Kosmin, L. *Directors' Duties* (2014) Second edition, Jordan Publishing, Bristol

Kettle, R. 'Balance Sheets and Accounts under the Companies Act, 1948' in Baxter, W.T. (Ed.) *Studies in Accounting* (1950) Sweet & Maxwell

Keynes, J. M. 'The General Theory of Employment' (1937) 51(2) *Economic Journal*

Khatri, N. and Ng, H.A. 'The Role of Intuition in Strategic Decision Making' (2000) 53(57) *Human Relations* 57–86

Kirkpatrick, D. *Facebook Effect: The Real Inside Story of Mark Zuckerberg and the World's Fastest Growing Comp*any (2012) The Random House Group, USA

Knight, F.H. *Risk, Uncertainty and Profit* (1911) Boston as quoted in Ferguson, N. *The Ascent of Money* (2012) Penguin Books, London

Knopf, H. *Security Interests in Intellectual Property* (2002) Thomson/Carswell, Toronto

Kono, T. (Ed.) *Security Interests in Intellectual Property: Perspectives in Law, Business and Innovation* (2017) Springer Verlag, Singapore

Kosfeld, M., Heinrichs M., Zak, P. J., Fischbacher, U. and Fehr, E. 'Oxytocin Increases Trust in Humans' (2005) 435 *Nature* 673–676

Kote, L. and Drehwing, E. 'The Interplay between IP and Sarbanes-Oxley – Outline & Background Material' (2005) *PLI's Course Handbook: Handling IP Issues in Business Transactions* at www.darbylaw.com

KPMG *An Overview of Risk and Disclosure* (15 May 2012) at www.kpmg-institutes.com/institutes/healthcare-life-sciences-institute/articles/2012/05/risk-and-disclosure-in-the-global-pharmaceutical-industry.html

Kraemer, G. Linden, G. and Dedrick, J. *Capturing Value in Global Networks: Apple's iPad and iPhone* (July 2011) at http://pcic.merage.uci.edu/papers/2011/Value_iPad_iPhone.pdf

Kramer, W.J. and Patel, C.B. 'Securitisation of Intellectual Property in the US Market' (6 June 2013) Marshall, Gerstein & Borun, Chicago, IL at www.ipo.org/wp-content/uploads/2013/04/Securitisation_of_IP_in_the_US.pdf

Lang, M.H. and Lundholm, R.J. 'Corporate Disclosure Policy and Analyst Behaviour' (October 1996) 71(4) *The Accounting Review* 467–492

Lee, J. 'Big Achievers Share The Greatest Risks They Ever Took' (3 July 2011) at www.forbes.com/2011/03/07/greatest-risk-they-ever-took-2011-entrepreneurs.html

Lee, L.A. and Tweedie, D.P. *The Private Shareholder and the Corporate Report: A Report to the Research Committee of the Institute of Chartered Accountants in England and Wales* (1977) Institute of Chartered Accountants in England and Wales, London

Lee. L.A. and Tweedie, D.P *The Institutional Investor and Financial Information* (1981) Institute of Chartered Accountants in England and Wales, London.

Lending Code (March 2011, revised 28th September 2015) available at www.lendingstandardsboard.org.uk/wp-content/uploads/2016/06/The-Lending-Code-Mar-2011-revised-2015-1.pdf

Leo, K. *Intangible Assets: Seeking Consistency* (November 1999) Australian CPA

Lerner, J. *The Architecture of Innovation: The Economics of Creative Organizations* (2013) Oxford University Press, Oxford

Lev, B. *Intangibles Management, Measurement, and Reporting* (2001) Brookings Institution Press, Washington D.C.

Lim, S.C., Macias, A.J. and Moeller, T. 'Intangible Assets and Capital Structure' (August 2014) *Baylor University Research Paper* p 14 at www.baylor.edu/business/finance/doc.php/231371.pdf.

Lin, Tom W.C. 'A Behavioral Framework for Securities Risk' 16 (April 2012) 34 *Seattle Law Review* 325 at http://ssrn.com/abstract=2040946

Lipton, J. 'Intellectual Property in the Information Age and Secured Finance Practice' (2002) *EIPR* 358

Lipton, J. *Security Over Intangible Property* (2000) LBC Information Services, London

Lloyd, R. 'New banking group launches with focus on improving patent quality' (15 October 2014) *Intellectual Asset Magazine blog* at www.iam-magazine.com/blog/detail.aspx?g=972D0D5D-D116-42FD-945D-82AC28C33B3A accessed 7 November 2014

Macneil, C. 'Personal Property Securities and Intellectual Asset Management: Thinking Outside the Box' (27 August 2014) Intellectual Asset Management at www.iam-magazine.com/reports/Detail.aspx?g=3b995832-b39d-41d0-a9d6-f50dfcf3a83d accessed 12 November 2014

Malone, S. 'Quantifying the Brave New World' (1999) *Hoover Digest*, 1999 No. 1

Manickavasagam, V. 'IP Best Practices in the Post Sarbanes-Oxley Act Era' (February 2011) at www.icisi.edu

Marenberg, B. 'What Corporate Directors Need to Know About Intellectual Property' (9 March 2010) *Life Science Leader Magazine* at www.lifescienceleader.com/doc/what-corporate-directors-need-to-know-about-intellectual-property-0001

Markesinis, B.G. (Ed.) *The Gradual Convergence: Foreign Ideas, Foreign Influences, and English Law on the Eve of the 21st Century* (1994) Clarenden Press, Oxford

Martin, D. and Beling, P. 'Patent Litigation Risk Characterization: Prospective identification of Financial Risk in Patent Holdings' (2004) M-Cam draft.

Maslow, A.H. 'A Theory of Human Motivation' (1943) 50(4) *Psychological Review* 370–96

Mason, S., French, D. and Ryan C. *Company Law* (2013–2014) Oxford University Press

Mathews, M. R. and Higson, A.W. 'Potentially Dysfunctional Impacts of Harmonising Accounting Standards: The Case of Intangible Assets' (2000) Massey University at http://hdl.handle.net/10179/2536

Maubussin, Michael J. *The Success Equation: Untangling Skill and Luck in Business, Sports, and Investing* (2012) Harvard Business Review Press, Boston Mass.

Mayer, R.C., Davis J.H. and Schoorman, F.D. An Integrative Model of Organizational Trust (1995) 20(3) *Academy of Management Review* 709–734

Michel, J. and Bettels B. 'Patent Citation Analysis' (2001) 51(1) *Scientometrics* 185–201

McDonald, L. and Drinkwater, R. *Realistic Valuations of Intellectual Property: Methods and Techniques for Valuing IP* (2004) Report commissioned by the Australian Institute for Commercialisation

McEachern, W.A. *Economics: A Contemporary Introduction* (2012) Tenth edition, Cengage Learning

McLaren, R. H. *Secured Transactions in Personal Property* (1989) Second edition. Looseleaf, Maxwell, Scarborough Ontario

McLaughlin, S. *Unlocking Company Law* (2015) Third edition, Routledge, Abingdon Oxfordshire

McLeod, S. A. 'Qualitative Quantitative' (2008) at www.simplypsychology.org/qualitative-quantitative.html

Medhurst, D. *A Brief and Practical Guide to EC Law* (1994) Second edition, Wiley, Oxford and London

Megginson, L.C. 'Lessons from Europe for American Business' (1963) 44(1) *Southwestern Social Science Quarterly* 3–13

Mehta, S.S. *Commercializing Successful Biomedical Technologies* (2008) Cambridge University Press, New York

Moberly, M.D. *Safeguarding Intangible Assets* (2014) Butterworth-Heineman, London

Munari, F. and Oriani, R. (Eds) *The Economic Valuation of Patents: Methods and Applications* (2011) Edward Elgar Publications Ltd, Cheltenham UK

Moore, J.F. *The Death of Competition: Leadership and Strategy in the Age* (May 1997) HarperCollins Publishers, New York

Moore, M. (QC) Opinion (2008) entitled, 'True and Fair Requirement Revisited' made to the Financial Reporting Council at www.frc.org.uk/accountants/accounting-and-reporting-policy/true-and-fair-concept

Moore, M. (QC) Opinion (2013) 'International Accounting Standards and the True and Fair View' made to the Financial Reporting Council at www.frc.org.uk/getattachment/5d0b34be-5742-41d8-a442-6ad22d2b878e/Martin-Moore-QC-Opinion-3-October-2013-sig.pdf

Morgan, R. and Hunt, S. 'The Commitment-Trust Theory of Relationship Marketing' (July 1994) 58(3) *The Journal of Marketing* 20–38

Mulcahy, D., 'Six Myths About Venture Capital Offer Dose of Reality to Startups' (16 April 2013) *Ewing Marion Kauffman Foundation* at www.kauffman.org/newsroom/six-myths-about-venture-capital-offer-dose-of-reality-to-startups-in-harvard-business-review-article.aspx

Munari, F., Odasso, M. and Toschi, L. 'Patent-backed Finance' in Munari, F. and Oriani, R. (Eds) *The Economic Valuation of Patents: Methods and Applications* (2011) Edward Elgar Publications Ltd, Cheltenham UK

Murphy, W., Orcutt, J. and Remus, P. *Patent Valuation Improving Decision Making through Analysis* (5 April 2012) Wiley, Hoboken USA

Nelson, S.L *Understanding the Basic Principles of Accounting* (2011) All-in-One for Dummies (US Edition) John Wiley & Sons, Hoboken USA

Nelson. K. and Pritchard, A. *Litigation Risk and Voluntary Disclosure: The Use of Meaningful Cautionary Language* (August 2007) Second Annual Conference on Empirical Legal Studies

Neuhausen, B., Schlank, R. and Pippin, R. *Accounting for Business Combinations, Goodwill, and Other Intangible Assets* (2007) CCH Incorporated

'New UK Annual Report and Requirements to Disclose Human rRghts, Diversity and Greenhouse Gas Emissions' (20 June 2013) Linklaters UK Corporate Update at www.linklaters.com/Insights/Publication1005Newsletter/UK-Corporate-20-June-2013/Pages/New-UK-annual-strategic-report-disclose-human-rights-diversity-greenhouse-gas-emissions.aspx

Ngah-King, E. L., and Folta, T. B. 'Going Public or Private? The Role of Patent Portfolio in Equity Financing for Biotechnology Start Ups' (2006) *Academy of Management Proceedings*

Nielsen, C. 'Dilemmas in the Usefulness of Business Reporting Narratives towards Investors and other Professional Decision-makers' Department of Business Studies, Aarlborg Universitet

Nielsen, C., Roslender, R. and Schaper, S. 'Continuities in the use of the Intellectual Capital Statement Approach: Elements of an Institutional Theory Analysis' (March 2016) 40(1) *Accounting Forum* 16–28

Nor Shaipah Abdul Wahab and Holland, K. 'Tax Planning, Corporate Governance and Equity Value' (June 2012) 44(2) *The British Accounting Review* 111–124 at www.sciencedirect.com/science/article/pii/S0890838912000212

Ordonez de Pablos, P. and Edvinsson, L. *Intellectual Capital in Organizations: Non-Financial Reports and Accounts* (2015) Routledge

Padfield, S.J. 'Who Should Do the Math? Materiality Issues in Disclosures that Require Investors to Calculate the Bottom Line' (2006) 34 *Pepperdine Law Review*, University of Akron Legal Studies Research Papers No. 6-11 at https://papers.ssrn.com/sol3/papers.cfm?abstract_id=928630

Palma, S. 'Is technology enough to plug the SME financing gap?' (2 October 2017) *The Banker* at www.thebanker.com/Transactions-Technology/Is-technology-enough-to-plug-the-SME-financing-gap

Palmer, V. 'From Lerotholi to Lando: Some Examples of Comparative Law Methodology' (2004)4(2) *Global Jurist Frontiers* Art. 1

Parker, R. H. and Nobes, C. *An International View of True and Fair Accounting (International Accounting)* (1994) Cengage Learning EMEA London and New York

Patent Litigation: Is it Worth the Expense? If Rights Are Uncertain, Pursuing Licensing with Alleged Infringer Might Be Best Option (1 April 2006) 26(7) *Genetic Engineering & Biotechnology News* https://www.genengnews.com/gen-articles/patent-litigation-is-it-worth-the-expense/1454

Patent Pools and Antitrust – A Comparative Analysis (March 0214) Prepared by the WIPO

'Perfecting Security over Intellectual Property rRghts and Registering Security at an Intellectual Property Register' Practice Note, *LexisPSL Banking & Finance* at www.lexisnexis.com/uk/lexispsl/bankingandfinance/document/391290/55KX-XBB1-F185-S0P1-00000-00/Perfecting-security-over-intellectual-property-rights-and-registering-security-at-an-intellectual-property-registry accessed on 11 November 2014

Perkins, J. 'Registration of Charges over Intangibles' (July 2010) 4(4) *Law and Financial Markets Review*

Phillips, J. 'The English Patent as a Reward for Invention: The Importance of an Idea' (1982) 3 *Journal of Legal History* 71

Phillips, J. 'Intellectual Property as Security for Debt Finance – A Time to Advance?' (1997) EIPR 276

Phillips, J. 'Katenomics 4: Where to look for an IP-oriented economists' (28 November 2008) *The IPK blog* at http://ipkitten.blogspot.co.uk/2011_11_01_archive.html

Phillips, J. 'IP finance: The trillion dollar tipping point: a report, and a product launch' (18 September 2014) *IP Finance blogspot* at http://ipfinance.blogspot.co.uk/2014/09/the-trillion-dollar-tipping-point.html

Pitkethly, R. 'Intellectual Property Awareness and SMEs: UK IP Awareness Survey 2006' (2006) UK IPO http://breese.blogs.com/pi/files/ipsurvey.pdf

Pletscher, T. 'Corporate Strategies for Managing, Exploiting and Enforcing IP rights' in WIPO National Seminar on IP for Export Competitiveness (1988) WIPO WIPO/IP/K/98/7 at www.wipo.int/edocs/mdocs/sme/en/wipo_ip_pk_98/wipo_ip_pk_98_7.pdf

Poltorak, A. and Lerner, P. 'Introducing Litigation Risks Analysis' (May 2001) Issue 109 *Managing Intellectual Property*

'Progress on Implementing the UPC and the Unitary Patent' (23 September 2014) Allen & Overy at www.allenovery.com/publications/en-gb/Unitary-Patent-System/Pages/Latest-News.aspx

Prudence and IFRS (August 2014) The Association of Chartered Certified Accountants at www.accaglobal.com/content/dam/acca/global/PDF-technical/financial-reporting/tech-tp-prudence.pdf

Rabinowitz, A.B. 'Keep Your Eye on Your Ball: Patent Holders' Evolving Duty to Patrol the Marketplace for Infringement' (Spring 2007) 5 Art. 1 *Northwestern Journal of Technology and Intellectual Property*

Ramb, F. and Reitzig *A Comparative Analysis of the Explanatory Power of Balance Sheet and Patent Information for Market Values of German Firms* (2004) Working Paper, Copenhagen Business School

Reilly, R.F. 'Attributes That Influence IP Value' (Spring 2015) *Forensic Analysis Insights* 3

Rhodes, T. and Campbell, M. *Syndicated Lending: Practice and Documentation* (2009) Fifth edition, Euromoney Institutional Investor, Inc., Foreword by Sir Andrew Large

Rivette, K.G. and Kline, D. *Unlocking the Hidden Value of Patents: Rembrandts in the Attic.* (2000) Harvard Business School Press, Boston, Massachusetts

Rivette, K.G. and Kline, D. 'Discovering New Value in Intellectual Property' (Jan–Feb 2000) 78(1) *Harvard Business Review*

Robson, C. *Real World Research* (1993) Blackwell, Oxford

Roos, J., Roos, G., Edvinsson, L. and Drognetti, N. *Intellectual Capital: Navigating in the New Business Landscape* (1998) Palgrave Macmillan, UK at www.palgrave.com/us/book/9780333694794

Rubinfeld, D. L. and Maness, R. 'The Strategic Use of Patents: Implication for Antitrust' in Leveque, F. and Shelanski, H. *Antitrust, Patents and Copyright: EU and US Perspectives* (2005) Edward Elgar, Northampton

Ruddick, G. 'Suspended Tesco executive to return as Dave Lewis overhauls team' (1 December 2014) *The Telegraph* at www.telegraph.co.uk/finance/newsbysector/epic/tsco/11266257/Suspended-Tesco-executive-to-return-as-Dave-Lewis-overhauls-team.html

Savage, G. et al 'Strategies for Assessing and Managing Organizational Stakeholders' (1991) 5(2) *The Executive*

Schell, C. 'The Value of the Case Study as a Research Strategy' (1992) *Manchester Business School* at www.finance-mba.com/Case%20Method.pdf

Schramm, C. and Bradley, H. 'How Venture Capital Lost Its Way' (2009) *BusinessWeek* at www.kauffmann.org

'Self-financing' (18 February 2014) *Trizle* at www.trizle.com/tips/20-self-financing

Shakespeare, C. 'SOX 2002 Five Years On: What Have We Learned?' (2008) *Journal of Business & Technology Law* 333

Shiller, R.J. 'Human Behaviour and the Efficiency of the Financial System' in Taylor, J.B. and Uhlig, H. (Eds) *Handbook of Macroecomics* (2016) Vol. 1, Elsevier, North Holland

Siems, M. 'Legal Origins: Reconciling Law and Finance and Comparative Law' (2007) 52 *McGill Law Journal* 55

Siems, M. and Cabrelli, D. *Comparative Company Law A Case-Based Approach* (2013) Hart Publishing Limited, Oxford

'Singapore: IP Financing Scheme Launched' (16 July 2014) *Managing IP* at *www.managingip.com/Article/3362420/Singapore-IP-financing-scheme-launched.html*

Stilwell, Frank. *Political Economy: The Contest of Economic Ideas* (2002) First Edition. Oxford University Press, Melbourne, Australia

Song Xianzhong and Liu Zhen, 'On Financing Efficiency of Technology Innovation of High-tech Enterprise', (2008) 8 *Journal of Accounting* 10–12

Stein, H. *Beyond the World Bank Agenda: An Institutional Approach to Development* (2008) University of Chicago Press

Striukova, L.,Unerman, J. and Guthrie, J. 'Corporate Reporting of Intellectual Capital: Evidence from UK Companies' (2008) 40 *The British Accounting Review 297–313*

Sullivan, P.H. *Value-Driven Intellectual Capital: How to Convert Intangible Corporate Assets into Market Value* (2000) Wiley, Hoboken USA

Sunjata, Das. 'Protecting ideas is crucial for eco-technology to succeed' (4 June 2010) *The Environment and Intellectual Property Financial Times Special Report*

Surowiecki, J. *The Wisdom of Crowds: Why the Many are Smarter than the Few* (2005) Abacus, New York

Susskind OBE, R. *The End of Lawyers? Rethinking the Nature of Legal Services* (2008) Oxford University Press, Oxford

Sveiby, K.E. *The New Organisational Wealth: Managing and Measuring Knowledge-Based Assets.* (1997) Berrett-Koehler, San Fransisco

Sykes, J. and King, K. *Valuation and Exploitation of Intellectual Property and Intangible Assets* (2003) Emis Professional Publishing, UK

Taylor Wessing Global IP Index 2014 at www.taylorwessing.com/ipindex/

'The Coalition: Our Programme for Government' (May 2010) *HM Government* at www.gov.uk/government/uploads/system/uploads/attachment_data/file/78977/coalition_programme_for_government.pdf

'The Expanding Market for IP Finance' (2010) *IAM Strategy*

'The Financial Reporting Standard for Smaller Entities' (July 2013) FRC at www.frc.org.uk/Our-Work/Publications/Accounting-and-Reporting-Policy/FRSSE-(effective-January-2015).aspx

'The International IR Framework' by the International Integrated Reporting Council, December 2013

'The Perfect Storm: Corporate Disclosure, Shareholders, and the Importance of Intellectual Property' at www.ipprospective.com/portfolio-potential/the-perfect-storm-corporate-disclosure-shareholders-and-the-value-of-intellectual-property/

'The Role of the Chief Intellectual Property Officer' (2013) INTIPSA at www.intipsa.com/wp-content/uploads/2013/01/INTIPSA-Tips-The-role-of-the-CIPO1.pdf

Thomas, L.C. 'A Survey of Credit and Behavioural Scoring: Forecasting Financial Risk of Lending to Consumers'(2000) 16(2) *International Journal of Forecasting* 149–72

Thomas, R.S. 'The Materiality Standard for Intellectual Property Disclosures' (2002) 42(2) *IDEA The Journal of Law and Technology* 205-226

Tier, M. *The Winning Investment Habits of Warren Buffett & George Soros* (2005) St. Martin's Press, NY

'Tighter banking rules will drain £1 tr from financial system study shows' (10 July 2010) *The Guardian*

'To hack or not to hack? A new report on patent thickets' (22 August 2013) *UKIPO Facto blog* at www.ipo.gov.uk/blogs/ipofacto/2013/08/22/to-hack-or-not-to-hack-a-new-report-on-patent-thickets/

'To manage and Account for Intangibles' (February 1999) Report of meeting in Brussels as quoted at www.ll-a.fr/intangibles/international accounting.htm

Tosato, A. 'Security Interests over Intellectual Property' (2011) 6 (2) *Journal of Intellectual Property Law and Practice*

Tricker, B. 'Re-inventing the Limited Liability Company' (July 2011) 19(4) *International Review*

Tronnberg, C. and Hemlin, S. 'Bankers' Lending Decision Making: A Psychological Approach' (2012) 38(11) *Managerial Finance*1032–1047

Tuncak, B. 'The WIPO nformation Meeting on IP financing: some notes' (1 April 2009) *IPKAT Finance blog* at http://ipfinance.blogspot.co.uk/2009/03/wipo-information-meeting-on-ip.html

Ughetto, E. 'The Financing of Innovative Activities by Banking Institutions: Policy and Regulatory Options' in Laperche, B. and Uzunidis, D. (Eds) *Powerful Finance and Innovation Trends in a High-Risk Economy* (2008) Palgrave Macmillan, UK

University of Cambridge Faculty of Law Research Paper No. 21/2017 available at SSRN: https://ssrn.com/abstract=2917219.

UK Corporate Governance Code (2010, 2012 and 2014) Financial Reporting Council at www.frc.org.uk/directors/corporate-governance-and-stewardship/uk-corporate-governance-code/history-of-the-uk-corporate-governance-code, and see www.frc.org.uk/Our-Work/Codes-Standards/Corporate-governance/UK-Corporate-Governance-Code.aspx

UK Stewardship Code (September 2012) Financial Reporting Council at www.frc.org.uk/getattachment/d67933f9-ca38-4233-b603-3d24b2f62c5f/UK-Stewardship-Code-(September-2012).pdf.

'United Kingdom: Telling Performance - Surveying Narrative Reporting in annual Reports in 2009' Deloitte Audit Group, London

'Using patents as collateral can free up funds for growing businesses' at www.ipnav.com/blog/using-patents-as-collateral-can-free-up-funds-for-growing-businesses

Van Houten, F. Speech (23 June 2014) IP Business Conference reported at www.newscenter.philips.com/main/standard/news/speeches/20140624-speech-by-frans-van-houten-at-ip-business-conference.wpd

Walmsley, J. *Patenting Finance: Financing Patents* (2001) International Securities Market Association, Zurich.

'We've acquired Motorola Mobility' *Google Official Blog* at https://googleblog.blogspot.co.uk/2012/05/weve-acquired-motorola-mobility.html

White, C. 'SME Cases up by 68%' (24 May 2017) *Intellectual Property Magazine*, available at www.intellectualpropertymagazine.com/patent/sme-cases-up-by-68-at-ipec-124252.htm accessed on 30 May 2017

'Why don't companies with huge compliance departments have anyone looking at patents' (April 2014) *Intellectual Asset Management blog* at www.iam-magazine.com/blog/Detail.aspx?g=61ae47f6-df41-4f41-8b31-98de9c888157

Wilkof, N. 'The Nokia-Microsoft transaction: further thoughts on strategy and valuation' (11 September 2013) *IP Finance blogspot* at http://ipfinance.blogspot.co.uk/2013/09/the-nokia-microsoft-transaction-further.html

World Intellectual Property Indicators 2016 Economics and Statistics Series, World Intellectual Property Organization at www.wipo.int/edocs/pubdocs/en/wipo_pub_941_2016.pdf

Yeoh, P. 'Narrative Reporting: the UK Experience' (2010) 52(3) *International Journal of Law and Management* 211–231

Yin, R.K. *Case Study Research: Design and Methods* (1984) Sage Publications, Newbury Park

Zich, J. 'Business 911: Triage for Trying Times' (June 1994) *Stanford Business School Magazine at www.gsb.stanford.edu/insights/about/magazine*

Zipf, G.K. *Human Behaviour and the Principle of Least Effort* (1949) Addison-Wesley, Cambridge Mass

Reports

A Guideline for Intellectual Capital Statements: A Key to Knowledge Management (2000) Danish Agency for Trade and Industry, Ministry for Trade and Industry

Accounting Standards are part of Legally Binding Corporate Reporting Framework (3 October 2013) FRC at https://frc.org.uk/news/october-2013/accounting-standards-are-part-of-legally-binding-c

Action Program concerning enhancement of Relationship Banking Functions (Background and Basic Policy Concept) (28 March 2003) Japanese Financial Services Agency, English version at www.fsa.go.jp/news/newse/e20030328-1a.pdf

Analysing Intellectual Capital Statements (2003a) Danish Ministry of Science Technology and Innovation ISBN: 87-91258-52-9 at https://pure.au.dk/ws/files/217/analyse_uk.pdf

Australian Intellectual Property Report (2013) Australian Government p 25 Table 3

*Banking on IP: An Active Response (*2014) United Kingdom Intellectual Property Office

Basel Committee on Banking Supervision (2000) *Report to G7 Finance Ministers and Central Bank Governors on International Accounting Standards* at www.iasplus.com/resource/basel1.pdf

Brassell, M. and King, K. *Banking on IP? The role of Intellectual Property and Intangible Assets in Facilitating Business Finance Final Report* (6 November 2013) Independent report commissioned by the UK Intellectual Property Office

Brassell, M. and Maguire, J. *Hidden Value: A Study of the UK IP Valuation Market* (August 2017) Independent Report Commissioned by the UK Intellectual Property Office

Clear & Concise: Developments in Narrative Reporting (December 2015) Financial Reporting Council

Conceptual Framework for Financial Reporting: Summary of Tentative Decisions (2017) IFRS Foundation at www.ifrs.org/-/media/project/conceptual-framework/current-stage/summary-of-tentative-decisions-june-2017.pdf

'Confidential Treatment Requests' (28 February 1997, addendum 11 July 2001) SEC Division of Corporation Finance Staff Legal Bulletin No. 1

'Considering the Effects of Accounting Standards: An Australian Response to the European Financial Reporting Advisory Group' (2012) *Institute of Public Accountants*

Corporate Insolvency in the UK: A Decade of Change (2002) Association of Business Recovery Professionals Tenth Report p 9

Copyright and the Value of the Public Domain: An Empirical Assessment (February 2015) Independent Report Commissioned by the UKIPO carried out by CREATe

Creating a financial market for IPR Final report for EU Tender (6 December 2011) No3/PP/ENT/CIP/10/A/N02S003, University of St Gallen and Frauhofer Moez,at https://publications.europa.eu/en/publication-detail/-/publication/afdc8beb-866f-400e-913b-23f4c018e58b

Dyson, J. *Ingenious Britain Making the UK the Leading High Tech Exporter in Europe: A Report by James Dyson* (March 2010) Commissioned by the UK Conservative Party

Disclosure Initiative – Principles of Disclosure (2017) IASB Discussion Paper DP/**2017**/1 at www.efrag.org/Activities/322/Disclosure-Initiative---Principles-of-Disclosure?AspxAutoDetectCookieSupport=1

Facilitating Interdisciplinary Research (2004) Committee on Facilitating Interdisciplinary Research, Committee on Science, Engineering and Public Policy, National Academic Press, Washington

Federation of Small Businesses Quarterly Report (18 June 2013) Independent report produced by the Centre for Economic and Business Research (CEBR) for the FSB

Finance for Small Firms A Seventh Report (22 February 2000) Bank of England at http://webarchive.nationalarchives.gov.uk/20100114112406/http://www.bankofengland.co.uk/publications/financeforsmallfirms/fin4sm07.pdf

FRC's Culture Coalition (2016) Financial Reporting Council at www.frc.org.uk/News-and-Events/FRC-Press/Press/2016/July/Corporate-culture-key-to-sustainable-growth.aspx

Guidance on the Strategic Report (June 2014) Financial Reporting Council at www.frc.org.uk/getattachment/2168919d-398a-41f1-b493-0749cf6f63e8/Guidance-on-the-Strategic-Report.pdf

Final Report of the National Commission on the Causes of the Financial and Economic Crisis of in the United States (January 2011) The Financial Crisis Inquiry Commission Pursuant to Public Law 111–21, Washington DC

Final Report form the Expert Group on Intellectual Property Valuation (March 2014) European Union at http://ec.europa.eu/research/innovation-union/pdf/Expert_Group_Report_on_Intellectual_Property_Valuation_IP_web_2.pdf

Fraser, S. *The Impact of the Financial Crisis of Bank Lending to SMEs: Economic Analysis from the EU Survey of SME Finances* (July 2012) University of Warwick, Report prepared for the Breedon Review of Business Finance for the Department of Business Innovation and Skills

From Ideas to Growth: Helping SMEs get value from their intellectual property (April 2012) UK IPO at www.ipo.gov.uk/business-sme.pdf

G20/OECD Principles of Corporate Governance (30 November 2015) ISBN: 9789264236882 at http://dx.doi.org/10.1787/9789264236882-en

GlaxoSmithKline plc Annual Report 2012 at www.gsk.com/media/2694/annual-report-2012.pdf.

Goodridge, P. et al *UK Investment in Intangible Assets: Report for NESTA* (2011) NESTA Working Paper No. 14/02 p 15

Goodridge, P., Haskell, J. and Wallis, G. *UK Intangible Investment and Growth: New Measures of UK Investment in Knowledge Assets and Intellectual Property Rights* (September 2016) Independent Report commissioned by the UK Intellectual Property Office ISBN: 978-1-910790-25-0

Gower, A. *Gowers Review of Intellectual Property* (December 2006) HM Treasury on behalf of the Controller of Her Majesty's Stationery Office

Guide to Evidence for Policy (2011 updated in 2013) UKIPO at http://webarchive.nationalarchives.gov.uk/20140603093549/http://www.ipo.gov.uk/consult-2011-copyright-evidence.pdf

Guidelines for the Management and Reporting of Intangibles (2002) MERITUM at www.pnbukh.com/files/pdf_filer/MERITUM_Guidelines.pdf

Guthrie, J, Petty, R and Ricceri, F. *Intellectual Capital Reporting: Lessons from Hong Kong and Australia* (2007) at http://icas.org.uk/guthrie/

Hall, B.H., Helmers, C.,. von Graevenitz, C. and Rosazza-Bondibene, C. *A Study of Patent Thickets* (2013/26) Research commissioned by the UK Intellectual Property Office at www.gov.uk/government/uploads/system/uploads/attachment_data/file/311234/ipresearch-thickets.pdf

Hargreaves, I. *Digital Opportunity: A Review of IP and Growth* (May 2011) Independent report commissioned by the UK Prime Minister

Haskel, J., Goodridge, P., Pesole, A., Awano, G., Franklin, M. and Kastrinaki, Z., *Driving Economic Growth Innovation, Knowledge Spending and Productivity Growth in the UK* (2011) NESTA

Influences on Corporate Governance B853-2 Issues in International Financial Reporting (1 March 2016) The Open University, Amazon Media EU S.à r.l.

Innovation in Access to Finance for SMEs (February 2014) The Association of Chartered and Certified Accountants

Intellectual Capital Statements – The New Guideline (2003b) Danish Ministry of Science, Technology and Innovation ISBN: 87-91258-52-9 at https://pure.au.dk/ws/files/217/analyse_uk.pdf.

Intellectual Property and Eco-innovation for Small and Medium Businesses (2011) Research Report conducted by Inngot for Ecomind, co-funded by the European Union under the Interreg IVA 2 Seas Cross-Border Programme 2008–2011

Inventors' Rights (2013) Report of CIPA seminar at www.cipa.org.uk/pages/Inventors-Rights

Intellectual Property Rights Index 2016 Tenth edition, Property Rights Alliance, available at http://internationalpropertyrightsindex.org/blog

IP Attaché Evaluation Report: Programme Review (October 2014/39) Research commissioned by the UKIPO carried out by Tonic Insight Ltd at www.gov.uk/government/uploads/system/uploads/attachment_data/file/365195/ip-attache-_evaluation-report.pdf

'Japanese Guidelines for Disclosure of Intellectual Assets Based Management' No English reference

Kingston, W. *Enforcing Small Firms Patent Rights* (2000) Publications Office of the Commission of the Commission of the European Communities, Luxembourg

Kote, L. et al (2005); *Report and Recommendations Pursuant to Section 401(c) SOX 2002. On Arrangements with Off-Balance Sheet Implications, Special Purpose Entities, and Transparency of Filings by Issuers* at www.sec.gov/news/studies/soxoffbalancerpt.pdf

Leveraging Knowledge Assets Reducing Uncertainty for Security Interests in Intellectual Property (2004) Law Commission of Canada (Ottawa) at www.ulcc.ca/en/cls/index.cfm?sec=2&sub=2j

Lomax, S. and Davies, E. *Small and Medium Sized Enterprise (SME) Journey towards raising external finance* (October 2013) A Report by BMG Research commissioned by the UK Department of Business, Innovation & Skills

Louder than Words: Principles and Actions for Making Corporate Reports Less Complex and More Relevant (June 2009) UK Financial Reporting Council available at www.frc.org.uk/getattachment/53bf7b4b-0dbb-4586-b85b-b548ef28ca9e/FRC_DiscussionPaper_020609.pdf

Options for an EU Instrument for Patent Valorisation (2012) Prepared by the Expert Group on IP Valorisation, European Union at http://ec.europa.eu/enterprise/policies/innovation/files/options-eu-instrument-patent-valorisation_en.pdf

Patent Applications Guide UK Intellectual Property Office at www.ipo.gov.uk/p-apply.pdf

Patent Backlogs and a System of Mutual Recognition (January 2010) Prepared by London Economics for the UK Intellectual Property Office

Patent Thickets – An Overview (25 November 2011) UK Intellectual Property Office Informatics Team at www.gov.uk/government/uploads/system/uploads/attachment_data/file/312540/informatic-thickets.pdf

Phillips, J. (Ed) *The Trillion Dollar Tipping Point AISTEMOS Report* (September 2014) AISTEMOS, London, p 8 at https://aistemos.com/2014/09/17/report-trillion-dollar-tipping-point-exploiting-untapped-value-patents/

Pierrakis, Y. and Collins, L. *Banking on Each Other: Peer-to-Peer Lending to Business: Evidence from the Funding Circle* (April 2013) NESTA

Reference Guideline for Intellectual Property Information Disclosure in the Pursuit of Mutual Understanding between Companies and Capital Markets through Voluntary

Registration of Security Interests: Company Charges and Property other than Land (2002) Law Commission Consultation Paper No 164 at paras 2.6–2.19

Report of the Oulton Committee on Patent Litigation (November 1987) Lord Chancellor's Department

Rising to the Challenge: A Review of Narrative Reporting by UK Listed Companies in 2008/2009 Accounting Standards Board at www.frc.org.uk/Our-Work/Publications/ASB/Rising-to-the-Challenge/Rising-to-the-challenge.aspx

Royal Philips Annual Report 2013 at www.philips.com/philips/shared/assets/Investor_relations/pdf/PhilipsFullAnnualReport2013_English.pdf

Sanchex, P. Castrillo, R. and Elena, S. *VII The Intellectual Capital Report for Universities* in the ICU Report at www.uam.es/personal_pdi/economicas/palomas/THE%20INTELLECTUAL%20CAPITAL%20REPORT%20FOR%20UNIVERSITIES.pdf

SME Finance: Help to Match SMEs Rejected for Finance with Alternative Lenders (29 October 2014) Consultation Outcome, Department for Business Innovation & Skills, p 1at www.gov.uk/government/consultations/sme-finance-help-to-match-smes-rejected-for-finance-with-alternative-lenders/sme-finance-help-to-match-smes-rejected-for-finance-with-alternative-lenders accessed 20 November 2014

The Innovation Index: Measuring the UK's Investment in Innovation and the Effects (2009) NESTA at www.nesta.org.uk/library/documents/innovation-index.pdf

The Run on the Rock Fifth Report of Session 2007–2008 House of Commons Treasury Committee (2008) Vol. 1, House of Commons, The Stationer Office Ltd, London

True and Fair (July 2011) Financial Review Council at www.frc.org.uk/getattachment/55214e7d-6e34-4c11-af51-1b0533ec0c95/Paper-True-and-Fair1.pdf

True and Fair (June 2014) at www.frc.org.uk/getattachment/f08eecd2-6e3a-46d9-a3f8-73f82c09f624/True-and-fair-June-2014.pdf

UKIPO Facts and Figures 2010 and 2011 Calendar Years

UKIPO Facts and Figures 2012 and 2013 Calendar Years at www.gov.uk/government/uploads/system/uploads/attachment_data/file/318346/Facts_and_Figures.pdf

Wiles, I. *Encouraging Employers to use Human Capital Reporting: A Literature Review of Implementation Options* (2013) UK Commission for Employment and Skills at www.gov.uk/government/publications/human-capital-reporting-literature-review

WIPO 'Competition and Patents: Introduction, Studies and Articles' www.wipo.int/patent-law/en/developments/competition.html

WIPO IP Facts and Figure 2013 Economics and Statistics Series at www.wipo.int/edocs/pubdocs/en/statistics/943/wipo_pub_943_2013.pdf

WIPO *IP Advantage* database at www.wipo.int/ipadvantage/en/details.jsp?id=2689

Press Releases

'Bank of England and HM Treasury Announce Extension to the Funding of Lending Scheme' (April 2013) News Release available at www.bankofengland.co.uk/publications/Pages/news/2013/061.aspx

'Better and Simpler Company Reporting' (12 June 2013) BIS at www.gov.uk/government/news/better-and-simpler-company-reporting

'EPO Welcomes Historic Signing of the Unified Patent Court Agreement' (19 February 2013) European Patent Office Press Release

'Lenovo to Acquire Motorola Mobility from Google' (29 January 2014) Google Investor Relations Press Announcement at https://investor.google.com/releases/2014/0129.html.

'New IP Attaché in China will Support UK Businesses' (8 December 2011) UKIPO at www.gov.uk/government/news/new-intellectual-property-attache-in-china-will-support-uk-businesses

'New Figures Published Today show that UK Business is Building Success through Knowledge and Created Asset' (21 March 2014) Department Business, Innovation and Skills at www.gov.uk/government/news/uk-knowledge-investment-continues-to-grow

Oblack, S. 'Patent Quality Initiative Launched to Facilitate Better Patents and Fewer Disputes' (15 October 2014) The Clearing House at www.patentqualityinitiative.com/news/press%20releases/2014_oct%2015_pqi%20launch

'Patent Right Pledge Financing Amounted to 25 Billion Yuan' (3 March 2014) *IP China News* as reported in English at www.chinaipr.gov.cn/policyarticle/policy/statistics/201403/1801673_1.html

'Patents: Realising and Securing Value – An International Conference in London' (15 August 2006) UKIPO *at www.prnewswire.com/news-releases/patents-realising-and-securing-value---an-international-conference-in-london-69963807.html*

'Plans Unveiled to Support IP-rich Businesses get Funding' (17 October 2013) Department for Business, Innovation & Skills, Intellectual Property Office and the Rt. Hon Dr Vince Cable MP at www.gov.uk/government/news/plans-unveiled-to-support-ip-rich-businesses-get-funding

'Silicon Valley Bank's UK Brank Opens for Business' (11 June 2012) *Silicon Valley Bank* Press Release at www.svb.com/News/Company-News/Silicon-Valley-Bank%E2%80%99s-UK-Branch-Opens-for-Business/

'Singapore Continues Stride Towards Becoming an Intellectual Property Hub of Asia, Launches First-Ever IP Management and Value Lab' (26 August 2014) Intellectual Property Office of Singapore at *www.ipos.gov.sg/MediaEvents/Readnews/tabid/873/articleid/284/category/Press%20Releases/parentId/80/year/2014/Default.aspx*

'Singapore Launches S$100M Intellectual Property Financing Scheme & First One-Stop IP Service Centre' (8 April 2014) Intellectual Property Office of Singapore at www.ipos.gov.sg/MediaEvents/Readnews/tabid/873/articleid/272/category/Press%20Releases/parentId/80/year/2014/Default.aspx

'Singapore Ranks Tops in Asia for IP Protection' (12 September 2014) at www.ipos.gov.sg/MediaEvents/Readnews/tabid/873/articleid/288/category/Press%20Releases/parentId/80/year/2014/Default.aspx

'Sweeping Reforms to IP Court Save BusinessesTtime and Money' (1 Oct 2013) BIS and UKIPO at www.gov.uk/government/news/sweeping-reforms-to-ip-court-save-businesses-time-and-money

'UK SMEs Earmarked for EU Grants to Help Them Innovate' (27 July 2014) European Commission at http://ec.europa.eu/unitedkingdom/press/frontpage/2014/14_77_en.htm

'SEC Proposes Amendments to Update and Simplify Disclosure Requirements as Part of Overall Disclosure Effectiveness Review' (6 April 2016) US Securities and Exchange Commission at www.sec.gov/news/pressrelease/2016-141.html

'WIPO Meeting to Explore IP as a Financing Tool' (5 February 2009) WIPO Press Release MA/2009/47

Websites

www.amazon.com
http://blog.crowdfunder.co.uk/2010/11/08/147/
www.cipfa.org/about-cipfa
www.colleripmanagement.com/news/ip-finance-toolkit
http://ec.europa.eu/research/horizon2020/index_en.cfm
www.doingbusiness.org/rankings
www.edmpublications.com
www.epo.org
www.faveo.co.uk
www.fiveoffice.org
www.forbes.com
www.frc.org.uk
www.fsa.gov.uk/consumerinformation/product_news/saving_investments/crowdfunding
www.grameen.com
http://forumblog.org/2012/02/the-2012-top-10-emerging-technologies/

www.geox.com
www.geox.biz
www.gov.uk/business-finance-explained/loans
www.hm-treasury.gov.uk/patent_box.htm
www.iasplus.com
www.ifrs.com
www.ilf-frankfurt.de
www.imf.org
www.independent.co.uk
ipfinance.blogspot.co.uk
www.ipfinance-institute.com
www.ipkat.com
https://twitter.com/Ipkat
ipkitten.blogspot.co.uk
www.ipos.gov.sg
www.justice.gov.uk
www.kickstarter.com
www.law.qmul.ac.uk
http://lexicon.ft.com
www.londonstockexchange.com/specialist-issuers/debts-bonds/how-to-issue/listingcosts/debt-price-list.pdf
www.qfinance.com
www.santanderbreakthrough.co.uk/advice/finance/funding-options-mezzanine-finance
http://securedtransactionslawreformproject.org
www.wipo.int/ipadvantage/en/details.jsp?id=2689
www.ll-a.fr/intangibles/international accoutningh.htm
www.wipo-int/meetings/en/details
www.cdb.com.cn/web

Biography and list of publications

Dr Janice Denoncourt is graduated from McGill University in Montreal, Quebec in 1988. She relocated to Australia where she completed her law degree was a law clerk in the Western Australian Supreme Court. Janice began her professional legal career in 1995 with international commercial law firm Freehills. She has worked as in-house counsel for a publicly listed Australian company and senior associate heading the Intellectual Property department of Minter Ellison's Perth Office. On being awarded the British Council Britain-Australia Chevening Landerer Commercial Law Scholarship in 2003 Janice relocated to the UK where completed her LLM in Intellectual Property Policy & Management at Bournemouth University (with Distinction) and qualified as a solicitor of England and Wales. Janice was awarded a PhD from the University of Nottingham in 2015 for her thesis 'Patent-backed Debt Finance: Should Company Law Take the Lead to Provide a True and Fair View of SME's Patent Assets?' She co-chairs the European Intellectual Property Teachers' Network (EIPTN) and is a Senior Fellow of the Higher Education Academy. Janice regularly presents her work and ideas at international peer-reviewed conferences around the world including Oxford, Lund, Bocconi and Tokyo universities, the Chartered Institute of Patent Attorneys (CIPA); the Academy of Legal Business Studies (ALSB); the Society for Legal Scholars (UK) and the Association for Teachers and Researchers in Intellectual Property (ATRIP). She the Editor of the *Nottingham Law Journal*, a founding member of the *Nottingham Creative IP Project*, leads Nottingham Law School's *IP Research Group*, and is the Director of Studies for several PhD candidates in the IP law field.

Selected list of relevant publications

Denoncourt, J, Chapter 1: 'IP Debt Finance and SMEs: Revealing the Evolving Conceptual Framework Drawing on Initiatives from Around the World' in Kono, T. (Ed.) *Security Interests in Intellectual Property: Perspectives in Law, Business and Innovation* (2017) Springer Verlag, Singapore.

Denoncourt, J., proposal: 'Corporate Disclosure of IP Rights' is noted in Part 4 – Further Potential Projects, *Thirteenth Programme of Law Reform*, Law Commission (2017), 35–36

IP, Brexit and Beyond –Opportunities and Challenges: Report of an IPAN Panel and Workshop on 15th March, 2017; J. Denoncourt contribution at 21–22

Denoncourt, J. 'Unblocking the Arteries at the Heart of IP-backed Debt Finance' (26 September 2017) *Oxford Business Law Blog* at https://www.law.ox.ac.uk/business-law-blog/blog/2017/09/unblocking-arteries-heart-ip-backed-debt-finance

Denoncourt, J. 'Corporate Governance and Intellectual Property Assets' (2016) *Expert Guide Intellectual Property 2017*, CorporateLiveWire

Part 6, Chapter 20: 'Intellectual Property Rights' in Kelly, D., Hammer, R., Hendy, J. and Denoncourt, J., *Business Law* (3rd edn) (2016) Routledge, London.

Denoncourt, J. 'True and Fair Intellectual Property Information: A Corporate Governance Issue' (2016) (1) *Journal of Business Law*, 47–72

Denoncourt, J. 'Patent Attorneys IPO due diligence' (April 2016) 45(4) *CIPA Journal* 52–54

Denoncourt, J. 'Shining a light on China's Innovation Ecosystem': Review of *Innovation and Intellectual Property in China: Strategies, Contexts and Challenges* by Shao, K. (Ed.) and Feng, X.' (2015) (24) *Nottingham Law Journal* 167–170

Denoncourt, J. 'Patents and Value: A Dialogue: Distinguishing Dogs from Diamonds' (23 September 2014) *IP Finance* at http://ipfinance.blogspot.co.uk/search?q=Denoncourt

Denoncourt, J. 'Intellectual Property and Venture Capital: The Secrets to Building Innovation Ecosystems: A Special Report' (9 September 2014) *IP Finance* at http://ipfinance.blogspot.co.uk/search?q=Denoncourt

Denoncourt, J. 'Financial Reporting for IP Intangibles: Protecting Investors from Infringement Risks' (20 August 2014) *IP Finance* at http://ipfinance.blogspot.co.uk/search?q=Denoncourt

Denoncourt, J. 'Financial Reporting for Intangibles: Why IP Intangibles Remain Invisible' (17 August 2014) *IP Finance* at http://ipfinance.blogspot.co.uk/search?q=Denoncourt

Denoncourt, J. 'Financing Technological Innovation, Intellectual Property Rights and the Financing of Technological Innovation: Review of *Public Policy and the Efficiency of Capital Markets* by Frey, C. B., 2013' (2014) 23 *Nottingham Law Journal*161–163

Denoncourt, J., Legislation Commentary: 'Reform to the UK Company Registration of Charges Scheme, The Companies Act 2006 (amendment of Part 25) Regulations 2013 (SI 2013/600)' (2013) 22 *Nottingham Law Journal*, 138–140

Denoncourt, J .Review of *Valuation of Patents* by Wurzer, J. et al. 20012' (2013) 22 *Nottingham Law Journal*, 160–162

UK Intellectual Property Office (IPO) Research Report, contribution Denoncourt, J and Soetendorp, R. 'Appendix A IP, Education and Training' *Banking on IP?'* research report (2013) commissioned by the UK Intellectual Property Office and the Department of Business Innovation and Skills (BIS) at 220–221, at http://www.ipo.gov.uk/ipresearch-bankingip.pdf

Denoncourt, J., Legislation Commentary: 'Impact of the America Invents Act 2011 on the UK: "First to File" Rules" (2012) 21 *Nottingham Law Journal* 133–135.

Denoncourt, J. 'Review of *Secured Transactions in Intellectual Property*' (2008) 20(1) *Denning Law Journal*

Denoncourt, J. 'Hanging on Every Word – Capturing Invention Information' *Managing IP* (April 2002) Euromoney International Plc, London

Denoncourt, J. 'Managing Risk to Protect Your Rights' *Managing IP* (May 2002) Euromoney International Plc, London

Brandrill Group, Australia (delisted) Company Annual Report conceptual creator and author (1998–2001)

Index

www.ingramcontent.com/pod-product-compliance
Ingram Content Group UK Ltd.
Pitfield, Milton Keynes, MK11 3LW, UK
UKHW022012180926
475701UK00003B/330
9780367591410